Verdi and the French Aesthetic

Verse, stanza, and melody in nineteenth-century opera

Focusing on Verdi's French operas, Andreas Giger shows how the composer acquired an ever better understanding of the various approaches to French versification while gradually bringing his works in line with French melodic aesthetic. In his first French opera, *Jérusalem*, Verdi treated the text in an overly cautious manner, trying to avoid prosodic mistakes; in *Les Vêpres siciliennes*, he began to apply more freedom, scanning the verses against some prosodic accents to convey the lightheartedness of a melody; and in *Don Carlos*, he finally drew on the entire palette of prosodic interpretations. Most of Verdi's melodic accomplishments in the French operas carried over into the subsequent Italian ones and set the stage for what later would be called operatic verismo. Drawing attention to the significance of the operatic libretto for the stylistic and dramatic development of nineteenth-century French and Italian opera, this book illustrates Verdi's gradual mastery of the challenges he faced and their historical significance.

ANDREAS GIGER is Associate Professor of Music at Louisiana State University. His research interests have concentrated on nineteenth-century Italian opera and the work of Leonard Bernstein. He is the author of *Verismo* (2004) in the Handwörterbuch der musikalischen Terminologie and articles in many books and journals, including *The Cambridge Companion to Verdi*, the *Journal of the American Musicological Society*, and the second edition of the *New Grove Dictionary of Music and Musicians*. He is also coeditor of *Music in the Mirror* (2002) and founder of the Internet database *saggi musicali italiani*.

Verdi and the French Aesthetic

Verse, stanza, and melody in nineteenth-century opera

―

ANDREAS GIGER
Louisiana State University

CAMBRIDGE UNIVERSITY PRESS
Cambridge, New York, Melbourne, Madrid, Cape Town,
Singapore, São Paulo, Delhi, Tokyo, Mexico City

Cambridge University Press
32 Avenue of the Americas, New York, NY 10013-2473, USA

www.cambridge.org
Information on this title: www.cambridge.org/9780521349543

© Andreas Giger 2008

This publication is in copyright. Subject to statutory exception
and to the provisions of relevant collective licensing agreements,
no reproduction of any part may take place without the written
permission of Cambridge University Press.

First published 2008
First paperback edition 2011

A catalog record for this publication is available from the British Library

Library of Congress Cataloging in Publication data

Giger, Andreas, 1965–
Verdi and the French aesthetic : verse, stanza, and melody in nineteenth-century opera / Andreas Giger.
    p.   cm.
Includes bibliographical references and index.
ISBN 978-0-521-87843-2 (hardback)
1. Verdi, Giuseppe, 1813–1901 – Criticism and interpretation.   2. Opera – Italy – 19th century
3. Opera – France – 19th century   4. Music – Philosophy and aesthetics.   I. Title.
ML410.V4G53   2008
782.10944'09034-dc22   2007045344

ISBN 978-0-521-87843-2 Hardback
ISBN 978-0-521-34954-3 Paperback

Cambridge University Press has no responsibility for the persistence or
accuracy of URLs for external or third-party internet websites referred to in
this publication, and does not guarantee that any content on such websites is,
or will remain, accurate or appropriate.

In memory of Harold S. Powers

Contents

Acknowledgments [*page* ix]

Introduction [1]

PART I: VERSIFICATION AND MELODIC AESTHETICS

1 Rhythm and stanza in French and Italian librettos [7]

2 French and Italian melodic aesthetics and practice ca. 1830–1870 [43]

   Episode: Design, middleground rhythm, and phrase [78]

PART II: FRENCH MELODY IN VERDI'S OPERAS

3 *Jérusalem* and its influence on the subsequent Italian operas [91]

4 *Les Vêpres siciliennes* and its influence on the subsequent Italian operas [121]

5 *Don Carlos* and after [182]

   Appendix: Principal theoretical texts cited (arranged in chronological order by date of publication) [229]

Notes [233]
Bibliography [271]
Index [287]

Acknowledgments

During the twelve years of working on this project, I have been able to count on the help of many wonderful colleagues and friends. The journey began at Indiana University (IU), where I had decided to write a dissertation on a topic related to Giuseppe Verdi. My advisor, George J. Buelow, offered to ask Philip Gossett whether he might be willing to help supervise the project. Not only did he generously agree, but he has been an unfailing supporter ever since, lending his enormous expertise and providing encouragement whenever necessary. After I had been working on the project for a couple of years, the late Harold Powers came to IU to give a presentation on Verdi and Shakespeare. By that time, I had made my first interesting discoveries. Professor Powers agreed to meet with me and take a look at what I had found; his reaction conveyed the impression that I had just cut the Gordian knot. Since then, he has never failed to take a sincere interest in my work.

Completing the group of mentors is Thomas J. Mathiesen, who, although not a Verdian, has had as substantial an influence on this book as anyone. His interest in my findings (however undeveloped they may have been at the time) encouraged me to discuss any issue with him and show him as many drafts as it took to get it right. Without his care (which ranged from solving computer problems to discussions on versification and musical analysis to editorial help), this book would never have seen the light of day. Whatever problems remain are, of course, my responsibility alone.

I am further grateful to my friends and colleagues in the field of nineteenth-century Italian opera for taking an interest in my ideas, reading drafts, or simply lending biographical help: Scott L. Balthazar, Martin Chusid, Mark Everist, Denise P. Gallo, Anselm Gerhard, Helen M. Greenwald, Gregory W. Harwood, Steven Huebner, Jeffrey Langford, David Lawton, Roberta M. Marvin, Hilary Poriss, David Rosen, Jesse Rosenberg, Emanuele Senici, Mary Ann Smart, Sebastian Werr, and the anonymous reviewers of earlier versions of this book. A very special thank-you goes to Francesco Izzo, who, as archivist of the American Institute for Verdi Studies, photocopied numerous sources for me and who has remained a dear colleague and friend ever since.

Completion of this book was made possible by a grant from the National Endowment for the Humanities (NEH), which allowed me to take a leave from teaching at Louisiana State University (LSU). I am very grateful to the NEH for its generous support, without which publication of this book would have been much delayed. My leave from teaching put a considerable burden on my colleagues in the musicology department (headed by Jan Herlinger) and in administration (headed by Dean Ronald D. Ross). My thanks go to all of them for allowing me to complete this book in a timely manner. I am also very fortunate to count among my friends a few opera enthusiasts in LSU's English department: Susannah Monta, Lisi Oliver, and Malcolm Richardson. They have made the final stretch of this project much more pleasant than it otherwise would have been, and I am very grateful for their friendship and support.

Last, but not least, I must thank my family: my godmother, Gertrud M. Giger; my brothers Christian and Matthias; and my parents, Urs and Gilberte, who first made possible the pursuit of my dreams in the New World.

A note on the musical examples

Whenever possible, the musical examples are taken from the critical vocal scores of *The Works of Giuseppe Verdi* or Ursula Günther's earlier critical edition of *Don Carlos* (all listed in the bibliography). The examples taken from these editions include Exx. 2.1; E.4; E.6; 3.3; 3.4; 3.11; 4.3; 4.9a; 4.14a–b (Italian version); and Exx. 5.1–5.10. If the full score but not the vocal score of the critical edition is published, the example is taken from a published vocal score with emendations according to the critical edition.

Introduction

Success at the Paris Opéra had a strong allure for Italian composers in the first half of the nineteenth century, not least for Giuseppe Verdi, whose ambition of matching Giacomo Meyerbeer's triumphs there is well known.[1] Having just arrived in Paris from London in late July of 1847, Verdi hoped for some time to relax with Giuseppina Strepponi and become acquainted with the musical scene, but almost immediately, he was approached by the directors at the Paris Opéra with a request to compose a new opera for the Fall season. Verdi accepted and proceeded with the project immediately, reworking one of his early successes, *I lombardi*, into *Jérusalem*, which he completed in less than two months. Five years later, he signed a contract to produce, in collaboration with librettist Eugène Scribe, an entirely original work, *Les Vêpres siciliennes*. This time, Verdi planned his project very carefully and hoped to land "a decisive coup" by which he meant "to succeed or to be done forever."[2] Although he scored a success when *Les Vêpres siciliennes* was produced in 1855, it was still no match in public popularity with Meyerbeer's works. At last, in 1867, three years after Meyerbeer's death, *Don Carlos* firmly established Verdi among the top composers of French grand opera. Gioachino Rossini could now ask Tito Ricordi to "tell [Verdi] from me that if he returns to Paris he must get himself very well paid for it, since – may my other colleagues forgive me for saying so – he is the only composer capable of writing grand opera."[3] In only three tries, Verdi had successfully adapted his style to the conventions at Europe's most prestigious opera house.

When Verdi began to set French librettos for a French audience, he faced the twin challenge of understanding French poetic rhythm and adjusting to French taste as it had been shaped by composers before him.[4] Understanding the effect of such a challenge on a composer's melodic style has remained elusive for several reasons. While some aspects of French opera – innovations of staging, form, instrumentation, ballet, and dramaturgy – have been successfully described, we do not yet have an adequate understanding of the melodic style nineteenth-century critics considered to be distinctly French. Furthermore, when studying Verdi's handling of French prosody, scholarship has focused on arbitrarily selected theories of French versification, ignoring the highly diverse and often contradictory theories in circulation during the nineteenth century. And, finally, French prosody has been studied only in the form of isolated melodic fragments but not in the broader musical and aesthetic context.

In determining the relationship between French poetic rhythm, musical style, and drama, the operas of Verdi provide the perfect objects for investigation. This book addresses these topics as they relate to Verdi's gradual mastery of French melody from *Jérusalem* to

Don Carlos. It focuses on the mechanics of French verse and stanza and the ways in which they serve to illuminate Verdi's musical development and, by extension, the works of other nineteenth-century composers in the orbit of French and Italian opera.

Italian composers repeatedly complained about the limited rhythmic patterns of Italian verse because these patterns restricted the invention of new and original melodies.[5] By contrast, they realized that French melodies featured greater rhythmic variety because French versification allowed for accents in a greater variety of positions. In praising Verdi's second French opera, *Les Vêpres siciliennes*, the renowned Italian composer, librettist, and journalist Arrigo Boito attributed its success to this flexibility:

> French verse, being less measured than our own, and having smoother and less definite accents, has helped the music since it has removed the tedium of cantilena of symmetry, of that mighty dowry and mighty sin of Italian prosody which generates a meanness and poverty of rhythm within the musical phrase.[6]

The rhythmic relationship between verse and melody turns out to be more complex than might seem to be the case at first.[7] We cannot simply pull from the shelf a manual of French versification and expect to find an explanation of all the prosodic interpretations possible in a particular opera. Theorists espoused conflicting systems of versification, and even those who described basically the same system still disagreed on details, thus impeding the formation of a clear-cut taxonomy. Nevertheless, this book groups the various theories into three broad categories prevalent in the nineteenth-century: an approach based on regular scanning, another based on a fixed number of accents per verse, and a third based on naturalistic declamation oriented to syntax and sense. This variety of interpretations offered composers specific prosodic possibilities, some of which were used for distinct dramatic purposes. In lighthearted, picturesque, and often strophic arias typical of French opera, for instance, Verdi tends to scan the text mechanically, often against tonic accents, whereas in agitated narratives, he tends to respect a greater number of tonic accents than required and to avoid melismas and word repetition. To some degree, it is thus possible to postulate a "rhetoric of prosody," a theory that attributes dramatic meaning to certain prosodic interpretations.

Both the distinction of prosodic theories and the choice of melodic samples must follow a clear system if they are to be useful in developing an analytical method. Here, the poetic stanza will be helpful to us because it identifies passages generally intended for formal lyricism. Unlike its Italian counterpart, the stanza in a French libretto is often anything but clear. French librettists did not necessarily arrange their verses in visually clear stanzaic structures, that is, by indenting all lines following the first verse of each stanza; in their librettos, indention served to indicate verses of lesser syllable count. Recognizable stanzaic forms, however, are paramount in an opera libretto because composers usually set them to formal melodies, while they set non-stanzaic lines in a freer melodic style or in recitative.

Analysis of stanzaic form has had a long tradition in French literary history. But the available prosodic theories are only of limited use in the libretto, a complex genre mixing stanzaic and non-stanzaic structures. By demonstrating the ways in which French stanzaic forms suggest a melodic style flexible in phrasing and rhythm, I will propose a set of criteria essential to the analysis of a literary genre that has been neglected until now.

Further, the distinct characteristics of a French melody do not necessarily derive from prosody but may reflect broader aesthetic principles. When describing the melodic quality of *Les Vêpres siciliennes*, for instance, Abramo Basevi was able to draw on the nature of French verse only vaguely,[8] while other critics did not mention French verse at all. In the reformist journal *L'armonia*, for instance, Pietro Torrigiani missed the "transitions and the unity of the melodic ideas" but, at the same time, praised Verdi for having given up those trivial melodies that had titillated the ears of uneducated audiences.[9] Likewise, Hector Berlioz noted progress in Verdi's melodic style when he referred to the "penetrating intensity of melodic expression," which surpassed that of the popular *Il trovatore*.[10] Even though such general observations are not usually discussed in relation to prosody and stanzaic theory, a surprising number of them can, in fact, be traced to structural aspects of the libretto. The absence of "trivial melodies," for example, may be related to the presence of fewer strongly patterned accompaniments (which in turn derived from the lack of a strong tonic accent in French speech) or to the innovative melodic structures derived from the distinct forms of some French stanzas. In other words, the musical characteristics vaguely described by some critics may bear a closer relationship to poetic rhythm and stanzaic form than has been recognized so far. The lack of a systematic study devoted to French and Italian melodic aesthetics has hampered meaningful interpretation of the innumerable observations scattered among well-known and obscure nineteenth-century journals. Now that new bibliographic tools have provided access to specific information, classification and interpretation of these observations have become feasible.[11] The most important sources (whether theoretic or aesthetic) are listed in the Appendix, with brief references to their content.

His growing experience with French opera and familiarity with its melodic aesthetics allowed Verdi, with each of his French operas, to take a clearly defined step toward exploiting the full range of prosodic options. *Jérusalem* shows an overly cautious approach; *Les Vêpres siciliennes* is freer, especially in numbers of a popular tone; and *Don Carlos* draws on the full palette of musical solutions. By the time he wrote *Don Carlos*, Verdi had mastered the various approaches to French prosody so fully that even when the rhythmic structure of the verse or stanza was irregular, he was able to write a formal melody, while at the same time imbuing it with just the right expressive character. This newly acquired virtuosity left clear traces in his work when Verdi returned to Italian verse in *Aida*.

Verdi most probably did not learn about French prosody from manuals but through his knowledge of French operatic repertoire – from which the information in the manuals was, of course, derived – and by setting French text himself. True, he occasionally pretended not to understand what he heard in French theaters, writing to his friend Clarina Maffei on September 6, 1847: "Yesterday I went to the Opéra: I was bored to death but also stunned by the *mise en scène* – they gave *La Juive* by [Jacques Fromental] Halévy."[12] Seven years later, Verdi reported: "I went to the first performance of [Meyerbeer's] *Étoile du nord*, and

I understood little or nothing [of it], while [the Parisian] audience understood *everything* and found it all beautiful, sublime, divine!!!"[13] Like many of Verdi's remarks, however, such statements must be taken with a grain of salt. In fact, he liked to promote himself as a person of "somma ignoranza musicale" who owned hardly any music and never went to a library or a publishing house to examine a work by someone else.[14] His tendency to downplay both his musical interest and knowledge, which thereby absolved him from the charge of influence, stands in contrast to the holdings of his library at Sant'Agata, his astute observations on other composers' music, and the evidence in his own compositions.[15]

Clearly, Verdi realized very early in his career that much of the inspiration for creating exciting and original new works had to come from outside the Italian peninsula. In reaction to a warning by poet Giuseppe Giusti to focus on topics relevant to Italians, Verdi replied: "Oh, if we had a poet who knew how to devise a drama such as you have in mind! But unfortunately (you will agree yourself) if we want something that is at least effective, then we must, to our shame, resort to things that are not ours."[16] This statement obviously refers to drama, not to melody. But, as we shall see, Verdi subconsciously also appropriated and mastered French melody and, in this process, the idiosyncrasies of French verse played a crucial role.

PART I

Versification and melodic aesthetics

1 | Rhythm and stanza in French and Italian librettos

French versification

The French have long taken great pride in the verse forms of their lyric, epic, and dramatic literature. Opera librettos form an important subclass of this corpus, so it is somewhat surprising that comprehensive theoretical works analyzing French verse largely exclude operatic texts. Several reasons may account for this exclusion.

First, librettos are not generally considered to be autonomous works but rather texts subservient to music. Throughout most of the nineteenth century, French librettos were written entirely in verse but at the same time had to provide enough variety of poetic meter, accentual pattern, and stanzaic structure to accommodate the musical style envisioned by the composer.[1] In recitatives, the meters were generally longer and changed more frequently, whereas in arias, they tended to be shorter, more uniform, and more regularly accented to allow for regular rhythms and phrases.

Second, librettos followed neither French drama in maintaining a uniform meter throughout an entire work nor lyric poetry in relying exclusively on stanzas. Thus, the mixture of stanzaic, non-stanzaic, and hybrid forms, as well as the greater freedom librettists took with traditional rules, seem to have caused theorists to regard the French libretto as an unsuitable genre for illustrating the principles of versification, even though many parts of these librettos would have been sufficiently traditional to illustrate particular points. Moreover, there is in fact no single "theory" of French versification.[2] The treatises reflect a wide variety of approaches, some more or less compatible with each other, others contradictory. To understand these approaches, it is indispensable to begin with a brief preliminary survey of syllable counting, which is relatively easy to master with the help of a few basic rules. Then we will sort out the differences among the theories, concentrating on those aspects that are potentially significant for the relationship between text and music.

The length of a verse (the poetic meter, in French terms) is determined by the number of syllables, which normally equals the number of vowels. This basic rule, however, has numerous exceptions due to the *e muet* (mute "e"), contraction of adjacent vowels into one syllable (syneresis), and separation of adjacent vowels into two syllables (dieresis). The *e muet* can appear in three different positions: at the end of a verse, at the end of a word in the body of the verse, or in the body of a word. The position determines whether or not the *e muet* counts as a separate syllable. At the end of a verse, it does not count, as in this example:³

1 2 3 4   5 6 7 8   [ ]
O mes amis, mes frères d'armes   (*Jérusalem*, III,6)

If the *e muet* appears at the end of a word within a verse and precedes a vowel, it elides and does not count as a separate syllable. If, however, it precedes a consonant, it does count as a syllable. The following two examples illustrate each of these two cases (with underlined numbers highlighting the syllable in question):

1 2 3   4 <u>5</u> 6   7 8
Et je l'implore à vos genoux.   (*Jérusalem*, III,6)

1   2 3   4   5 6 7 <u>8</u> 9 10 [ ]
Et devant Dieu l'innocente victime   (*Jérusalem*, III,6)

An *e muet* in the body of a word counts as a syllable if it follows a consonant, but not if it follows a vowel or diphthong; if, within the body of a verse, it concludes a word by immediately following a vowel, it must elide with the opening vowel of the subsequent word:⁴

 1   2 <u>3</u> 4 5 6 7   8 9 10
Vous chargera de votre iniquité.   (*Jérusalem*, III,6)

1 2 3   4 5   6 7 [ ] 8
Payer un pareil dévouement?   (*Les Vêpres siciliennes*, III,2)

1 2 3 <u>4</u>   5   6   7 8   9 10   11 12 [ ]
L'infami<u>e</u>! ... O mon Dieu! prenez, prenez ma vie!   (*Jérusalem*, III,6)

Cases where two or more vowels follow each other within a word frequently cause problems in determining whether they are subject to syneresis or dieresis. Contemporary critics admitted the lack of clear rules and thus the necessity to examine models of the way in which the most prestigious poets handled a particular case.⁵ Except for the *e muet*, no final vowel of a word may elide with any opening vowel of the subsequent word. Such sequences of vowels are subject to hiatus, a phenomenon censured by classical theorists but treated more liberally in the nineteenth century.

In their attempts to form a coherent theory of verse, nineteenth-century critics and theorists were confused by the fact that poets of the preceding three centuries had explored a variety of approaches. Some of these poets had applied the quantitative meters of classical Greek and Latin to French verse, while others, as a reaction, proposed a system based on stress accents.⁶ As a consequence, nineteenth-century theorists often used terminology from both systems but failed to clarify how the two related to one another or, of greater importance, what this duality meant for a composer. For instance, Alexandre Choron, the French theorist, publisher, and composer, emphasized that French syllables have both a "valeur fixe et inaltérable [a fixed and unchanging value]" and either a stress or no stress, but then he continued to use quantitative terminology ("short" vs. "long") and qualitative terminology ("strong" vs. "weak") seemingly without discrimination.[7] Castil-Blaze, the French critic, translator, and librettist, similarly concentrated on a system relying on regular patterns of stress accents but nevertheless drew on quantitative terminology.[8]

In mid-nineteenth-century France, the leading theorists emphasized stress over quantity. The following passage appears in Louis-Marie Quicherat's widely known *Traité de versification*:

But the principle was found and this principle is irrefutable: "In the verses of whatever language, it is impossible to admit any harmony without rhythm, *nor any rhythm without accent.*" ... The modern system differs essentially from the ancient one in that accent has been substituted for quantity: instead of *long* syllables, one took accented syllables, and weak syllables instead of short syllables.[9]

Antonio Scoppa tries to reconcile the two views. He does not deny that French knows both quantitative accents and stress accents but claims that because a contradiction of the two would offend the ear, they must always coincide, with the stress accent submerging the quantitative one.[10] This approach does not reflect the fine shades of recited verse, where lengthening or shortening a syllable can refine the recitation, but it does suggest the priority of stress accent. It may, in fact, have been Scoppa's goal to convince the French of this priority: in an attempt to prove that French verse could be just as musical as Italian verse, he superimposed on French verse Italian principles of versification, including the concept of a dominant stress accent.[11]

In contrast to nineteenth-century studies, current scholarship has attempted to prove that the main French accent is primarily one of duration and not stress. In his *Dictionnaire de poétique*, Henri Morier defines "accent tonique ou temporel" as a "natural accent of spoken French that consists of a more or less perceivable lengthening of the final sounding vowel in a rhythmic measure. It is thus an accent of duration."[12]

The nineteenth-century theoretical sources usually agree that the tonic accent (i.e., the accent of a short rhythmic group consisting of a polysyllabic word, article plus noun, pronoun plus noun, pronoun plus verb, etc.) falls on the ultimate syllable of rhythmic groups not ending with an *e muet* and on the penultimate syllable of those ending with an *e muet*. Not all theorists adopted this view without qualification, however. The French tonic accent is so weak that it was sometimes perceived as falling on the first or second syllable of polysyllabic words, especially those with a circumflex accent.[13] Even in the following words, devoid of circumflex accents, Jules Combarieu, a late nineteenth-century French musicologist, suggested accentuation on an early syllable: "be<u>au</u>té," "ét<u>e</u>rnité," "r<u>e</u>fuser," "c<u>ou</u>rroux," and "b<u>ou</u>rgeois."[14]

In cases of two adjacent accented syllables, the one with the stronger accent takes precedence and weakens the other. In such cases, the strength is determined by the accent's position (at the end of a syntactic group, at the caesura, or at the rhyme) or its function as *accent oratoire* or *logique* (discussed below). The syllables in question appear in boldface; the stronger one is also underlined:[15]

Mon dern**ier** j**ou**r me sera doux	(*Jérusalem*, III,6)
Laiss**ez**-m**oi**, laissez-moi mourir!	(*Jérusalem*, III,6)

While theorists generally agree on the position of the accent in an individual word, no such agreement exists in regard to the obligatory accents in an entire verse. Theorists take four basic approaches to accentuation: they avoid the issue; they discern regular patterns of metric feet, the approach most commonly occurring in musical writings; they observe a set number of accents per verse, which fall on the most important syllables; or they see irregular rhythmic groups, defined by syntax and sense, as punctuated by accents. Those who avoid the issue describe French verse primarily in terms of syllable count, rhyme, and caesura. They concur with most authors that accents highlight both rhyme and caesura, but they do not take their discussion of rhythmic aspects beyond this point.[16]

Theorists discussing regular patterns of metric feet, that is, those who scan the verse, operate from two distinct traditions. The first one, French in origin, takes into account not only the accent of a word but even more especially the rhythm created by the regular recurrence of an accent within the verse, called *ictus* or *temps fort*. Louis Benloew's *Précis d'une théorie des rythmes* of 1862 perfectly describes this type of scanning:

We must not confound with the strong syllable another element that contributes even more than this accent to the harmonious movement of the verse; I mean the *temps fort*. It too makes itself felt, like the modern accent, by an emphasis, a vocal stress; and when – as this happens very often – it falls on an accented syllable, it completely escapes the superficial observer. It is only when it falls on a weak syllable that it becomes sensible even to the least-trained ear ...

One would read
   il **e**st un D**ieu** devant l**ui** je m'inc**li**ne
   p**au**vre et cont**e**nt sans lui demand**er** r**ie**n.

But one would sing
   il **e**st un D**ieu** dev**a**nt lui j**e** m'inc**li**ne
   pauvre **et** cont**e**nt sans **lui** dem**a**nder r**ie**n ...

This causes a strongly marked discrepancy between strong syllables and *temps fort* ... But it is evident that this discrepancy cannot be absolute. At the caesura and at the rhyme, *temps fort* and strong syllable always coincide, [but] this correspondence does not necessarily have to occur elsewhere ...

When a reciter of a verse wishes to appeal mainly to the intelligence, he would emphasize the strong syllables, neglecting a bit the *temps forts*. When, on the other hand, he wishes to flatter the ear (and even more so when he wishes to sing), he would inevitably scan. The strong syllable is inherent to the word, to the sense: it is always the same. The *temps fort* is inherent to the rhythm and is positioned indifferently on strong syllables or on weak syllables, on meaningful or empty words. The strong syllable has a logical value; the *temps fort* has only a poetic and musical value.[17]

This method of scanning takes as its point of departure either the iamb or trochee, but these metrical feet can be neutralized for expressive purposes, so long as the accents at the rhyme and caesura still coincide. Indeed, composers often did not follow the *temps forts* but adjusted their setting to the sense of the verse. Without citing any concrete evidence, some sources suggest that the "poetic and musical" way of scanning (occasionally also labeled "monotonous") was still commonly taught at schools in the nineteenth century.[18] Modern attempts at describing French versification in librettos have completely ignored this theory, which in its flexibility has far-reaching implications for the musical setting.

The second tradition of scanning, Italian in origin, came to France through the writings of Scoppa. In the context of the general insecurity regarding the nature of the French accent, Scoppa's straight-forward approach must have had particular appeal. From Italian verse, he not only appropriated the priority of the stress accent mentioned earlier but also the predilection for equal placement of these accents in all verses of a stanza. With his unwillingness to accept the inherent accentual irregularity of French verse, Scoppa influenced a large number of French theorists, all of whom began to advocate verse based on regular accentual patterns.[19] Like Benloew, they considered poetry in which accents coincided with the *temps forts* as particularly appealing to the ear. But unlike Benloew, they criticized verses without such perfect correspondence as lacking in harmony and thus as "rhymed prose." Castil-Blaze offers the following quatrain of regular anapests as a model:

Si j'ai f<u>ai</u>m, si j'ai s<u>oi</u>f, mon cour<u>a</u>ge déc<u>a</u>mpe;
Le des<u>ir</u> est mu<u>et</u>, l'amour n'<u>a</u> plus de f<u>eu</u>x.
Oubli<u>ez</u> de rem<u>e</u>ttre un peu d'h<u>ui</u>le à la l<u>a</u>mpe,
Le ray<u>on</u> qui brill<u>ait</u> va s'ét<u>ei</u>ndre à vos y<u>eu</u>x.[20]

These verses show, however, that interest in rhythmic regularity led in at least one instance to awkward accentuation: the tonic accent of am<u>our</u> in the second verse was forfeited and given to the subsequent "empty" syllable "n'<u>a</u>."

The ease with which Scoppa's theory took hold must be seen in the context of the popularity of Italian opera in Paris. It seems that this popularity and the presence of many prominent Italian composers in Paris at the time led some critics to believe that an adaptation of certain Italian principles of versification might help boost the popularity of French opera. Even Meyerbeer, whose melodies of French grand opera have often been contrasted with those of Italian opera, occasionally demanded from Scribe that prosodic accents be placed with strict regularity, exactly as he would have expected in an Italian verse of the same length:

All rhythms are good if the interior points of repose are regular. For the points of repose to be regular, not only must the point of repose in the second line occur after the same number of syllables as in the first, but it is also necessary that the syllable at the break be long, if it was long in the first line, or short, if it was short in the first line.

For example:　　La fl<u>a</u>mme / rap<u>i</u>de
　　　　　　　　　d'un p<u>eu</u>ple / perf<u>i</u>de –

this is an example of regular points of rest.

But if instead of this there were:
　　　　　　　　　La fl<u>a</u>mme / rap<u>i</u>de
　　　　　　　　　de ce r<u>o</u>c / perf<u>i</u>de –

although the hemistich would have the same number of syllables, the point of repose would be irregular for the musician because the syllable that marks the point of repose in the first line is short while that which marks the point of repose in the second line is long.[21]

The French, and Camille Saint-Saëns most prominently among them, later came to lament this Italianization of French verse and, as a consequence, melody.[22]

The third general approach to accentuation focuses not on regular metric accent but rather on a set number of tonic accents per verse. Longer verses generally include more accents than shorter verses, with one accent falling on the rhyme, one on the caesura, and any additional ones on words distinguished by their rhetorical importance. Quicherat stresses that "it will sometimes happen that one will not be in agreement on the place of the accents; [but] one will always be [in agreement] on their number."[23] Analyses in musicological writings have tended to add to the accents required by Quicherat, evaluating the composer's prosodic accuracy by unrealistic standards. In the following alexandrine, for example, Jeffrey Langford located six accents, while Quicherat would have required only four:

J'<u>ai</u> de ce pr<u>i</u>x sangl<u>a</u>nt | | pay<u>é</u> la p<u>ai</u>x du m<u>o</u>nde　　(Langford)[24]
J'ai de ce pr<u>i</u>x sangl<u>a</u>nt | | pay<u>é</u> la paix du m<u>o</u>nde　　(interpretation according to
　　　　　　　　　　　　　　　　　　　　　　　　　Quicherat)

Quicherat's required accents may be summarized as shown in Table 1.1.

Like the third basic approach to accentuation, the fourth appears mainly in theoretical sources concerned with declamation rather than musical setting. Nevertheless, in the second half of the nineteenth century it became the subconscious ideal by which the prosody of French melodies was measured. Even though the third and fourth approaches may foster similar results, the latter follows, in part, different principles: it focuses on significant syntactic groups, the endings of which are punctuated by accents regardless of their position in the verse (except for the rhyme and the caesura, which most always coincide with the end of a syntactic group); and the accents do not have to fulfill a quota and may either add to the numbers related by Quicherat or subtract from them. None of the theorists consulted use our term "syntactic group," but their designations of "rhythmic group," "conceptually related words," or "segment" all imply a string of interrelated words (i.e., a syntactic group).

Like Benloew, Eugène Landry recognizes the duality of forces involved when performing verse (i.e., sense vs. rhythm), a duality that ultimately accounts for the ambiguity of

Table 1.1. Required accents according to Quicherat

Number of syllables	Number of accents and placement	Example (| | indicates the caesura)
12	4; caesura, rhyme, and one in each hemistich on any non-adjacent syllable	Vous détourn__ez__ les y__eux__ | | et mon aud__a__ce est gr__a__nde! (*Les Vêpres siciliennes*, II,3)
10	3; caesura, rhyme, and either the sixth, seventh, or eighth syllable	C'en est donc f__ai__t! | | Fat__a__les destin__é__es, (*Don Carlos*, I,6)[25]
9	3; caesura, rhyme, and either the fifth, sixth, or seventh syllable of the second hemistich	Il tomber__a__ (| |) sous le f__er__ sacr__é__![26] (*Don Carlos*, IV,1,6)
8	2 or 3; rhyme and one or two on any other non-adjacent syllable	Comm__e__nt, dans ma reconnaiss__a__nce Pay__er__ un par__ei__l dévouem__e__nt? (*Les Vêpres siciliennes*, II,3)
7	2; rhyme and either on the third or fourth syllable or – less frequently – on either the second or fifth	Je s__ui__s comme la beaut__é__ De la lég__e__nde du v__oi__le, (*Don Carlos*, III,1,2)
6	2; distributed as in the hemistichs of the alexandrine	Mon D__ieu__, brises mes ch__aî__nes. (*Jérusalem*, III,3)
5	2; rhyme and on an undefined interior syllable	Beau pa__y__s de Fr__a__nce! (*Les Vêpres siciliennes*, I,1)
fewer	1; rhyme	Dieu nous ent__e__nde, O vaillant c__oeu__r! (*Don Carlos*, I,6)

French prosody. Unlike Benloew, however, Landry gives considerably more weight to the sense:

> The sense, which here means the importance and the connection of the words, must accord with the rhythm – that is, with an artistic need – to determine the place of the emphatic accent, its force and return. Sense and rhythm play a role equally positive and negative, that is, of selection and exclusion. Here it is the sense, which first dictates its laws, both to the author and reciter, but these laws are less strict than those of rhythm. In general terms, they are in conflict. The sense demands varied accents, long and unequal groups. The rhythm tends to balance and multiply the accents and to create regular returns. In addition ... there is much uncertainty and latitude in this matter.[27]

This account seems to conform with the third approach. But while Quicherat observes a set number of accents that lend the verse its rhythmic pace, Landry sees accents as points of arrival at the end of an unspecified number of syntactic groups. He clarifies this concept by relating it to the alexandrine. The verse consists of incisions (*incises* – usually equivalent to hemistichs) and the incisions consist of rhythmic groups (*groupes*). But depending on the length and structure of the verse, a group may be equivalent to an incision or even an entire verse. In any case, the emphatic accent always falls on the end of a group, followed at most by one or more consonants or an unaccented (feminine) syllable.[28] "Rhythmic group" is never clearly defined, but occasional examples clarify the concept. Even though not in verse form, the following phrase from Landry illustrates how some potential accents are ignored with the purpose of letting the text flow to the punctuating accents at the end of syntactic groups: "est aussi le s**eu**l qui se glor**ifi**e de faire la l**oi** aux r**ois**."[29] In his introduction to French versification of 1879, the German scholar Otto Lubarsch provides a particularly telling example of this theory:

In French, the *Wortton* or the accentuation of an individual word is significantly reduced by the *Satzton*... The French *Satzton* groups a series of conceptually related words by assigning to the last limb of the chain a greater accent than to the other limbs. For example, the sentence

   Cette maison est agré**able**,

which forms a single conceptual chain, is pronounced in a way that the accent of its final word *agréable* stands out much more than all the other words of the sentence. The sentence becomes a regularly flowing sequence of syllables ending with the *Hauptton* of the final word while being structured by interior accents only weakly. For the same reason, the word *agréable* in the sentence

   C'est une agréable nou**velle**

has a much weaker accent than in the previously mentioned sentence because here, the *Satzton* falls on *nouvelle*.[30]

All accents other than the ones required by Lubarsch and Landry exist only in theory:

The simple accent of a word, which is a weak accent of stress and duration on the ultimate or penultimate vowel, plays in declamation as in other forms of French diction a purely intellectual role, which consists in separating the vocables, in distinguishing a compound from its components ...[31]

Both authors agree that the strongest accents appear at the end of syntactic groups, that in fact all other accents may be ignored. It is important to keep in mind, however, that Landry admits to considerable uncertainty and latitude in matters of accentuation.

The third and fourth approaches to accentuation may easily lead to similar results because they often require accents in the same places. The following quatrain from the act II duet between Élisabeth and Carlos consists of *octosyllabes*, which according to Quicherat include either two or three accents. These can be determined without any difficulty, except perhaps for the one on "fut," which can be left out:

Hél*a*s! sa doul*eu*r me déch*i*re.
Entre mes br*a*s, pâle et glac*é*,
D'am*ou*r, de doul*eu*r, il exp*i*re,
Cel*ui* qui f*u*t mon fianc*é*!

Analysis according to Lubarsch and Landry would not foster significantly different results except for omitting the accents on "fut" and the first "douleur." But neither Landry nor Lubarsch forbid occasional secondary accents, even if they do not actually require them.

Some theorists do not fall squarely within one of the four proposed approaches and may synthesize two theories into one. In his *Métrique naturelle du langage* of 1884, Paul Pierson takes as his point of departure a critique of Benloew's scanning for the purpose of singing. Like Benloew, Pierson objects to scanning when reciting verse; but unlike Benloew, he also objects to scanning in the context of music. The following excerpt appears in the chapter "Mesure musicale et mesure poétique":

This accentuation of two and two would be unbearable in a reading, especially when it would make an ictus fall on a naturally weak syllable; thus, in the declamation of a verse, it suffices today to make the last ictus of each hemistich heard, which must always coincide with a natural ictus of the voice. And most often, we hear within each hemistich another ictus voluntarily placed on the syllable most naturally indicated by the sense ... We must have the courage to admit that pronouncing French verse – not in the monotonous manner practiced at schools but with the full expression demanded by the sense of the phrase – no longer has any determined rhythm and no longer distinguishes itself in any way from simple prosaic declamation, with the possible exception of the style's allure. Besides, we should congratulate ourselves rather than complain: everyone agrees that there is no poorer rhythm than that of scanned verses. The more expression one puts in the declamation of verse, the more the indigence of the old rhythm disappears under the rich improvisation of the sentiment. In a word, the more the declaimed verses resemble beautiful prose, the more they please.[32]

This excerpt primarily recalls Quicherat's predetermined number of irregularly spaced accents but, in its analogy with prose, also alludes to Lubarsch and Landry's organization by punctuated rhythmic groups. In another section of the same book, discussing the hierarchy of accents based on "segments" determined by "pauses" and "rests," Pierson seems to draw on essentially the same idea as Lubarsch and Landry, giving considerably more weight, however, to secondary accents:

Each segment begins after the stopping point marked by the preceding caesura in order to head for a new stopping point marked by the caesura that ends [the segment] ... This is thus [a way of] proceeding at an entirely natural pace ... The word considered by itself, leaving aside the entire phrase of which it is a part, can constitute an ideal entity. But as soon as we want to transfer it from the abstract domain to a concrete organism, it loses its ideal individuality and is no more than an assembly of syllables working with the syllables of one or several other words towards forming a rhythmic entity, which we called *segment*... We already know that every segment has at its core a general accent of the period, which becomes the culminating accent of the segment ...; [hierarchically] below this culminating and unique accent, rule one or several comparatively weak accents, which, however, are individually endowed by a sufficient force to exert control over a system of weaker accents.[33]

Unlike most other theorists, Pierson provides musical realizations of his ideas. In light of the author's emphasis on the beauty of irregularity, it is not surprising that these musical examples (presumably of Pierson's own invention) do not fall within a regular meter (Ex. 1.1).

Example 1.1. Pierson's musical interpretation of prosody.

Because the vocal lines appear without accompaniment, the reader has to determine the accents solely on the basis of downbeats and lengthened notes. Pierson usually distinguishes "culminating" accents from lesser ones but reflects every possible accent with the exception of "sel<u>o</u>n," thus exceeding the number of accents proposed by either Quicherat or Lubarsch and Landry.

Besides the tonic accent (whether of duration or stress), some critics refer to two additional accents, *oratoire* and *logique*, both of which coincide with one of the obligatory accents of approaches 3 and 4. The first is determined entirely by the person who interprets the text, with the intention of rendering the delivery as lively as possible:

[The *accent oratoire*] consists in a certain inflection of the voice and in the imitative expression of the sentiment that emanates from this organ: it is everything that passion, vivacity, taste, and genius can add to the word to render it more striking, to imbue it with more life and vivacity, just as colors enliven and bring to bear the beauty of a drawing, in order to agitate the senses and to stimulate the imagination. It is not an attribute of the tongue that speaks, but of the heart that feels; it is not inherent in the words, but inherent in the passions.[34]

The *accent logique*, however, according to theorist and composer Antoine Reicha, is inherent in the verse and belongs to the word that best captures the sense of the entire phrase. Whether in recitation or in a musical setting, this central word needs appropriate emphasis:

These words are not very difficult to recognize and feel if one carefully reads the passage to be set to music. The highlighted words in the following verses, for example, require an *accent logique*:

(1) .... Dans un age si *tendre*
    Quel éclaircissement en pouvez vous attendre.
(2) Je vois que la sagesse elle *même* t'inspire.

In order to allow the reciter or singer to emphasize these words sufficiently, the composer must slightly lengthen the note and give it a relatively higher pitch.[35]

Despite Reicha's assurance to the contrary, the *accent logique* is by no means always obvious but, just like the *accent oratoire*, dependent upon interpretation. In Reicha's second example, for instance, one could easily make a point for an *accent logique* on "v<u>oi</u>s" or "t'insp<u>i</u>re." The subjectivity of defining both the *accents oratoire* and *logique* render them little useful for our prosodic analyses, especially because they already seem to be covered by the approaches outlined earlier.

This brief survey of accentuation suggests that a nineteenth-century composer had the choice of a variety of rhythmic theories, some very formulaic, others more strongly oriented to syntax and sense, and thus more expressive in a purely textual respect. None of our authors required all tonic accents to be observed, and it is important to keep in mind that some of them did not object to contradictions between tonic accents and *temps fort*, calling for correspondence only at the caesura and the rhyme.

Like the placement of the structural accent, the nature of the caesura was a subject of frequent debate. While the rhyme marks the end of a verse and a syntactic group, the caesura divides verses by a pause into two (and occasionally even three) hemistichs. The caesura must always fall on an accented syllable and, according to rigorous theorists, should not separate elements of a syntactic group, such as the article or the possessive pronoun from the noun, the preposition from its object, the auxiliary verb from an immediately succeeding participle or infinitive, etc.[36] Nonetheless, Adolphe Tobler, in agreement with practice, proposes greater open-mindedness in this matter:

To observe all rules of art in employing the caesura is one of the most difficult points of poetic technique, especially in poems that, from beginning to end, employ the same verse ... The principle ... is this: the caesura may separate even those parts of a phrase that are closely related, provided it is not unexpectedly followed by an even stronger pause, because in that case ... the nature of the verse might risk being misunderstood.[37]

The most elevated French verse, the alexandrine, traditionally has a caesura after the sixth syllable, which cannot be followed by an *e muet* unless it elides with the following word. Each hemistich in turn may divide into several parts, but those secondary accents are usually less marked, if at all, than the central one.

      6
Ce peuple qui s'indigne, | | impatient d'entrave,
Ne veut pas être libre | | et frémit d'être esclave!   (*Les Vêpres siciliennes*, II,2)

In the nineteenth century, Victor Hugo called for a freer type of alexandrine, one with displaced caesuras, to disguise the verse's rhythmic monotony.[38] He began to advocate unorthodox divisions (including the so-called Romantic alexandrine of 4+4+4 syllables), all of which occur in Verdi's French librettos. In the following examples, a caesura after the conventional sixth syllable would divide the verse in an unnatural manner:[39]

      4   8   12
De ces plaisirs, | | pour toi nouveaux, | | es-tu content?
                                                        (*Les Vêpres siciliennes*, I,4)

    4   12
Salut, ô Reine, | | épouse de Philippe deux!   (*Don Carlos*, I,5)
  3   12
A vos pieds, | | éperdu de tendresse, je meurs!   (*Don Carlos*, II,2,4)

As in the alexandrine, the caesura of shorter verses does not have a fixed position but only a recommended one, which according to nineteenth-century theorists renders the verse most harmonious. The *décasyllabe* (verse of ten syllables) has the obligatory caesura after the fourth and less often the fifth syllable, and the *vers de neuf syllabes* (verse of nine syllables) after the third or the fourth syllable. Critics disagree about some of these divisions, however: Reicha, for example, does not require a caesura for verses of fewer than ten syllables,[40] and Théodore de Banville accepts Wilhelm Ténint's view of 1844 that any verse may have its caesura in any conceivable place.[41] Nevertheless, most of the verses conform to the traditional structure:

   3   9
Levez vous! | | Et l'on vous soutiendra!   (*Les Vêpres siciliennes*, II,1)

    4   10
Et toi, Palerme, | | ô beauté qu'on outrage,   (*Les Vêpres siciliennes*, II,1)

     5   10
Je n'ai que ce coeur, | | ne m'en bannis pas!   (*Don Carlos*, II,1,3)

Even though they have a tonic accent on the fourth syllable, the two following examples depart from the established divisions:

 2   10
Lisez! | | au nom du salut de votre âme!   (*Don Carlos*, II,2,3)

       7   10
Que tardez-vous à frapper? ... | | me voilà!   (*Don Carlos*, III,3,3)

As stated earlier, a verse had to correspond to a syntactic group. But to avoid rhythmic monotony, poets and librettists drew on a technique called enjambment (or verse overflow) – that is, the completion of the syntactic group within the following verse.[42] Such a definition unfortunately provides no guidelines as to when we can consider a syntactic group to be complete. Tobler offers a useful paradigm, however, when he suggests that to avoid enjambment, the repose at the rhyme should be stronger than any repose within the verse.[43]

From the time of François Malherbe (1555–1628) and especially Nicolas Boileau (1636–1711) and extending into the nineteenth century, critics had censured enjambment, especially in the alexandrine.[44] The technique never completely disappeared, however, and with André Chenier (1762–1794) it again became more fashionable.[45] In shorter meters with less rhythmic variety than the alexandrine, enjambment did not meet as much resistance because the consistent correspondence of verse ending and sense could have led to considerable rhythmic monotony.[46] In spite of frequent censure, enjambment regularly occurred not only in drama and poetry but also in librettos, as in the following examples. (The completion of the significant syntactic group is marked by double vertical bars.)

Tu porteras ton opprobre et ton crime
Aux pieds de Dieu, | | qui voit l'iniquité.   (*Jérusalem*, III,6)

   Prince, si le Roi veut se rendre
   A ma prière ... | | pour la Flandre
   Par lui remise en votre main, | |
   Vous pourrez partir dès demain!   (*Don Carlos*, II,2,4)

   Concentration on the rhythmic aspects of verse has diverted attention from their stanzaic structures, and neither contemporary criticism nor recent scholarship has devoted significant attention to the way in which stanzas in nineteenth-century librettos are defined. Distinguishing stanzaic from non-stanzaic verse, however, can consciously or subconsciously be of great importance for a composer. Even though stanzas are by no means always set as formal melodies and non-stanzaic passages as recitatives, one of the composer's first tasks when setting a libretto was to recognize the distinction between texts intended for recitative and those for arias. This task involved two basic challenges, one inherent in the genre of the libretto, the other in the specific nature of the French libretto.

   Of the literary genres conceived in verse, only lyric poetry and librettos make notable use of stanzaic forms.[47] The former consists exclusively of stanzas, which the poet clearly identifies by regular repetition of rhyme scheme and verse patterns as well as by spatial separation. No reader of Victor Hugo's "L'Oiseau" from the posthumously published collection *Toute la lyre* (1888–1897) would have missed the division into three stanzas, each with a corresponding number of verses, rhyme scheme, and meter and each separated by additional line spacing:[48]

L'oiseau passe	a
Dans l'espace	a
Où l'amour vient l'enflammer;	b
Si les roses	c
Sont des choses	c
Faites exprès pour charmer,	b
Le ciel est fait pour aimer.	b

L'oiseau vole	a
Et console	a
Le désert et la maison,	b
Et les plaines	c
Et les chênes	c
Écoutent, quand sa chanson	b
Va de buisson en buisson.	b
Hymne et flamme,	a
Il est l'âme	a
Du bois, du pré, de l'étang,	b
Des charmilles,	c
Et des filles	c
Que dès l'aurore on entend	b
Ouvrir leur porte en chantant.	b

Librettos, on the other hand, mix stanzaic and non-stanzaic forms. Here, spaces separate not only stanzas but also the text for the various characters of the opera.

In Italian opera librettos, a composer would have found clear distinctions between *versi sciolti* (i.e., non-rhyming verses of seven or eleven syllables) and *versi lirici* (i.e., rhyming lyrical verses of uniform poetic meters grouped in stanzas). When turning to French librettos, a composer such as Verdi would have been looking for equivalent distinctions. French librettos of the time, however, consisted of nothing but rhyming verses and did not feature a type of verse corresponding to *versi sciolti*. Therefore, when looking for a textual distinction between verses for recitative and those for formal lyricism, the composer had to distinguish between stanzaic and non-stanzaic verse. Furthermore, unlike their Italian counterparts, French librettists did not indent all verses following the first one of each stanza for visual clarification. Because French librettos mix verses of various meters, they draw on indention to indicate verses of lesser syllable count, with those of adjacent meters (5/6; 7/8; 9/10; 11/12) usually sharing the same degree of indention.[49] The difference in layout between corresponding texts in an Italian and French libretto is apparent from the following juxtaposition:[50]

French original (Rossini, *Guillaume Tell*, III,1):	Italian translation by Calisto Bassi:
Pour notre amour plus d'espérance	Ah! se privo di speme è l'amore,
Quand ma vie à peine commence,	Non mi resta che pianto e terrore:
Pour toujours je perds le bonheur.	Infelice per sempre sarò.
Oui, Melcthal, d'un barbare	Un delitto a me toglie il mio bene,
Le forfait nous sépare;	Fa più acerbe le immense mie pene,
Ma raison, qui m'égare,	Né il suo duol confortar io potrò.
A compris ta douleur.	

Indention in the French original does not serve the purpose of delineating stanzas; rather, it indicates metric relationships. Depending on the context in which French verses appear, their identification as stanzaic might cause considerable difficulty, whereas Italian examples pose hardly any problems. A comparison between Giselda's prayer from *I lombardi* (1843) and the parallel passage from the French translation in *Jérusalem* (1847), here sung by Hélène, dramatically illustrates the difference. Giselda's text consists of eight *quinari doppi* (double verses of five syllables), Hélène's of an irregular sequence of verses ranging from four to ten syllables. Stanzaic analysis in the latter case poses an infinitely greater challenge.

<table>
<tr><td>

Salve Maria! – di grazie il petto
   T'empie il Signore – che in te si posa;
   Tuo divin frutto – sia benedetto
   O fra le donne – l'avventurosa!
   Vergine santa – madre di Dio,
   Per noi tapini – leva preghiera,
   One'Ei ci guardi – con occhio pio
   Quando ne aggravi – l'ultima sera!
               (*I lombardi*, I,6)[51]

</td><td>

Vierge Marie,
Ma voix te prie;
Taris mes pleurs.
O Vierge de douleurs,
Fais sur nous descendre
Ton regard si tendre,
Vois me terreurs!
Fais que la haine, en cette enceinte,
Tombe et s'efface avec ma crainte,
Et d'être heureuse enfin viendra le jour.
Vierge Marie,
Ma voix te prie,
Sur nous jette un regard d'amour.
          (*Jérusalem*, I,2)

</td></tr>
</table>

Any attempt at defining stanzas in nineteenth-century French librettos makes it clear that the investigation of a single parameter cannot suffice. It is the interaction of various factors, such as unity of thought, rhyme scheme, number of different meters, and spatial separation that help determine whether or not we can refer to a group of verses as a stanza.[52]

Stanzas require unity on two levels: unity of the verse and unity of the stanza. Unity of the verse means that a line of text should constitute a syntactic group; that is, it should not be broken up by a pause equal to or even stronger than that at the rhyme. The following lines from *Les Vêpres siciliennes*, for instance, include an alexandrine followed by three *octosyllabes*.

Et je suis dans les fers! ... Ah! n'importe à quel prix,
   Que je sois libre! ... un jour ... une heure! ...
   Que je délivre mon pays ...
   Et qu'après, ô mon Dieu! je meure! ...

[I am in chains! ... Ah! At any price whatsoever,
May I be free! ... for a day ... for an hour! ...
May I free my country ...
And then, oh my God! I die! ...]
                                                   (*Les Vêpres siciliennes*, IV,3)

The fragmentary nature of the excerpt does not conform with the stanzaic requirements: The pauses on "fers" in the opening alexandrine and on "libre!" in the subsequent *octosyllabe* are stronger than the pause on "prix." In fact, the former is also stronger than the pause after the second verse, the expected place of the stanzaic caesura. It is thus not surprising that Verdi set the passage as recitative. Unity of the stanza requires that a set of verses contain a complete sentiment or thought, terms the sources fail to define.[53] Furthermore, this requirement loses defining force once we learn that a stanza may include several complete sentiments or a suspended one. Jean François Marmontel writes in his *Élémens de littérature* of 1787:

The *stanza* is a symmetrically composed poetic period. It is true that quite often it includes several complete sentiments and that sometimes, too, the sentiment is but suspended; but I take [the stanza] to define it in its most regular form; and in terms of both aural and mental perception the most perfect stanza is the one that embraces a single thought and ends with it and like it by a full repose.[54]

In 1871, Gustave Weigand pointed out in his treatise of versification that for the sake of developing a thought freely, Romantic poets in particular took advantage of the license to disregard unity of thought, sometimes with great effect.[55] In determining the limits of a "thought," one might consider a librettist's use of punctuation. As the following example from *Les Vêpres siciliennes* shows, periods, exclamation points, and – with less conclusive force – question marks and ellipses may indicate the end of a thought, while commas, semicolons, and colons do not.[56]

Et toi, Palerme, ô beauté qu'on outrage,
Et toujours chère à mes yeux enchantés! ...
Lève ton front courbé sous l'esclavage,
Et redeviens la reine des cités!

[And you, Palermo, o beauty, which everyone insults,
And still dear to my enchanted eyes! ...
Raise your head, which was weighed down by slavery,
And become once again the queen of all cities!]   (*Les Vêpres siciliennes*, II,1)

Unfortunately, punctuation does not always define a stanza to any reliable degree. Poetic rhythm offers a more adequate and effective concept. Rhythm structures not only the verse – through the sequence of accented and unaccented syllables – but also the stanza, through patterns of rhymes and possibly alternation of meters. With the exception of the tercet (which never comprises a complete set of rhymes) and sometimes the quatrain (which may not comprise a complete set of rhymes), each verse should rhyme with at least one other verse in the stanza.[57] Whatever the rhyme scheme, it has to comply with the general rule of alternating feminine and masculine rhymes. Some critics did not permit rhyming couplets in stanzas, but the following excerpt shows that librettists allowed themselves considerable freedom.[58]

O mes amis, mes frères d'armes,
Mon coeur se fend, voyez mes larmes! ...
Le déshonneur! c'est trop affreux!
N'accablez pas un malheureux.
Mon dernier jour me sera doux,
E je l'implore à vos genoux.
Mais, par le ciel! moi, traître! ... infâme! ...
Je pleure, hélas! comme une femme.
C'est la pitié que je réclame ...
Par quels accents vous attendrir?
O mes amis! sans me flétrir,
Laissez-moi, laissez-moi mourir!

[My friends, my comrades in arms,
My heart is torn, watch my tears!
Dishonor! that's too horrible!
Don't overwhelm an unhappy man.
My last day is dear to me,
And I implore you on my knees.
But, Heavens! me, an infamous traitor! ...
I'm crying, alas, like a woman.
It is pity that I request ...
How can I move you?
Oh friends! without disgracing me,
Please, let me die!]   (*Jérusalem*, III,6)

This passage from *Jérusalem* features an initial distich with feminine rhymes; but both of the subsequent rhymes, "affreux"/"malheureux" and "doux"/"genoux" are masculine.

With the exception of the stanza of twelve verses (*douzain*), stanzas rarely exceed the number of ten verses (*dizain*). Longer forms are usually divided into subsections defined by the completion of a rhyme scheme and a corresponding repose. In other words, such subsections might be interpreted as stanzas in their own right.

Just like the longer poetic meters, stanzas of four or more verses tend to have a caesura. This stanzaic caesura always occurs at the end of the verse requiring the greatest pause and must coincide with the structural caesura of the rhyme scheme, which usually falls near the middle of the stanza.[59] The following excerpt from *Don Carlos*, for instance, does not qualify as a stanza because the rhyme scheme implies a stanzaic caesura after the second verse, where enjambment prevents repose.

Va, ne crains rien pour moi! Je suis la fiancée	a
De l'Infant don Carlos ... J'ai foi	b
Dans l'honneur Espagnol ... Page, suis ta pensée! ...	a
Ce seigneur peut garder la fille de ton Roi!	b (*Don Carlos*, I,3)

    Spatial separation may prove to be either an unreliable or a helpful tool in determining stanzas. It is unreliable when it also serves other functions, such as separating the text for one character from that for another and creating space for stage instructions; it is helpful, however, when it functions solely to create distinct stanzas, as in the following passage from *Don Carlos*:

Pour une nuit me voilà Reine,
Et dans ce jardin enchanté
Je suis maîtresse et souveraine.

  Je suis comme la beauté
  De la légende du voile,
  Qui voit luire à son côté
  Le doux reflet d'une étoile!

  Je vais régner jusqu'au jour.
  Sous les doux voiles de l'ombre,
  Je veux enivrer d'amour
  Carlos, le prince au coeur sombre!

[Here I am Queen for a night,
And in this enchanted garden
I am mistress and sovereign.

I am like the beauty
In the legend of the veil
Who saw shine at her side
The soft reflection of a star!

I will reign until dawn
Under the soft shadow of the veil,
I want to inebriate with love
Carlos, the prince with the somber heart!]   (*Don Carlos*, III,1,2)

If the libretto does not spatially separate two or more complete sets of rhymes, and if no other parameter clearly requires a division into two or more separate stanzas, the entire set of verses should be considered a single stanza. In the example from *Jérusalem* (III,6), discussed above in regard to alternation of masculine and feminine rhymes, the first half could easily be considered as a separate stanza of six verses, followed by a second one of equal length. But the lack of spatial separation and the overall unity of thought suggest a stanza of twelve verses, and Verdi's setting does indeed ignore the stanzaic caesura after verse 6.

In some cases, a set of verses is followed, without intervening space, by a second set in a new meter, with both sets encompassing four or more verses and complete sets of rhymes. The following two excerpts from *Les Vêpres siciliennes* include such a change, which can serve two formal functions: either it introduces a contrasting middle section of a large-scale ternary aria (as in "Au sein de la puissance") or it introduces a refrain (as in "Merci, jeunes amies").

>   Au sein de la puissance,
>   Au sein de la grandeur,
>   Un vide affreux, immense,
>   Régnait seul dans mon coeur!
>   Le ciel vient apparaître
>   A mes yeux rajeunis,
>   Et je me sens renaître
>   A ce mot seul: Mon fils!
>   Mon fils!
> La haine égara sa jeunesse,
> Mais près de moi, dans ce palais,
> Je veux conquérir sa tendresse
> Et le vaincre par mes bienfaits!
>   Au sein da la puissance, etc.
>
> [At the bosom of power,
> At the bosom of grandeur,
> A horrible, immense emptiness
> Has been reigning in my heart!
> But a new being appears
> Before my rejuvenated eyes,
> And I feel I'm reviving
> Just through this word: My son!
> My son!
> Hate misled his youth,
> But at my side, in this palace,
> I want to conquer his tenderness
> And to win him over by my kindness.
> At the bosom of power, etc.]   (*Les Vêpres siciliennes*, III,3)

>   Merci, jeunes amies,
>   D'un souvenir si doux!
>   Pour moi, ces fleurs jolies
>   Sont moins fraîches que vous.
>   Et l'hymen qui me lie
>   Est plus cher à mes yeux
>   Quand l'amitié chérie
>   L'embellit de ses voeux.
> Rêve divin! heureux délire!
> Mon coeur frissonne à vos accents!
> Hymen céleste! qui respire
> Les fleurs, l'amour et le printemps!
>   Rives siciliennes,
>   Sur vos bords enchanteurs,
>   Assez longtemps les haines
>   Ont désuni les coeurs.
>   D'espérance joyeuse,
>   Puissé-je [sic], ô mes amis,
>   Voir ma patrie heureuse
>   Le jour, où je le suis...
> Rêve divin! heureux délire! etc.

[Thank you, young friends,
For such a sweet memory!
For me, these pretty flowers
Are less fresh than you.
And the marriage that binds me
Is even dearer to me
When a cherished friendship
Embellishes it with good wishes.
Divine dream! happy delirium!
My heart is shivering with your sounds!
Celestial marriage! you who breathe
The flowers, love, and spring!
Sicilian coasts,
On your enchanting shores,
Hate has long enough
Disunited the hearts.
Joyous hope,
May I see, oh my friends,

My homeland happy
The same day I am happy, too ...
Divine dream! happy delirium! etc.]   (*Les Vêpres siciliennes*, V,2)

In both instances, the new meter coincides with a new thought and thus supports a subdivision into multiple stanzas. In "Au sein de la puissance," the character of Montfort changes thought twice: first from past feelings of emptiness in the first quatrain to feelings of rejuvenation by virtue of finding his son, then again at "La haine égara sa jeunesse," where the focus shifts to reconquering his son's affection. The lack of spatial separation between "Régnait seul dans mon coeur!" and "Le ciel vient apparaître" justifies an interpretation of the first nine verses as a single stanza, but the change of meter at "La haine égara sa jeunesse" in combination with the change of thought suggests the beginning of a new one. Hélène's "Merci, jeunes amies" is more straightforward: the initial focus on her wedding being a reality in the eight verses of six syllables contrasts with the delirium and joy expressed in the subsequent verses of eight syllables. The quatrain starting with "Rêve divin" thus constitutes a new stanza.

A few types of stanzas deserve particular emphasis. Some sources require that a stanza conclude with a masculine rhyme if it opens with a feminine one and vice versa, which means that neither the distich nor the tercet can count as a proper stanza. The tercet occurs frequently in opera librettos, usually in combination with a second tercet that provides the completion of the rhyme scheme.[60] Rare in both lyrical poetry and librettos is the *aaab* pattern of the quatrain;[61] like the tercet, it needs a complementary stanza:

Entendez-vous la trompette
Que l'écho des mers répète?
Pour nous la palme s'apprête,
Marchons nobles Portugais!

Conquérants du Nouveau-Monde,
La victoire nous seconde!
Des flots que Dieu nous réponde ...
Je vous réponds du succès!   (*Dom Sébastien*, I,4)[62]

In a *huitain* (stanza of eight verses), however, this rhyme scheme appears frequently:

Pour moi rayonne
Douce couronne.
Ton coeur pardonne
Au repentir.

Que la mort vienne
Briser ma chaîne! ...
Auprès d'Hélène
Je peux mourir!   (*Les Vêpres siciliennes*, IV,2)

In lyric poetry, stanzas rarely include more than two distinct meters (mainly because the ear would have difficulty grasping and retaining the rhythm),[63] while in librettos, they may include as many as three. Critics warn that not all metric combinations make for harmonious patterns; they recommend simple ratios of syllable count such as 1:2, 1:3, 1:4, and 2:3, less often 2:5 or 3:5.[64] In practice, 3:4 occurs regularly also:

Ne tremble pas, reviens à toi.	8
Ma belle fiancée:	6
En souriant, lève sur moi	8
Ta paupière baissée.	6 (*Don Carlos*, I,4)

Verses of odd syllable count often cannot be combined in these ratios. Instead, librettos may include verses of an odd number of syllables juxtaposed with those of either one syllable more or less. Such inharmonious combinations seem to indicate that a librettist did not intend to create a stanza, but this is by no means a safe conclusion. Sélika's "Air du Sommeil" from Giacomo Meyerbeer's *L'Africaine*, for instance, includes meters of five, six, and eight syllables. Despite the inharmonious ratios, Meyerbeer and his librettist Scribe clearly conceived this passage as a stanza: it demonstrates unity on the levels of verse and stanza, a complete rhyme scheme, and a restriction to no more than three meters.

Sur mes genoux, fils du soleil,	8
Enfant, dors sans alarmes;	6
Le frais lotus, d'un doux sommeil	8
Sur toi verse les charmes.	6
Le ramier frémit;	5
La brise gémit;	5
L'étoile scintille dans l'ombre;	8
Le Bengali dit	5
Son chant dans la nuit.	5
Sommeille en paix dans le bois sombre ...	8 (*L'Africaine*, II,1)

In the following example from *Don Carlos*, however, the rhyme-based set of verses includes four distinct and in part inharmonious meters (7, 6, 6, 8, 6, 10), which speaks against stanzaic interpretation. The fact that these verses sound like a series of fragmentary statements, thus lacking unity of thought and a clear stanzaic caesura, would support this conclusion:

A cette voix, je frissonne!	7
J'ai cru voir ... ô terreur!	6
L'ombre de l'Empereur!	6
Sous le froc cachant sa couronne	8
E sa cuirasse d'or;	6
Ici, dit-on, il apparaît encor! ...	10

[This voice, I'm trembling!
I thought I saw ... oh horror!
The ghost of the Emperor!
Hiding under the frock his crown
And his golden breast plate;
Here, they say, he still appears! ...]   (*Don Carlos*, II,1,2)

While stanzaic forms must comply with certain rules of rhyme and meter, their verses do not have to continue a once-established pattern of accents. Neither general efforts, such as Jean-Ambroise Ducondut's *Essai de rhythmique française* of 1856, nor specifically musical ones, such as those of Choron or Castil-Blaze, could change a system that for so long had counted irregular accentual structures among its most characteristic features. The caesura, however, received much more regular treatment than the accents. Not only does it maintain a once-established position, but this position is always the traditional one after the sixth syllable in the alexandrine, and after the fourth in the *décasyllabe*. An example of the former type appears in the excerpt from *Les Vêpres siciliennes*; an example of the latter in that from *Jérusalem*:

Près du tombeau peut-être | | où nous allons descendre,
A tant de dévouement | | je ne répondrais pas!
Non, et du haut des cieux, | | où tu dois nous entendre,
Mon frère! ... ô Frédéric! | | tu me pardonneras!   (*Les Vêpres siciliennes*, II,3)

Frappez bourreaux! | | je reprends ma fierté.
Mon sang versé | | pour vous fut mon seul crime,
Et devant Dieu | | l'innocente victime
Vous chargera | | de votre iniquité.   (*Jérusalem*, III,6)

In very rare cases, however, even the caesura changes position, although the verse usually allows for a technical although incorrect pause at the traditional spot. The quatrain from Donizetti's *La Favorite* exemplifies such a case with *décasyllabes*:

Pour tant d'amour | | ne soyez pas ingrate;
Lorsqu'il n'aura (| |) que vous | | pour seul bonheur,
Quand d'être aimé | | pour toujours il se flatte,
Ne le chassez jamais (| |) de votre coeur.   (*La Favorite*, III,3)[65]

Tobler recommends interpretation of such irregular verses as lacking a caesura "because it is contrary to the nature of strophic poetry to join verses of anything but a standard structure."[66] Verses of fewer than nine syllables (i.e., those that do not require a caesura) may nevertheless include strong points of repose, which a librettist may arrange in irregular fashion:

O Roi! | | J'arrive de Flandre,
Ce pays jadis si beau!
Ce n'est qu'un désert de cendre,
Un lieu d'horreur, | | un tombeau!
Là, | | l'orphelin qui mendie
Et pleure par les chemins,
Tombe, | | en fuyant l'incendie
Sur des ossements humains!   (*Don Carlos*, II,2,6)

It is undoubtedly significant that none of the stanzas cited in nineteenth-century sources, not even those dealing with opera, is distributed among two or more characters. Does this imply that stanzas must be recited or sung by a single character? One may argue that because they represent different points of view, statements made by more than one person cannot fulfill the principle of "unity of thought." Even though the following conversation from *Les Vêpres siciliennes* centers on a single issue (Henri's refusal to acknowledge Montfort [the French governor on Sicily] as his father because Henri's mother, who had been raped by Montfort, raised him to hate the French), the argument (and thus the thought) changes whenever the other character takes over.

> MONTFORT
> Quoi, ma tendresse, ma prière
> Ne pourront donc rien obtenir?
> HENRI
> Si vous m'aimez, laissez-moi fuir!
> MONTFORT
> Pas même le doux nom de père?
> HENRI
> Ah! je voudrais courir en vos bras! ... je ne peux!
> MONTFORT
> Qui t'en empêche, ingrat?

>   HENRI
>   L'image de ma mère
>   Qui se place entre nous deux!
>   MONTFORT
>   Mon fils! ...
>   HENRI
>   Elle fut ta victime!
>   Et déjà pour moi c'est un crime
>   Que d'hésiter entre vous deux!

>   [MONTFORT
>   What, my tenderness, my prayer
>   Cannot achieve anything?
>   HENRI
>   If you love me, let me escape!
>   MONTFORT
>   Not even the sweet name of father?
>   HENRI
>   I would like to throw myself into your arms! ... I can't!
>   MONTFORT
>   What does hold you back, ungrateful one?
>   HENRI
>   The image of my mother,
>   Which places itself between the two of us!
>   MONTFORT
>   My son! ...
>   HENRI
>   She was your victim!
>   And already it is a crime for me
>   To hesitate between the two of you!]
>   (*Les Vêpres siciliennes*, III, 4)

Another reason this passage does not qualify as a stanza lies in its dramatic character. Although critics seldom state it explicitly, stanzas are inextricably connected with reflection or narration and not with dramatic dialogue. Verbal exchanges such as the one in this example progress by abrupt reactions and not by the coherent development of a thought that would favor setting as a formal melody. But at what point does a passage of a dialogue become reflective enough to warrant formal melodic setting? Or when does a reflective passage become part of a dialogue, thus suggesting a declamatory setting or recitative?

The following excerpt from *Les Vêpres siciliennes* shows Hélène and Henri involved in a passionate dialogue, delivering a distich at a time. Subsequent distichs combine to form a quatrain with a complete rhyme scheme, and each quatrain conforms to all characteristics of a stanza, except perhaps unity of thought.

>
> Hélène
> Comment, dans ma reconnaissance
> Payer un pareil dévouement?
> Henri
> A vous, ma seule providence,
> A vous et ma vie et mon sang!
> Hélène
> Pour nous d'un tyran sanguinaire
> Vous avez bravé le courroux?
> Henri
> Sans trembler j'ai vu sa colère,
> Hélas! et tremble devant vous!
>
> [Hélène
> How, in my gratitude can I
> reward such devotion?
> Henri
> To you, my only providence,
> To you both my life and my blood!
> Hélène
> For us you defied the wrath
> of a bloodthirsty tyrant?
> Henri
> Without trembling I saw his anger,
> Ah! and I am trembling before you!] (*Les Vêpres siciliennes*, II,3)

It seems therefore that sets of verses may function as stanzas even when they are divided between two characters, but the change of character must occur at the stanzaic caesura – that is, at an incision marked simultaneously by the rhyme and by a point of repose. Nonetheless, if the portion either preceding or following the stanzaic caesura is itself divided, then the other, undivided portion would have to be of at least stanzaic length, namely a tercet or longer, in order to be considered a stanzaic unit.

All the aspects considered so far indicate that in librettos, stanzas cannot be defined by any absolute measure. Although stanzas share specific characteristics, these may be more or less pronounced. Table 1.2 summarizes the essential and recommended characteristics. To qualify as a stanza, a set of verses can reasonably be expected to violate none of the essential characteristics, no more than two different recommended characteristics, or no more than twice a single recommended characteristic.

Table 1.2. Essential and recommended characteristics of stanzas in French librettos

Characteristic	Essential vs. recommended
1. the stanza consists of three or more verses	essential
2. the stanza includes a complete rhyme scheme, except in the tercet, where one rhyme may be incomplete	essential
3. the strongest point of repose must coincide with the structural caesura of the rhyme scheme	essential
4. the stanza does not include more than three distinct meters	essential
5. the stanza is assigned to only one character, or if divided, the division coincides with a stanzaic caesura	essential
6. masculine and feminine rhymes alternate	recommended
7. individual verses correspond to a syntactic group	recommended
8. the stanza is unified by a single thought	recommended
9. the meters of a stanza are reasonably harmonious, that is, 1:2, 1:3, 1:4, and 2:3, less often 2:5 or 3:5 syllables	recommended

Comparing French and Italian versification

Italian versification of opera librettos, unlike its French counterpart, has been a frequent subject of investigation in both the nineteenth and twentieth centuries. The following discussion, therefore, does not intend to provide a complete survey of Italian versification or compare the two practices point by point. Rather, it intends to fill gaps and stress those differences that have potential implications for the musical setting.

Italian syllable counting largely follows the same rules as counting French syllables, with one basic exception: French versification counts through the last accented syllable of a verse, Italian versification through the subsequent unaccented syllable, whether it is actually present or not. An Italian verse of a specific length thus corresponds to a French verse of one less syllable (e.g., a *settenario* is equivalent to a *vers de six syllabes*). The following three examples all have the same syllable count in spite of their distinct endings: *sdrucciolo* (two syllables beyond the final accent), *piano* (one syllable beyond the final accent), and *tronco* (no syllable beyond the final accent).

1 2 3 4 5 6 7 [ ]
La mia letizia infondere   ´ ⌣ ⌣   (*sdrucciolo* ending)

1 2 3 4 5 6 7
Vorrei nel suo bel core!   ´ ⌣   (*piano* ending)

1 2 3 4 5 6 7
Dove mortal non va!   ´   (*tronco* ending)   (*I lombardi*, II,2)

As in French verse, a vowel at the end of a word elides with the one at the beginning of the subsequent word, even if the two are separated by a punctuation mark.[67] But because of the great number of words that either begin or end with a vowel, Italian verses contain many more elisions and thus subvert the effect of punctuation much more frequently than their French equivalents.[68]

Sono io stesso! A te davanti
Vedi, o donna, un infelice;   (*Oberto*, I,9)

The frequency of elision raises questions about the function of caesuras and other structural pauses. In nineteenth-century Italian versification, the caesura plays a subordinate role; it appears only in the *versi doppi* (i.e., in those cases where the librettist combines two verses in one to reduce the number of obligatory rhymes). In that context, the caesura always divides the verse in half, and it can fall after a *piano*, *sdrucciolo*, or – in theory – a *tronco* ending:[69]

Non basta una vittima – a questo codardo,   [*sdrucciolo*]
  Il padre e la figlia – vilmente egli uccide,   [*piano*]
  Rapisce l'onore, – insulta, deride ...   [*piano*]
  Oh stolto! una spada – so cingere ancor!   [*piano*]   (*Oberto*, I,10)

The term "caesura" thus carries different connotations in French and Italian prosody. In French, it denotes a syntactic pause on a syllable in a preferred (as opposed to obligatory) position. In Italian, it refers to a syntactic pause between two equal hemistichs and is almost always preceded by an unaccented syllable.

Syntactic pauses occur at points other than the caesura and in verses of any length. In Italian poetry, such pauses are rarely reinforced by an immediately following syntactic rest; instead, they are followed by an unaccented syllable or an elision, often across punctuation marks, thus obscuring the syntactic structure. A composer or reciter may, of course, disregard the elision but will do so only at the expense of destroying the characteristic rhythm of a particular type of verse. For instance, in the example from *Oberto*'s act I, scene 9, given above, disregarding the elisions would turn the verses from *ottonari* with obligatory accents on the third and seventh syllable into *quinari doppi* with obligatory accents on the fourth syllables of each hemistich. In French poetry, however, syntactic pauses are often reinforced by an immediately following syntactic rest, indicated by some kind of punctuation. In the following comparison, boldface letters indicate the obligatory accents, vertical lines the syntactic pauses, and bracketed vertical lines syntactic pauses subverted by elision. The example from *Les Vêpres siciliennes* includes only one instance (at "dire") where an accent is not immediately followed by a syntactic pause. In the excerpt from *I due Foscari*, on the other hand, all syntactic pauses are either subverted or followed by an unaccented syllable.[70]

Deh frenate quest'ira funesta	Pour moi, | | quelle ivresse inconnue
L'inveire,[| |] o infelici, | | non vale:	De contempler (| |) ses traits chéris!
S'eseguisca il decreto fatale ...	Et de me dire, | | l'âme émue:
Sparve il padre,[| |] ora il doge sol v'è.	Mon fils! | | mon fils! | | c'est là mon fils!
(*I due Foscari*, I,6)	(*Les Vêpres siciliennes*, III,4)

These characteristics point directly to one of the most marked differences between the two practices of versification. Italian verse focuses on rhythm and is defined by it as much as it is by the poetic meter, with the clear understanding of the text often hampered by frequent elisions and, as a consequence, suppressed syntactic pauses.[71] French verse, on the other hand, usually does not require a regular rhythm, emphasizing instead points of arrival at the end of syntactic groups. Choron seems to have recognized this distinction, drawing on the term "repose" for explanation. For him, "repose" has only rhythmic and no syntactic significance (in contrast to "caesura," which also has syntactic significance), and it is no coincidence that he illustrates it with examples from Italian librettos:

When the declaiming voice emphasizes the last syllable of a word in a verse, we call it a caesura;[72] when the syllable on which we pause is not the last but only a long one followed by short or mute ones and it carries an accent, we call it a *simple repose*, as in these Italian verses:

    1 2 3
    Così bollono, etc.
    1 2 3
    Le lor gelide, etc.

The syllables *bol* in *bollono* and *ge* in *gelide* are long and carry the accent; it is on these that the voice pauses. The following ones are short and belong to the second hemistich. The voice could rest on them as little as on the French *e muet*. The same applies to the syllables that elide due to the succession of two vowels, as in *or che niega i doni*. The syllable *ga* is subsumed with the following *i*, as if it were *or che nieg' i doni*, etc.[73]

It is thus possible to conclude that "reposes" are characteristic of Italian, syntactic pauses of French prosody. Italian reposes tend to create a regular rhythm, which ideally corresponds to the regular alternation of strong and weak beats; French syntactic pauses create points of arrival that often occur at irregular intervals.

Choron's argument raises questions about the character of the Italian accent. Nineteenth- and twentieth-century writers have always emphasized stress over quantity, asserting that the accent's strength contributed significantly to the rhythmic effect of the verses. Authors such as Gianbattista Bisso (1712–1787) argue that any stressed syllable is automatically lengthened:

But as a consequence of the invasion of the Vandals and the Goths, the Latin idiom became corrupted and lost the knowledge and the true application of quantity and accents. Thus, our Italian language,

Table 1.3. Accented syllables in Italian versification (numbers in parentheses indicate less frequent positions)

Type of verse	Giuseppe Baini	Bonifazio Asioli	Carlo Ritorni
Quinario	1,4	1 or 2,4	4
Senario	2,5	2,5	2,5
Settenario	2,4,6 or 4,6	4,6 or 2,4,6 (or 2,6)	4,6 (or 3,6 [not recommended])
Ottonario	3,7	3,(5),7	3,7
Novenario	2,5,8 or 4,8	3,5,8	
Decasillabo	3,6,9	3,6,9	3,6,9
Endecasillabo	6,10 or 4,6,8,10 or 4,7,10	6,10 or 4,8,10 or 4,6,8,10	6,10 or 4,(6),8,10 (or 4,7,10)

which took from Latin its laws or beginning, no longer knew how to sense the distinction between accent and quantity of a syllable. On the contrary, by confounding the two, the acute accent and the long syllable became one and the same thing, and this applies also to the grave accent and short syllable. For example, in the word *favore*, only the syllable *vo* is acutely accented and at the same time long; the other two syllables, *fa* and *re*, remain with a grave accent and pass as short.[74]

Others claim that stress lends rhythmic structure to the verse, while duration in part follows the stress and in part adds expressive emphasis.[75]

Even if an author still uses quantitative terminology, the context suggests that accentuation is the intended meaning.[76] This confusion recalls the controversy in French sources. But in Italy the terminological discrepancy is purely a residue of classical metrics, whereas in France it reflects a conflation of classical practice, Italian influence, and actual French properties. Landry's characterization of the French and Italian accents confirms the differences between the two practices of versification as outlined above (i.e., a focus on duration in French verse and a focus on stress in Italian verse):

[The alexandrine] has more breadth and variety than the *endecasillabo*, but less force, and this difference responds to that of the accent, which with us, as an emphasis, is more marked in terms of duration, and with other romance people is marked more in terms of energy ... The force of the [Italian] accents has the effect of giving more intelligible and independent rhythmic divisions ... This force ... multiplies the pauses.[77]

While a particular verse in French features a wide variety of possible accent patterns, the Italian system relates each type to only one (in the case of verses with an even number of syllables) or at most three (in the case of verses with an odd number of syllables). Table 1.3 lists these patterns as documented by three leading Italian theorists.[78] Carlo Ritorni distinguishes between *accenti obbligati* and *accenti casuali* (only the former appear in his column), whereas Giuseppe Baini and Bonifazio Asioli also include the most typical *accenti casuali*. *Accenti obbligati* generally remain constant within one type of verse and thus represent its essential rhythmic character. *Accenti casuali* – that is, all other possible accents, which must leave at least one unaccented syllable between themselves and the individual *accenti obbligati* – may vary from verse to verse. Ritorni thus interprets the verses overall as more rhythmically unified than do either Asioli or Baini.[79]

Italian librettos of the period under consideration distinguish between two fundamental types of verses: those based on rhyme, homogeneous rhythm, and stanzaic organization; and those lacking these traits (called *versi sciolti* or free verses). The former have sometimes been labeled *versi lirici*, possibly because Verdi himself used the term.[80] The term does not figure in the standard vocabulary of Italian prosody, however. In fact, *versi lirici* might be confused with *metri lirici* (for lyric poetry), which are seen in opposition to *metri drammatici* (for sacred and secular dramatic venues including opera) and thus would exclude stanzas in dialogues.[81] The term *versi sciolti* primarily refers to the unrhymed *endecasillabi piani* (blank verse),[82] but in opera librettos, it has come to indicate the free combination of *endecasillabi* and *settenari* with an obligatory rhyme only in the final pair of verses.[83] These are exactly the characteristics of *versi in selva*, a term that would more accurately describe what is now commonly called *versi sciolti*.[84]

Italian librettos mark the beginning of a stanza by indenting all verses following the first. This visual aid applies even to those passages where verses are distributed among several characters. Following the respective principles outlined in the section on French versification, we limit this study to unbroken stanzas of at least three verses or subsequent unbroken distichs. This limitation would make it easy to determine the appropriate stanzas were it not for inconsistencies and errors as they appear in the original printed librettos. We thus must first determine the characteristics of a stanza and then suggest a solution for these problems.

A comparison of French and Italian verse has shown that the Italians relied on a few determined accentual patterns regardless of syntax, while the French often took into account the syntactic structure and allowed for a wide variety of patterns. Moreover, at the level of the stanza, Italian theory is characterized by mechanical principles rather than a combination of mechanical and content-related ones. None of the theoretical sources consulted requires "unity of thought," but all list the type and number of verses and the structure of the rhyme as essential formal parameters.[85] At least one source mentions that stanzas usually conclude with a pause greater than the one following each verse.[86] An Italian theorist would not ask, "What makes a stanza a stanza?" but rather, "What makes an *ottavarima* an *ottavarima*, a sonnet a sonnet, or a *canzona* a *canzona*?" The operatic stanzas derive from yet another form, the *canzonetta*, a genre that allows for considerable variety in terms of rhyme scheme, number of verses, and their length.

The *canzonetta* as conceived by Gabriello Chiabrera (1552–1637) includes the following characteristics: (1) short verses with a distinct rhythm, (2) short stanzas of rarely more than six verses, and (3) the use of *versi tronchi* and *sdruccioli* to provide structure through acceleration and interruption.[87] Carlo Innocenzo Frugoni (1692–1765) in particular played an important role in the further development of the *canzonetta* by introducing, among others, the forms of short coupled stanzas linked by a final *tronco* rhyme:[88]

La bella nave è pronta:
   Ecco la sponda e il lido,
   Dove nocchier Cupido,
   Belle, v'invita al mar.
Mirate come l'ancora
   Già da l'arena svelsero
   Mille Amorin, che apprestansi
   Festosi a navigar.

This construction, without a complete set of rhymes in either stanza, became the prototype for Verdi's early- and middle-period librettos and allowed for variation in terms of rhyme scheme and length of both verse and stanzas. In fact, the length of the stanzas can be so unbalanced that the question arises whether the arrangement of the verses really highlights the stanzas or rather the structure provided by *versi tronchi*. In other words, should we describe the following cabaletta from Alzira's cavatina as one stanza or two?

Nell'astro che più fulgido
   La notte in ciel sfavilla,
   Ivi è Zamoro, e palpita
   Fatto immortal scintilla.
   Conversa in luce ascendervi
   A me fia dato ancor,
E seco unirmi, e vivere
   Vita d'eterno amor.   (*Alzira*, I,3)[89]

W. Theodor Elwert has pointed out that the *verso tronco* interrupts the rhythm and articulates a stanza, which would suggest an interpretation of two stanzas.[90] But the punctuation after the sixth verse does not appear strong enough to conclude a stanza and, most important, we do not count distichs as independent stanzas. To reflect the position of the *versi tronchi*, we will thus call this structure a stanza of six plus two verses.

The original printed librettos sometimes ignore the structural importance of *versi tronchi* for the layout of a stanza. Because those by Verdi's two most experienced librettists (Felice Romani and Salvadore Cammarano) lack such inconsistencies, and because Verdi's two most frequent early librettists (Temistocle Solera and Francesco Maria Piave) had little experience in this genre, their inconsistencies might be explained as carelessness, especially because there are often no convincing reasons to justify the alternate arrangements. The following examples show how such cases should be emended.

Printed Libretto	Emended Version

Jacopo e Lucrezia *a due*   Jacopo e Lucrezia *a due*
     Ah padre! ...   Ah padre! ...
Doge   Figlio ... Nuora ...   Doge   Figlio ... Nuora ...
Jac.   Sei tu?   Jac.   Sei tu?
Luc.   Sei tu?   Luc.   Sei tu?
Dog.   Son io.   Dog.   Son io.
          Volate al seno mio.   Volate al seno mio.
a tre   Provo mia gioja ancor.   *a tre*   Provo mia gioja ancor.
Dog.   Padre ti sono ancora,   Dog.   Padre ti sono ancora,
         Lo credi a questo pianto;   Lo credi a questo pianto;
         Il volto mio soltanto   Il volto mio soltanto
         Fingea per te rigor.   Fingea per te rigor.
           (*I due Foscari*, II,3)

Odabella   Odabella
        Io t'ho salvo ... il delitto svelai ...   Io t'ho salvo ... il delitto svelai ...
        Da me sol fia punito l'indegno.   Da me sol fia punito l'indegno.
Attila   Io tel dono! Ma premio più degno,   Attila   Io tel dono! Ma premio più degno,
        Mia fedele, riserbasi a te: Mia fedele, riserbasi a te:
        Tu doman salutata verrai   Tu doman salutata verrai
        Dalle genti qual sposa del re.   Dalle genti qual sposa del re.
              (*Attila*, II,6)[91]

Such inconsistencies may have two principal reasons: either the *tronco* ending began to lose its structural significance, or any of the responsible parties in the process of producing a printed libretto (librettist, copyist, or typesetter) was careless. The sources provide examples for both categories. Those of the former can easily be verified in manuscript librettos (if available);[92] for those of the latter, the exact source of inconsistent alignment is sometimes difficult to determine due to missing copies in the chain leading to the printed version. Even a cursory examination of the available manuscript librettos, however, suggests that sloppy handwriting and careless alignment allowed for easy misreading of the librettist's autograph.[93]

    Verdi's early librettos also include stanzas without concluding *versi tronchi*. They must, however, have a complete set of rhyme:

Salve Maria! – di grazie il petto
   T'empie il Signore – che in te si posa;
   Tuo divin frutto – sia benedetto
   O fra le donne – l'avventurosa

>   Vergine santa – madre di Dio,
>   Per noi tapini – leva preghiera,
>   Ond'Ei ci guardi – con occhio pio
>   Quando ne aggravi – l'ultima sera!   (*I lombardi*, I,6)

The only exception to this rule concerns verses with *sdrucciolo* endings: due to the limited repertoire of *sdrucciolo* words, these can be paired even if they do not rhyme.[94]

In the strict sense, stanzas are defined – as in French – by at least one repetition of a set of characteristics.[95] Such a requirement, however, would exclude too many stanzas marked by indention in the published librettos. The following passage clearly consists of *versi lirici*, the stanzaic arrangement of which is indicated only by the *versi tronchi*:

>   PIRRO
> Molti fidi qui celati
>   Pronti agli ordini già stanno.
>   PAGANO
>   Ch'io li vegga! ... In tutti i lati
>   Essi il fuoco spargeranno.
>   SCENA V.
>   Di perigli è piena l'opra! ...
>   Molti servi Arvin ricetta;
>   Ma per me chi ben s'adopra
>   Largo è il premio che l'aspetta.
>   SGHERRI
>   Niun periglio il nostro seno
>   Di timor vigliacco assale;
>   Non v'è buio che il baleno
>   Nol rischiari del pugnale;
>   Piano entriam con piè sicuro
>   Ogni porta ad ogni muro;
>   Fra le grida, fra i lamenti,
>   Imperterriti, tacenti,
>   D'un sol colpo in paradiso
>   L'alme altrui godiam mandar!
> Col pugnal di sangue intriso
>   Poi sediamo a banchettar!   (*I lombardi*, I,4–5)

Librettists frequently distribute a set of *versi lirici* among two or more characters. Such structures may appear as part of a complex marked by indention and a concluding *verso tronco* but may be disqualified as a stanza or stanzaic unit due to asymmetrical distribution of the text among the characters. The following example illustrates the manner by which a coherent group of verses is extrapolated in such cases and adapted to our purposes as a stanzaic unit. (The excerpt is quoted as it appears in the original printed libretto).

Giselda	Teco io fuggo!		
Oronte		Tu! ... che intendo!	[*versi piani*]
Giselda	Vo' seguir il tuo destino.		
Oronte	Infelice! ... è un voto orrendo,		
	Maledetto è il mio cammino.		
	Per dirupi e per foreste		
	Come belva errante io movo;		
	Giuoco ai venti e alle tempeste		
	Spesso albergo ho un antro, un covo!		
	Avrai talamo l'arena		
	Del deserto interminato,		
	Sarà l'urlo della jena		
	La canzone dell'amor!	[*verso tronco*]	
	Io, sol io sarò beato	[*verso piano*]	
	Nell'incendio del mio cor.	[*verso tronco*]	

broken-up quatrain (*abab*) (excluded)

extrapolated stanza of 8+2 verses (based on the structure provided by the *versi tronchi*)

(*I lombardi*, III,3)

Polymetric stanzas had been declining before Verdi's time and remained rare in his Italian operas through *Aida*.[96] Those that do occur represent three types: (1) they end with a shorter verse, (2) they mix verses with their *doppio* form, and (3) they regularly alternate rhyming *settenari* and *endecasillabi*.[97] The first polymetric stanza that goes beyond these basic types appears in *Aida* and will be analyzed in Chapter 5.[98]

While *versi tronchi* continued to play an important role through Verdi's last two operas, the Italian system of indention had disappeared, with stanzas often being separated from each other by a space. Boito occasionally reverted to Italian indentions, but he, the copyist, or the publisher failed to follow the system consistently. In the following perfectly symmetrical form from *Otello*, the first eight verses correspond to the second eight. To reflect visually the stanzaic symmetry of the two parts, either the third verse should be indented or the indention of the eleventh verse removed. This is how the text appears in the original printed libretto:[99]

Dio! mi potevi scagliar tutti i mali	11
Della miseria, – della vergogna,	5 × 2
Far de' miei baldi trofei trionfali	11
Una maceria, – una menzogna ...	5 × 2
E avrei portato la croce crudel	11
D'angoscie e d'onte	5
Con calma fronte	5
E rassegnato al volere del ciel.	11

Ma, o pianto, o duol! m'han rapito il miraggio	11
Dov'io, giulivo, – l'anima acqueto.	5 × 2
Spento è quel sol, quel sorriso, quel raggio	11
Che mi fa vivo, – che mi fa lieto!	5 × 2
Tu alfin, Clemenza, pio genio immortal	11
Dal roseo riso,	5
Copri il tuo viso	5
Santo coll'orrida larva infernal!	11 (*Otello*, III,3)

Our comparison between French and Italian versification of librettos during Verdi's time has shown that Italian librettos generally took a more formulaic approach to the structure of both verses and stanzas. Accents fall on specific metric positions, lending each meter a distinct rhythmic quality regardless of the verse's syntactic structure. Stanzas (at least through *Aida*) are determined by *tronco* verses and marked by indention, whether in unstructured dialogue or symmetrical quatrains. In French verse, on the other hand, the accentual positions are, at least according to some theorists, determined by the syntactic structure of the verse, and stanzas, according to our definition, are determined by unity of thought and a variety of other formal parameters.

In the last third of the century, principles of French and Italian versification began to merge, especially with the arrival of Arrigo Boito, who greatly admired French verse for its structural variety. Before we can turn to Verdi's musical responses to the challenges of French verse, however, we must investigate nineteenth-century perceptions of French and Italian melody. When Verdi agreed to set French librettos, he not only had to cope with a new type of verse but also with a new set of melodic conventions.

2 | French and Italian melodic aesthetics and practice ca. 1830–1870

> Music intended to fit a libretto requires of a critic all the attention and study regarding suitable melody, phrasing, rhythm, cut, harmony, and accompaniment.[1]
> – Abramo Basevi

Some of the conventions a composer had to follow when writing for the Paris Opéra have long been well known: a four- or five-act design, grand emotions (i.e., a focus on issues that concern a large segment of society rather than isolated individuals), ballets, extended choral sections, musical forms that complied with French expectations (such as ternary aria forms), and certain dramatic requirements. But when it comes to defining French melody in the broadest sense, including consideration of rhythmic and harmonic characteristics, relationship to prosody and accompaniment, and principles of melodic development, opinions have been vague and often contradictory. One nineteenth-century critic for the *Gazzetta musicale di Milano*, for example, questioned whether the melodic style even at the Opéra could truly pass as French. In reaction to a review in a Berlin paper that detected French influences in Verdi's *Rigoletto*, the critic responded:

Of what French opera does the Berlin paper speak here? We cannot recognize the true physiognomy of French melody except in comic operas. In serious opera, of which the major temple is the grand *Opéra*, as someone else observed, French music is cosmopolitan; and in fact, quite rarely are we given the chance to perceive in the grand works performed in that theater the vices inherent in the melody and the music of the French in general.[2]

On a later occasion, Achille de Lauzières confirmed that musical "Frenchness" could be found only in *opéras comiques*, of which he accepted only those of Daniel-François-Ésprit Auber (1782–1871) as truly successful. In other words, he found very little French music worth mentioning and therefore in his reviews for the *Gazzetta musicale di Milano* preferred the phrase "la musica in Francia" over "la musica francese."[3] The most radical voices even maintained that French music did not exist at all, basing this assessment on the notion that revered composers of French opera came from other parts of Europe. The refutation of this argument by a contributor to *La France musicale* abounds with typically vague generalities:

We have just talked about French music, school, and style; in this regard we hear tell that French music in the strict sense is a myth and does not exist ... because the most beautiful works we call our own are for the most part due to foreign compositions. They cite Grétry for comic opera and Gluck for [tragic] opera.

From this point of view, it is true, our baggage would consist only of more or less clever borrowings made on the one hand from Italy, this divine melodious source, on the other from Germany, this land of harmony. But it is otherwise; while assimilating the qualities of the Italian and German schools, French music has always known how to bring out its originality: grace, elegance, taste, above all spirit are always there. Gluck was German, but it is only in the French language that he encountered a prosody at the same time firmer and more accentuated than the Italian one, sweeter and more harmonious than the German one – the only prosody to which he was able rigorously to apply his dramatic theory.[4]

Such opinions allow for two preliminary assertions: first, it would be wrong to limit potential models of French music to native French composers, because foreigners may have mastered or even defined the idiom to a greater degree than the natives; and second, some nineteenth-century critics agreed, if only by implication, that a French style did indeed exist, although a precise definition remained elusive.

Regarding the first assertion, Meyerbeer is undoubtedly the most obvious example because his activity in Paris overlapped with Verdi's and because he held the most prominent position among those who wrote for the Opéra. The Italians either saw in Meyerbeer a German, not a French composer or otherwise counted him in the general category of the *oltremontani* (those from north of the Alps), most of whom they believed suffered from similar melodic deficiencies.[5] Even for the Italians, however, Meyerbeer embodied success at the most prestigious French musical institution, thus setting the standard for serious French works. Other composers whose operas were occasionally performed in Italy did not come even close to eliciting the extensive critical response accorded to Meyerbeer.[6]

Several Italian critics believed that their composers had much to learn from Meyerbeer's skills. The most astute observer of his style, Abramo Basevi, declared in the reformist journal *L'armonia*: "We are of the opinion that music as we see it employed by the sublime talent of Meyerbeer could alone serve as a model for the Italians to escape from this state of transition that threatens decline and enter into a period of regeneration of musical art."[7] Unlike the majority of their Italian colleagues, French critics saw in Meyerbeer a French composer, even if they rarely said so explicitly. Their overall enthusiasm for his works and the vocabulary they used in describing his melodies imply a complete identification of his style with French principles. In reviewing *Le Prophète*, for example, François-Joseph Fétis even provided an instance of explicitly praising Meyerbeer for "having made excellent French music."[8]

When describing French melody between 1830 and 1870, we must, of course, keep in mind that it had been influenced previously by Italian composers. First, Gaspare Spontini (at the Opéra) and Luigi Cherubini (at the Opéra comique) imbued the traditionally simple French melodic style with greater harmonic and lyrical expressivity, which earned them both criticism and praise.[9] Then, in the second and third decades, Rossini introduced the French to vocal virtuosity and effective rhythmic devices while at the same time matching his predecessors in melodic expressivity and harmonic audacity.[10] Ironically, some melody-supporting parameters later praised as distinctly French (such as sophisticated harmony and orchestration) came to France through Italian composers, a process that is still only partially understood.

The implicit recognition by nineteenth-century critics of a French melodic style, the subject of our second assertion, emerges from a study of representative French and Italian operas and their discussion in the nineteenth-century musical press. Operas by Halévy, Meyerbeer, Berlioz, Gounod, and even Auber shared features that were seen as distinct from works by Italian composers, even though all except Berlioz and Gounod studied at some point with an Italian teacher.[11] The many illustrative quotations from primary sources on the subsequent pages indicate that critics north and south of the Alps judged melody from distinct perspectives: while in Italy melody had to please as a self-sufficient entity, in France it constituted a musical complex that included harmony, accompaniment, and, on occasion, even orchestration. As a consequence, the two groups often evaluated each other's style inadequately, drawing on a vocabulary of clichés. Alberto Mazzucato, for example, compared the two styles in a review of Le Prophète for the Gazzetta musicale di Milano, emphasizing rhythm, symmetry, and the development of melody:

Our melody is smooth, fluid, [composed] of proportions that are said to be architectonic; it is symmetrical, respondent in its various phrases, round, periodic, concluding. It has a homogeneous beginning, middle, and end. In short, it flows naturally in carrying out its two elements, that is, tonality and rhythm.

Melody north of the Alps shuns this naturalness, this spontaneity with study, almost as it seems with affectation, even repugnance... As to rhythm and specifically its natural carrying out, the musical period, the whole thing proceeds very differently. In the melodies of Le Prophète, with a few exceptions, there is no ordinary regularity, no rigor of proportions, no symmetry, no rhythmical correspondence of phrases, no roundness of periods, no natural conclusions. More often, the melody stops, breaks off, is truncated; and if not always at the beginning, then certainly in the middle or unfailingly toward the end.[12]

Mazzucato's terminology is vague enough to allow for various interpretations. A fluid melody, for example, might suggest a non-repetitive rhythm that is difficult to grasp; but, such a definition surely does not reflect what the author had in mind. Rather, Mazzucato meant regular and naturally spaced rhythmic patterns with close correspondence of textual and musical accents, an ideal no different from that of many French, who would have objected to a description of their music as truncated and lacking in symmetry.[13] One of the most prominent, Fétis, upheld symmetry as an essential characteristic and praised Meyerbeer for observing it.[14] "Declamation" was another of the terms used to denigrate each other's melodic style. According to some French critics, Verdi and Bellini overused "exaggerated declamation," whereas Italian authors attributed this defect to the oltremontani.[15] Such assessments can be explained at least in part by rivalries among publishers who also issued their own journals with the goal of promoting their artists;[16] it is equally plausible, however, that the various authors used the same terms but with distinct meanings and implications.

The renowned Italian critic Filippo Filippi recognized this state of affairs and the resulting difficulty of intelligently discussing melody; in his review of *Don Carlos*, he preferred not to talk about melody at all because of the seemingly irreconcilable concepts attached to it:

As to melody, I would rather not talk about it; of this essential musical element, there are so many diverse concepts that, when judging an opera, it is impossible ever to ascertain or deny whether melody is present or lacking. For some, the melody is the trivial motive that tickles the ear and for which is reserved the final honor [of being played] on hurdy-gurdies; for others, the melody is any musical phrase that penetrates the fiber of the heart, that touches them and makes them cry – and those are the ones with a better concept; for Wagner, the melody is the infinite, the murmur of the forest, melopoeia without rhythm, without proportions, without returns, that wanders and digresses, and that can produce a metaphysical excitement, leaving the ear dissatisfied and the heart arid.[17]

Undaunted by Filippi's argument for not discussing melodic styles in greater detail, we shall attempt here to bring together the essential traits discussed in French and Italian sources. Excerpts from operas by representative composers whose works Verdi knew or probably knew – Grétry, Auber, Halévy, Berlioz, Meyerbeer, and Gounod – will illustrate the points made in the writings of the time, rendering in more specific musical terms the features recognized – implicitly or explicitly – as French. As will become abundantly clear in the course of this chapter, neither the French nor the Italians presented a unified view of the characteristics and quality of their respective melodic style, although each implied that their tradition embraced distinct tendencies. Moreover, by the mid-nineteenth century, the ongoing stylistic exchange between French and Italian opera had led to a large common set of musical characteristics, which further impeded a clear distinction between the two traditions. Nevertheless, a study of the focal points of reviews and theoretical sources, words of encouragement to emulate or avoid melodic aspects of certain operas,[18] and the music itself suggests the existence of two basic philosophies of melody that are able to accommodate the distinct views of individual critics.

Music and verse

Chapter 1 introduced the various approaches to French and Italian versification in opera librettos from a purely textual standpoint. While these approaches may seem to be perfectly clear in isolation, they raise new issues when seen in a musical context, for example when and why certain accents might be ignored. Some authors (such as Reicha and Geremia Vitali) required the observation of *accent logique*[19] but without providing musical illustrations; they probably realized that melodic writing relied on a certain structural autonomy. Reicha's formulaic rule of musically reflecting this accent by a relatively longer and higher note taken together with the frequent violation of this rule in practice might explain why he exemplified the *accent logique* in an alexandrine (a meter often associated with recitative), implying that lyrical passages did not require such a narrowly defined corresponding musical emphasis.[20]

One of the most controversial issues in French and Italian melodic aesthetics concerns the discrepancy between the accentual structure of the text and the musical ideal. The rhythm of the verse did not always correspond with the musical rhythm a composer had in mind, which led to frequent discussions of how to align textual and musical (usually metric) accents.[21] In this regard, and based on the rhythmic properties of their respective verse, the emphases of Italian and French writers emerge at least in part as distinct: while the Italians aimed at a melodic rhythm that corresponded with the underlying meter, the French tended to stress a melody's originality and expressive quality, which often came at the expense of symmetry or resulted in rhythmic-metric ambiguity.

Italian writings present a relatively uniform picture of the relationship between textual and musical accents, with discrepancies only in verses of odd syllable count (*quinario*, *settenario*, and *endecasillabo*). While Baini and Asioli do not distinguish between migrating accents (i.e., those that vary from verse to verse) and fixed accents and require all of them to be observed, Ritorni considers migrating accents as "almost useless for the poetic ear."[22] His description of the verse-music relationship implies that migrating accents may be disregarded, allowing for rhythmic-metric correspondence and enabling easy reproduction of a melodic pattern from verse to verse.[23] Ritorni illustrates this principle in an *endecasillabo*, among other meters (*A* stands for arsis, *T* for thesis):[24]

A | T A   T A| T   A   T   A|T [A]
Càn-to l'àr-mi pie-tò-se e il Ca-pi-tà-no.

This mechanical kind of scanning against tonic accents recalls Benloew's approach but, to the best of my knowledge, does not appear in Italian settings of *endecasillabi*. Baini and Asioli would have censured it, without offering, however, a solution for cases of odd syllable count with migrating accents.[25] Because such accentual migration occurred frequently in verses of odd syllable count, composers had the choice of either following Ritorni's recommendation or accommodating the change of pattern through musical adjustments. Verdi's setting of the first four *settenari* of Zaccaria's prayer in *Nabucco* exemplifies both options. The accentual pattern in the text varies from verse to verse; only syllables 4 and 6 are stressed throughout.

D'Egitto là sui lidi	[2,4,6]
Egli a Mosè die' vita;	[1,4,6]
Di Gedëone i cento	[4,6]
Invitti ei rese un dì ...	[2,4,6]

Verdi misaccented "Egitto" in the first verse and accented "Di" in the third to make the rhythmic pattern of the first three verses correspond but introduced an upbeat and a new rhythmic design for the fourth verse (Ex. 2.1).[26] This setting is in line not only with Ritorni's theory but also with Italian practice in general.

This excerpt features perfect rhythmic-metric clarity, both in the melody and in the accompaniment. To relieve the potential rhythmic monotony, theorist Melchiorre Balbi suggested occasional accentuation of weak syllables by an *accento apparente*, which would

Example 2.1. Verdi, *Nabucco*, Part I,2, "D'Egitto là sui lidi" (Zaccaria).

animate the tranquil flow created by the three principal accents (the *accento minore*, on a weak beat in relation to any subdivision of that beat; the *accento maggiore*, on the first beat of the measure; and the *accento massimo o metrico*, on the first beat of every other measure):

> The use of these accents [*minore, maggiore, massimo*, and *apparente*] produces in the music a *qualifying* condition of great relevance, since the regular uniformity of the first three renders the expression equable and *tranquil*, and the *accento apparente* [also called *accento eccezionabile*] breaks in a certain way the monotonous equability and renders the expression more *fluctuating* and *agitated*.[27]

By *accento apparente*, Balbi mainly meant syncopations, which occur more prominently in Italian than in French opera, frequently – although by no means exclusively – coinciding with weak syllables. Because they do not fall on a metrical accent or the beginning of an accompanimental pattern, they do not create the impression of prosodic negligence; rather, such accents add rhythmic vitality as long as they are not overused. In the following example, *accenti apparenti* appear on "disprezz<u>o</u>," "<u>il</u> rigor," and "<u>un</u> amante" (Ex. 2.2).

These examples suggest that the variations in the prosodic approach of Italian theorists were relatively insignificant for the melodic style. On the other hand, French concepts of versification – less compatible with each other than their Italian counterparts – potentially have much greater consequences. For example, interpretation according to Benloew allows for much rhythmic freedom, including superimposed regular musical patterns – with the resulting prosodic flaws – and "expressive" rhythms that follow the accentual structure as described by Quicherat; scanning according to Scoppa and his followers implies rhythmic

Example 2.2. Donizetti, *Anna Bolena*, I,12, "Meco obblia" (Percy).

symmetry as in Benloew's scanning, with the sole difference that the text lends itself to such scanning; and the approach of Lubarsch and Landry with its focus on the syntactic groups results in rhythmic diversity, irregular phrasing, or both.[28]

Scanning in the manner of Benloew goes back at least to Grétry's *opéras comiques*, which critics have tended to hold up as models of prosody.[29] It is hard to believe that these critics – who claimed that Grétry followed true declamation – did not recognize the frequent scanning, but they never mentioned it, probably out of embarrassment.

In *opéra comique*, mechanical scanning was not confined to lighthearted couplets, the strophic songs with refrains so typical of the genre. One of the most famous examples appears in Grétry's *Richard Coeur-de-Lion* (1784) when Blondel, at the parapet of the castle of Linz, intones a *romance* to signal his imprisoned master, King Richard, that he will do everything he can to free his King (Ex. 2.3). A version of the opening distich with highlighted tonic accents (on the left) is juxtaposed with a version as scanned by Grétry (on the right):

Une **fiè**vre brû**lante**   Un**e** fièv**re** brûlante
Un **jour** me terrass**ait** ...   Un **jour** me t**e**rrass**ait** ...

In an equally serious moment from act III of *Le Domino noir* (1837), the novice nun Angèle is torn between her plans to become an abbess and her love for Horace. Having returned from an encounter with Horace after the gates of the convent had already been locked, she is relieved to have gained access with the help of a confidante and without being seen by

Example 2.3. Grétry, *Richard Coeur-de-Lion*, II,4, "Une fièvre brûlante" (Blondel).

Example 2.4. Auber, *Le Domino noir*, III,4, "Flamme vengeresse" (Angèle).

her superior. Soon, however, her feelings give way to her love for Horace in an interpolated bravura waltz, the music of which is rather incompatible with the passionate text and the seriousness of the dramatic situation. Auber scans the text in anapests, accepting violations of numerous tonic accents, including some at the rhyme (Ex. 2.4). The stanza accentuated according to Quicherat (on the left) is juxtaposed with the version as accented by Auber (on the right):

Fl**a**mme venger**e**sse,	Flamme v**e**ngeress**e**,
Tourm**e**nt qui m'oppr**e**sse,	Tourment q**ui** m'oppress**e**,
Am**ou**r qui sans esp**oi**r me l**ai**sse,	Amour q**ui** sans esp**oi**r me l**ai**sse,
Tu v**oi**s ma faibl**e**sse,	Tu vois m**a** faibless**e**,
Hél**a**s! pauvre abb**e**sse,	Hélas! p**au**vre abbess**e**,
Devant t**oi** mon pouv**oi**r se b**ai**sse.	Devant t**oi** mon pouv**oi**r se b**ai**sse.

Example 2.5. Adam, *Le Brasseur de Preston*, II,18, "Tout-à-l'heure tant bien que mal" (Daniel Robinson).

Such settings were in line with French practice and sanctioned by theorists such as Benloew, because they allowed for more memorable melodies. They had nothing to do with negligence or even caricature; if a composer intended to make fun of a character, he would go out of his way to abandon a working pattern for the purpose of greater prosodic distortion. In *Le Brasseur de Preston* (1838), when the beer brewer Daniel Robinson fills in as an army officer for his deserted twin brother while having absolutely no clue about the duties or the behavior appropriate to the position, Adolphe Adam abandons the pattern established in the first verse, creating total prosodic chaos. A version of the quatrain from Daniel's "Air du cheval" – in which he reports how, in spite of himself, he led the troups to victory – with the accents highlighted according to Quicherat (on the left) is juxtaposed with Adam's distortion (on the right) for comic effect. The result does not correspond, even remotely, with any of the standard prosodic approaches (Ex. 2.5).

Tout-à-l'h**eu**re tant b**ien** que m**al**	T**ou**t-à-l'h**eu**re t**a**nt bien que m**al**
Le serg**ent** me h**i**sse à chev**al**	L**e** sergent m**e** hisse **à** chev**al**
Et, sans att**en**dre mon sign**al**,	**Et**, sans att**en**dre mon sign**al**,
Je v**oi**s s'él**an**cer l'anim**al**;	J**e** vois s'él**an**cer l'**a**nim**al**;

In grand opera, mechanical scanning fulfills a relatively clear dramatic function, including the establishment of lighthearted contrast and local color or the association of a singer with a certain social or religious group.[30] When the Catholic Valentine in Meyerbeer's *Les Huguenots* does not dare to ask her Huguenot lover Raoul to marry her, Queen Marguerite of Valois offers to ask him on her behalf. Raoul, who unjustly believes that Valentine has betrayed him, appears before the Queen and is unable to conceal the effect her beauty has

Example 2.6. Meyerbeer, *Les Huguenots*, II,5, "Si j'étais coquette!" (Marguerite).

on him. To deflate the tension, Marguerite strikes a playful tone for the second movement of the duet, in which the music mirrors the trochaic rhythm of the text. When Raoul, to revenge Valentine's ostensible betrayal, throws himself at the Queen's feet in admiration, she attempts to deflate the tension once again, this time with a coquettish melody that superimposes a trochaic rhythm on irregularly accented text (Ex. 2.6). With this melody, she not only disarms Raoul but also herself, realizing that she is taken by the young man even though she is meeting him to help Valentine. The version of the stanza on the left shows the verses as printed in the libretto and with all tonic accents highlighted; the version on the right shows the text as set by Meyerbeer and with the regular accents superimposed by the music. The realization of the trochaic rhythm required the addition of some words and the repetition of "non" in the final verse:

Si j'étais coquette,	Si j'étais coquette! Dieu!
Pareille conquête,	Pareille conquête, Oui,
Serait bientôt faite;	Serait bientôt faite,
Mais, non! ... et je dois[s]	Mais, non, non, non, et je dois

Despite abundant examples of scanning, Quicherat's fixed number of accents in partly flexible positions has usually been presented in musicological writings as the sole standard against which a composer's handling of prosody is measured. While Quicherat's approach is obviously not the only standard, it has worked well, especially when we allow for additional accents created by the metric structure of the music. In the following example from Halévy's

La Juive (1835), Cardinal Brogni begs Rachel, the adopted daughter of the Jew Éléazar, to convert to Catholicism and thus save herself from being burnt at the stake. Brogni does not yet know that Rachel is his daughter, whom Éléazar had saved from a fire in Rome before being banished from the city. For the *octosyllabes* of Brogni's quatrain, Quicherat requires an accent at the rhyme and one or two additional interior accents. Halévy disregards only the first accent of the second verse, which Quicherat would have preferred to be observed, even though the minimum of two accents is met.

En mon âme une voix secrète   [3,6,8]
Parle pour elle et la défend?   [1,4,8]
Et lorsque son bûcher s'apprête   [2,6,8]
Je tremble du sort qui l'attend.[31] [2,5,8]

Although this quatrain consists of *octosyllabes* throughout, the distribution of the accents within each verse changes. Instead of forcing this structure into the straitjacket of parallel *a,a'* phrases with at least similar rhythmic patterns, Halévy decided against rhythmic regularity on nearly all levels. In addition, the lack of clear melodic and accompanimental patterns makes it difficult for the listener to grasp the meter and thus determine where the most prominent textual accents would normally fall (Ex. 2.7). The disregarded accent of "parle" leads us directly to the approach of Lubarsch and Landry, the irregular groups of syllables flowing to punctuating accents at the end of each group. Pure examples of this approach appear rarely in stanzaic passages at this time, not only because it was described with recitation rather than opera in mind but also because metric and durational emphases stress syllables theoretically not requiring an accent. Such additional emphases, of course, do not contradict Lubarsch and Landry, but they do bring the accentual interpretation closer to the other approaches. In the following excerpt from Ambroise Thomas's *Mignon* (1866), Mignon takes an interest in Lothario's past, asking him whether he had to suffer (accentuation follows Lubarsch and Landry):

As-tu souffert? as tu pleuré?
As-tu langui sans espérance?
L'âme en deuil, le coeur déchiré
Alors tu connais ma souffrance!

Out of grief over the abduction of his daughter, who will turn out to be Mignon, Lothario has been traveling as a minstrel, subconsciously searching for her. At this point, though, neither he nor Mignon knows the identity of the other. Thomas supports all the occurrences of "tu," the first syllables of "âme," and "coeur" by a "redundant" metric accent, thus virtually scanning the text in some places ("As-tu souffert? as tu pleuré? As-tu langui ... "). Nevertheless, the effect of basically even notes flowing toward the main accent at the end of a syntactic group and the complete disregard for the tonic accent on "connais" (which would have been obligatory according to Quicherat), thereby creating a particularly

Example 2.7. Halévy, *La Juive*, IV,3, "En mon âme" (Brogni).

long group in agreement with syntax and sense, perfectly reflects Lubarsch and Landry (Ex. 2.8).

The examples presented so far have illustrated the main prosodic approaches with relative clarity. In opera, however, they do not commonly appear in pure form for more than a few measures, usually because the musical style to some degree imposes its own laws. The clear metric organization of opera, for instance, particularly in the first half of the nineteenth century, creates accents in excess of those described by the theorists, who point out only the *required* accents and not any additional ones that might be tolerated in a musical setting. These additional accents – or any other accents incompatible with a particular approach – can usually be explained as the result of mixing approaches, which may occur within a single verse; Benloew's description of scanning, for example, easily covers the ground left open by the other theorists, especially when

Example 2.8. Thomas, *Mignon*, II,2,2, "As-tu souffert?" (Mignon).

scanning is taken to include not only the iamb and trochee but also the dactyl and anapest. As we have seen in the duettino between Brogni and Rachel mentioned earlier (see Ex. 2.7), neither Quicherat's nor Lubarsch and Landry's approach fit perfectly (Quicherat requires an accent on "Parle," Lubarsch and Landry do *not* require an accent on "voix"). If we took Lubarsch and Landry as the point of reference, Halévy would have supplemented the obligatory accents with one (on "voix") derived from scanning:

(a) Landry and Lubarsch
   En mon âme une voix secrète
   Parle pour elle et la défend?
(b) Benloew (scanned iambs)
   En mon âme une voix secrète
   Parle pour elle et la défend?

(c) Halévy
En mon âme une voix secrète
Parle pour elle et la défend?

Only the light accent on "En," caused by the relative durational stress of the dotted note c', cannot be justified by any of the standard prosodic approaches because scanning the verse in trochees would lead to an unacceptable clash at the rhyme. Theorists focusing on music, such as Castil-Blaze or Choron, make it clear that redundant accents on unaccented syllables are permissible if they allow for transposition of a rhythmic pattern from one verse to the next, but in the case of "En mon âme," symmetry was clearly not Halévy's goal.[32] Rather, his interest lay in the invention of an original rhythmic design, an issue to be addressed more fully later.

Even though French theorists did not require musical reflection of all tonic accents, they repeatedly stressed the importance of verses with corresponding patterns of accents to allow for rhythmically corresponding phrases.[33] But librettists often did not provide the regular rhythmic structures demanded by Castil-Blaze, Fétis, and others, and depending on the dramatic situation, a composer simply may not have felt comfortable with the method of scanning described by Benloew, with its potential discrepancy between tonic accents and *temps forts*. And if the syntactic approach described by Lubarsch and Landry, which frequently would have resulted in rhythmically irregular musical solutions, could not offer a feasible alternative, the composer had to resort to some kind of compromise, adjusting the music, modifying the verses, or finding a way by which violations of prosody could be rendered barely perceptible. This situation seems to have caused considerable uncertainty as to the licenses that might be taken. René Brancour expressed this sentiment in his article "Mélodie" for the *Grande encyclopédie*:

There is ... an accommodation between the rhythm of a verse and that of the sounds that must be realized at the risk of compromising the harmony of their association. [These are] mysterious and complex rapports, the laws of which nearly completely escape analysis, which one must feel and not research with toil.[34]

Brancour's "mysterious and complex rapports" can be broken down into four basic solutions for setting irregular verses: the first downplays the problem, claiming that it would be perfectly all right partly to disregard prosody for the sake of melody; the second capitalizes on the ambiguous nature (stress vs. duration) of the French accents; the third suggests slowing down the musical pace in order to conceal prosodic "mistakes"; and the fourth proposes following the rhythms of verse at the cost of regular musical structures.

It is not surprising that the suggestion to ignore textual accents for the sake of melodic interest appears only rarely in critical writings (Benloew is a rare exception); it would have reflected badly on an author had he dared to condone the distortion of the French language. Nevertheless, the frequency with which prestigious composers disregarded strict correspondence of musical and textual accents indicates that melodic interest justified a

Example 2.9. Auber, *Le Domino noir*, II,7, "Chanson aragonaise" (Angèle).

free handling of prosody. Adrien de La Fage expressed this view in a critique of Charles Beauchemin's *Méloprosodie française, ou guide du chanteur* (1847), with the restriction only that such licenses not be pushed to an extreme. The various examples of scanning discussed earlier would be acceptable to La Fage:

In a language as the one spoken in France, is there such a great disadvantage in making a prosodic mistake in order to obtain a melodic phrase of a successful and new design? And the musicians of our day, are they so wrong in shaking off the chains with which the poets liked to burden them? I do not think so.[35]

As to the second solution, French theorists sometimes distinguished between accents of stress and duration but often confounded the two, whereas Italian theorists always maintained that syllables are accented simultaneously by stress and duration. This state of confusion in French treatises and criticism made it possible for a composer to draw on duration or stress with equal justification. In the following excerpt from *Le Domino noir*, Angèle, in disguise, sings a Spanish song as part of the evening's entertainment in the rooms of Count Juliano, one of her lover's friends (Ex. 2.9). Auber combines aspects of scanning with durational accents on metrically weak beats to accommodate verses of irregular length (the lengthened accents are highlighted).[36]

La belle Inès
    Fait flores;
Elle a des attraits,

Des vert<u>u</u>s;
Et bien pl<u>u</u>s,
Elle a des éc<u>u</u>s.

With regard to the third solution (slowing down the musical pace), a certain A. Fleury cites a set of three options from an unidentified text by Castil-Blaze, who, however, considers only the third one acceptable:

[The musician] would have to choose among these three possibilities: either changing the rhythm for each verse, which would be unbearable; violating the prosody by truncating notes and placing good notes on bad syllables, which is hardly less vicious; or finally creating a *vague melody without determined character* that does not create too much sense of rhythm and does not shock the prosody too much. This last procedure is the *least bad*, but *it is not good*.[37]

Castil-Blaze's suggestion to not "create too much sense of rhythm" does not seem as inappropriate to a language with generally weak tonic accents as he would have liked his readers to believe. French composers increasingly drew on this solution, but it is not always clear whether "vagueness" was the result of irregular accentuation, the composer's expressive ideal regardless of accentual structure, or both. In writing such melodies, a composer might continuously vary the rhythm or use equal note values in order to distribute the weight of the syllables evenly; he might introduce broad meters and accompaniments, draw on melodic and harmonic rather than rhythmic patterns, or avoid patterns altogether; or he could make use of accentual devices such as pitch and duration to neutralize the underlying metric structure with its implied accentual positions.

In the following excerpt from Halévy's *Le Juif errant* (1852), Ashvérus, the wandering Jew, has just saved an infant girl from a group of brigands and is contemplating her while she is sleeping. The beginning of this aria features the kind of irregularity Castil-Blaze suggested should be concealed by a vague melody (all tonic accents are highlighted):

<u>A</u>h! sur ton fr<u>o</u>nt de r<u>o</u>se,   [1,4,6]
Mon p<u>au</u>vre et b<u>e</u>l enf<u>a</u>nt,   [2,4,6]
Que mon **oeil** se rep<u>o</u>se,   [3,6]
Hél<u>a</u>s! un s<u>eu</u>l inst<u>a</u>nt!   [2,4,6]

Halévy set these verses in perfect rhythmic symmetry at the cost of prosodic inaccuracies in several cases (Ex. 2.10): the textual accents on "rose" and "repose" (the strongest ones in their respective verses from the standpoint of versification) have no metric and only a relative durational stress in the music, and the accent on "oeil" has neither a metric nor a durational stress. Four elements help to conceal the prosodic "deficiencies," all by preventing patterns that would forcefully establish strong and weak beats: a melodic design with a variety of rhythmic elements such as dotted figures, triplets, and tied notes sets up a minimum of repetition;[38] a subdued accompaniment avoids strong accents to beats 1 and 3; a diastematic accent on "repose" distracts attention from the empty syllable "se" on the downbeat; and irregular spacing of the durational accents on "Ah!," "pauvre," and "enfant" contributes to the vague quality Castil-Blaze may have had in mind.

French and Italian melodic aesthetics and practice ca. 1830–1870   59

Example 2.10. Halévy, *Le Juif errant*, I,8, "Ah! sur ton front de rose" (Ashvérus).

A particularly prominent example of a "vague" melody opens Raoul's *romance* from *Les Huguenots*, in which he recalls the feelings he had when he first saw Valentine. Although irregular accentuation does characterize the verse, the mood expressed by the text may better account for the overall quality of the melody.

Plus bl<u>a</u>nche que la bl<u>a</u>nche herm<u>i</u>ne,   [2,6,8]
Plus p<u>u</u>re qu'un j<u>ou</u>r de print<u>e</u>mps.   [2,5,8]

In a metrically clear and strongly accented context, Meyerbeer's interpretation of the prosody – with *e muets* on downbeats in both verses – would be terrible, but the nature of the accompaniment and his use of diastematic accents both alleviate the problem and reinforce the melancholy atmosphere of the text (Ex. 2.11). The solo viola accompaniment avoids any rhythmic pattern; only the harmonic implications provide some subtle sense of meter. In combination with the diastematic emphasis on the first "bl<u>a</u>nche" and on "herm<u>i</u>ne," Meyerbeer de-emphasizes the stress on the *e muets* of these two words, even though they fall on relatively longer notes and on harmonically defined downbeats. Furthermore, the slow tempo allowed him to repeat the first three syllables of the second verse in a natural fashion and thus to adjust the textual rhythm to the musical flow.

It seems that if irregular accentuation had indeed been a problem for a composer, he would have rewritten the verses or requested new and regular ones from the librettist, as both Meyerbeer and Halévy frequently did;[39] or he could have made minor adjustments to the musical rhythm in order to accommodate additional syllables. Such adjustments could be made more naturally in moderate and slow tempos where additional notes were less likely to necessitate a rushed delivery. When Jean-Jacques Rousseau complained about

Example 2.11. Meyerbeer, *Les Huguenots*, I,2, "Plus blanche" (Raoul).

the generally slow tempo of French music, he attributed it mainly to the inert quality of the French consonants, but the same result could also be justified by the irregular patterns of accent: "The pace of our music must be slow and boring. However so little one would like to accelerate its movement, the swiftness would resemble that of a hard and angular body rolling on the street."[40]

The fourth solution – accommodating irregular accentual rhythms by an irregular musical structure – suggests that changing rhythmic structures of the verse should be mirrored by new rhythms or an entirely new melody, probably along the lines of Example 2.7. Henri Blanchard, a contributor to the *Revue et gazette musicale*, censured the regular structure of Italian verses, which he believed led only to musical monotony:

The intellectual servility of Italy's *signor poeta* must cease, because the monotony of verse and rhythm of complaisance necessarily produce melodic monotony; and only mediocre composers should desire the continuation of lyric verses as they are made to this day. Such verses [are]

Casually clad in half a rhyme,
In unrelated and parallel lines they're cast,
With their uniform cadence, the ear is blast,
Or, inflated with great words that shock us through,
One dependent on the other, they drag on two by two.

The old masters of our musical school, and Gluck in particular, have proven themselves scrupulous observers of prosody and the rules of declamation in their melody, which often is not even balanced; and in this they are more truthful than our modern composers, for whom learned harmony is nearly everything.[41]

The previous examples have shown various musical responses to the challenges posed by irregularly accented verse. Italian composers faced such challenges to a lesser extent but nevertheless acknowledged, at least occasionally, French solutions as a chance to broaden their own vocabulary. One prominent statement comes from Arrigo Boito. As is so often the case in writings of the time, his remarks are vague. But the issues of prosody discussed above offer a better context for understanding what the composer may have had in mind:

[Verdi's *Les Vêpres siciliennes*] includes passages of exquisite elegance of harmony and elegance of rhythm not frequently found in the other works of the great composer; French verse, being less measured than our own, and having smoother and less definite accents, has helped the music, since it has removed the tedium of cantilena and of symmetry, that mighty dowry and mighty sin of Italian prosody that generates almost inevitably a meanness and poverty of rhythm within the musical phrase. But practically all our greats knew how to free themselves from this defect when they set French texts.[42]

Like Boito, Basevi embraces French verse as a way for Italian composers to enlarge their rhythmic vocabulary but unlike Boito goes so far as to accept prosodic "mistakes," citing Meyerbeer as a model:

To achieve the effective union of poetry and music, Meyerbeer broke those chains under the weight of which our masters seem willing to write. This independent action earned Meyerbeer the charge of strange and capricious [behavior] by those who, in order to walk, always look back and never ahead. On the other hand, those who, deprived of good taste, want slavish imitation and nothing more in the fine arts (and even in music for that matter) demand that song resemble declamation to such a degree as to confound the two. But operatic music would not have any reason to exist if this were its intention, and comedy and tragedy would have to chase the intruder opera from the stage altogether, as some advise.[43]

All these elaborations have shown the myriad of consequences prosody may have for the musical setting, depending on the chosen prosodic approach and, in the case of irregular verse, the strictness with which a composer was willing to accommodate the irregularity. The following pages will discuss aesthetic principles that focus on musical issues rather than on prosody, although some of the arguments will recall and corroborate aesthetic points already made.

Rhythmic design, phrase, and melodic development

Concern with regularity and symmetry pervaded discussions of not only the verse–music relationship but also rhythm and phrasing. Critics on both sides of the Alps advocated an ideal of regularity and symmetry, but French authors were more likely to propagate variety and freedom than their Italian colleagues and praised rhythmic ambiguity, especially if it suited a particular dramatic situation. The combination of diverse rhythms to soften metric stress has been mentioned earlier. The subdivision of downbeats followed by longer notes on weak beats – another prominent rhythmic feature of French melody – has a similar effect, as Désiré Beaulieu points out in his detailed study of musical rhythm:

The subdivision of the strong beat [of a measure], like that of the weak beat, can be done into two, three, four, six, etc. [This subdivision] results in a complete change of the rhythm's character because it inverts the natural order born of the need for regularity in the innate movement of man. [The subdivision] deprives the strong beat of its force, passing it on to the weak beat, and – in triple meter – even to the weakest of the three beats, the second. Furthermore, according to the various degrees of tempo and according to the character of the melody, [the subdivision] is appropriate to express everything that is opposed to order, from simple negligence to most absolute disorder ... [The following example is stamped] by this *laisser-aller*, this graceful negligence, the expression of which has so much charm:[44]

Hérold, *Le Pré-aux-Clercs,* Act I, no. 5, finale.

In Paris, original melodic invention was a prime concern. Hector Berlioz demanded greater rhythmic variety and challenged French and especially Italian composers to abandon the simple and uniform rhythms.[45] Fétis, while accusing Verdi of lacking melodic inventiveness, repeatedly praised Meyerbeer's achievements in this regard. His astute description of an excerpt from *Le Prophète* explains the composer's approach:

Few composers have to the same degree as Meyerbeer the feeling for rhythm at once original and regular. I find an example worthy of comment in this romance for two voices, the harmony of which I indicate from memory [Meyerbeer, *Le Prophète*, I,5]:

According to ordinary rhythmic tradition, one should have divided the first verse as follows:

Un | jour dans les | flots de la | Meuse, etc.

But the author of Le Prophète, instead of beginning on the upbeat of the measure, found a much more original form by beginning on the second beat, which gives the entire first part of the musical phrase an unusual and piquant character. But due to this arrangement, the second verse, "J'allais périr ... Jean me sauva," would have produced a phrase of only two measures and poorly cadenced with the four-measure phrase of the first. Meyerbeer, by repeating two new rhythms, gave the entire phrase its complete balance, while preserving a free allure for his original rhythms. Within the general effect of a large-scale musical work, the audience does not realize these results of an art very attentive to detail, but the connoisseur values them in an artist.[46]

Meyerbeer's setting – which is not as balanced with its nine-measure period as Fétis would have us believe – creates rhythmic-metric ambiguity because the strongest notes of the phrase often do not coincide with the strongest positions of the 3/8 meter. The f'' on "jour" is approached by a dotted figure and a leap of a fourth, a pattern usually associated with an upbeat and consequently perceived as leading to an accented note. The c'' and f'' on "pér<u>ir</u>" are accented by duration and by coinciding with a structural accent of the text, both notes again falling on metrically weak beats. And finally, Meyerbeer succeeds in packing three distinct rhythmic ideas into a nine-measure phrase. He was by no means the only composer of French opera playing with the audience's expectations; the examples by Halévy and Auber quoted earlier draw on the same principle, but Meyerbeer went further than his French colleagues in practically every respect.[47]

The Italians usually criticized the artful melodies of the French but on occasion pointed to them for inspiration. In his account on the general state of music in Italy, for instance, Raimondo Boucheron recognizes the need for rhythmic diversity, and although he does not expressly mention the French, his reference to artfulness and appropriate dramatic expression evokes French ideals:

Does beauty in dramatic melody lie only in the ease with which it engraves itself in the memory so that one can repeat this or that motive after the first hearing? We cannot believe it; rather, we estimate that a certain freedom, a certain artful nonchalance better befits the drama, provided that it is directed toward adding clarity to expression, dignity to the character, and novelty to the [musical] idea.[48]

The novelty of melodic invention mentioned by Boucheron became a particular problem toward the middle of the century when the trend toward syllabic text setting, itself associated with France,[49] made it increasingly difficult to conceive rhythmically original ideas while at the same time maintaining the rhythmic-metric clarity and immediate melodic intelligibility expected in Italy.

Italian composers indeed made attempts at inventing original rhythmic ideas, but usually without creating rhythmic-metric ambiguity. As early as the 1820s, Giovanni Pacini tried to find new solutions for his cabaletta themes, which earned him the nickname of "maestro delle cabalette." Unlike Meyerbeer, though, Pacini seemed to regret that rhythmic originality came only at the expense of naturalness:

> My *cabalettas* did not flow like limpid water from the purest well, but they were rather the fruit of some meditation, since I looked for a way to give poetic meters a different accent in order not to fall into melodies that recalled some other idea – something that is easy to verify, especially in the *first measure*. I advance the example of the manner in which the *quinario* was treated by the great Rossini and by me:

> I nearly always put the same system into practice for all other meters, trying at the same time to obtain more uniformity of thought between the first part of the theme and the second.[50]

It was with pride, however, that Pacini pointed to Italian superiority in regular phrasing, attributing it to the homogeneity of Italian verse:

> [I] only say that those [French composers] whom I admired most were Méhul [and] Boieldieu, because they were more melodious and balanced than the others in their compositions, insofar as their native language allowed it. And in this respect, may I observe that no other nation will ever take from us primacy in terms of inspiration; because our sweet idiom and by consequence our poetry, regulated by rhythm and uniformity of verse, are the principal causes for our melodic phrasing.[51]

Only those Italian critics with a weak spot for the *oltremontani* censured the overuse of symmetric phrases in the melodies of their composers. As with artful rhythms, Boucheron's emphasis on variety of phrasing and proper dramatic expression indicates that he had French models in mind:[52]

> Restricting the periods to eight, twelve, or sixteen measures as is often done, pairing rhythms and phrases so that each is followed by a corresponding second one – if this can be indispensable in ballet music or in other genres of small proportions, it can often harm a grand composition and be inappropriate for the dramatic concept, which requires that all means be subordinate to the scope of depicting the action represented with the greatest possible illusion. From this servility, to a great extent, comes the uniformity that spoils many modern melodies and the difficulty of creating new

Example 2.12. Gounod, *Faust*, III,4, "Salut! demeure chaste et pure" (Faust).

ones; from this, the exclusion of some meters in dramatic poetry, which could provide an opportunity for furthering expression, and the nearly always arbitrary laws with which the composers frequently torment the poets.[53]

Such observations might easily give a distorted picture of the melodic conventions for the time under consideration. In terms of symmetry and regularity, the melodies by Auber, Halévy, and Meyerbeer do not show as radical a difference from those of their Italian colleagues as the critical writings indicate. On the other hand, composers of the "old school," such as Gluck, as well as later progressive artists, such as Berlioz and Gounod, more readily abandoned regularity and symmetry.[54] The middle section of Faust's "Salut! demeure chaste et pure," for instance, features both irregular phrasing and a complete absence of symmetry (Ex. 2.12). The first three-measure phrase is followed by one of four measures, and although the remainder of the section consists of two- and four-measure phrases, Gounod avoids rhythmic repetition, paying close attention to the structure of the text.[55]

Italian critics also objected to the short-windedness of French melodies, maintaining that their own were longer and better developed. A German review of Verdi's *Rigoletto* recognized and deplored the presence of such short-winded melodies as a distinctly French influence: "The influence of French opera is felt in Verdi's operas more than in those of any other Italian composer. This new element reveals itself not only in the harmony but also penetrates the melody, disturbing the smooth flow with short rhythms and harsh accents."[56] Boucheron regretted this trend in Italian music in general:

Finally, we will say a word about the structure of melody, which ever more seems to approach the forms of the canzonetta instead of assuming a broad conception, which befits dramatic [melody], especially when dealing with a serious plot.[57]

The reviewers seem to have in mind the style of *opéra comique* with its parallel phrases of two measures in long meter (such as 4/4 and 6/8) or four measures in short meter (such

Example 2.13. Auber, *Le Domino noir*, I,6, "Une fée, un bon ange" (Angèle).

Example 2.14. Halévy, *La Juive*, I,5, "Loin de son amie" (Léopold).

as 2/4 and 3/8). In act I of *Le Domino noir*, for example, Angèle responds to Horace's questions about her identity with couplets that combine parallel rhythmic patterns into two-measure phrases in long meter (Ex. 2.13), and in act I of *La Juive*, Léopold serenades Rachel with strophes that combine parallel rhythmic patterns into four-measure phrases in short meter (Ex. 2.14). These kinds of phrases, however, do not appear in French opera as often as the critics imply, and it is possible that they were actually objecting to the rhythmic quality of the motives, the manner in which they are developed, or the nature of the accompaniments, rather than to the phrase length.

The concept of phrasing inevitably leads to the issue of "conducting a melody": that is, the question when to develop an existing idea and when to introduce a new one. A prime feature distinguishing French from Italian melody appears in what the Italians criticized as "frasi spezzate" or "frasi troncate" (broken-up or truncated phrases)[58] in contrast to their own "longer, better-felt, and more connected melodies."[59] Several characteristics may explain their perception of French melodies as broken: the orchestra and not the vocal part provides the melodic coherence (*parlante melodico* in Basevi's terminology), symmetry or the development of a theme is interrupted either too early or too often, or a melody consists of loosely connected fragments.

Rachel's act II *romance* from Halévy's *La Juive* illustrates all of these characteristics (Ex. 2.15). Anxiously awaiting the return of her mysterious lover Samuel (who in reality

Example 2.15. Halévy, *La Juive*, II,5, "Il va venir ... " (Rachel).

Example 2.15 (*Continued*)

Example 2.15 (*Continued*)

is Prince Léopold), Rachel is initially unable to utter a coherent melodic thought, punctuating the perfectly balanced phrases in the orchestra with mere fragments. One measure of orchestral transition (m. 9) announces a melodic idea new in rhythm, contour, and accompaniment (m. 10). After four measures, Halévy seems to repeat the phrase (m. 14) but breaks off after only two measures, a perfect example of what Mazzucato calls truncated melodies, "if not always at the beginning, then certainly in the middle [as in this particular case] or unfailingly toward the end." The third melodic idea – again new in rhythm, contour, and accompaniment – spans two clearly separated fragments of uneven length ("et cependant il va venir, cependant" [m. 16] and "il va venir" [m. 19]) and, when freely repeated (m. 20), is extended by an additional motive. As Mazzucato observed, "if [the phrase] does not break off, it is transformed into a new design, sets out for a new and unexpected path, so that its second part seems no longer to have any regular connection with the first."[60] This process continues until the recapitulation of the original theme (m. 37), with the melodic line becoming ever more declamatory.

The irregular accentual structure of the verse can explain the irregular setting only in part. To maintain phrase parallelism in the second melody ("D'une sombre..."), Halévy slightly altered Scribe's original text, as shown in Table 2.1. (The accents are highlighted according to Quicherat.) Halévy accommodated the distinct rhythmic features of the first two verses by assigning the melody to the orchestra, but the structure of the subsequent four verses, especially after the textual emendation, would have allowed for perfectly balanced

Table 2.1. Accentuation and phrasing in "Il va venir"

Music	Version of the libretto in Scribe's collected works	Variations of the text as set by Halévy	
a	Il va ven<u>i</u>r! ... il va ven<u>i</u>r!		[4,8]
a'	Et d'effr<u>oi</u> je me s<u>e</u>ns frém<u>i</u>r!		[3,6,8]
b	D'une s<u>o</u>mbre et tr<u>i</u>ste pens<u>é</u>e;		[3,5,8]
	Mon <u>â</u>me, hél<u>a</u>s! est oppress<u>é</u>e;		[2,4,8]
b'	Mon c<u>oeu</u>r ne bat p<u>a</u>s de plais<u>i</u>r,	Mon coeur b<u>a</u>t ... mais non de plais<u>i</u>r ...	[3,8]
c	Et cepend<u>a</u>nt ... il va ven<u>i</u>r.[61]		[4,8]

phrases (because neither the rhythmic patterns of verses 3 and 5 nor those of verses 4 and 6 clash). The contrast implied in the text by the word "cependant [however]" must have suggested a contrasting melody, a procedure that led to extensive text repetition in order to balance phrase c.[62]

In Paris, developing or conducting a melody assumed a wide variety of meanings with an overall greater emphasis on expressing the sentiment of the text.[63] Implications of the term "development" ranged from motivic fragmentation, counterpoint, and harmonic peroration in order to create extended formal sections, to the concept of "developing the passions" through contrasting, although not diametrically opposed melodic ideas.[64] It seems that a critic from the *Journal des débats* had the latter primarily in mind when he denied Italian composers in general and Verdi in particular any ability to develop an idea:

It is not easy to analyze Mr. Verdi's score, and what particularly renders our task laborious is the capital flaw for which we allow ourselves to reproach him first of all: Mr. Verdi ... is a TRUE ITALIAN for whom dramatic expression has been until now only a very secondary accessory, and who especially lacks the knowledge of how to develop an idea ... I would like to talk of this art [of development], of which LES HUGUENOTS and ROBERT LE DIABLE offer us such admirable models.[65]

The Italians had a rather different concept of development. Vitali, for example, believes that a thought, once introduced by a few phrases, should be developed and completed in the subsequent phrases, implying that the composer should confine development to the voice and not assign it, even if only in part, to the orchestra. Development thus meant maintaining melodic interest and coherence over an extended period of time.[66] In conducting their melodies, Italians expected from their composers that they sustain a once-established rhythm to render a melody more homogeneous, natural, and thus easy to grasp and remember.[67] This ideal tended to lead to what is now known as "mid-century lyric form," a prototype with many possibilities for variation and often an extended coda on previously stated text. Mid-century lyric form is based on eight verses (usually grouped 4+4 or 6+2) with each *a* phrase covering two verses and each *b* phrase one, as in this example from *Anna Bolena* (Ex. 2.16):[68]

Example 2.16. Donizetti, *Anna Bolena*, I,5, "Anna pure" (Enrico).

Anna pure amor m'offria,	*a*
Vagheggiando il soglio inglese ...	
Ella pure il serto ambìa	*a'*
Dell'altéra Aragonese ...	
L'ebbe alfin; ma l'ebbe appena,	*b*
Che sul crin le vacillò.	*b'*
Per suo danno, per sua pena,	*a"*
D'altra donna il cor tentò.	

This form, with its many possibilities for variation (such as replacing the final *a"* phrase by a *c* phrase, extending or compounding sections, etc.), accounts for a large portion of lyrical passages in Italian opera. The excerpt from Donizetti's *Anna Bolena* shows not only a pure example of mid-century lyric form but also how a short melodic idea can be developed into a sixteen-measure period, which in turn comes to a satisfying close. This approach perfectly reflects the aesthetic ideal of symmetry, balance, and principal focus on melody that prevailed in Italy at the time. But for the admirers of Meyerbeer, mid-century lyric form led to the dramatic "non-sense" of repeating old music with new text,[69] a pitfall that was easier to avoid when setting French librettos, because their forms challenged Italian composers to invent new ways of conducting a melody:

> The true difficulty for an Italian [composer] writing on a French libretto consists in having to set pieces that require new forms; because poetry destined for cantabile is now too short, now too long, sometimes it is repeated many times, and sometimes it is interrupted with recitatives. This and many other things impede the adaptation of musical forms accepted in Italy today. The change of form inevitably entails a change in the conduct of the pieces, from which it arises that where one intends to remain in the Italian style, one is obliged to pass quickly over verses when they exceed the scope required in the Italian form or linger too long where there are too few. Thus, italianizing a French libretto means in every respect amplifying Italian music, overloading it with musical pleonasms.[70]

Harmony and accompaniment

The interest French theorists took in harmony affected their concept of melody. While they tended to view melodic and harmonic components as equally important, if not inseparable, Italian critics expressed the concern that nothing should distract attention from the vocal line. Pietro Siciliani maintained as late as 1868 that Italian melody had to preserve its independence from harmony: "Here is what characterizes Italian song, the melodic element of our music: it is independent from everything that is not song, that is to say, from harmony; and nevertheless it is beautiful, always beautiful in its substance, whether you hear it sung by the uncouth voice of a yokel or by the most able artist."[71] Not all Italian critics espoused an aesthetic in which melody reigned at the expense of harmonic interest, but French writings consistently praised the way in which French composers used original harmony to intensify melodic charm or achieve other effects.[72] Fétis referred to this perfect union of the two parameters as *mélodie harmonique*, a concept he believed Italians had resisted for a long time. And although he conceded in 1853 that during the previous forty years Italian composers had caught up to some degree, he made it clear that it was only when Rossini "touched the French soil that his tendencies of transformation took a more decisive determination: *Guillaume Tell* is the highest manifestation of these tendencies.[73] There, Rossini fully enters the realm of attractive harmony, and his melodies assume a harmonic character."[74] Rossini, however, defended the viewpoint that Italian melody was expected to please even if the underlying harmonies consisted only of tonic and dominant. An anecdote in *L'Art musical* vividly illustrates this point:

"Maestro [Rossini]," said [an unknown composer], "I have come to show you my grand work for double choir and double orchestra entitled *The Last Judgment* and ask you, as a service, to tell me frankly whether I am born for composition and whether I should persist in pursuing this career. I ask you in particular to pay attention to the high point of my work. At the moment where the dead rise from the tomb, one hears a piece that will be frightening due to the fact that it is scored entirely for brass instruments playing in eight real parts, with eight pairs of timpani, eight piccolos, and a children's chorus of three hundred, which until then has not uttered a sound."

Rossini cast a suspicious glance at the author of *The Last Judgment*, examined the score, and said: "Very good; now, write me a short aria accompanied on the piano by only two chords, the chord of the tonic and the chord of the dominant, and I will see whether you are born for composition and whether I should in good conscience encourage you to pursue this career."[75]

Indeed, Italian composers generally kept their harmonic vocabulary simple, especially when introducing a melody at the beginning of an aria; they occasionally employed the subdominant, the supertonic, the submediant, and secondary dominants but did not go out of their way to find particularly unusual or chromatic harmonic progressions. Rossini's argument, of course, does not imply that Italian melodies should avoid harmonies other than the tonic and the dominant. In fact, we find quite regularly melodic expositions over more sophisticated progressions, such as Amina's "Ah! vorrei trovar parole" from Bellini's *La sonnambula* (1831), in which the heroine cannot find words to express to Elvino her feelings of love. The harmonies constantly change both within the phrases and from one phrase to the next (Ex. 2.17).

French melodies may demonstrate somewhat greater harmonic interest than their Italian counterparts, but the difference is not as significant as the critics want us to believe. For the period after Rossini, not even Fétis distinguishes any longer between the two traditions, accusing both French and Italian composers of tormented harmony.[76] And when Halévy or Meyerbeer resort to more sophisticated harmony, one often senses a conscious effort to be original, due at least in part to the discrepancy between adjacent inventive and uninventive progressions. A melody as simple as Brogni's *cavatine* from Halévy's *La Juive*, with its short meter and repetitive rhythm, receives much of its interest from the harmonic underpinning, but after all the activity through m. 8, the static alternation between A major

Example 2.17. Bellini, *La sonnambula*, I,5, "Ah! vorrei trovar parole" (Amina).

and D minor in mm. 9–12 sticks out as rather dull. Still, the tonic does not return until m. 14 and a strong cadence not until m. 16, contributing to what Fétis called *largeur du style* (Ex. 2.18).[77]

With regard to the accompaniment, the distinctions between French and Italian opera resemble those applied to rhythm, phrasing, and harmony. The goal of providing a melody with a solid rhythmic-metric foundation often led Italian composers to choose accompaniments with regular rhythmic or melodic patterns, which let the melody shine because of their consistency and formulaic nature. Fétis was particularly harsh in criticizing formulaic accompaniments, not so much those of the subdued type of Bellini's "Ah! vorrei trovar parole," but rather those of the rhythmically forceful character often found in Verdi:

If the fashionable maestro [Verdi] lacks originality and invention in melody, his imagination is no richer in the orchestration and rhythm of his accompaniments. There is only one manner, one formula for each thing, and from his first score to the latest, he shows himself everywhere the same, with a desperate obstinacy. For his arias and duets, he seized a form of accompaniment for the themes put in use by Bellini and Donizetti. This form is always as follows:[78]

Example 2.18. Halévy, *La Juive*, I,4, "Si la rigueur" (Brogni).

Fétis does not seem to have accepted that such patterns establish both the necessary metric clarity and the character's agitation, most typically in cabalettas, but he was not the only French critic slamming Verdi for "musical violence." Gustave Bertrand found the orchestration just as objectionable as the rhythms:

> Since his first works, since *Ernani* and *I lombardi*, one noticed this hot and impetuous inspiration which forgets to be refined, this violence of rhythm and sonority, which often dispenses with melodic invention ... When his *romances* speak of love and sighs, we must not believe a word: deep down it shouts: To arms![79]

A poem published in the *Revue et gazette musicale* confirmed that if Verdi intended to compete with the most successful composers in Paris, he had to refine his orchestration:

> Vraiment l'affiche est dans son tort;
> En faux on devrait la poursuivre.
> Pourquoi donc annoncer *Nabucodonos-or*
> Quand c'est *Nabucodonos-cuivre*.[80]

[The lies of the poster are really too bold,
We cannot allow them to pass.
How can they announce *Nabucodonos-gold*
And play *Nabucodonos-brass*?]

Fétis and Bourges, among others, recognized that orchestration could play an important role in creating original, less aggressive accompaniments and thus influence our perception of the melody. It is from this perspective that orchestration will be primarily considered.[81]

Although rhythmic patterns occur in French opera as well, they tend to be broader and less accentuated, often relying on harmony more than on any other parameter.[82] Maurice Bourges, a contributor to the *Revue et gazette musicale*, naturally singled out Meyerbeer as a model for imaginative accompaniments:

> Meyerbeer does not restrict himself, like the Italians, to lodging all interest in the vocal melody, of which he nevertheless cultivates to the highest degree the forms, allures, and rhythms definitely suited to the subject. He does more: he entrusts to the accompaniment a role that is always important. For him, accompaniment is a game of physiognomy, gesture, eloquent pantomime that reveals all that the voice does not say and could not say. Of the accompaniment he makes a skilled interpreter, a paraphrase, an intelligent gloss that details all the sensations and sets in relief the accessories without pushing meanwhile to the abuse of the picturesque, this scourge of contemporary art. Also, [there are] no banal formulas, fripperies dragging on under the craziest Italian and French thoughts and even in German *Lieder* of recent years.[83]

Bourges's inclusion of French composers among those who were writing formulaic accompaniments must not hide the fact that the solutions of other artists, such as Halévy and Berlioz, are also more complex than those generally found in Italian opera. Ashvérus's contemplation "Ah! sur ton front de rose" from *Le Juif errant* (Ex. 2.10) illustrates this distinction: in the accompaniment, harmony rather than rhythmic or melodic patterning establishes the meter in both the first and second themes, and harmony, although just as effective as rhythm in marking the meter, is usually less obtrusive and thus more in agreement with French aesthetic.

The stylistic features of French melody discussed in this chapter – prosody, rhythm, and phrasing; vocal and orchestral dialogue; and emphasis on harmonically interesting and expressive accompaniments – may explain why French critics characterized the melodies of their composers as "charmant," "mélancolique," "naturel," "tendre," "plein de grâce," "suave," and, of course, "expressif." These adjectives contrast markedly with those chosen by Mazzucato to characterize Italian melody: "fluida," "simmetrica," "rotonda," "periodata," "ben ritmato." And although French composers drew on characteristics appropriated by the Italians and vice versa, we can distinguish the respective conventions on the basis of the distinct priorities attributed to these characteristics. Because Meyerbeer, in the eyes of the French, found the most daring but also the most successful balance, he inevitably set the standard against which Italian composers writing for the Opéra were measured. Progressive Italian authors accordingly embraced him as the genius who showed the path to the future:

> But then, more and more, evening by evening, pricking up its ears, the audience noticed that the dawn of Münster had something beautiful and true that was not in the electric staging, in the flapping flags, in the silvery ice, but in a certain aura, in a certain atmosphere, in a certain ...
>
>   indistinct unknown ...

that was fluttering in the orchestra, in the choruses, in the rhythms, in the potent notes; and they sensed in their heart the mysterious contact with a very new genius.[84]

Despite the significant differences between French and Italian melodic aesthetics and practice, the constant intellectual and musical exchange between the two traditions will never allow a complete distinction. Nevertheless, the trends outlined here provided a clear sense of the direction Verdi had to take when writing for the Paris Opéra.

Episode: Design, middleground rhythm, and phrase

A cursory examination of the analytical literature on Verdi's music is sufficient to reveal a fundamental methodological problem: the concept of the phrase, one of the most important musical building blocks in Verdi analyses, lacks a clear definition. This is hardly surprising, for the application of a strict system tends to lay open methodological deficiencies, either because it does not produce results that are adequately detailed or because it superimposes an analytical system that dissects the music in an unnatural and thus meaningless way. Nineteenth-century French and Italian writers struggled with this problem to such an extent that their theories can at best suggest basic approaches,[1] while more recent scholars have tended to use the term "phrase" loosely. In his analysis of Paolo's *racconto* "L'atra magion vedete" from the Prologue of *Simon Boccanegra*, for example, Joseph Kerman interprets the following excerpt as consisting of phrases *a*, *a'*, and *b* (Ex. E.1).[2] The opening four measures, which exactly repeat a two-bar thematic idea, receive the label *a*, the distinct concluding idea of a single gesture the label *a'* ("Una beltà infelice"). The subsequent transition of eight measures ("Sono i lamenti suoi"), which picks up the rhythm of phrase *a* exactly, is labeled *b*; nothing accounts for its subdivisions or the proximity to *a*.

The term "phrase" calls for a definition that is both clear and sufficiently flexible. We will take as our point of departure Antoine Reicha's "design" and develop it into a concept of phrasing by drawing on later definitions of cadence types and the rhythmic theories by Grosvenor Cooper and Leonard Meyer, Maury Yeston, and Joel Lester,[3] always striving for practicality. Much of what follows in later chapters, especially the prosodic interpretations, can be followed without this theoretical episode; however, certain interpretations of musical parameters reflecting general French aesthetics, whether influenced by prosody or not, will make more sense in light of the following methodological clarifications. These are not hard and fast rules and may be modified according to the purpose of a particular analysis. But even a flexible concept must be followed consistently if it is to generate reliable results.

The perception of a phrase depends on a variety of factors, most notably a certain length, harmonic and melodic cadences, and parallelism. A single note, for example, cannot make up a phrase because it lacks movement and thus a concluding gesture. Two notes (as those on "Ami" in Ex. E.2 below) could theoretically make up a phrase, but in most cases, this would hardly correspond with the listener's perception. And even with strings of more than two notes, it is the conclusiveness of the cadence or the existence of a subsequent parallel

Example E.1. *Simon Boccanegra*, Prologue, 4, "L'atra magion vedete" (Paolo), with phrasing according to Kerman.

idea that evokes the decisive perception. Nineteenth-century Italian theorists recognized the importance of cadence in analyzing phrases, but their definitions are inadequate for our purposes, because the various parameters are not defined with sufficient clarity.[4] A combination of nineteenth-century ideas with a modern definition of cadence, however, does offer a sufficiently clear and consistent system.

Let us begin with the cadence and define it as a relatively conclusive gesture with the following combination of harmonic and melodic aspects (Table E.1):[5] For a cadence to define a phrase ending, it must have the strength of at least a half cadence or a deceptive cadence, whether in a clearly defined key or a local tonic. Such cadences can, however, be subverted, for example, when the note concluding the cadence ties over to the subsequent harmony. In her *romance* from *Les Vêpres siciliennes*, Hélène's languor emerges in part in the elevated cadential notes, especially in the last, most passionate one at "grande peine," which carries over from the half cadence on a subdominant C-minor harmony into the subsequent dominant D-major harmony, creating a single three-measure phrase (Ex. E.2).[6]

In his *Traité de mélodie*, Reicha required that a phrase (called *rhythme* or *membre*) consist of at least one or two designs (i.e., short melodic ideas punctuated by a cadence):[7]

If a melodic design is very short and if it has only a weak [melodic] cadence, it must at least be repeated, with other pitches, and the repetition must have a more strongly marked [melodic] cadence; thus the melody will have a more determined sense because this repetition reinforces it ... We call such a parallel repetition a *rhythme*...

Episode: Design, middleground rhythm, and phrase

Table E.1. Typology of cadences

Cadence type	Cadence strength	Conditions (all cadences require a point of rest in the melody)
Full	strong	IV-I or V-I harmonic progression; root progression in the bass; melodic cadence on the root of the chord
	weak	IV-I or V-I harmonic progression; penultimate or ultimate chord in inversion (this includes vii-I cadences) or melodic cadence on a note other than the root of the chord
Half	strong	I-IV or I-V harmonic progression; root progression in the bass; melodic cadence on the root of the chord
	weak	I-IV or I-V harmonic progression; penultimate or ultimate chord in inversion or melodic cadence on a note other than the root of the chord
Deceptive	strong	surprising cadence, but otherwise with the same attributes as the strong cadences above
	weak	surprising cadence, but otherwise with the same attributes as the weak cadences above
Quarter[8]		a) the melody rests, but the harmonic progression does not fit any of the above types b) full or half harmonic cadences: (1) with the penultimate or ultimate chord in inversion and the melodic cadence on a note other than the root of the chord; (2) with the penultimate and ultimate chords in inversion and the melodic cadence on the root of the chord

Example E.2. *Les Vêpres siciliennes*, IV,2 "Ami! ... le coeur d'Hélène" (Hélène).

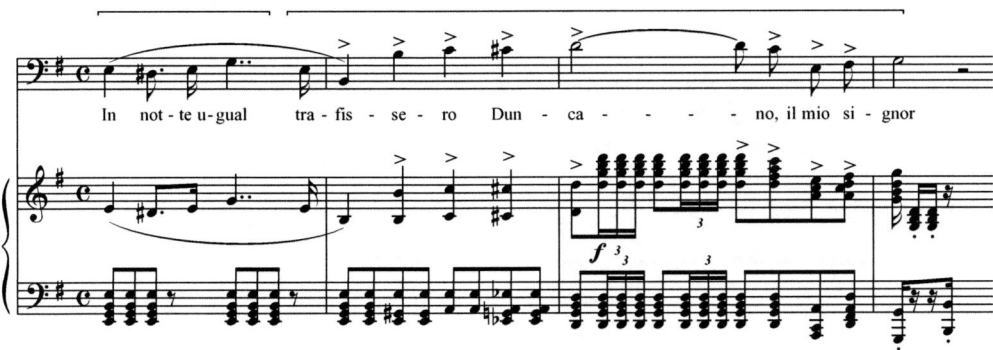

Example E.3a. *Macbeth*, II,4 "Come dal ciel precipita" (Banco).

In order to distinguish a design from the subsequent design, it must have at least a [melodic] quarter cadence, that is, a little point of repose resulting from (1) a rest or (2) a longer note. In short, there must be something at the end of each design, however small this difference may be, that distinguishes it from the beginning of the next.[9]

In determining designs, Reicha draws on two musical elements: melodic repetition (which must include aspects of contour or rhythm), and punctuating longer notes and rests. He first tried to ignore harmonic characteristics but then, in the supplement of the *Traité*, conceded that these cannot be ignored.[10] Only the consideration of all these elements together produces convincing results, and if ambiguity remains, the structure of the text may provide the solution. An example from *Macbeth* illustrates the way in which the harmonic structure articulates and differentiates two very similar melodic ideas (Ex. E.3a). In Ex. E.3a, the first design could not end on the *B* of "tra*fis*sero," despite the slur and the subsequent contrast in register. The lack of harmonic closure, the articulation, and the text all indicate that the *B* functions as the beginning rather than the end of a melodic gesture. In Ex. E.3b, on the other hand, the strong harmonic cadence on "terror" together with the contrast in articulation and register creates a clear incision completing a design, even if the final note is neither relatively longer nor followed by a rest. The example also shows that designs are distinct from motives in that they are marked by articulating elements or points of repose, whereas motives can be of any size as long as they maintain their rhythmic identity (see, for example, the beginning of Ex. E.3b as marked in brackets below the text).

Determining the end of a design is somewhat more involved in the case of musical *sdrucciolo* and *piano* endings, where the crucial longer notes fall on the penultimate or antepenultimate position of a potential design. In theses cases, the concluding shorter notes must be separated from what follows in some way: they may coincide with the end of a word or mark the end of some kind of pattern or a change in contour, and they certainly must not require resolution on a subsequent harmony. In Ex. E.4a, incisions fall after

Example E.3b. *Macbeth*, II,4 "Come dal ciel precipita" (Banco).

Example E.4a. *La traviata*, II,1 "De' miei bollenti spiriti" (Alfredo).

Example E.4b. *La traviata*, III,7 "Parigi, o cara" (Alfredo).

"immemore" (*sdrucciolo* ending, followed by a break in contour due to the repeated A♭′) and after "quasi" (*piano* ending and break in contour); in Ex. E.4b, symmetry reinforces the structure suggested by the *piano* ending.

Reicha does not specify the minimum length of a design. He does, however, point out that in some cases designs and phrases can be equivalent (several examples from his *Traité* serve as evidence).[11] Thus, it would seem more reasonable to focus on the minimum length of a design rather than the minimum length of a phrase and to investigate the circumstances under which a design can count as an independent phrase. In determining the minimum length of a design, we will draw on the concept of middleground rhythm.[12]

Unlike surface rhythm, which takes into account every note, middleground rhythm encompasses a variety of levels from the dominant foreground pulse to slower-rate changes of phrase, texture, or key area. For our purpose, a foreground pulse is considered dominant if it adds fewer notes *to* the surface rhythm of a design or ignores fewer notes *of* the surface rhythm than any other possible pulse. In the pattern ♩♩|♫♩, for example, a whole-note pulse ignores three foreground attacks and adds none (a deviation of three notes); a quarter-note pulse would ignore one foreground attack and add four (a deviation of five notes). No pulse leads to a lower sum of added and ignored attacks than that of the whole-note (and thus dominant) pulse. A rest following a design and the notes of the subsequent design covered by the last pulsation of the predecessor count as deviations from the pulse; in ambiguous cases, preference will be given to the faster pulse. Ex. E.5 provides an illustration: here, a half-note pulse dominates in the first design (by ignoring five foreground attacks, including the d' on the second "Au"), a quarter-note pulse in the second (ignoring three foreground attacks and adding one). Although the melodic pulse tends to be closely related to the designated meter, the meter signature itself does not always adequately determine the pulse but rather provides the composer's metric interpretation of a longer musical section. It thus makes more sense to infer the pulse not from the metric signature but from inherently musical characteristics.

Example E.5. *Les Vêpres siciliennes*, III,3 "Au sein de la puissance" (Montfort).

Example E.6. *Ernani*, II,3 "Oro, quant'oro ogn'avido" (Ernani).

Several parameters can group pulses into distinct middleground rhythms: harmonic change, relative dynamic stress, changes of contour or register, obligatory prosodic accents, and accompanimental patterns. Because a musical passage includes a variety of middleground levels, we must decide on which one to focus. For the purpose of this study, it is most practical to stick closely to the surface (i.e., to a level that groups some of the pulses into middleground beats). This step is perhaps the least obvious but usually fairly straight-forward: the various kinds of patterns and accents tend to leave little doubt about the immediate grouping of the pulses. The following examples illustrate the theory in some relatively tricky cases.

In Ex. E.6, the melody features a quarter-note pulse, which the accent on <u>a</u>vido and the harmonic rhythm (bracketed below the system) group into a clearly perceivable middleground pattern of ♩♩|♩ ♩. The next two measures introduce a new middleground rhythm of ♩♩|♩. Suspensions, essentially dividing one harmonic progression into two, cannot support two middleground beats unless other middleground-defining parameters reinforce the harmonic resolution or the resolution conflicts with the previous middleground pattern;

Example E.7. *Les Vêpres siciliennes*, III,3 "Au sein de la puissance" (Montfort).

Ex. E.6, for instance, includes first a conflicting suspension (on "avido"), then a non-conflicting one (on "desio"). The latter could possibly be interpreted as its own middleground beat, based on the accentuation provided by the accompanimental pattern, in which case "puote saziar desio" would break into two designs. But because we have thus far grouped according to the harmonic rather than the melodic accompanimental pattern, a three-quarter middleground beat on "desio" makes more sense.

Middleground rhythm provides a helpful frame of reference for determining the minimum length of a design. Reicha's theory fails to establish clear guidelines, but a minimum of two middleground beats proves meaningful for our purposes. For instance, the first two notes of Ex. E.6 (♩♪), separated from the following ones by a rest, might be considered a design, but they cover only one middleground beat. The first two notes of Ex. E.7 (♩│♩) similarly make up a potential design, in which a dominant quarter-note pulse seems to be grouped into a subsequently repeated design (♩│♩ and ♫│♩). But harmony, the main force in grouping the pulse in this case, suggests otherwise. The harmony of the introductory measure begins earlier than the opening c♯ of the vocal line, causing it to be interpreted as an upbeat to a middleground beat (marked above the staff) rather than a middleground beat itself. The f♯ is thus the actual beginning of the middleground pattern.

Determining the first design raises further issues. It could not end on "ap[-paraître]" (i.e., with the third middleground beat), because the a♯ does not conclude a word. The three notes on the textual repetition of "à mes yeux," of course, cover only one middleground beat and thus do not qualify as a separate design. Ex. E.7 should therefore be interpreted as a single design.

To answer the question as to why a design is sometimes perceived as a complete phrase and sometimes as only part of one, we must consider the forces of phrase parallelism and unifying melodic gestures. Parallelism here refers to phrases that include identical or nearly identical interval patterns and functionally identical harmony (see Ex. E.1) or antecedent-consequent phrases (see the first three measures of Ex. E.8). In Verdi's operas, parallelism occurs at the beginning of most aria sections, either as exact or modified

Example E.8. *Les Vêpres siciliennes*, II,3 "Ah! l'ai-je bien" (Henri).

repetition commonly labeled *a* and *a'*. They may occur at two levels, if *a* and *a'* themselves include subordinate parallel structures. In such cases, the higher level of parallelism will be given precedence.

Overarching gestures, too, may group short phrases (whether defined by parallelism or cadences) into a longer phrase, especially when the phrases are tightly connected due to weak cadences and the absence of a clear separating rest. The beginning of Henri's "O jour de peine" is a good example (Ex. E.9). The opening two designs, punctuated by a strong cadence on F major, initiate an arch and will be interpreted, together with the two subsequent designs, as a single phrase *a*. Neither *a*, *a'* nor *a*, *b* would describe the first eight measures in a meaningful way.

Example E.9. *Les Vêpres siciliennes*, IV,1 "O jour de peine" (Henri).

As this episode has shown, rhythmic, harmonic, and melodic aspects must be taken into account when formulating a clear concept of phrasing. Equipped now with a thorough understanding of French prosody and the musical tools to describe its impact, it is time to embark on the journey through Verdi's three French operas, interpreting them first in light of their responses to French prosody and melodic aesthetics and then in terms of their influence on his subsequent Italian works.

PART II

French melody in Verdi's operas

3 | *Jérusalem* and its influence on the subsequent Italian operas

After conducting the premiere of *I masnadieri* in London, Verdi traveled to Paris, where he hoped to finally lead the life he wished.[1] He had little time to relax, however: within a week of his arrival on July 28, 1847, the new directors of the Opéra, Nestor Roqueplan and Charles Duponchel, succeeded in convincing the composer to provide an opera for the fall season. Such short notice did not allow Verdi time to compose a new work, and so he negotiated a contract that would let him rework *I lombardi*, an opera first performed in 1843. Eugène Scribe suggested that Verdi collaborate with librettists Alphonse Royer and Gustave Vaëz, who agreed to fit a modified plot to existing music. We know very little about the collaboration between librettists and composer. With Verdi living in Paris, the parties involved could discuss emerging issues face to face and did not have to rely on the postal system. Unfortunately, the constant presence of two librettists, two impresarios, and two editors (Léon and Marie Escudier) not only deprived posterity of insightful correspondence regarding the project but sufficed to drive Verdi mad, as he himself confessed in a letter to a friend.[2] As to the music, Verdi rearranged some of the numbers, omitted others, composed a few new ones, and replaced transitions where necessary.

Although the librettists had to adapt the *Lombardi* libretto to a modified plot, they aimed at a free translation, often preserving only key words and the overall sense. In instances where a free translation was not feasible, they tended to preserve at least the overall affect, accentual structure, and verse length. A comparison of "La mia letizia infondere" with its French remake, "Je veux encor entendre," shows, however, that the librettists occasionally changed not only the dramatic situation but also prosodic characteristics. In *I lombardi*, the aria is sung by the Muslim Oronte, son of the tyrant of Antioch. He has fallen in love with Giselda – who had been captured while on a crusade led by her father – and wishes he could find a way to get her to return his feelings. In *Jérusalem*, the protagonist is Gaston, who, after having been exiled from France for alleged murder, was captured by the Emir of Ramla. Having learned that his love Hélène is among the crusaders in the vicinity, Gaston expresses his desire to see her again. The first three verses of the French perfectly copy the structure of the original's tonic accents. But the fourth, sixth, and eighth verses change the accentual structure and, in the case of the former two, the poetic meter as well.

La mia letizia infondere	[2,4,6]	Je veux encor entendre	[2,4,6]
Vorrei nel suo bel core!	[2,4,6]	Ta voix, ta voix si tendre.	[2,4,6]
Vorrei destar coi palpiti	[2,4,6]	Pour fuir il faut attendre	[2,4,6]
Del mio beato amore	[2,4,6]	Les ombres du soir.	[2,5]
Tante armonie nell'etere,	[1,4,6]	Ange vers qui s'envole	[1,4,6]

Example 3.1. *I lombardi*, "La mia letizia infondere" (Oronte) with a hypothetical French text underlay and inserts from *Jérusalem*, II,7, "Je veux encor entendre" (Gaston), reflecting Verdi's solution.

Quanti pianeti egli ha;	[1,4,6]	Mon rêve d'espoir,	[2,5]
Ir seco al cielo, ed ergermi	[2,4,6]	Bel ange, mon idole,	[2,6]
Dove mortal non va!	[1,4,6]	Je veux encor te voir.	[2,4,6]
(*I lombardi*, II,2)		(*Jérusalem*, II,7)	

Example 3.1 (*Continued*)

It seems that Royer and Vaëz either expected Verdi to adjust the music to the new text, or they knew that their verses fit the music despite the prosodic changes. A hypothetical underlay of the French text in the Italian score shows what they could have had in mind, and in most cases, Verdi followed this solution (Ex. 3.1). He must have objected, however, when in the sixth verse (mm. 11–12), the pronoun "mon" fell on the downbeat, pushing the accented syllable of "rêve" to the second quarter of the measure. Nevertheless, the hypothetical text underlay would perfectly conform with French aesthetics because the accented syllable of "rêve" would still receive a rhythmic and harmonic emphasis from the accompaniment. In Verdi's solution, the first syllable of "rêve" falls on the downbeat, but the second syllable now receives the same harmonic and rhythmic accents as the first.

The setting of the last verse presents a more complex case. Accentuation of "je" over "veux" would not be possible according to any theorist. But Royer and Vaëz could have envisioned a belated entry of the voice to make "veux" fall on the third quarter of the measure, which, because the orchestra doubles the voice, would not have significantly altered the melodic experience. On the other hand, the librettists may have assumed Verdi would add the upbeat he indeed ended up adding. Once again he seems to have played it safe, putting tonic accents in relief by aligning them with a downbeat.

The following pages will investigate the significance of the melodic characteristics of *Jérusalem* by comparing borrowed and reworked portions with their sources, by investigating melodic peculiarities of the original portions, and by interpreting the findings in the context of the surrounding Italian operas. It will become clear that the influences of French prosody and aesthetics, while apparent in detail, did not lead to an inherently French work, and it is thus not surprising that *Jérusalem*'s influences on the subsequent Italian operas remained minimal. Verdi's approach to prosody at this point shows him overly concerned with reflecting every tonic accent and not yet in command of the variety of options that might have helped renew his style.

Comparing reworked and borrowed portions

Jérusalem has particular importance for our purposes. In other *rifacimenti*, such as *Macbeth*, *Stiffelio/Aroldo*, *Simon Boccanegra*, and *Don Carlos*, a gap of seven or more years separates the revised version from the original. *Jérusalem*, on the other hand, followed *I lombardi* after only four and a half years, which means that stylistic differences are more likely to have resulted from adapting the opera for Paris than from the composer's artistic development.[3] Borrowed and reworked portions of *Jérusalem* abound with minor revisions, and many can be explained by Verdi's response to French aesthetics.

In turning Pagano's "Sciagurata! hai tu creduto" into Roger's "Oh! dans l'ombre dans le mystère," Verdi made only minor changes. The two movements fulfill the same dramatic function of conveying the reason for the protagonists' murderous intentions: they are unable to overcome their love for a woman who belongs to someone else. Several of the musical revisions are mentioned in earlier literature but usually without prosodic interpretation.[4] The most significant of these, besides the transposition from C major to B-flat major, undoubtedly concerns the accompaniment. The French version is not only less busy and lighter overall, showing Verdi's awareness of his reputation in France as a noisy composer, but also smoother (Ex. 3.2a). David Kimbell explains the latter characteristic by the emotional content of the text, which, he claims, evokes "a secret passion," whereas the Italian version expresses "a frenzy of rage."[5] But this argument could easily be turned around (the French talks about vengeance and death, the Italian about pain), and Verdi might well have considered the original accompaniment as an appropriate evocation of "mystère (mystery)" and "feu coupable (guilty fire)."

Example 3.2a. *I lombardi*, I,4, "Sciagurata! hai tu creduto" (Pagano) and *Jérusalem*, I,6, "Oh! dans l'ombre dans le mystère" (Roger).

Certainly, the abundance of *e muets* and the concern that they not be overly stressed explain the changes more convincingly. The pattern of the Italian accompaniment creates two strongly marked beats at the beginning and in the middle of the measure, and beats 2 and 4 receive rhythmic accents by means of articulation and harmonic suspension. In agreement with French practice, Verdi broadened the accompanimental pattern by repeating it only every measure (instead of every half measure), omitted the accent on beat 2, and replaced the accent on beat 4 by one that does not stand as sharply in relief as in the Italian version. The new arrangement thus reduces stress on the fourth syllable of each verse, which in the French text often coincides with an *e muet*, the weakest of all syllables. With a less-accented accompaniment, Verdi succeeded in avoiding too strong an emphasis on the endings of "ombre," "mystère," "coupable," "encore," "angoisses," "tendresse," and "vengeance."

Oh! dans l'ombre, dans le mystère
Feu coupable que j'ai su taire,
Reste encore caché à la terre
    Mes angoisses, mes remords.
    Mais redoute ma colère,
    Toi, l'amant qu'elle préfère!
    Ta tendresse en vain espère,
    Ma vengeance veut ta mort.

Other musical changes can also be explained, at least in part, by prosody. For the contrasting b and b' phrases, for instance, Royer and Vaëz provided verses that most French composers of the time would have accepted as perfectly compatible with the Italian melody. But Verdi preferred to de-emphasize *e muets*, accepting word repetition in return.[6] The following hypothetical text underlay (added to the Italian score in Ex. 3.2b) would have perfectly agreed with Benloew's system of scanning.[7]

M**ai**s red**ou**te m**a** col**è**re, b
T**oi**, l'am**a**nt qu'ell**e** préf**è**re. b'

For the cabaletta, Pagano's "O speranza di vendetta" gave way to Roger's "Ah! viens! démon! esprit du mal!," which preserves only the original's concluding stretta. Nevertheless, the French movement cannot be considered truly new. David Rosen and David Lawton have suggested that Verdi modeled the music on Silva's "Infin che un brando vindice" from *Ernani* (I,9), which, as Roger Parker has subsequently discovered, was written for the bass Ignazio Marini as part of a substitute aria for an 1841–1842 *Oberto* production in Barcelona.[8] A prosodic analysis of "Ah! viens! démon!" confirms that borrowing took place. It is difficult to imagine that at this stage of his artistic development Verdi would have accepted a stanza of irregular meter for such a standard lyrical section as a cabaletta.[9] Although the text can be scanned in iambs throughout (especially with the word "Ah" added

Example 3.2b. *I lombardi*, I,4, "Sciagurata! hai tu creduto" (Pagano) and *Jérusalem*, I,6, "Oh! dans l'ombre dans le mystère" (Roger).

Example 3.2b (*Continued*)

at the beginning of the penultimate verse), the juxtaposition of eight- and six-syllable lines would have been a novelty for Verdi; in fact, such a combination does not even occur in pertinent passages of Verdi's next French opera, *Les Vêpres siciliennes*.

Ah! viens! démon! esprit du mal!
    Il t'a livré sa vie.
Ah! viens au coeur de mon rival
    Porter le coup fatal.
À cet amour qui le perdra
    Tout son bonheur se fie,
    [Ah!] C'est le ciel qu'il prie,
    L'enfer lui répondra.

It seems more likely that the composer provided his librettists with the rhythmic structure of the cabaletta he had in mind (i.e., with the theme – or at least its beginning – of "Infin che un brando vindice") and asked them to provide suitable verses. The French text fits the Italian melody without violating any accents (Ex. 3.3).

Why then did Verdi not adopt the melodic rhythm of "Infin che un brando vindice" exactly? Several possible answers come to mind: (1) he had provided his librettists not with the exact rhythm of "Infin che un brando vindice" but with that of "Ma fin che un brando vindice" (i.e., the substitute cabaletta for *Oberto*, an autograph of which has not survived) or even "Ah! viens!"; (2) he wanted to avoid exact rhythmic borrowing by introducing

Jérusalem *and its influence on the subsequent Italian operas*   99

Example 3.3. *Ernani*, I,9, "Infin che un brando vindice" (Silva; melody only) with added French text.

occasional changes; or (3) he was once again more concerned than his librettists with the balance of the accents. In the second design of Ex. 3.4a, for instance, Verdi recognized the iambic structure ("Il t'a livré sa vie") and may have felt the need to emphasize the second syllable ("t'a") over the first ("Il"), even though none of our theorists would have required accentuation on any of the first three syllables. Prosody here can explain the melodic change only in part; Verdi could easily have added an upbeat without changing the rest of the melodic line.[10] In Ex. 3.4b, Verdi correctly identified "amour" as the most important interior accent, and the natural way of adding emphasis to that syllable consisted in preceding it by a dotted note. Yet once again, his adjustments are purely cosmetic and show a composer overly preoccupied with reflecting all tonic accents.

As in Pagano's "Oh! dans l'ombre," Verdi considerably altered the accompaniment in Hélène's "Non...votre rage," but instead of lengthening the pattern, he omitted the downbeat, thus reducing its metrical weight (Ex. 3.5). The dramatic situation of the two versions is once again very similar, indicating that Verdi's changes were motivated either by the French language or by his greater maturity rather than by the dramaturgy: while Giselda lashes out at her father for having caused a blood bath when storming Antioch with his crusaders, Hélène directs her anger at all the crusaders for dragging her falsely accused lover to his execution.

Hélène's melody shows two additional changes that indicate a stylistic shift toward French aesthetics. While Verdi preserved the syncopation on "spargere" in m. 4 (probably due to its vivid expression of "outrage [insult]," the dominating emotion of the passage), he removed the syncopation on "pio" three measures later. Agreeing here, apparently, with the greater emotional charge of the French words ("delirium" and "agony" as opposed to "pious sentiment") as well as filling the melodic "gap" that resulted from omitting

Example 3.4a. *Ernani*, I,9, "Infin che un brando vindice" (Silva) with added vocal line from *Jérusalem*, I,7, "Ah! viens! démon! esprit du mal!" (Roger).

Example 3.4b. *Ernani*, I,9, "Infin che un brando vindice" (Silva) with added vocal line from *Jérusalem*, I,7, "Ah! viens! démon! esprit du mal!" (Roger).

the syncopation, he introduced an unexpected harmonic shift to N^6 with the appropriate diastematic adjustment of the melody.[11] The careful observer will have noticed that in the case of "votre délire," Verdi decided not to adjust the rhythm of the upbeat to avoid the diastematic and durational accent on the *e muet* of "votre." But he had already accented the word correctly in the first measure, and by the time of its return, the listener, under the spell of the repeating rhythmic pattern, is unlikely to notice the inconsistency. Moreover, Verdi did not commit a prosodic error: the setting still conforms with Benloew's method of scanning.

In his rhythmic revisions, Verdi went beyond reducing the number of syncopations and accented *e muets*, smoothing out the rhythm in several instances. Such changes usually have nothing to do with prosody and reflect other aesthetic concerns, including the rejection of "noisy" accompanimental patterns, more direct vocal lines, or dramatic accuracy.[12] All three elements come together in a brief section of the famous act III trio in which

Example 3.5. *I lombardi*, II,9, "No!...giusta causa" (Giselda) and *Jérusalem*, III,5, "Non...votre rage" (Hélène).

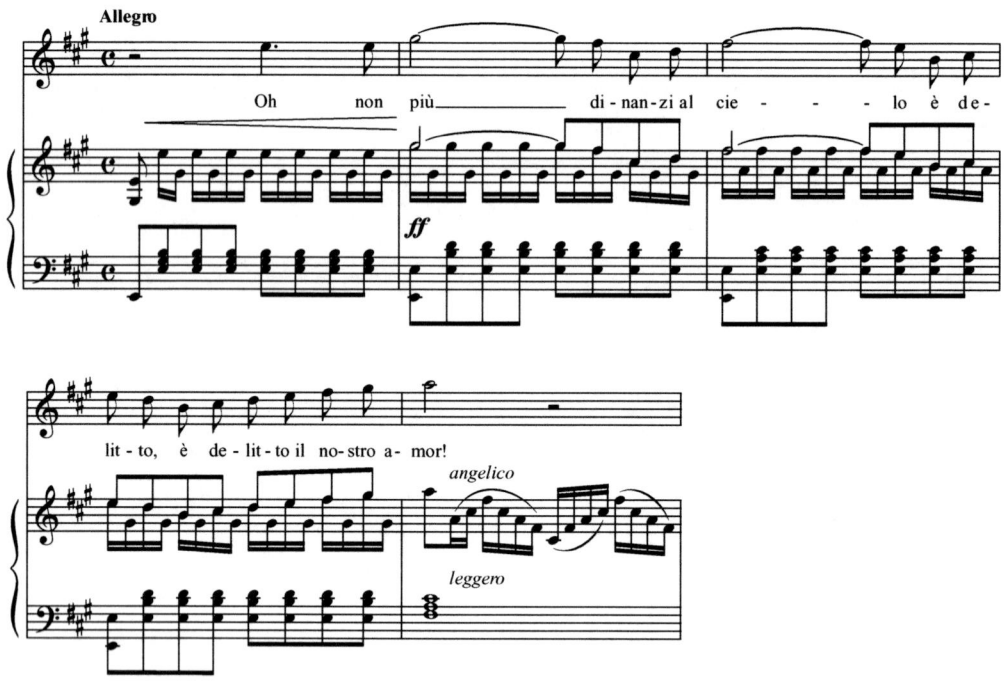

Example 3.6a. *I lombardi*, III,7, "Oh non più dinanzi al cielo" (Giselda).

Example 3.6b. *Jérusalem*, IV,4, "O bonheur! ton innocence" (Hélène).

Oronte, mortally wounded, consents to being baptized, and Giselda, overjoyed, expresses her relief that their love is no longer sinful (Ex. 3.6a). In *Jérusalem*, Royer and Vaëz placed the passage in a drastically different context while maintaining the general affect: Gaston, wrongly accused of attempted murder, is given a chance to fight alongside the crusaders, and Hélène expresses her joyful hope that his innocence will yet be proven. Verdi changed the uneven rhythms of the *Lombardi* passage to even quarter notes and the strongly patterned *ff* accompaniment to tremolos, a technique frequently used for transcendental feelings, especially in France (Ex. 3.6b).

Although Verdi in most cases did not significantly alter the borrowed melodies, the changes he did make usually conformed with French aesthetics. A look at the original portions of *Jérusalem* will confirm the picture of a composer who continued writing in an Italian style while making some adaptations to French taste.

The original portions of *Jérusalem*

Composers and scholars alike have commented on the importance of a libretto's structure for stimulating musical innovation. The stimulus may have come from French stanzas lacking an equivalent Italian meter (such as the *octosyllabe*) or from polymeters resulting in particularly unusual patterns of accent. The original portions of *Jérusalem*, however, present remarkably few of these traits. Polymeters, for instance, are confined to short stanzas, such as quatrains and tercets, which usually lack "unity of thought" and thus tend to be set as recitative. Those that do feature unity of thought are more regular than their appearance suggests, because individual verses, when split or merged, create regular meters, as in the Count of Toulouse's invitation to Gaston, early in the opera, to kneel with him at the altar as a symbol of their families' reconciliation. Were it not for the requirement that all verses rhyme, the tercet's alexandrine would be divided into two verses to create a metrically regular quatrain.

Tous deux agenouillés à la table de Dieu,
    Scellons dans ce saint lieu
    Notre amitié sincère.

Tous d**eu**x agenouill**és**	[2,6]
À la t**a**ble de D**ieu**	[3,6]
Scell**o**ns dans ce saint **lieu**	[2,6]
Notre amit**ié** sinc**è**re.	[4,6]

Here, the only possibility for true irregularity lies in the accentual pattern. It resembles that of the Italian *settenario* with its fixed accent on syllable 6 and, depending on the theorist, one or two additional accents on syllables 2 and 4.[13] While in his early Italian operas Verdi sometimes disregarded one or the other interior accents, he reflected all of them in his first French opera. This rigor does not necessarily imply significant rhythmic innovation, however; in most cases, he could accommodate accentual irregularity with only minor musical adjustments, such as introducing or omitting an upbeat or a note within the subsequent measure. Verdi's setting of "Tous deux agenouillés" perfectly illustrates this procedure. From the viewpoint of a composer accustomed to symmetry, the tercet consists of four verses of six syllables with changing positions of accents (Ex. 3.7).[14] All accents fall on strong positions of the measure, coinciding either with a harmonic change, the beginning of an accompanimental pattern, or both. Verdi needed to make only minor

Example 3.7. *Jérusalem*, I,4, "Tous deux agenouillés" (Le Comte).

rhythmic adjustments to accommodate the accentual irregularity. In the second measure, he added a note to the upbeat, compensating the anticipation of a syllable by omitting a note in the following measure. For the final design ("notre amitié sincère"), he omitted the upbeat altogether, adding instead a note within the next measure; the rhythmic flow remains largely regular. This procedure is by no means new, but Verdi applies it with greater consistency than in his early Italian operas.

It was more difficult to make such an adjustment naturally while at the same time maintaining a basically regular pattern if verses of varying syllable count added to the accentual irregularity. The quatrain "Noble guerrier" consists of three distinct meters. Here the Count of Toulouse, after having taken Jerusalem with his crusaders, asks a particularly brave soldier, whose face is concealed by the lowered visor of his helmet, about his name. It is Gaston, still a guilty man in the eyes of most.

Noble guerrier,	[1,4]
Qui plantas le premier	[3,6]
L'étendard de la foi sur la cité conquise,	[3,6,10,12]
Quel est ton nom?	[4]

The accents of this stanza are more regular than the bracketed numbers at the end of each verse imply because the text through "la foi" in the third verse, if scanned across verses, consists of perfect dactyls. But to maintain correspondence of textual accents and strong metrical positions while balancing the opening four-measure phrase with one of equal length, Verdi had to squeeze in an extra note at "sur la cité" and then stretch the

Example 3.8. *Jérusalem*, IV,5, "Noble guerrier" (Le Comte).

first syllable of "conquise" over two notes (Ex. 3.8). Then, having completed two balanced phrases, he still had one verse of four syllables to set. Verdi used it for a cadential phrase, which turned out to be unusually short, despite the repetition of words.

While the two original passages considered so far show Verdi's overly cautious approach to French prosody, they do not really reflect the kinds of French melodic features outlined in our chapter on aesthetics. In fact, typically French passages occur only rarely in *Jérusalem*. The most interesting among non-transitional sections is without doubt the slow movement of Gaston's act III aria, "O mes amis," in which Gaston laments his fate of being falsely accused of attempted murder and begs his comrades at arms to let him die. The textual rhythm is unique in Verdi's oeuvre up to that time. It consists of *octosyllabes*, the equivalent of the Italian *novenari*, which due to their irregular accentual structure do not occur in Italian librettos of the time. In practice, the Italian meter most closely related to the *octosyllabe* (and the one used when translating it into Italian) is the *quinario doppio*.[15] In his translation, Calisto Bassi made no exception:

Original by Royer and Vaëz:

1   2 3 4
O mes amis, mes frères d'armes
Voyez mes pleurs, voyez mes larmes! ...
Le déshonneur! c'est trop affreux!
N'accablez pas un malheureux.

Translation by Calisto Bassi:

1   2 3 4 5
O miei diletti – compagni d'armi
Non isdegnate – di sollevarmi:
Dal disonore ... – ah! per pietà!
Nessun di voi – mi salverà?

Example 3.9. Rhythmic comparison of "O mes amis" with related melodies.

Although Bassi followed the French rhythm as much as the *quinario doppio* allowed, the *piano* endings at the caesura considerably change the rhythmic character of the original by adding an extra syllable. Bassi's clever solutions for verses 3 and 4 allow for *de facto tronco* endings, in the third verse by singing "disonor" instead of "disonore" and in the fourth by pronouncing "voi" as a monosyllabic word; the first two verses, however, require an extra note in the middle of the verse. A comparison of the first measures of "O mes amis" and rhythmically related melodies from earlier Verdi operas illustrates the uniqueness of the French rhythm; the Italian rhythms are similar but never exactly the same (Ex. 3.9).

"O mes amis" furthermore includes several stylistic peculiarities that, when taken in isolation, would not sufficiently characterize the music as French; in combination, however, they clearly add a French flavor not previously encountered in Verdi's operas. Some critics singled out the "degradation scene" – which includes "O mes amis" – as the only one in *Jérusalem* conforming with French taste. Here is the pertinent passage from the review in the *Journal des débats*:

This scene is the degradation scene, which does not figure in *I lombardi* and which the composer wrote entirely in collaboration with Royer and Vaëz. Success has crowned this alliance. The great superiority of the fifth tableau over all the others is a good omen of Verdi's lyric future and reveals to us what we may expect from his talent if he no longer worked exclusively on an Italian canvas but on a libretto and with advice from Scribe. Here at least, everything is profoundly dramatic: the funeral march of the cortège, which has just assembled around the stake; the prayer so feelingly addressed by Gaston to his comrades at arms; his rage, his desperation; and when everything on earth eludes him, this appeal to God, his last, his only refuge! Mr. Verdi understood and mastered every detail of this beautiful situation; he found a simple and penetrating tone for the prayer, a surge of indignation for the offended honor, and above all, he for once followed the rule of which we spoke above: he was the faithful interpreter of his character's passion. He has followed it in all its developments, rejecting the entire academic tradition, the entire routine of a system. In a word, he has been true, and he now must feel what can come of emotions and power from this sacred source, from which he may have drawn for the first time.[16]

One does not need to rely on subjective evaluations of dramatic accuracy to determine the novelty of "O mes amis." A comparison with a similar melody, Riccardo's act II *romanza* from *Oberto*, may illustrate the uniqueness of the French setting on purely musical grounds (compare examples 3.10a and 3.10b). The first phrase of both arias consists of four rhythmically uniform melodic designs over a short accompanimental pattern a quarter note in length. Nevertheless, a closer look reveals interesting differences. In Gaston's aria (Ex. 3.10a), the harmonic and melodic middleground rhythms correspond (♩ ♩), whereas in Riccardo's aria they are more independent (♩ ♩ ♩ for the melody; ♩♩♩♩ for the harmony). The harmonies in the parallel opening phrases of "O mes amis" are often inverted, which not only weakens the cadences but also distracts from the rhythmic pattern by rendering the bass line more linear. Furthermore, the harmonic vocabulary is less predictable than in *Oberto* (Ex.10b), drawing on secondary dominants and the relatively rare second scale degree. Finally, Verdi breaks up the rhythmic pattern in the French aria by introducing a transitional measure after the *a* phrase. Such an interruption does not conform with the Italian preference of melodies that are *ben ritmato*.

An essential difference between the two settings lies in the conduct of the melody. In *Oberto*, after the opening parallel phrases, follows the contrasting, rhythmically related but less periodically organized middle section of the lyric form ("Ah si fugga! ...) and then a cadential phrase ("l'ultimo lamento") that brings the melody to a satisfying close with a strong cadence. In *Jérusalem*, however, Verdi introduces at the end of phrase *a'* a deceptive cadence, continuing with two measures of transition. Thus, after only four verses, the first melody is suspended, and a new one ensues in a new key (A major), with an entirely new accompaniment, in a slower tempo, and based on a longer design. Prosody cannot explain the rhythmic change; a continuation of the opening design (♪ ♫ ♩) would have fit the accentual structure at least as well as the new idea. Rather, Verdi recognized the subtle change of affect (from the plea for pity to a plea to be released from suffering). Knowing French practice, Verdi dared to introduce a new melody without the customary development of the first. The two melodies draw on the same motives, but their new arrangement and beginning on the downbeat evoke the sense of something new.

Second melody ("Mon dernier jour"): 3/4 ♩ ♪.♪|♩. ♪♪♪|♩. ♫♪.♪|♩

Motives from the first melody: 3/4 ♪♪.♪|♩ ‖ ♪♪♪|♩. ‖ ♪♪.♪|♩

Verdi eventually also introduces a new theme in Riccardo's *romanza* but with the essential difference that the original one is developed and brought to a conclusion on a strong cadence before the new one begins. As in "O mes amis," the new theme features designs of double length and receives an entirely new accompaniment, but the rhythm is more obviously related to the beginning of the aria by drawing on the same dotted upbeat while incorporating a rhythmic idea from the cadential section.

Original melody "Ciel che feci": c ♪.♪|♩ ♩ ♪, ♫|♩♩♪

Rhythmic idea from the cadential section: c ♩♩♩♩ |♩ ♪♪♪♪|♪.♪

New melody "Ciel pietoso": c ♪.♪|♩ ♪♪♪♪|♪.♪

Example 3.10a. *Jérusalem*, III,6, "O mes amis" (Gaston).

Example 3.10a (*Continued*)

Example 3.10b. *Oberto*, II,7, "Ciel che feci! ... " (Riccardo).

Jérusalem and its influence on the subsequent Italian operas 111

Example 3.10b (*Continued*)

Example 3.11a. *Nabucco*, II,8, "Chi mi toglie il regio scettro" (Nabucco), fast section.

Example 3.11b. *Nabucco*, II,8, "Chi mi toglie il regio scettro" (Nabucco), slow section.

Even though the emotions evoked in the text of the *romanza*'s first and second parts are more strongly contrasted than in "O mes amis" (Riccardo first cannot believe that he has just killed an old man in a duel and then asks Heaven for forgiveness), the French version introduces a more distinct musical change. In line with French practice, "O mes amis" eventually even introduces a third melody, "C'est la pitié," once again in a new key and a slower tempo. But the affect – the pleading for death – remains the same as in the second melody, and similarities in accompaniment and melodic rhythm raise the question, whether the melody can count as truly new.

A comparison with two other arias may illustrate the unique melodic structure of "O mes amis" in Verdi's work to date. The first, "Chi mi toglie il regio scettro?" concludes the second part of *Nabucco* (II,8) and shows the title character wavering between fear of a supernatural power that has just struck him with lightning and profound sadness of being abandoned by everyone. Here, in contrast to the example from *Jérusalem*, the musical themes stand in stark contrast to each other. The first (Ex. 3.11a) is set as an allegro, the second (Ex. 3.11b) as an adagio; the first features a strongly accented accompaniment, the second a smooth one. Despite these differences, the rhythms of the two themes are closely related by their motivic content in general and the rhythm of the upbeat in particular. Such themes expressing diametrically opposed emotions did not agree with French aesthetics, as the critic Charles Beauquier made clear in his study on music and drama: "A piece of verse destined for music must, insofar as possible, be only the development of the same sentiment or similar sentiments and present only a few images or images without great contrast and of the same general character as that of the piece."[17] Unlike "Chi mi toglie il regio scettro," "O mes amis" perfectly conforms with this ideal.

A comparison with an excerpt from act I of *Attila* further reveals distinct characteristics of "O mes amis." In this scene, Pope Leo leads a procession to stop Attila from attacking Rome. Attila is at once dumbfounded and overwhelmed, especially because he dreamt the night before what is now unfolding before his very eyes. His stanza shares with "O mes amis" a similar poetic meter (*quinario doppio* in *Attila*, *octosyllabe* in *Jérusalem*) and a melodic structure of dotted figures and four equal rhythmic designs per phrase (Ex. 3.12). After parallel phrases and a half cadence in F minor, a new melody ensues in a new key, on a new rhythm, and with a new accompaniment. Attila's stanza differs from Gaston's in a crucial respect: it begins in a declamatory style, here created by fermatas after each design, its undeveloped repetition of the first design, and the lack of a sustained accompaniment. The declamatory beginning thus assumes the function of an introduction, the new melody that of a lyrical climax. This combination is common in Italian arias and has nothing to do with French aesthetics.[18]

Verdi sometimes introduces a new melody that neither strongly contrasts with the first nor functions as a lyrical climax after a declamatory beginning. In these cases, however, it tends to retain certain of the first melody's characteristics, such as a rhythmic element, the contour, or the accompanimental pattern. In poetic meters with fixed accents (such as the *ottonario* or the *decasillabo*), it may only take a rhythmic reinterpretation of the upbeat (typically from ♫ ♩ to the broader ♩ ♩ ♩) to create the impression of something new. The *romanza* "Di ladroni attorniato" from *I masnadieri* exemplifies several of these characteristics as Carlo directs his thoughts from his misery as leader of a troupe of brigands to his beloved. Despite the difference in key (F minor vs. A-flat major), the relationship between the two melodies is apparent (Ex. 3.13): both consist of one-measure designs (marked below the text), both start on c' followed by an upward gesture, and the second designs begin with a similar dotted figure followed by a descending cadential one. And although the accompanimental pattern of the A-flat major section moves at a faster pace, the rhythmic characteristics are similar, starting on a longer note value followed by faster and then slower ones.

Despite all the stylistic traits that bring "O mes amis" into the aesthetic orbit of French opera, its overall character remains Italian. In fact, one might argue that this movement shows a conscious attempt on Verdi's part to adopt certain French elements rather than to write a truly French aria from beginning to end: nearly each phrase has its symmetrical counterpart; the rhythmic-metric relationship is always clear; the foreground rhythm flows regularly and predictably; the harmonic vocabulary of the main theme – although not the

Example 3.12. *Attila*, I,6, "No!... non è sogno" (Attila).

Example 3.13. *I masnadieri*, II,6, "Di ladroni attornïato" (Carlo).

one commonly used in Italy – does not go beyond what Verdi had used in earlier operas; and the relationship between the various themes remains recognizable despite the new arrangement of the motives. Significant changes in these respects will not appear until Verdi's next French opera.

The second and only other entirely new formal section in *Jérusalem*, the cabaletta following "O mes amis," does not include any significant stylistic innovations. Two aspects are nevertheless worth pointing out. First, the opening harmonic progression avoids the usual I-V and V-I progressions, replacing them by the rare progression (in Italian opera of the time) from the first to the sixth scale degree. And second, Verdi faced the challenge of writing a cabaletta on a single quatrain. The result perfectly matches Basevi's observation that the often unusual form of French stanzas forces the composer to either cover a lot of text too quickly or, as in this case, "linger too long" if the text is too short.[19] Verdi's attempt to write a lyric form on only four verses leads not only to word repetition but also to awkward accentuation, because repeated words occasionally fall first on a metrically strong position and immediately after that on a weak one (note especially the treatment of the words "Je" and "seul"). Nevertheless, the somewhat unnatural delivery fits Gaston's emotional state as, after the degradation of the *tempo di mezzo*, he regains his pride, telling the executioners that his only crime was to have shed his blood for them. Ex. 3.14 shows the opening parallel phrases on the first two verses.

In evaluating the prosody of *Jérusalem*, we can safely say that Verdi did not take advantage of the variety of approaches available to composers of French opera, either because he was not aware of them or because he tried to play it safe and avoid mistakes critics would most certainly have held against him. In 1847, the approach of Lubarsch and Landry would not yet have found significant attention in French opera, but scanning against tonic accents certainly did.[20] For Verdi to draw on such scanning to any significant extent, however, he would have required texts, so common in French opera, for lighthearted songs or passages conveying local color. Lighthearted songs are missing in *Jérusalem*, with the possible exception of Hélène's "polonaise" "Quelle ivresse" in act II. The generic title is misleading, however: even though the accompanimental pattern and the divided downbeat of the melodic line belong to the typical characteristics of the polonaise, the 4/4 meter and strong upbeat do not. "Quelle ivresse" is in fact a reworking of the "cabaletta della visione" "Non fu sogno" from *I lombardi* and with its brilliant coloratura reflects Verdi's early style rather than lighthearted French song. When incorporating the cabaletta into *Jérusalem*, Verdi rendered it more serious, adding between the two statements a short transition justifying the conventional repeat.[21]

In the wake of *Jérusalem*

The few changes in melodic style that can be detected in the Italian operas immediately following *Jérusalem* do not seem to originate from characteristics first related to French

Example 3.14. *Jérusalem*, III,6, "Frappez bourreaux!" (Gaston).

prosody, a conclusion not surprising in light of Verdi's conservative handling of prosody in his first French work.[22] Verdi spent most of the time between July 1847 and July 1849 in Paris, and some of the stylistic changes that do appear in the ensuing operas are more convincingly attributed to his contact with the French operatic scene than with the experience gained from writing *Jérusalem*. The final section of this chapter will focus on two stylistic features of the operas following *Jérusalem*: symmetry and conducting the melody.

Understanding the subtle changes of phrasing in the operas following *Jérusalem* requires a point of reference (henceforth called prototype) regarding the melodic structure at the beginning of lyrical sections (henceforth called thematic block). Such sections usually open with parallel phrases of four or eight measures, with each phrase starting out on the

Table 3.1. Thematic block of lyrical sections (prototype)

Original phrase				Parallel phrase			
m. 1	m. 2	m. 3	m. 4	m. 5	m. 6	m. 7	m. 8
T/D	T/D	X/T/D	T/D	T/D	X/T/D	X/T/D	R/T
[1]		[2]		[1]		[2/x]	

Example 3.15. *La battaglia di Legnano*, III,4, "Digli ch'è sangue italico" (Rolando).

same melodic material and the same harmony (either the tonic [T] or the dominant [D]). Each phrase consists of two basic designs ([1] and [2]), which may be identical, related, or completely different.[23] In the second half of each phrase, the composer may draw on basic or extended harmonic vocabulary (X) or modulate to a related key (R) and introduce cadential melodic material ([x]). Table 3.1 illustrates this prototype.[24]

Several of the arias in the operas following *Jérusalem* depart from this prototype in that they begin with a primarily tripartite structure instead of the parallel bipartite one: the first design presents the thematic material; the second introduces harmonic variation; and the third further develops the material harmonically or rhythmically, initiating a phrase that usually encompasses several designs. In most cases, this model leads to a period of 2+2+4 measures (a,a',a''/b) instead of 4+4 (a,a').

Rolando's "Digli ch'è sangue italico" from *La battaglia di Legnano* is a particularly beautiful example (Ex. 3.15). The first design cadences on the tonic of G minor, whereas

Jérusalem *and its influence on the subsequent Italian operas*

Example 3.16. *La battaglia di Legnano*, I,2, "Ah! m'abbraccia ... d'esultanza" (Rolando).

the second one, albeit starting on the same melodic pitch as the first, is set to the dominant harmony. The third design moves to V/III and through a "soft" syncopation on "giudice," connects with the fourth design, ending with a half cadence in the original key.

This tripartite thematic block occasionally also appears before *Jérusalem* but emerges with increasing frequency in the post-*Jérusalem* works.[25] It would be misleading, however, to attribute the higher number of tripartite themes to Verdi's work on *Jérusalem*, inasmuch as its new portions do not make use of this structure even once.[26] The concentration of tripartite themes in *La battaglia di Legnano*, an opera written in 1849 during one of Verdi's extended sojourns in Paris, might suggest a French influence (see Ex. 2.18). But such themes are not particularly prominent in French opera, and Verdi could easily have found models in the works of his Italian predecessors (see Ex. 2.2). Departures from the symmetry of the prototype were more frequent north of the Alps, however, and it is certainly possible that the French operatic scene inspired Verdi to greater structural variety in his melodies.

Unlike examples of tripartite thematic blocks, those of melodies conducted in the French way remain rare in the operas immediately following *Jérusalem*. The only reasonably good example appears early in *La battaglia di Legnano* when Rolando rejoices over the return of his friend Arrigo, whom he believed to be dead. Although titled *romanza*, a term usually applied to arias lacking a cabaletta, Rolando's aria initially resembles a cabaletta rather than a slow movement and begins with parallel phrases on even quarter notes (Ex. 3.16). At "O buon Dio," the emotion changes from joyful welcoming to a prayer of thanksgiving, and a new melody ensues in a new key (D minor), in a slightly slower tempo, in a new rhythm, and with a new accompaniment. The novelty of this melody differs fundamentally from the customary contrasting *b* phrases of the lyric form because it consists of a self-contained musical period resembling the tripartite structure discussed earlier.[27] The new melody essentially functions as the middle section of a French ternary form with its typical return of the opening text and music.[28] Yet as so often in Verdi's early operas, the rhythmic structure of the second melody bears some resemblance to the first in that both start with two quarter notes of upbeat.

Just as the melodic innovations of *Jérusalem* itself were relatively insignificant, their immediate impact was minimal and may have derived equally from Verdi's study of French works while he was in Paris as from his own contribution. In the following years, he composed a series of masterworks – from *Luisa Miller* (1849) to *La traviata* (1853) – that introduced fundamental and widely discussed dramaturgical changes. For melody, however, it was *Les Vêpres siciliennes* that marked a turning point, and it is to this work that we will now turn.

4 | *Les Vêpres siciliennes* and its influence on the subsequent Italian operas

Scribe and Verdi discussed the *Vêpres* project as early as 1853 and may have met in person before rehearsals began on November 16, 1854.¹ Evidence regarding Verdi's prosodic concerns, however, is limited to a few extant letters, which also debunk the long-standing assumption that the composer, with his supposedly inferior knowledge of French, readily accepted Scribe's verses without requesting changes.² In fact, the letters portray a composer actively involved in structuring the libretto – from its dramatic pace down to details of poetic meter and accentual rhythm – and a librettist aware of Verdi's talent and graciously complying with his wishes.³

On at least three occasions, Verdi requested regularly accented verses. Two of these requests refer to choral sections, and in both cases the composer was looking for meters corresponding with two of the most regularly accented Italian equivalents, the *vers de sept syllabes* (corresponding to the Italian *ottonario*) and the *vers de cinq syllabes* (corresponding to the Italian *senario*). In a letter of June 7, 1854, Verdi elaborated:

I come to ask your kindness for a small change in the second act. I would need the chorus "O bonheur! O délice!" to have verses of *eight* instead of verses of *seven*, as for example [the highlighted syllables reflect Verdi's intentions]

   *O mart_y_r de la patr_ie_*
   *Pour bris_er_ la tyrann_ie_*

You can keep – if it suits you – the same ideas, the same rhymes, only be so good to change the rhythm to verses of *eight*.⁴

In a letter of August 29, 1854, Verdi described his preferences for the beginning of act V:

Eight verses for the Sicilians, eight for the French (or, if you like, only eight verses for the French and Sicilians together), plus eight verses for the women who present the flowers to Hélène. I should like the rhythm to be like these verses [the highlighted syllables reflect Verdi's intentions]

   Fort_u_ne cru_e_lle
   Tu v_i_ens m'accabl_er_:
   Mais _u_n seul mot d'_e_lle
   Peut m_e_ consol_er_!

They lend themselves very well to 3/8.⁵

The latter example presents a particularly interesting case because it illustrates that Verdi – probably at the stage of sketching act V but before having received the requested addition to the libretto – already had a rhythm in mind, which he presented as a model for the eventual verses. The highlighted syllables (the ones Verdi considered structurally important here) do not represent the strongest accents ("seul" in the third verse is stronger than "un," and "Peut" in the fourth verse stronger than "me"); instead, the composer interpreted the prosody precisely as he would have done in an Italian *senario*, with regular accents on the second and fifth syllables.[6]

Verdi's third reference to rhythmic regularity (in an undated letter) concerns a passage for one of the solos:

For the moment, I would need to have a beautiful cantabile in place of "Tout respire un air de fête." With three verses, it is impossible for me to make a melodic phrase. I would need four – that is to say, 8. Try to give them a more moving turn, and that the rhythm be like [the highlighted syllables reflect Verdi's intentions]

   Am<u>i</u>! le coeur d'Hél<u>è</u>ne,
   Pard<u>o</u>nne au repent<u>i</u>r –[7]

It seems that Verdi (perhaps with the melody already in mind) was looking for *vers de six syllabes* that would allow for scanning in iambs in the manner of Scoppa and Castil-Blaze.[8] Scribe, however, responded by sending lines with irregular patterns of accents that matched only in part those of "Ami! le coeur d'Hélène." Verdi treated the text in a manner that accords with the prosodic approach of Benloew, scanning it against some of the tonic accents (Ex. 4.1):[9]

Version with highlighted tonic accents	Verdi's interpretation
Merci, jeunes amies,	Merci, jeunes amies,
De ces présens si doux!	De ces présens si doux!
Dont les fleurs si jolies	Dont les fleurs si jolies
Sont moins fraîches que vous.	Sont moins fraîches que vous
O chaîne fortunée	O chaîne fortunée
Et plus chère à mes yeux,	Et plus chère à mes yeux,
Alors que l'hyménée	Alors que l'hyménée
S'embellit de vos voeux.	S'embellit de vos voeux.

Verdi did not object to this irregularity. By the time of *Les Vêpres siciliennes*, he had learned that scanning against some tonic accents was perfectly acceptable in arias intended to convey a lighthearted atmosphere or local color.[10] The beginning of act V indeed focuses on these characteristics. To save the life of his love (Hélène) at the end of act IV, the young Sicilian Henri openly admitted that Montfort, the despised French Governor on Sicily, is his father. In return, Montfort consented to the union of Henri and Hélène, not only as a favor to his son but to reconcile the French occupants and the Sicilian people. Act V takes place in the rich gardens of Montfort's palace with castanets adding a Spanish flavor to the celebratory opening chorus. Spanish local color continues through Hélène's "Merci, jeunes amies" and is apparent in the accompanimental pattern and arched melodic gesture typical of the Bolero;[11] the scanned verse is not only in line with the focus on local color but also reinforces the lighthearted atmosphere of the celebration. Unlike in other numbers of

Example 4.1. *Les Vêpres siciliennes*, V,2, "Merci, jeunes amies" (Hélène).

this kind, however, the rhythmically diverse theme undermines to some degree the effect of the prosodic scanning. The reason surely lies in the nature of the Bolero and the attempt at painting as multifaceted a musical celebration as possible rather than in an effort to hide the violation of tonic accents. Had Verdi been concerned about such violations here, he would certainly have tried to disguise them in the subsequent "La brise souffle" as well. Nor were reviewers of the first production concerned, praising "Merci, jeunes amies" as "gracieux," "charmant," "ingénieux," and "délicieux."

The focus on lightheartedness continues in Henri's "La brise souffle," where scanning in the manner of Benloew is underscored by an equally uniform musical rhythm (Ex. 4.2). The poetic meter, alexandrine with the customary caesura after the sixth syllable, corresponds to the Italian *settenario doppio*, at least as far as the syllable count is concerned. The high number of masculine endings at the caesuras (six out of eight) and the irregularity of the

Example 4.2. *Les Vêpres siciliennes*, V,2, "La brise souffle au loin" (Henri).

accentual structure, however, go far beyond what Verdi would have encountered in Italian librettos:

Version with highlighted tonic accents
La brise souffle au loin, | | plus légère et plus pure
Et de parfums plus doux | | l'air paraît embaumé.
L'onde plus mollement | | et serpente et murmure,
Et d'un rayon divin | | tout me semble animé!

Verdi's interpretation
La brise souffle au loin, | | plus légère et plus pure
Et de parfums plus doux | | l'air paraît embaumé.
L'onde plus mollement | | et serpente et murmure,
Et d'un rayon divin | | tout me semble animé!

The musical accents fall on the wrong syllable of "légère" in the first verse, "paraît" in the second, and "onde" in the third. In the fourth verse, Verdi transfers the emphasis on "semble" to the pronoun "me." In one instance, however, he shifts briefly to trochees and then uses syncopation on "serpente" to shift back to iambs. Here, Verdi clearly abandoned the rhythmic regularity of the *temps fort* for expressive purposes, exactly as described by Benloew. As with Hélène's aria, critics did not comment on the prosody but pointed to the elegance and tenderness of the melody. The reviewer of *La vérité*, Sylvain St.-Étienne, remarked on the relationship between text and music, and even though he did not specifically refer to prosody, he acknowledged the composer's success in capturing the verses' grace and style:

Henri's romance continues the harmonious and sweet genre adopted by the musician throughout this beginning of the act. Here the verses, without being rivals of those by Lamartine, had a certain grace of style that could up to a point inspire him.
    La brise souffle...
This is Racan[12] or Segrais[13] at its purest. Verdi could only follow this path and write in the picturesque and imitative genre: he perfectly succeeded and his orchestration is very pleasantly colored.[14]

The composer's choice of scanning the text in the manner described by Benloew undoubtedly contributes to the gracefulness of the setting because it leads to binary rhythms without subdivision in a moderate tempo (i.e., exactly those rhythmic characteristics that, according to Beaulieu, elicit the emotions described by the critics).[15] The asymmetry created by the longer note values at the end of each phrase not only preserves the conventional four-measure phrasing but also perfectly reflects the unpredictability of the gently blowing breeze.

Act V has a complicated history, which can be told in full only once all the manuscript sources are available. The beginning was originally conceived as a duo between Hélène and Procida and later as a chorus, an aria for Hélène, and a *romance* for Henri, all meant at least in part to revive the ominous tone of the preceding acts.[16] Once Verdi had completed acts I through IV, however, he began to request dramaturgical changes in act V that eliminated from its first half any hint of foreboding and led to a string of numbers, not even connected by recitative, unambiguously focusing on the carefree anticipation of Hélène and Henri's wedding.[17] Whether this solution primarily reveals a problematic imbalance of public and private spheres, as Anselm Gerhard has suggested, or an effective application of "the calm before the storm" cannot be objectively answered.[18] But at the beginning of act V, neither Hélène nor Henri knows about Procida's plans of using the wedding bells as a signal for the final massacre, and Verdi must have felt that a carefree celebration – along the lines of the adjacent gypsy and matador choruses in the recently completed *Traviata* – would be dramatically more appropriate. Thus, he chose lighthearted music of local color and frequently scanned the text against tonic accents, not only in the two solos but also in the act's opening chorus ("Célébrons ensemble / L'hymen glorieux / Dont l'espoir rassemble / Deux peuples heureux!"). Such deliberate scanning in this type of dramatic context marks the beginning in Verdi's French works of a rhetoric of prosody (i.e., the use of prosody as a dramatic tool).

The rhythmic discrepancies between the French meters of "Merci jeunes amies" and "La brise souffle au loin" on the one hand and their closest Italian equivalent on the other did not bother Verdi: he knew that lightheartedness and local color allowed him to scan against tonic accents. An altogether different situation emerged when he was confronted with verse lacking an Italian equivalent that also appeared in a dramatic situation in which extensive scanning against tonic accents would have been inappropriate. In such cases, the musical setting almost always led to new rhythmic solutions. The most prominent French verse without Italian equivalent – at least in practice – is the *octosyllabe*; the Italian relative, the *novenario*, existed only in theory until Arrigo Boito began to use it in his librettos. The *octosyllabes* of "O mes amis, mes frères d'armes" from *Jérusalem* (see Ex. 3.10a) closely resembled Italian *quinari doppi*, but those of *Les Vêpres siciliennes* often lack such resemblance and must have challenged Verdi with their irregular accents. To conceal the irregularity, he would occasionally follow Castil-Blaze's suggestion of resorting to vague melodies that do not "create too much sense of rhythm."[19] Melodies of even note values over a metrically weak accompaniment, for instance, produced such an effect.

The first stanza of *octosyllabes* appears in Hélène and Henri's act II duet. Henri has just offered his support for Procida's plan of inciting the Sicilians to a rebellion against the French occupants. After Procida's departure, Hélène expresses her gratitude, and Henri confirms his devotion. (Accents are highlighted in the manner of Quicherat.)

Hélène:
    Comment, dans ma reconnaissance   [2,8]
    Payer un pareil dévouement?   [2,5,8]
Henri
    A vous, ma seule providence,   [2,4,8]
    A vous et ma vie et mon sang!   [2,5,8]
Hélène:
    Pour vous d'un tyran sanguinaire   [2,5,8]
    Vous avez bravé le courroux?   [3,5,8]
Henri
    Sans trembler j'ai vu sa colère   [3,5,8]
    Hélas! et tremble devant vous!   [2,4,8]

Verdi could have set the first quatrain in triple meter with accents on [2,5,8], violating only one tonic accent (on "seule"). A setting in regular triple meter, however, would not have conformed at all with this passionate dialogue, and aligning obligatory accents with the strongest metrical beats would have been difficult in the fast tempo of this movement. Verdi responded to the unusual rhythmic qualities of the text with predominantly neutral note values over a metrically weak accompaniment. Only the end of each verse provides some distinction between longer and shorter syllables and thus greater metric clarity (Ex. 4.12, mm. 1ff), while the unusually long upbeat of three quarter notes, the chromatic harmony at the beginning of the first two distichs, the lack of symmetry within the four-measure

Les Vêpres siciliennes *and its influence on the subsequent Italian operas* 127

Example 4.3. *La traviata*, III,7, "Gran Dio! ... morir sì giovine" (Violetta).

phrases, and the metrically vague accompaniment all contribute to the sense of instability. The accompaniment plays a particularly crucial role in this process, because the pattern, shortened to the duration of a single quarter note and thus stressing every melodic note to the same degree, does not lend any structural support.

A comparison with an earlier Italian setting of a similar type may help clarify the uniqueness of "Comment, dans ma reconnaissance." In act III of *La traviata*, Violetta realizes the imminence of her death and the hopelessness of a new life at Alfredo's side. The melody consists of predominantly regular quarter notes and a fairly neutral accompanimental rhythm, just as in the example from *Les Vêpres siciliennes* (Ex. 4.3). Despite these corresponding characteristics, Violetta's melody displays much greater rhythmic regularity. The *settenario* verses can easily be scanned in iambs, a feature Verdi fully exploits, and the

Example 4.4. *Les Vêpres siciliennes*, V,4, "De cette voix" (Henri; Hélène's and Procida's interjections are omitted).

harmony tends to group the pulsating accompaniment into a half-note pattern, reinforcing the iambic character of the text and thus contributing to the structural clarity so typical of Italian melodies.

Gran D<u>i</u>o! ... mor<u>i</u>r sì g<u>io</u>vin<u>e</u>,
  Io ch<u>e</u> pen<u>a</u>to ho t<u>a</u>nto! ...
  Mor<u>i</u>r sì pr<u>e</u>sso a t<u>e</u>rger<u>e</u>
  Il m<u>io</u> sì l<u>u</u>ngo p<u>ia</u>nto!

Castil-Blaze's solution of not creating too much sense of rhythm also fits the setting of "De cette voix," the magnificent melody early in the act V trio for Henri, Hélène, and Procida (Ex. 4.4). Procida has just informed Hélène that the ringing of the wedding bells will signal the beginning of the massacre and thus Henri's death. The trio then juxtaposes Hélène's desperation, Procida's admonishment that she put duty over love, and – oblivious to Procida's plans – Henri's longing for a reassuring word from Hélène. Once again the crucial passage consists of *octosyllabes* with irregularly spaced accents (the prosodic interpretation follows Quicherat).

De cette voix qui m'est si chère	[4,8]
Qu'un mot vienne me rassurer![20]	[1,8]
Parlez! cédez à ma prière	[2,8]
Ou d'effroi je vais expirer.	[3,8]

It cannot have escaped Verdi's notice that despite the irregular pacing of the obligatory accents, much of the quatrain could be scanned in iambs as long as he scanned across the first and third line breaks and made the necessary adjustments to accommodate the change of rhythm at the end of verses 2 and 4. In addition, the text lent itself to perfect parallel phrases, with verses 1 and 2 corresponding to verses 3 and 4:

1. De cette voix qui m'est si chère 2. Qu'un mot vienne me rassurer!
2. Parlez! cédez à ma prière 4. Ou d'effroi je vais expirer.

Such an interpretation, however, had its pitfall, because obvious scanning would not have been entirely appropriate in this passage: Henri's feelings, although more positive than either Hélène's or Procida's, certainly do not fall in the category of "lighthearted." Verdi thus balanced the inherent iambic nature of the verses by irregular rhythmic and harmonic accents in the accompaniment, especially in the first phrase, and by repetition of text. None of the repetitions would have been necessary for prosodic reasons, but they break the even pace of the melodic line and, in the context of the slow tempo and irregularly structured accompaniment, sound perfectly natural. Henri's melody takes on a sentimental tone and stands in relief against the surrounding, more declamatory sections.

Prosodic challenges did not necessarily lead to settings of lesser rhythmic or metric definition. With *Les Vêpres siciliennes*, however, Verdi began to reflect irregular rhythmic groups in the manner of Lubarsch and Landry,[21] letting the syllables flow evenly toward the punctuating accents on the strongest beats of the meter. This approach tends to result in declamatory passages, which, if too frequent, would have been problematic in formal sections of both French and Italian opera. In introductions to arias or in transitions, however, interpretation in the manner of Lubarsch and Landry was perfectly acceptable.[22] A good example of such a transition occurs in Hélène's act I aria "Viens à nous, Dieu tutélaire." Pressured by the French soldiers to sing for them, Hélène responds with a full-fledged aria, telling the story of sailors about to be shipwrecked (introduction), their prayer (*adagio*), and God's charge to take destiny into their own hands (*tempo di mezzo*), followed by a rousing call to action (cabaletta), with the text, of course, functioning as a substitute for the Sicilians' own seemingly hopeless situation. In the *tempo di mezzo*, the crucial passage here, Verdi could have scanned the verses in iambs, which, however, would have been dramatically inappropriate (because scanning is reserved for lighthearted passages).

A declamatory setting in the manner of Lubarsch and Landry works much better for this brief speech:

Et Dieu dis<u>ai</u>t | | dans ses décrets supr<u>ê</u>mes:
N'avez-vous donc d'esp<u>oi</u>r | | qu'en des secours div<u>in</u>s?
    Vos j<u>ou</u>rs dépendent de vous-m<u>ê</u>mes;
      Votre sal<u>u</u>t est dans vos m<u>ai</u>ns...

Verdi perfectly accommodates the irregular spacing of these accents, and in most cases reflects even the secondary ones ("Dieu," "décrets," "donc," "secours," and "dépendent") all of which fall on secondary accents created by the accompaniment. Only in the case of "votre [salut]" does the accompanimental emphasis fall on the weak syllable of the word, which does not offend the ear in any way, due to the short and evenly flowing note values (Ex. 4.11, mm. 28ff).

The challenges of setting irregular French verse increase as soon as a composer tries to write a symmetrical melody over a regular accompanimental pattern in a clear rhythmic-metric context. The approach of Lubarsch and Landry does not lend itself well to these circumstances, because the irregular pace of the prosodic accents is generally incompatible with the regular pace of meter and phrase. In such cases, Verdi usually compromises by repeating text and by mixing prosodic approaches as seen in the slow movement of the duet between Hélène and Henri in act II. After Hélène's expression of gratitude, Henri declares his love and implores her to let him fight and die for her. Hélène accepts his devotion, and Henri, aware of his lower social standing (she is a duchess, he without rank), is overwhelmed. The text Verdi eventually set departs somewhat from the printed libretto, transforming the original verses into a configuration resembling a stanza.

Version in the printed libretto	Version set by Verdi
HENRI	
L'ai-je bien entendu?...moi! ma noble maîtresse!	<u>A</u>h! L'ai-je bien entend<u>u</u>?... m<u>oi</u>! ma noble maît<u>re</u>sse!
Moi qui n'ai ni rang, ni richesse...	M<u>oi</u> qui n'ai ni r<u>a</u>ng, ni rich<u>e</u>sse...
Moi, qui, simple soldat, vous ai voué ma foi?	M<u>oi</u>, pauvre et simple sold<u>a</u>t, vous acceptez ma f<u>oi</u>,
Et mon obscure misère...	Et mon obscure mis<u>è</u>re...
HÉLÈNE	
Henri!... vengez mon frère?	
Et vous serez pour moi	
Plus noble que le roi!	

Scribe did not conceive Henri's verses as a stanza or stanzaic unit; the necessary characteristics – a complete rhyme scheme coinciding with the conclusion of a thought – require a potential stanza to extend through "ma foi" in the third verse (because tercets do not need to comprise a complete rhyme scheme) or "roi" in the seventh verse.[23] Verdi, however, seems to have been determined to set the first four verses as a formal melody for Henri, despite the quatrain's incomplete rhyme scheme and thought. By substituting a comma for a question mark at "ma foi," he considerably diminished the point of repose, turning

Henri's fourth verse into an extension of the third, postponing the stanzaic caesura until "misère," and thus completing a thought. In addition to regrouping the verses, Verdi preceded the first hemistich with the exclamation "Ah!" to balance the exclamation "moi!" at the beginning of the second hemistich. This change turned the original alexandrine into a verse of thirteen syllables, rendering the sequence of meters irregular [13,8,12,7] but allowing for convincing melodic parallelism. After having created for himself a poetic structure that allowed for parallel phrases, Verdi was still faced with distinct rhythmic groups in the second half of verses 1 and 3 and throughout verses 2 and 4. But instead of employing an approach that follows the manner of Lubarsch and Landry throughout the entire stanza, he did so consistently only at the beginning of each phrase. After that, he repeated text (with the repetitions treated in the manner of Lubarsch and Landry), scanned a few words ("M**oi**, qui n'**ai** ni r**a**ng"), and misaccentuated "acceptez" in return for a sustained melodic arch. In other words, he mixed prosodic approaches (Ex. 4.12, mm. 65ff).

Mixture of prosodic approach and repetition of text also characterize Verdi's only setting in *Les Vêpres siciliennes* of a stanza of *décasyllabes*. While the rhythm of the *décasyllabe*, with its uneven hemistichs of four and six syllables, could theoretically be replicated by the Italian *endecasillabo*, it was, in stanzaic contexts, usually translated into a *quinario doppio* (the *endecasillabo*, with its irregular accentual structure was not yet commonly used in lyrical sections).[24] In "Et toi, Palerme," probably the opera's most famous number, Procida encourages his native city of Palermo to stand up to her oppressors and once again become the queen of all cities (Ex. 4.5). Verdi must have noticed that with relatively few violations of tonic accents, the quatrain lends itself to scanning in dactyls, but he also knew that extensive scanning (a) would have been dramatically inappropriate in such a solemn situation:

(a) Et toi, Pal**e**rme, | | ô beaut**é** qu'on outr**a**ge,
    Et toujours ch**è**re | | à mes y**eu**x enchant**é**s!...
    L**è**ve ton fr**o**nt | | courbé s**ou**s l'esclav**a**ge,
    Et redevi**e**ns (| |) la rein**e** des cit**é**s!

On the other hand consistent interpretation in the manner of Quicherat (b) and Lubarsch and Landry (c) would have rendered the setting too declamatory or incompatible with the regularly patterned accompaniment.

(b) Et toi, Pal**e**rme, | | ô beaut**é** qu'on outr**a**ge,
    Et toujours ch**è**re | | à mes y**eu**x enchant**é**s!...
    Lève ton fr**o**nt | | courb**é** sous l'esclav**a**ge,
    Et redevi**e**ns (| |) la r**ei**ne des cit**é**s!
(c) Et **toi**, Palerme, | | ô beauté qu'on outr**a**ge,
    Et toujours ch**è**re | | à mes yeux enchant**é**s!...
    Lève ton fr**o**nt | | courbé sous l'esclav**a**ge,
    Et redeviens (| |) la r**ei**ne des cit**é**s!

Example 4.5. *Les Vêpres siciliennes*, III,1, "Et toi, Palerme" (Procida).

Verdi uniformly interprets the first hemistichs as dactyls and the second hemistichs in the manner of the following approaches: in verse 1, he basically accords with Quicherat but adds an additional accent by ignoring the elision and turning "ô" into an *accent logique*; in verse 2, he accords with Lubarsch and Landry by letting a long group of syllables flow evenly toward the major accent at the rhyme; and in verses 3 and 4, he scans in iambs in the manner of Benloew. In verse 4, he also repeats text, introducing an idiosyncratic accent on the article "la." The irregular length of the hemistichs, the irregular accentual structure within each hemistich, and Verdi's mixing of prosodic approaches lead to unusually diverse melodic designs.

A final example of the challenges Verdi faced when setting irregularly accented texts in *Les Vêpres siciliennes* appears once again in the act II duet between Hélène and Henri, when Henri declares his love and pleads for permission to fight and die for her. As in "Ah! l'ai-je bien entendu," the text in the score differs from that of the printed libretto; it is arranged as a complete stanza, thus facilitating the composition of a formal melody.

Text as it appears in the printed libretto	Text as set by Verdi
	(with accentuation in the manner of Quicherat)
Hélène	Henri
[Qu'ai-je entendu?]	
Henri	
Je sais que mon audace est grande!	Vous détourn<u>ez</u> les y<u>eux</u> || et mon aud<u>a</u>ce est gr<u>a</u>nde,
Mais qu'un rayon d'espoir en mon âme descende,	Q'un s<u>eu</u>l rayon d'esp<u>oi</u>r || en mon <u>â</u>me desc<u>e</u>nde,
Hélène... je vous aime et n'implore à genoux,	Hél<u>è</u>ne... je vous <u>ai</u>me || et n'impl<u>o</u>re à gen<u>oux</u>,
Que le droit de combattre et de mourir pour vous!	Que le dr<u>oi</u>t de comb<u>a</u>ttre || et de mour<u>i</u>r pour v<u>ous</u>!

Once again, Verdi could have scanned much of the quatrain in iambs but instead undermined their rhythm with accentual interpretation in the manner of Quicherat and Benloew, brief melismas, and repetition of words. A comparison of these alexandrines with their most likely Italian equivalent, the *settenari doppi*, may illustrate Verdi's challenge. *Settenari* with an interior accent on the fourth syllable often have an additional accent on the second syllable, which favors the following alignment with the musical meter: the accent on the second syllable falls on the downbeat, the accent on the fourth syllable on the secondary accent of the meter, and the accent at the rhyme on the next downbeat.[25] Furthermore, *settenari* at the beginning of a stanza almost always have a *piano* or *sdrucciolo* ending, which can easily reach far into the second measure. Many of the hemistichs of "Vous détournez," however, offer neither additional accents on the second syllable nor *piano* or *sdrucciolo* endings. When setting the first verse to music, Verdi felt he could (as a result of scanning in iambs) afford to emphasize the second syllable ("Vous dé̱tournez"). With the second hemistich, however, this solution became more problematic, because a downbeat on "mon" would have created too much of a rhythmic void in the second measure and reduced activity there to a level customary in declamatory passages but not in cantabiles (Ex. 4.6). By filling the void in the second measure with the syllables "et mon au[dace]," Verdi shifted it to the

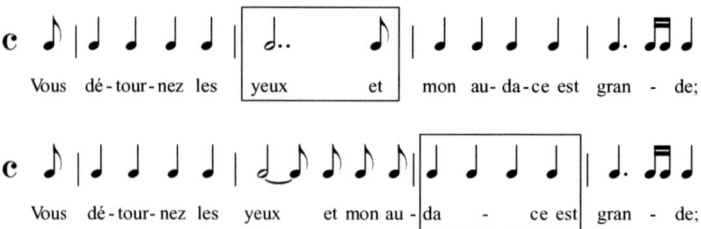

Example 4.6. *Les Vêpres siciliennes*, II,3, hypothetical and actual settings of "Vous détournez les yeux" (Henri).

subsequent measure, which now includes only two syllables ("[au]dace est"). He solved the problem by filling the measure with a three-note melisma that sounds less intrusive in the middle of a verse than at the end. The same problem recurs in the second verse, where Verdi avoids a drop in rhythmic activity by repeating the entire first hemistich "Qu'un seul rayon d'espoir" (see Ex. 4.12, mm. 28–30). In the third verse, he abandons scanning and regular four-measure phrases, following the manner of Quicherat for the rest of the stanza with perfect naturalness. Is it possible that what appears to be somewhat awkward prosodic treatment was intended to show Henri's initial inhibitions, which he then sheds in verse 3 ("Hélène! Je vous aime!")?

Damien Colas has justly singled out this melody as particularly innovative.[26] The reason lies at least in part in the subtle middleground shifts leading to and from Henri's outburst in verse 3.[27] The naturalness (i.e., the technical perfection) with which Verdi achieves them is impressive. The established middleground rhythm of a whole note accelerates in m. 30 with an additional emphasis on beat 3 ("âme"). In the next measure, beat 3 becomes even stronger than the subsequent downbeat, due to diastematic, prosodic, and durational emphases. The result could be illustrated as follows. (The rhythm of only the strongest middleground beats is notated above the text).

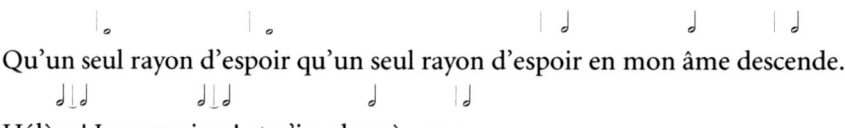

The originality of this melody derives from yet another important aspect of French versification: accents of duration. We remarked earlier on the discrepancy of opinion among the theorists and concluded that durational accents played a greater role in French than Italian verse.[28] Although Italian theorists always maintained that syllables were accented at the same time by stress and duration, Verdi's Italian operas indicate that he often accented strong syllables by stress alone. This practice did not fundamentally change with *Les Vêpres siciliennes*, but Verdi must have realized that a greater use of durational accents

Les Vêpres siciliennes *and its influence on the subsequent Italian operas* 135

Example 4.7. *Les Vêpres siciliennes*, IV,5, "Adieu, mon pays, je succombe" (Procida).

could help him accommodate the prosodic irregularities so typical of French librettos. When judged on the basis of durational accents, the phrase "Hélène! je vous aime" actually makes perfect sense, because duration highlights important accents more convincingly than metric position.

The act IV quartet "Adieu, mon pays" illustrates the role of durational accents in greater detail (Ex. 4.7). Procida, on the way to his execution, launches the quartet with a farewell to his homeland, regretting his inability to free it from its French oppressors. The quatrain consists of irregularly accented *octosyllabes*, which once again call for either textual or musical adjustments if parallel phrasing and reasonably regular rhythms are to be maintained. Verdi decided on a small mid-century lyric form and set the first two verses to parallel *a* and *a′* phrases, part of the third verse to shorter *b* and *b′* phrases, and the remaining text to a concluding cadential phrase.[29] On a textual level, this arrangement required word repetition in two instances ("sans briser" and "Je meurs sans vengeance"); on a musical level, phrase parallelism, the solemn pace suggested by the meaning of the text, and avoidance of misaccentuations required interpretation of prosodic accents as accents of duration. Verdi accordingly set strong syllables to longer notes or groups of notes, with exceptions only in the cadential flourish at the end. In this way, he was able to interpret beat 3 as an accented or unaccented position depending on the prosodic quality of the syllable falling on it. In most cases, the syllable on the third beat required a relatively longer note, but the unaccented "Sans" in the second verse and "et" in the third verse did not. In addition, the tonic accent of "succombe" is primarily reflected only by duration. (The prosodic interpretation follows Quicherat).

Ad<u>ieu</u>, mon pa<u>y</u>s, je succ<u>o</u>mbe
Sans bris<u>er</u> ta captivit<u>é</u>!
Je m<u>eu</u>rs sans veng<u>ea</u>nce! et ma t<u>o</u>mbe
Est c<u>e</u>lle de ta libert<u>é</u>!

Most of our examples from *Les Vêpres siciliennes* have thus far featured either compound meter or duple meter with dominant triple subdivision of the beat. The prominence of compound meters, explicit or implied, in settings of challenging poetic meters is hardly surprising. They allow for smoother accommodation of irregular accentual rhythms than any other standard meter because rhythmic groups of any length can be easily set to multiples of eighth notes. While duple and triple meters, too, can accommodate irregular rhythmic groups, the result usually does not match the smoothness of the compound meters. In fact, when Aimé Victor Becq de Fouquières, in his treatise of versification, illustrated the rhythmic possibilities of French verse, he invariably used 6/8 meter.[30] Two examples comparing the setting of related verses from *Un ballo in maschera* and *Les Vêpres siciliennes* may illustrate the greater smoothness of the French settings:

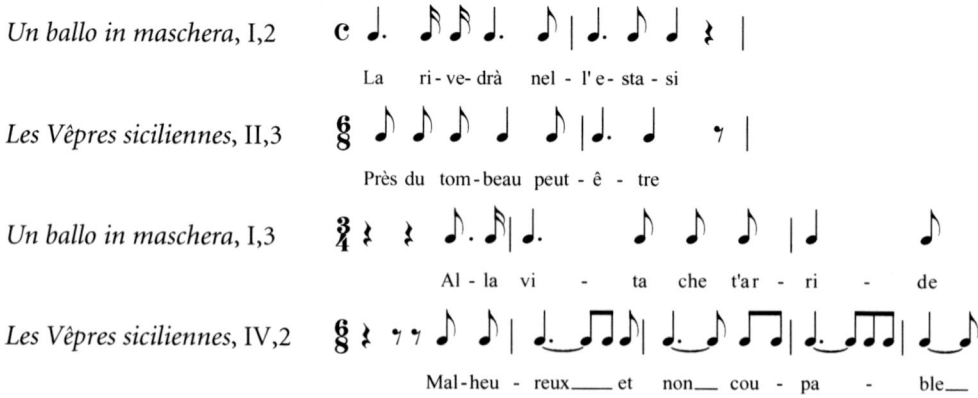

Verdi clearly had learned how to set French verse, even if the occasional awkward melisma and repetition of words attest to the challenge. He loosened the metric definition to soften the impact of irregular or overly regular accentuation, mixed prosodic approaches, and drew on accents of duration when accents of stress alone could not suitably reflect an irregular accentual structure. Even though Verdi occasionally complained to Scribe about verse lacking the rhythmic regularity he needed for "a well rhythmicized melody [un motif bien rhythmé],"[31] he rose to the challenge and wrote melodies of exceptional beauty, originality, and dramatic accuracy.

Aspects of rhythm and phrasing with questionable connection to prosody

Some melodic characteristics of *Les Vêpres siciliennes*, although in perfect conceptual agreement with French prosody, can be more convincingly explained by French aesthetics in general. On occasion, they caught the attention of leading critics. Alberto Mazzucato, for instance, who defended *Les Vêpres siciliennes* against accusations of sterility, lack of inspiration, and excessive declamation, and who described the melodies as perfectly in line with Italian tradition, was willing to admit that Italians, when writing for Paris, may "transform their spontaneous and boiling manner by rendering it more calm and moderate."[32] His assessment continues:

> Let us talk about the rhythmic pathos. And indeed it is necessary to agree that even though the melodies of *Giovanna de Guzman* [the title under which *Les Vêpres siciliennes* was first performed in Italy] are quite far from the excesses of dimension for which we have repeatedly reproved the school of Mercadante, they present nevertheless a *breadth* of ideas noticeably more marked than in all the previous scores of Verdi. Thus, an increase of severity, solemnity, and consequently a certain decrease of popularity, impetus, conciseness.[33]

With "breadth," Mazzucato most probably did not mean "variety," even though this trait counted among the stylistic aspects emphasized by some critics.[34] Breadth seems to refer here to the sense of a melodic grandness evoked by the tranquil flow of the music and broadened or altogether abandoned formulaic accompanimental patterns. Hélène's "Viens à nous, Dieu tutélaire" (see Ex. 4.11, mm. 17ff), the prayer section of the "song" the French soldiers force her to sing, is a good example: the melody begins with quarter notes and triplets and "broadly" flows over a metrically vague accompaniment of steady triplets in the flutes and clarinets and tremolo in the strings (the punctuations in the bass of the vocal score represent the sustained tremolo of the double basses).

A sense of breadth can also emerge when the distinction between a melody's pulse and its middleground rhythm is eliminated. As Henri defies Montfort in act I and prepares to accept the consequences, for instance, Verdi expresses Henri's lofty attitude in a "cantabile grandioso" with an initial half-note pulse (marked above the staff). The accompanimental

Example 4.8. *Les Vêpres siciliennes*, I,5 "Punis mon audace" (Henri; Montfort's interjections are omitted).

pattern, which usually groups the melodic pulse into a slower middleground rhythm, is here identical to the melodic pulse and reinforces the grandiose affect (Ex. 4.8). Although occasionally present in Verdi's earlier Italian operas as well, this correspondence of pulse and middleground rhythm appears more frequently in *Les Vêpres siciliennes*.[35]

Breadth also characterizes *Les Vêpres siciliennes* in regard to the variety of its melodic ideas. As we have shown earlier, the operas following *Jérusalem* occasionally begin a new melody with a tripartite structure *a*, *a'*, *b* instead of the thematic prototype *a*, *a'*. In *Rigoletto* through *Les Vêpres siciliennes*, Verdi not only continues to increase the number of tripartite themes but diversifies the beginning of his melodies in other ways as well. He may melodically or harmonically develop a parallel phrase as early as in the first design (Table 4.1, type 1); abandon parallel phrases altogether or relegate them to the orchestra (types 2–4), thus allowing for freer rhythm in the vocal line; abandon not only parallel phrases but also regular two-, four-, or eight-measure phrases (type 5); or begin with basically unaltered repetitions of a single melodic design (type 6) or with long, rhythmically diverse phrases of more than two distinct designs (type 7). A comparison of the four operas from *Rigoletto* through *Les Vêpres siciliennes* shows that the last surpasses its predecessors in almost every category, thus marking a significant step toward greater melodic variety.[36]

Abramo Basevi, the most astute Italian observer of stylistic subtleties, explicitly remarks on the aspect of non-developmental phrases (type 6) in his review of *Les Vêpres siciliennes*:

> The theme *Deh tu calma* ["Viens à nous, Dieu tutélaire"; see Ex 4.11, mm. 17ff] appears in a broad tempo [and] in the form often adopted by Verdi, which consists in repeating the gesture of a theme without resolving it, creating in this way the first phrase of the very same theme. This form, besides being contrary to the dramatic expression most of the time, reveals by itself great poverty of imagination.[37]

True, such non-developmental beginnings become more prominent in *Les Vêpres siciliennes*, but when searching for potential models of this stylistic peculiarity, we are led directly to Meyerbeer.[38] Was Basevi aware that he indirectly criticized a typical feature of his

Table 4.1. Thematic blocks in the operas from *Rigoletto* through *Les Vêpres siciliennes*

Type 1. Instant development of a thematic idea in the parallel phrase
   Rigoletto
      "Caro nome" (I,13)
      "Parmi veder le lagrime" (II,1)
      "Piangi, fanciulla" (II,6)
   Il trovatore
      "Deserto sulla terra" (I,3)
      "E deggio ... e posso crederlo" (II,4)
      "D'amor sull'ali rosee" (IV,1)
      "Ah! sì, ben mio" (II,6)
   La traviata
      "De' miei bollenti" (II,1)
      "Un dì, quando le veneri" (II,5)
   Les Vêpres siciliennes
      "Courage! ... du courage" (I,2)
      "Fidèle à ses leçons" (I,4)
      "Vous détournez les yeux" (II,3)
      "La haine égara" (III,3)
      "Adieu, mon pays" (IV,5)
Type 2. No phrase parallelism
   Rigoletto
      "Culto, famiglia" (I,9)
      "Ebben piango... " (II,4)
      "Tutte le feste" (II,6)
      "Solo per me l'infamia" (II,6)
   Il trovatore
      "A te credei rivolgere" (I,5)
      "Parlar non vuoi?... " (IV,4)
      "Prima... che d'altri" (IV,4)
   La traviata
      "Dite alla giovine" (II,5)
      "Ah sì!... che feci" (II,15)
      "Ogni suo aver" (II,14)
   Les Vêpres siciliennes
      "A quoi bon" (I,2)
      "Saint amour" (II,1)
      "Près du tombeau" (II,3)
      "O jour de peine" (IV,1)
      "Écoute un instant" (IV,2)
      "La brise souffle" (V,2)
      "La bannière de France" (V,4) [39]
Type 3. Including *ad libitum* portions
   Les Vêpres siciliennes
      "Le ciel vient apparaître" (IV,3)

Table 4.1 (*Continued*)

Type 4. Phrase parallelism only in the orchestra
    Il trovatore
        "Asserì che tirar" (I,1)
    Les Vêpres siciliennes
        "Et Dieu disait" (I,2)
        "Quand ma bonté" (IV,4)

Type 5. Irregular phrasing[40]
    Rigoletto
        "Tutte le feste" (II,6)
        "De' scudi, già dieci" (III,6)
    Il trovatore
        "Prima... che d'altri" (IV,4)
    La traviata
        "Se una pudica vergine" (III,8)
        "Morrò!... la mia" (II,5)[41]
    Les Vêpres siciliennes
        "A quoi bon" (I,2)
        "Le ciel vient" (III,3)
        "Ami, le coeur" (IV,2)
        "La bannière" (V,4)

Type 6. Short initial, basically unaltered parallel phrases of only one design but more than one measure in length
    Rigoletto
        "Bella figlia dell'amore" (III,3)
        "Lassù in cielo... " (III,10)
    Il trovatore
        "Ah, che la morte ognora" (IV,1)
    La traviata
        "Prendi, quest'è l' immagine" (III,7)
        "Se una pudica vergine" (III,7)
    Les Vêpres siciliennes
        "Viens à nous, Dieu tutélaire" (I,2)
        "Quoi, ma tendresse" (III,4)
        "Autour de moi" (IV,1)
        "Tout un peuple en prière" (IV,5)
        "Trahison! imposture!" (V,4)

Type 7. Long phrases with more than two distinct rhythmic designs
    Il trovatore
        "Vivrà!... contende il giubilo" (IV,2)
    La traviata
        "Morrò!... la mia memoria" (II,5)
    Les Vêpres siciliennes
        "Et toi, Palerme" (II,1)
        "Adieu, mon pays" (IV,5)

artistic idol, Meyerbeer, or did he primarily intend to depreciate Verdi's accomplishments for the benefit of Meyerbeer's reputation?

In the same review, Basevi also objects to the harmonies of "O jour de peine," calling them "studied and not natural [ricercate, e non naturali]."[42] As we have pointed out earlier, studied harmony was seen as a characteristic of French rather than Italian opera, even though critics tended to exaggerate the differences. Basevi's criticism is off the mark not only because Verdi conceived his opera for a French audience (and thus could allow himself greater harmonic experimentation) but also because the harmony, even if considered unnatural, perfectly fits Henri's pain at having betrayed his conspirator friends to save his father, Montfort. As if to balance the expressive harmony, Verdi couched the melody in a simple arch of a single repeated design. Two years earlier, in *La traviata*, he had written a similar melodic arch for the passage in which the desperate Violetta asks Germont to remind his daughter of her sacrifice. But while he set "Dite alla giovine" to only the most basic harmonies, in Henri's melody, he draws on the lowered seventh scale degree and the Neapolitan before returning to the tonic (Ex. 4.9a–b).[43]

Conducting a melody

With his first original work for Paris, Verdi adapted to French taste not only by varying his thematic blocks but also by developing them according to French practice. Our comparison of French and Italian aesthetics distinguished between two concepts of development. While the Italians focused on building an extended formal section from a memorable rhythmic idea, the French emphasized appropriate reflection of the dramatic course by a series of distinct melodies. In the eyes of Italian audiences, therefore, French arias or duets seemed to lack unity, appearing incoherent, fragmented ("spezzate"), and constantly contrasting. Both French and Italian reviews noted such characteristics in *Les Vêpres siciliennes* – either as praise or criticism, depending on the point of view.[44] One might expect that a Meyerbeer-biased, reformist journal such as *L'armonia* would have praised this stylistic aspect; the fear of portraying Verdi as Meyerbeer's equal, however, seems to have deterred critic Pietro Torrigiani from too positive an evaluation. Torrigiani recognized the new melodic quality of *Les Vêpres siciliennes* but blamed Verdi for poor craftsmanship:

Among the noticeable defects of this score, the capital one refers to the lack of a nexus and a connection between the melodic ideas; so that rather than fused they sooner appear stitched together, to the detriment of the musical language, which, though composed of very regular parts in itself, seems to proceed without any aim.[45]

Two reasons may account for the introduction of a new melody: a change of prosody or a change of affect. We have repeatedly seen that changes of a verse's accentual structure can be either ignored or accommodated by minor adjustments of musical rhythm. When such changes appear in conjunction with a new thought, however, or when they involve not only the accentual structure but the poetic meter, Verdi, in agreement with French

142 French melody in Verdi's operas

Example 4.9a. *La traviata*, II,5, "Dite alla giovine" (Violetta).

Example 4.9b. *Les Vêpres siciliennes*, IV,1, "O jour de peine" (Henri).

taste, would continue with a new melody. In "Ami!... le coeur d'Hélène," for instance, Hélène has just learned from Henri that Montfort is his father, whom he had protected out of filial duty rather than affection. Under these mitigating circumstances, she can forgive him for having thwarted the conspiracy against Montfort. With the fifth verse, she shifts her thoughts from forgiveness to love, and at the same time, the text introduces a new accentual structure:

Ami!... le coeur d'Hélène	[2,4,6]
Pardonne au repentir:	[2,6]
Et ma plus grande peine	[4,6]
Était de te haïr!	[2,6]
Abjurant ma colère	[3,6]
Et mon ressentiment,	[2,4,6]
Je t'aime!... heureuse et fière	[2,4,6]
De mourir en t'aimant.	[3,6]

Verdi could have modified the dominant design of the first quatrain (♪ ♫♪.♪|♩♩ *Le coeur d'Hé-lè-ne*) to fit the text of the second (e.g., ♪♪ ♫ ♪.♪|♩♩ *Ab-ju-rant ma co-lè-re*). The change of emotion, however, from fairly detached "forgiveness" to the much stronger "rejection of anger" and "confession of love" explains the melodic contrast more convincingly. As shown in connection with innovative aspects of *Jérusalem*, introduction of a new melody after a few verses and a turn from the minor to the major mode, all while basically preserving the accompanimental pattern, occur regularly in Italian opera of the time. But the type of melodic change here (an expressive shift rather than direct contrast), the fact that the new melody follows a lyrical as opposed to a declamatory section, and the function of the melody as a refrain instead of a culminating final phrase, are all typical features of French opera in the main (Ex. 4.10).

A chain of stanzas with distinct poetic meters almost always leads to a chain of distinct melodies, but such chains occur more frequently in French than in Italian librettos. Italian librettos tend to separate stanzas of arias and duets by transitions in *versi sciolti* or by non-stanzaic verse.[46] In addition, immediately subsequent parallel stanzas are often set to the same music, especially in Verdi's early works. French librettos, on the other hand, may link several stanzas without transitions, thus suggesting a sequence of contrasting melodies. Alberto Mazzucato, the prestigious critic of the *Gazzetta musicale di Milano*, seems to have been confused by this distinction between French and Italian librettos when he discussed the structure of Hélène's act I aria "Viens à nous, Dieu tutélaire":

We do not have the French text in front of us: but it seems that in the exit piece for the soprano, Scribe intended for the composer to design one of those arias based on strophes or *couplets* that are fairly common in the French theater and probably not used too often in Italian opera: we say "it seems"; because, to tell the truth, in the Italian translation the poetic structure of the three *couplets* does not appear, with regard to the meter, symmetrical as it should be, as the first pair of strophes has a different meter from the other two pairs. And furthermore, considering the latter two separately, the

Example 4.10. *Les Vêpres siciliennes*, IV,2, "Ami!... le coeur d'Hélène" (Hélène).

sentiment of the first four verses of the one [pair] is too much opposed to that of the first four verses of the other in order to support an identical or at least similar melody, since the first is a sentiment of courage, the other of sorrow. It is nevertheless obvious that the piece should have presented the lyrical, symmetrical form of the ode, the ballad, the *canzone*, the hymn.[47]

Mazzucato is correct about the poetic structure but wrong about Scribe's intention of providing couplets. On the surface, couplets may indeed seem appropriate in a song meant to entertain the French soldiers, but the text makes it clear that Hélène does not mean to entertain but to rally her compatriots; couplets clearly would have been out of place here. A comparison of the passages from the French and Italian librettos helps explain Mazzucato's confusion. Because the first two stanzas of the Italian translation appear without spatial separation and because all stanzas except for "Iddio risponde... " are equally indented, Mazzucato failed to notice that the first couplet, too, consists of distinct meters.

French text with its formal sections
[*tempo d'attacco*; m. 5]
    Au sein des mers et battu par l'orage,
    Voyez ce beau vaisseau prêt a faire naufrage.
    Malgré le bruit des vents et la fureur des flots,
    Entendez-vous les cris des matelots?

[*adagio*; m. 17]
    Viens à nous, Dieu tutélaire
    Apaise enfin ton courroux!
    Exauce notre prière!
    Sauve-nous?... protège-nous!

[*tempo di mezzo*; m. 28]
    Et Dieu disait dans ses décrets suprèmes:
N'avez-vous donc d'espoir qu'en des secours divins?
    Vos jours dépendent de vous-mêmes;
    Votre salut est dans vos mains...

[cabaletta, A Section; m. 51]
    Courage!... du courage!
    Et, pour braver l'orage,
    A l'ouvrage!... à l'ouvrage!
    Le ciel vous guidera!
    Oui, vaillant équipage,
    Ne perdez pas courage!
Veuillez être sauvés, et Dieu vous sauvera!

[cabaletta, B Section]
    A quoi bon des prières vaines?
    N'est-il plus de sang dans vos veines?
    D'effroi, de stupeur accablés,
    Devant le danger vous tremblez!
    Debout! au fracas des tempêtes
    Qui vont mugissant sur vos têtes,
    Réveillez-vous! réveillez-vous!
    Levez-vous tous!!!

Italian text with Mazzucato's sections[48]
[first "couplet"]
    In alto mare, e sbattuto dai venti, [*endecasillabi*]
    Mira quel pino in sen degli elementi.
    A naufragar già presso, ascolti il pianto
    Del marinar dal suo navile infranto?
    Deh! tu calma, o Dio possente, [*ottonari*]
    Col tuo riso e cielo e mar;
    Salga a te la pace ardente,
    In te fida il marinar!

Iddio risponde in suo poter sovrano: [*endecasillabi*]
"A chi fida in sè stesso il cielo arride;
Mortali, il destin vostro è in vostra mano."

[second "couplet"]
    Coraggio, su coraggio,   [*settenari*]
    Del mare audaci figli;
    Si sprezzino i perigli,
    È il gemere viltà!
    Al ciel fa grave offesa
    Chi manca di coraggio:
    Osate! e l'alta impresa
    Iddio proteggerà!

[third "couplet"]
    Perchè vane preci ascolto?   [*ottonari*]
    Perchè pallido è ogni volto?
    Nel più forte del cimento
    Voi tremate di spavento?
    Su, su forti! al mugghiare dell'onda [*decasillabi*]
    E agli scrosci del tuono risponda,
    Si desti il vostro ardor,   [*settenario*]
    Invitti cor!   [*quinario*]

Example 4.11. *Les Vêpres siciliennes*, I,2, "Viens à nous, Dieu tutélaire" (Hélène).

The indention in the French libretto, on the other hand, makes it easy to grasp the form of this aria. Verdi had no problems recognizing it, setting each stanza to at least one distinct melody and matching the degree of lyricism to the degree of the text's metric regularity. Only the second distich of the third stanza ("Et Dieu disait") is repeated to create a transition to the subsequent melody; all other themes make up a tight chain of basically unrelated or only loosely related short ideas. Many Italian critics would have considered them poorly developed or "stitched together," even if the form of the traditional Italian multi-movement aria remained clearly recognizable (Ex. 4.11).

Example 4.11 (*Continued*)

Example 4.11 (*Continued*)

Les Vêpres siciliennes *and its influence on the subsequent Italian operas* 149

Example 4.11 (*Continued*)

Example 4.12. *Les Vêpres siciliennes*, II,3, "Comment dans ma reconnaissance" (Hélène-Henri).

A similar chain of melodies appears in the act II duet "Comment dans ma reconnaissance" between Hélène and Henri (Ex. 4.12). Once again, the structure of the text invites continuous lyricism:

Comment, dans ma reconnaissance Payer un pareil dévouement? A vous, ma seule providence, A vous et ma vie et mon sang!	[melody 1, mm. 1ff]
Pour vous d'un tyran sanguinaire Vous avez bravé le courroux? Sans trembler j'ai vu sa colère Hélas! et tremble devant vous!	
Vous détournez les yeux et mon audace est grande! Qu'un seul rayon d'espoir en mon âme descende, Hélène... je vous aime et n'implore à genoux, Que le droit de combattre et de mourir pour vous!	[melody 2, mm. 24ff]

Example 4.12 (*Continued*)

Près du tombeau peut-être où nous allons descendre,   [melody 3, mm. 48ff]
A tant de dévouement je ne répondrais pas!
Non, et du haut des cieux, où tu dois nous entendre,   [melody 4, mm. 57ff]
Ô mon frère... ô mon frère! tu me pardonneras!

Example 4.12 (*Continued*)

Ah! l'ai-je bien entendu?... moi! ma noble maîtraisse!   [melody 5, mm. 65ff]
   Moi qui n'ai ni rang, ni richesse...
Moi, pauvre et simple soldat, vous acceptez ma foi
   Et mon obscure misère...

With the adjustments in stanzas 3 and 5, discussed earlier, Verdi essentially turned the text into a string of quatrains, each of which is set to an independent melody; only stanza 2

Les Vêpres siciliennes *and its influence on the subsequent Italian operas* 153

Example 4.12 (*Continued*)

Example 4.12 (Continued)

Example 4.12 (*Continued*)

continues the melody of stanza 1, and stanza 4, with its contrasting topics of "tombeau [grave]" and "cieux [Heavens]," is set to two melodies. Further, only stanzas 1–2 and 3 significantly develop the material, without, however, bearing strong resemblance to mid-century lyric form, and only "Non, et du haut des cieux" and "Ah! l'ai-je bien entendu" come to a satisfying harmonic close.[49] Chaining together short independent melodies did, of course, allow for perfect adjustment to changing emotions, but it also led to Torrigiani's criticism of a lack of connection between the themes. Basevi, on the other hand, considered the duet one of the best numbers of the opera.[50]

Of all the numbers, Basevi acknowledged only Montfort's "Au sein de la puissance" to be "to a certain point" composed according to French taste, although he had some reservations even here. (In the Italian version of the opera, titled *Giovanna de Guzman*, Montfort becomes Vasconcello.)

> Vasconcello's aria, in the movement *In braccio alle dovizie* ["Au sein de la puissance"], reminds us of the *Congiura* in Meyerbeer's *Huguenots*. After all, this aria is well conducted, and it is the only one that, to a certain point, can be called "to French liking"; in fact, it was little appreciated by the [Italian] public. It lacks the variety of rhythm by which alone pieces of a certain length become acceptable; and thus [this aria] turns out somewhat monotonous.[51]

The libretto with its two contrasting stanzas sets up the musical ABA′ form typical of large-scale French arias.

Au sein de la puissance,	[melody 1, mm. 1ff]
Au sein de la grandeur,	
Un vide affreux, immense,	
Régnait seul dans mon coeur!	
Le ciel vient apparaître	[melody 2, mm. 21ff]
A mes yeux rajeunis,	
Et je me sens renaître	
A ce mot seul: Mon fils!	
Mon fils!	

La haine égara sa jeunesse,	[melody 3, mm. 33ff]
Mais près de moi, dans ce palais,	
Je veux conquérir sa tendresse	
Et le vaincre par mes bienfaits!	
Au sein de la puissance, etc.	

The French influences go beyond this large-scale formal characteristic, however. The aria consists of three distinct melodies, each with a distinct accompaniment not based on conventional rhythmic patterns and each appropriate to Montfort's emotion at any given time: the void in his heart, the heavenly revelation as he realizes he is the father of a courageous young man (Henri), and his determination to turn his son's hate into tenderness. Although Verdi developed both the first and third themes beyond their thematic block, they do not come to a satisfying close before a new melody begins. The frequent changes of tempo greatly contribute to the impression of a chain of distinct melodies (Ex. 4.13).

Example 4.13. *Les Vêpres siciliennes*, III,3, "Au sein de la puissance" (Montfort).

Revisions for Paris: *Le trouvère* and *Macbeth*

During the ten years following the premiere of *Les Vêpres siciliennes*, Verdi revised two works for the Opéra: *Il trovatore* (1857; as *Le trouvère*) and *Macbeth* (1865). Unlike the reworking of *Stiffelio* into *Aroldo*, which was intended to rescue an opera from oblivion by eliminating some of its most progressive features,[52] the revisions of *Il trovatore* and *Macbeth* specifically targeted the Parisian audience and as such are potentially significant for our purposes. Production at the Opéra required a French libretto and thus a translation of both works, a task completed by Émilien Pacini for *Le trouvère* and by Charles Nuitter and Alexandre Beaumont for *Macbeth*. In the case of the former opera, translation preceded the musical revisions: in the case of the latter, it followed them.

In a letter of January 28, 1891, to Giulio Ricordi, Verdi wrote that Pacini had made "all the changes, additions, [and] modifications required by the demands of [the Paris Opéra]."[53] This claim and the lack of an extant autograph have led to speculations about the actual author of the musical revisions. David Lawton has concluded, however, that despite the vagueness of Verdi's words in the letter to Ricordi, evidence in the review of the premiere in *La France musicale*, annotations in Verdi's hand in the part-book for Léonore, and Verdi's contract with the Opéra seem to confirm his authorship.[54]

For Verdi's mastery of French melody, the *Trouvère* revisions are of minor importance because they primarily concern portions that are not the focus of this study (i.e., the new

Example 4.13 (*Continued*)

Example 4.13 (*Continued*)

ballet, ensemble passages, and transitions based on non-stanzaic structures). The most relevant changes concern the accompaniment, where Verdi repeatedly replaced simple patterns by somewhat more sophisticated and less accentuated ones. Two passages from the act III trio "Je vivais pauvre et sans peine" may serve as examples. In Azucena's invented explanation for her presence in Count di Luna's camp, the accompanimental pattern of the Italian version, while not disappearing entirely, becomes less formulaic (Ex. 4.14a) and, a few measures later, harmonically richer while abandoning the melodic accentuation of the downbeat (Ex. 4.14b).[55]

The revisions for *Macbeth*, although more extensive than those for *Le trouvère*, still have only limited significance for our examination of Verdi's melodic development.[56] Apart from the replacement of an entire aria ("Trionfai! securi alfine") with a more modern one

Example 4.14a. *Il trovatore/Le trouvère*, III,4, "Giorni poveri vivea"/"Je vivais pauvre et sans peine," E-minor section (Azucena).

Example 4.14b. *Il trovatore/Le trouvère*, III,4, "Giorni poveri vivea"/"Je vivais pauvre et sans peine," E-major section (Azucena).

Les Vêpres siciliennes *and its influence on the subsequent Italian operas* 161

Example 4.15. *Macbeth* (1865), II,1, "La luce langue" (Lady Macbeth).

("La luce langue"), the revised passages based on stanzaic structures offer little that could be explained by French melodic aesthetics. In most cases, the changes derive from Verdi's developed sensitivity to the dramatic requirements of the text rather than from French taste;[57] after all, by 1865 the original *Macbeth* lay eighteen years in the past.

Nevertheless, the one new aria, Lady Macbeth's "La luce langue," does draw on two of Verdi's achievements in *Les Vêpres siciliennes*: the French way of conducting a melody (Ex. 4.15) and reducing formulaic accompaniments. After having convinced Macbeth to kill Banquo and Banquo's son, Lady Macbeth launches into gloomy reflections on a darkening night that would facilitate the planned murders and then rejoices in her regal

Example 4.15 (*Continued*)

power. The accompaniment, although occasionally still formulaic in nature, is hardly perceived as such because its harmonic, melodic, and dramatic interest obscures the formulaic character. The text consists of two quatrains of *quinari doppi* and a stanza of four plus two *settenari*, suggesting a slow and then a fast movement, each of which might be set to a single melody in traditional Italian manner. Verdi's setting, however, includes at least four distinct melodies, which in traditional French manner feature little development and in most cases connect without a transition. Even though the poetic meter changes only once, Verdi introduces distinct melodies within both parts. In the first part, he distinguishes between

Les Vêpres siciliennes *and its influence on the subsequent Italian operas* 163

Example 4.15 (*Continued*)

Example 4.15 (*Continued*)

reflections on the gloomy night (melody 1); the necessity of the murders (transition); and the peace of the deceased, who are indifferent to power (melody 2). In the second part, however, he sets the same text twice. The reason for this choice is unclear; Verdi may have decided to interpret the text from two complementary angles (indicated in the score as "con trasporto [ecstatically]" and then "con voce pianissima e un po' oscillante [with a very soft and somewhat wavering voice]") or he may have wanted to cater to French taste.

Example 4.15 (*Continued*)

In light of Verdi's reluctance to compromise in artistic matters, he probably wanted both. Since he revised the opera to an Italian libretto (and thus cannot have reacted to rhythmic subtleties of French verse), the original Italian text is provided here:

La luce langue, il faro spegnesi [melody 1, mm. 1ff]
    Ch'eterno corre per gli ampî cieli!
    Notte desiata provvida veli
    La man colpevole che ferirà.

Nuovo delitto! È necessario!	[transition, mm. 20ff]
Compiersi debbe l'opra fatale.	
Ai trapassati regnar non cale;	[melody 2, mm. 35ff]
A loro un requiem, l'eternità.	
O voluttà del soglio!	[melody 3, mm. 45ff] [melody 4, mm. 55ff]
O scettro, alfin sei mio!	
Ogni mortal desìo	
Tace e s'acqueta in te.	
Cadrà fra poco esamine	
Chi fu predetto re.	

Between *Les Vêpres siciliennes* and *Don Carlos*

With *Simon Boccanegra* (1857), *Un ballo in maschera* (1859), and *La forza del destino* (1862), Verdi returned to verse with which he had long been familiar. Gone was the need for a weakened sense of rhythm to smooth over irregular and unfamiliar patterns of accent, gone the need for new melodic solutions to reflect the rhythm of typical French poetic meters, and gone the tradition of scanning against tonic accents to express lightheartedness or local color.[58] Reduced – at least – was also the need to set irregular rhythmic groups in the manner of Lubarsch and Landry, an approach that would not have been appreciated in formal melody in Italy and was still rare even in France. Nevertheless, some of Verdi's achievements in *Les Vêpres siciliennes* carried over to his subsequent Italian works, especially in accompaniment, harmony, conducting the melody, and variety of thematic blocks.

The first new opera after *Les Vêpres siciliennes* was *Simon Boccanegra*, a work generally counted among Verdi's more innovative ones.[59] The abundance of fresh melodies was probably the result of Verdi's newly gained experience in setting French verse for a French audience as the following three examples will illustrate. In the first one, Jacopo Fiesco bemoans the death of his daughter, whom he locked up in his palace after she had borne Boccanegra's illegitimate child. Taken in isolation, none of the characteristics of this *romanza* would make a particularly convincing case for French influence, but in combination, they do: the *romanza* consists of two independent melodies; the first lacks opening parallel phrases while the second begins with the short non-developmental phrases criticized by Basevi in *Les Vêpres siciliennes*; the accompaniment is not patterned but sustained and eventually draws on the tremolos so typical of French prayers; and the harmony – with its progression to the flat third scale degree and back to the tonic through an unexpected shift to a cadential six-four chord – features the kind of interest a French audience would have appreciated (Ex. 4.16).

With *Simon Boccanegra*, Verdi also begins to apply to Italian verses of fixed accents – and of an accordingly high threshold for melodic innovation – solutions tested or perfected in *Les Vêpres siciliennes*, especially Castil-Blaze's reduced sense of rhythm and the greater

Example 4.16. *Simon Boccanegra*, Prologue, 5, "Il lacerato spirito" (Fiesco): thematic blocks of the two melodies (choral interjections omitted).

Example 4.17. *Simon Boccanegra*, Prologue, 6, "Se concedermi vorrai" (Fiesco).

diversity of thematic blocks. In our second example from *Simon Boccanegra*, still the prologue, Fiesco names the price of forgiving Boccanegra for having seduced his daughter: the return of their off-spring, Maria (Ex. 4.17). Verdi expresses Fiesco's initial inner agitation by underlaying a vocal line of even quarter notes with an accompaniment that avoids clear structural support because it moves at the same pace as the melody but implies contradictory musical meters. While the harmonic structure – in agreement with prosody – suggests duple meter, the shift from unison to chordal accompaniment on "conce**der**mi" and "innocen**te**" suggests triple meter, seemingly confirmed by the syncopation on "nasce**a**," which by that time is no longer perceived as a syncopation. In addition to this ambiguity, the melody features other prominent stylistic characteristics of *Les Vêpres siciliennes*: the short non-developmental opening phrases and the early introduction of a new melodic rhythm and accompaniment at "Io che ancor."

Finally, in the act I duet between Boccanegra and Amelia, the *ottonari* also receive an unorthodox setting in a somewhat ambiguous meter. By ignoring the elisions in the first three verses of "Se la speme, o ciel clemente," Verdi in effect turns the *ottonari* into *novenari*, a rhythmically awkward poetic meter not used in Italian opera at the time. As a consequence, the verses' second accent falls not on the fourth but the fifth eighth-note of the 6/8 meter, implying a 3/4 meter in agreement with the added dynamic stress. The tremolo of the accompaniment favors neither interpretation, while the broken triads give preference to an interpretation in 6/8.[60] The resulting metric ambiguity beautifully matches the affect

Example 4.18. *Simon Boccanegra*, I,7, "Se la speme" (Boccanegra).

of Boccanegra's aside, as he begins to realize that Amelia may in fact be his long-sought daughter, Maria (Ex. 4.18).

Finding new solutions to setting standard poetic meters, especially the regularly accented ones, became an even bigger challenge in *Un ballo in maschera*, where *decasillabi* abound.[61] One of the most prominent numbers based on *decasillabi* is "Ma dall'arido stelo divulsa," in which Amelia is torn between her forbidden love for Riccardo and collecting the herb that will cure her of this love. Three stanzas of six *decasillabi* set to one of the traditional rhythms associated with this poetic meter would have sounded trite. Once again, Verdi resorted to an unusual rhythm in a vaguely defined musical meter, thus imbuing the beginning of this aria with the appropriate expression of indecision. In a traditional setting of *decasillabi*, the second accent (here "stelo") would have fallen on the fourth eighth-note of the measure, the third accent on the subsequent downbeat. The second accent does indeed fall on the fourth eighth-note but coincides with the beginning of a set of relatively shorter note values, which are associated with weak metric positions in Italian opera (unlike in French opera).[62] The third accent (on "divulsa") falls not on a downbeat but on a weak metric position of the measure. The lengthening of the accent on "divulsa," on the other hand, suggests a metric interpretation in 3/4, with which the preceding sixteenth-note triplets would conform. In other words, the passage can be understood in either 6/8 or 3/4. Only with the fourth verse ("Quell'eterea sembianza morrà") does a more straightforward solution clarify the meter

Example 4.19. *Un ballo in maschera*, II,1, "Ma dall'arido stelo divulsa" (Amelia).

in favor of 6/8. Finally, the unusual initial harmonic progression from i to VI to IV^7 to V and back to i lends this opening, in line with French aesthetics, a distinct character while at the same time supporting the drama (Ex. 4.19).

The French quality of *Un ballo in maschera* derives from the style of the French *couplets*, rather than from a metrically ambiguous setting of standard verses.[63] With their short meters, often short phrases, and accompanimental rhythm tied to the melody, the *couplets* are primarily associated with the character of Oscar, who with his unfailingly positive perspective inadvertently contributes to the downfall of his master, Riccardo. In his act III *canzone*, "Saper vorreste," he teasingly dares Renato to identify Riccardo among the disguised guests at the grand ball, not realizing that Renato is seeking Riccardo's life. The *canzone* includes all the attributes of French couplets: two stanzas with refrain, short meter and phrases, and an accompanimental rhythm tied to the melody. The phrasing appears particularly short, because each phrase is subdivided into two designs, which themselves would count as individual phrases were it not for the overarching parallelism of *a* and *a'*.[64] In addition, the text consists of the short poetic meters (here *quinari*) typical of *couplets* especially in French opera. Although Italian composers frequently scan *quinari* against interior accents (here "Quand<u>o</u> l'è c<u>o</u>sa"), scanning in this dramatic situation would also be perfectly in line with French practice (Ex. 4.20).

Oscar is not the only character singing *couplets* (first in his *ballata* [I,4], then in his *canzone* [III,8]): when Riccardo, disguised as a fisherman, challenges Ulrica to prophesy

Example 4.20. *Un ballo in maschera*, III,8, "Saper vorreste" (Oscar).

his future, he, too, resorts to *couplets* (in his *canzone* "Di' tu se fedele"). They have the lighthearted tone of Oscar's but lack the typical short phrases and melody-derived accompanimental rhythm. Shortly after having heard Ulrica's unexpected prediction of having to die by the hand of a friend, he tries to diffuse the tension, "con eleganza," in the quintet "È scherzo od è follia." Riccardo's phrases fit the character of a *couplet* perfectly but no longer follow a strophic form; rather, they serve as a dramatic contrast to Ulrica's warning of the conspirators Samuel and Tom, their fear of her insights, and the perplexity of the people. In this quintet, the *couplets* no longer exist in pure form, but their characteristics serve a dramatic function within the number.

La forza del destino includes no clear examples of metric ambiguity and only rare examples of passages influenced by *couplets* (e.g., Trabuco's "A buon mercato"). It does, however, continue the development toward greater expressive intensity through a combination of harmonic richness and constantly changing accompaniments as required by the drama. When Leonora laments her fate at having to abandon family and fatherland to be with the person she loves ("Me pellegrina ed orfana" [I,2]), she begins by reciting on a single pitch over an accompaniment that follows the rhythm of the melody (rather than a clear pattern) and links the phrases by an arpeggiated tonic, first in F major, then in F minor. Beginning with "fato inesorabile [inexorable fate]," the melody descends chromatically over rich harmonies and confirms the key of F minor by a ii-V-i cadence. At "colmo di tristi immagini," the melody works its way up chromatically, supported by chromatic and

Example 4.21a. *La forza del destino*, I,2, "Me pellegrina ed orfana" (Leonora).

dissonant harmonies, until it culminates on g'' over a sustained diminished seventh chord. After a half cadence on "pianto," a second chromatic ascent, considerably more agitated than the first, ensues over predominantly diminished harmonies, now climbing up to bb'' (Ex. 4.21a).

Toward the end of the aria, as Leonora realizes that her suffering will never end ("Per me non avrà termin sì gran dolor"), Verdi intensifies the accompaniment by switching to tremolo (a popular French feature) and sustaining, both in the bass and treble, an often dissonant C. The climactic a'' is approached by a leap of an octave right into the dissonance of a diminished seventh chord, which does not resolve on the downbeat but is prolonged into an even stronger dissonance. Only on the third eighth note of the measure does

Example 4.21a (*Continued*)

the tension resolve as the melody approaches the cadence in F major. Budden justifiably compared this kind of intensity to verismo, a comparison that might be extended to the very beginning of the aria with its fairly monotonous declamation that eventually builds to a final climax (Ex. 4.21b).[65]

Just how much the intensity of Verdi's music continued to increase can be seen in a comparison of the climax from "Me pellegrina ed orfana" with a similar passage from *Un ballo in maschera*. Toward the end of Amelia's "Ma dall'arido stelo divulsa," Verdi similarly switches to tremolo as the melody climbs up to c''', but the harmony remains more conventional: the dissonances on the ab''s are immediately resolved, and the c'''

Example 4.21b. *La forza del destino*, I,2, "Me pellegrina ed orfana" (Leonora).

is consonant with the supporting harmony (Ex. 4.22). Such a comparison may indicate that Verdi's language would have developed as it did even had he not written *Les Vêpres siciliennes*, especially because the music does not sound particularly French. On the other hand, his handling of the accompaniment as well as his focus on harmonic sophistication reflect concepts promoted by the French, and once they were applied to a work such as *Vêpres*, they continued to develop over subsequent works.

One of the most unusual numbers of *La forza del destino* is undoubtedly the *melodia* "Pace, pace," in which Leonora begs God for inner peace. The text consists of alternating

Example 4.22. *Un ballo in maschera*, II,1, "Ma dall'arido stelo divulsa" (Amelia).

and rhyming *endecasillabi* and *settenari*, a combination Verdi had first encountered in choruses of *I lombardi* ("Gerusalem!... Gerusalem!... ," III,1), *La battaglia di Legnano* ("Fra queste dense tenebre," III,1), and later in an aria from *Il trovatore* (Ferrando's racconto "Di due figli," I,1). The most interesting rhythmic solution of these appears in the chorus from *I lombardi*, where Verdi accommodated the unusual poetic structure by an irregularly phrased *a cappella* invocation, followed by regularly paced six-measure phrases ("Deh! per i luoghi"), irregularly paced four-measure phrases ("Gli empi avvinsero"), and a scanned transitional passage ("Sovra quel colle il Nazaren piangea"). Neither the example from *La battaglia di Legnano* nor that from *Il trovatore* adds anything that could be explained by French practice. The solution in "Pace, pace," on the other hand, *is* new, and even if it cannot be traced directly to his accomplishments in *Jérusalem* or *Les Vêpres siciliennes*, it may have been inspired by other French models. Like the middle section of Faust's "Salut! demeure chaste et pure" (Ex. 2.12), Leonora's melody unfolds with a minimum of parallelism and repetition, sometimes in regular, sometimes in irregular phrases, albeit over a more formulaic accompaniment and with none of the orchestral countermelodies found in the French passage.

Regarding thematic blocks, however, Verdi forged ahead, maintaining the diversity he had developed in *Les Vêpres siciliennes*. As Table 4.2 shows, the works through *La forza del destino* contain a basically constant number of non-standard thematic blocks.[66]

Table 4.2. Thematic blocks in the operas from *Les Vêpres siciliennes* through *La forza del destino*

Type 1. Instant development of a thematic idea in the parallel phrase
   Les Vêpres siciliennes
      "Courage!... du courage" (I,2)
      "Fidèle à ses leçons" (I,4)
      "Vous détournez les yeux" (II,3)
      "La haine égara" (III,3)
      "Adieu, mon pays" (IV,5)
   Simon Boccanegra
      "Cielo di stelle orbato" (I,1)
      "Cielo pietoso rendila" (II,5)
      "Perdono, Amelia" (II,9)
      "Delle faci festanti" (III,5)
   Un ballo in maschera
      "Eri tu" (III,1)
   La forza del destino
      "Urna fatale" (III,5)
      "Del mondo i disinganni" (IV,3)
Type 2. No phrase parallelism
   Les Vêpres siciliennes
      "A quoi bon" (I,2)
      "Saint amour" (II,1)
      "Près du tombeau" (II,3)
      "O jour de peine" (IV,1)
      "Écoute un instant" (IV,2)
      "La brise souffle" (V,2)
      "La bannière de France" (V,4)
   Simon Boccanegra
      "Il lacerato spirito" (P,5)
      "Come in quest'ora" (I,1)
      "Dimmi, perchè in quest'eremo" (I,7)
      "Mi baciò" (I,7)
      "E alla Ligure" (I,11)
      "All'ora istessa" (II,7)
      "Piango, perchè mi parla" (III,5)
      "Gran Dio li benedici" (III,6)
   Un ballo in maschera
      "La rivedrà nell'estasi" (I,2)
      "Re dell'abisso" (I,6)
      "È lui, è lui!" (I,7)
      "Chi voi siate" (I,10)
      "Odi tu, come fremono cupi" (II,3)
      "Di che fulgor" (III,4)
      "Ma se m'è forza perderti" (III,5)
      "Sì, rivederti Amelia" (III,6)
      "Ella è pura" (III,6)

Table 4.2 (*Continued*)

 La forza del destino
  "Ah per sempre" (I,3)
  "Al suon del tamburo" (II,2)
  "Madre, pietosa Vergine" (II,5)
  "Infelice, delusa" (II,9)
  "La Vergine degli Angeli" (II,10)
  "Leonora mia" (III,1)
  "Con voi scendere" (III,2)
  "Non io, fu il destino" (III,11)
  "Morte, ov'io!... " (III,11)
  "Vissi nel mondo" (IV,5)
  "Pace, pace" (IV,6)

Type 3. Including *ad libitum* portions
 Les Vêpres siciliennes
  "Le ciel vient apparaître" (III,3)

Type 4. Phrase parallelism only in the orchestra
 Les Vêpres siciliennes
  "Et Dieu disait" (I,2)
  "Quand ma bonté" (III,4)
 Simon Boccanegra
  "Dimmi, perchè in quest'eremo" (I,7)

Type 5. Irregular phrasing
 Les Vêpres siciliennes
  "A quoi bon" (I,2)
  "Le ciel vient" (III,3)
  "Ami, le coeur" (IV,2)
  "La bannière" (V,4)
 Simon Boccanegra
  "Cielo di stelle orbato" (I,1)
  "All'ora istessa" (II,7)
  "Perdono, Amelia" (II,9)
  "Come fantasima" (III,5)
  "Piango, perchè mi parla" (III,5)
  "Gran Dio li benedici" (III,6)
 Un ballo in maschera
  "Dunque signori" (I,5)
  "Eri tu" (III,1)
  "Ella è pura" (III,8)
 La forza del destino
  "Madre, pietosa Vergine" (II,5)
  "Con voi scendere" (III,2)
  "Morte, ov'io!... " (III,11)
  "Pace, pace" (IV,6)

Table 4.2 (*Continued*)

Type 6. Short initial, basically unaltered parallel phrases of only one design but more than one measure in length
    Les Vêpres siciliennes
        "Viens à nous, Dieu tutélaire" (I,2)
        "Quoi, ma tendresse" (III,4)
        "Autour de moi" (IV,1)
        "Tout un peuple en prière" (IV,5)
        "Trahison! imposture!" (V,4)
    Simon Boccanegra
        "L'atra magion" (P,4)
        "Se concedermi vorrai" (P,6)
        "Nell'ora soave" (I,12)
        "Sento avvampar" (II,5)
        "Sgombra dall'alma" (II,6)
    Un ballo in maschera
        "Su, fatemi largo" (I,8)
        "A tal colpa" (III,1)
    La forza del destino
        "Me pellegrina" (I,2)
        "Anco una volta" (I,3)
        "Guai per chi si lascia illudere" (II,9)
        "Se voi scacciate" (II,9)
        "Del mondo i disinganni" (IV,3)
        "Se i rimorsi" (IV,5)
Type 7. Long phrases with more than two distinct rhythmic designs
    Les Vêpres siciliennes
        "Et toi, Palerme" (II,1)
        "Adieu, mon pays" (IV,5)
    Un ballo in maschera
        "È lui, è lui!" (I,7)
        "Eri tu" (III,1)
        "Sì, rivederti, Amelia" (III,6)
    La forza del destino
        "Ti lascio, ahimè" (I,2)
        "Pace, pace" (IV,6)

The return to longer sections of uniform Italian verses naturally diminished the need to change the melodic rhythm and thus to conduct melodies as described in several excerpts from *Les Vêpres siciliennes*. Nevertheless, soloistic sections with more than two independent melodies also begin to appear in Verdi's Italian works. Alvaro's "O tu, che in seno agli angeli" from *La forza del destino*, for instance, consists of three stanzas of *settenari* and opens with two four-measure parallel phrases (a,a') followed by two shorter ones (b,b'), just as in many arias based on mid-century lyric form, except that the b phrases repeat text from the first quatrain and forgo any development. The second melody then introduces an entirely new rhythm and a distinct though still formulaic accompaniment, coming

Example 4.23. *La forza del destino*, III,1, "O tu, che in seno agli angeli" (Alvaro).

to a halt on the dominant after only a parallel statement (i.e., without any Italian-style development). The third melody ("Leonora mia, soccorrimi"), once again on a distinct rhythm and accompaniment, abandons even the parallel phrases of the first two themes and cadences after only six measures, this time on the tonic (Ex. 4.23).[67] Before *Les Vêpres siciliennes*, Verdi would probably not have set the first two stanzas to distinct melodies. The affect does not significantly change from Alvaro's envious reflection on Leonora's supposed carefree existence among the angels to his plea to her not to forget him, for he is still alive and miserable; the separation of the two stanzas by a mere comma supports their close connection. The last distich, set to the third melody is at least separated by ellipses but basically still continues Alvaro's plea. Evidently, Verdi's experience with *Les Vêpres siciliennes* had led him to use a chain of distinct melodies even if the text did not require it.[68]

Oh tu, che in seno agli angeli	[melody 1; mm. 1ff]
Eternamente pura	
Salisti bella, incolume	
Dalla mortal jattura,	
Non iscordar di volgere	[melody 2; mm. 11ff]
Un guardo a me tapino,	
Che senza nome ed esule,	
In odio del destino,	

Example 4.23 (*Continued*)

Example 4.23 (*Continued*)

Pugno anelando, ahi misero,
    La morte d'incontrar…
    Leonora deh soccorrimi,   [melody 3; mm. 19ff]
    Pietà del mio penar.

Compared with *Jérusalem*, Verdi's setting of French verse in *Les Vêpres siciliennes* marks a great step forward in assimilating French aesthetics. He added to his repertoire such techniques as the scanning against tonic accents, weakening the sense of rhythm to accommodate unfamiliar accentual structures, interpreting textual accents in the manner described by Lubarsch and Landry (albeit only tentatively), greatly diversifying his thematic blocks, and further increasing the number of melodies conducted in the French manner. Despite its significance for Verdi's artistic development, *Les Vêpres siciliennes* was viewed as one of his less successful works and one more refined than spontaneous.[69] Emphasis on refinement was, of course, characteristic of French opera at the time, and if spontaneity meant easily memorable tunes based on repeated rhythmic patterns, then a lack of spontaneity, too, should be counted among the French characteristics. Judged in this light, *Vêpres* should fare well, reflecting a melodic style based on French aesthetics in general and French verse in particular. Alhough unique in Verdi's oeuvre so far, it was to be joined twelve years later by one of the true masterworks of the operatic repertoire, *Don Carlos*.

5 | *Don Carlos* and after

> This is Meyerbeer! said the crowd while exiting, after having applauded.[1]
> *Le petit journal*, March 13, 1867
>
> All in all, the work was what it was supposed to be, a French opera, not an Italian opera.[2]
> *La Patrie*, March 18, 1867

Aspects of versification and Verdi's musical response

In 1865, Verdi was in frequent contact with Léon Escudier, his publisher in France, about the revisions of *Macbeth* for the Paris Opéra. Although Émile Perrin, the Opéra's director, preferred to mount this revised opera rather than revive one from the repertoire, he still hoped to entice the maestro to compose an entirely new work. Verdi refrained from committing himself but sent signals, though negative overall, that left a door open for a new commission; it was clear that the final decision would depend on a suitable libretto.[3] Perrin accordingly dispatched Escudier to Busseto, along with a libretto titled *Cleopatra* and a scenario for *Don Carlos*. Of these and other possible topics, Verdi considered *Don Carlos* the best by far, and by the end of August 1865, the Opéra and the composer had come to a basic agreement for a new production. At the beginning of December, Verdi joined Joseph Méry and Camille Du Locle in Paris to work on the libretto for *Don Carlos*, and by the time the composer returned to Sant'Agata in March 1866, the libretto was nearly complete, except for the final version of act V.[4]

Just as in 1847 with *Jérusalem*, Verdi's presence on site rendered written correspondence between librettists and composer unnecessary. Again as a consequence, posterity has been largely deprived of documentation pertaining to his influence on the libretto in general and its rhythmic and stanzaic properties in particular. Nevertheless, some documents do exist and attest to Verdi's significant input:[5] the library at Sant'Agata holds drafts of the libretto that are covered with corrections in his hand,[6] and the letters he wrote during his brief return to Sant'Agata contain some very specific requests. For instance, in his letter of June 16 to Du Locle (Méry had passed away), Verdi asked for consistent placement of the accents on syllables 4 and 8 in Eboli's stanza in the act IV quartet, for which he had already composed the music.[7]

In a letter of June 21 regarding the subsequent scene between Élisabeth and Eboli, Verdi provided a model in Italian, asking Du Locle to preserve "accento e ritmo."[8]

Verdi's model   Du Locle's solution

      Élisabeth   Élisabeth

Pace perd<u>o</u>n dal Ci<u>e</u>lo   Ah que le ci<u>e</u>l pard<u>o</u>nne
Invocher<u>ò</u> per L<u>ei</u>.   A vos am<u>e</u>rs regr<u>e</u>ts
Piet<u>o</u>so Ei st<u>e</u>nda un v<u>e</u>lo   Que sa bont<u>é</u> vous d<u>o</u>nne
Sui f<u>a</u>lli di cost<u>ei</u>.   L'espér<u>a</u>nce et la p<u>ai</u>x

      Eboli   Eboli

Ah n<u>o</u>; il perd<u>o</u>n dal Ci<u>e</u>lo   Mon coeur bris<u>é</u> friss<u>o</u>nne
Chiam<u>a</u>r non oser<u>ei</u>.   De doul<u>eu</u>rs, de regrets,
Stender non pu<u>o</u>te un v<u>e</u>lo,   Dieu jam<u>ai</u>s ne pard<u>o</u>nne
Son tr<u>o</u>ppi i f<u>a</u>lli m<u>iei</u>.   A de par<u>ei</u>ls forf<u>ai</u>ts!

Verdi's model consists of *settenari* with obligatory accents on the fourth and sixth syllables; on the second, fourth, and sixth syllables; or on the second and sixth syllables, depending on the theorist.[9] At first glance, it seems that Du Locle chose to follow accentuation on only the fourth and sixth syllables. In verse 4 of Élisabeth's quatrain and verses 2 and 3 of Eboli's quatrain, however, he placed the first accent on the third syllable, which is unaccented in every verse of the Italian model. Verdi accepted Du Locle's solution without rhythmic changes but accommodated the irregularity either by repeating text or by introducing some rather awkward melismas. The textual and musical adjustments, however, hardly offend the ear because they are submerged in vocal polyphony.

    The process of revision extended right up to the premiere, and the modifications seem to indicate that the composer's approach to prosody had not significantly changed since *Les Vêpres siciliennes*. Nevertheless, our understanding of prosody's dramatic function helps to reveal Verdi's compositional subtleties. In the act I duet, for example, Verdi reassigned Élisabeth's line "Ah! prince! Ah! Carlos!..." to Don Carlos, with a partially modified text,[10] a change that, among other effects, strengthened the prosodic rhetoric. From a purely technical standpoint, the setting of Carlos's line is no improvement: Lubarsch and Landry would not have required an accent on "Dieu,"[11] and while the *e muet* of "même" in the earlier version is indeed lightly accented, it still receives a lesser emphasis than the word's tonic accent on the first syllable (Ex. 5.1).

    Furthermore, in Élisabeth's line, each exclamation ("Ah Pr<u>i</u>nce" and "ah Carl<u>o</u>s") is correctly accented, whereas in Carlos's line, "je" is accented over "Ah!" Still, the prosody of Carlos's line makes a dramatic point. Like Élisabeth's effusion at the beginning of the preceding stanza ("De qu<u>e</u>ls transp<u>o</u>rts poign<u>a</u>nts et d<u>ou</u>x"), Carlos's reaction scans in iambs. In addition, the scanning (albeit not against tonic accents) is more obvious than Élisabeth's, because the musical rhythm is simpler. We know from later developments in the opera that Carlos's emotional control – in contrast to Élisabeth's – leaves much to be desired, and although his declaration of love at this point cannot count as a lighthearted moment,

Example 5.1. *Don Carlos*, I,4, "Ah! je vous aime".

it certainly conveys a moment of bliss too good to be true. Aware of this distinction, Verdi does not scan against tonic accents; he simply scans in line with the prosodic properties and (in contrast to lighthearted numbers) underlays the melody with a rhythmically neutral accompaniment to convey a feeling of bliss or even ecstasy.

While working on *Les Vêpres siciliennes*, Verdi had repeatedly asked Scribe for changes of poetic rhythm and meter. In contrast, the correspondence regarding the 1867 *Don Carlos* contains hardly any such requests. It seems as if Verdi was finally ready to accept without objection the challenges of a truly French libretto, the rhythmic and metric variety of which surpasses by far *Les Vêpres siciliennes*.

French reviews of the first production of *Don Carlos* implicitly accepted Verdi's prosody by not even raising the issue for the most part. The few exceptions usually did not criticize specific examples and conceded that the "mistakes are not frequent, and they do not even exist for the public or for the majority of composers."[12] The critics' evaluation of the opera as a whole, however, was highly mixed, with consensus only on two points: *Don Carlos* surpassed all of the composer's previous works in complexity and could not be adequately judged on the basis of a single hearing, and the work marked the beginning of a new style for Verdi, especially in regard to melody.

Critics had a reason beyond the opera's complexity to delay their verdict. They seemed to protest Verdi's decision to close the dress rehearsals to outsiders – which would normally have allowed the critics to familiarize themselves with the music – because he felt that the performers were not yet ready.[13] Verdi's precaution is particularly understandable in light of the highly charged atmosphere surrounding the premiere.[14] One critic who missed the first act of the premiere due to confusion over curtain time voiced frustration in his review:

We will not report on the first act of *Don Carlos* for the simple reason that we have not seen it. The bill announced the beginning for half past seven, which according to custom seemed to give the public half an hour of latitude to arrive. Only this time, the administration was not able to grant its invitees this favor. The curtain rose and the performance began at the announced time, in spite of the noise created by the doors of the loges, in spite of the mute language of the empty stalls of which the velvet arm rests seemed to mime a protest.[15]

Regardless of the numerous negative reviews, *Don Carlos* was a great success, beginning with the second performance when the polemics surrounding the premiere began to dissipate and the audience was able to concentrate on the music. Still, after forty-three performances, *Don Carlos* disappeared from the Opéra's schedule. Ursula Günther has shown that the proceeds, which were on occasion even higher than those for Meyerbeer's *L'Africaine*, could not have provided a sufficiently strong reason for the opera's demise. Rather, after Verdi had departed for Italy on March 13, some flaws of casting became increasingly obvious, especially the weakness of Jean Morère in the title role and the rivalry between Marie-Constance Sasse (Élisabeth) and Pauline Gueymard (Eboli), which seriously diminished the opera's dramatic impact.[16]

Commentary on Verdi's new melodic style pointed to the influence of Meyerbeer and especially Richard Wagner. References to the former are certainly not surprising in light of Verdi's long-standing goal of surpassing Meyerbeer at the Opéra. References to Wagner, on the other hand are tangled in a complex web of musical and political forces to be discussed later. In short, the progressive elements first detected in reviews of *Les Vêpres siciliennes* now seemed to prevail to a degree that reminded critics of Meyerbeer, Wagner, or both:

We must first remove the name of the author, dispel the memories of *Il trovatore*, *Rigoletto*, and *La traviata*, not look in *Don Carlos* for the violent, brutal, passionate but always captivating Verdi with [his] gust of inspired melodic ideas. This Verdi no longer exists. The composer we have before us has broken with the formulas of the Italian school. Meyerbeer himself seems old-fashioned in respect to him. Like Wagner, he tends toward mélopée and lyric declamation.[17]

Other writers, too, were convinced that Verdi had successfully changed his style and finally written a truly French opera.[18] Because the most innovative melodies are linked to typically French metric and stanzaic structures, as we shall see, it seems appropriate to draw on aspects of versification for explanation.

As we have seen, most French meters have a corresponding Italian meter of equal syllable count: a *vers de cinq syllabes* corresponds to the *senario*, a *vers de six syllabes* to the *settenario*, a *vers de sept syllabes* to the *ottonario*, etc. Our comparison between French and Italian versification has shown, however, that within corresponding meters, French versification allowed for greater variety of accented positions. Verdi had already dealt with such stanzas in *Les Vêpres siciliennes* and had usually responded either by scanning in the manner of Benloew, by avoiding a strong sense of rhythm, or by mixing prosodic approaches.[19]

Verdi's solutions in *Don Carlos* for stanzas with an approximate metric equivalent in Italian prosody are not fundamentally different from those in *Les Vêpres siciliennes*, but they are more pronounced. Élisabeth's farewell to the Countess d'Aremberg, for example, takes to an extreme Castil-Blaze's suggestion to not "create too much sense of rhythm" when accommodating what he considered "musically poor verses." The first quatrain of the farewell consists entirely of *vers de six syllabes*. In the corresponding Italian meter, the *settenario*, Verdi would have found the first accent on either the second or the fourth

Example 5.2. *Don Carlos*, II,2,5 "O ma chère compagne" (Élisabeth).

syllable; here, conforming to the theory of Quicherat,[20] it may fall on any of the first four syllables (Ex. 5.2).

O ma ch**è**re comp**a**gne   [or: **O** ma chère comp**a**gne]
Ne pleure p**as**, ma s**oeu**r...
On te ch**a**sse d'Esp**a**gne,
Mais non p**as** de mon c**oeu**r.

Regular alignment of obligatory accents on subsequent downbeats without repetition of text would have led to awkward pacing with a lot of activity in the third measure ("[com]pagne ne pleure") and hardly any in the fourth ("pas ma"). To incorporate the word repetition as naturally as possible while maintaining the melancholy atmosphere, Verdi created a metrically vague accompaniment of steady eighth-note triplets over which the verses could unfold naturally in spite of the unusual position of their accents. Furthermore, by adding a musical accent on the first syllable of "c**o**mpagne," by temporarily reinforcing the melody with instrumental forces on the second syllable of the same word, and by setting the final syllable at a slightly higher pitch, Verdi stressed all syllables to a nearly equal degree. Thus, rather than the notated 3/4 meter, the listener could easily hear a 3/4 meter with downbeats on "O" and the first syllable of "compagne"; or a 2/4 meter with downbeats on the first syllable of "chère" and on the first and last syllables of "compagne." While Verdi's rhythmic solution in this *romance* does not need to cover up any misaccentuations (the accentual irregularity is accommodated by means of word repetition), the ambiguity

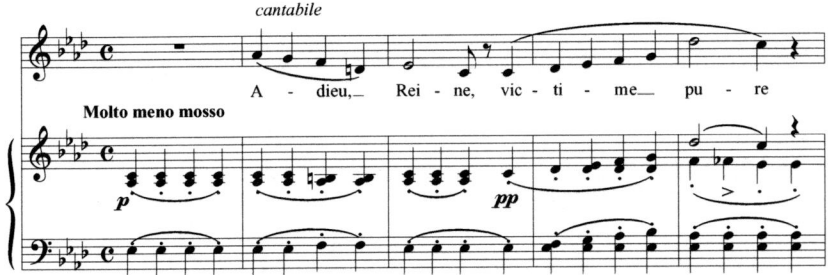

Example 5.3. *Don Carlos*, IV,1,6 "Adieu, Reine" (Eboli).

of its metric effect seems to be a direct consequence of the text's challenging accentual rhythm. The absence of what Bertrand called (and Fétis implied to be) rhythmic violence significantly contributes to the Frenchness of Élisabeth's aria.[21]

As in *Les Vêpres siciliennes*, the *octosyllabe* is the most frequent monometric stanza in *Don Carlos*. A comparison of isolated unbroken quatrains of *octosyllabes* in the two operas shows that many of the stylistic innovations of the former opera are greatly enhanced in the latter:[22] the phrase structure is much more varied, with more than half of the formal lyrical passages including irregular opening phrases or lack of parallelism; the middleground rhythm is more varied and less clearly defined; the melodies touch on keys beyond the dominant or relative major; and the accompanimental patterns are less formulaic. Eboli's "Adieu, Reine," for instance, with its clear traces of mid-century lyric form, might at first seem conventional but upon closer inspection emerges as yet another example of Castil-Blaze's advice to avoid a strong sense of rhythm. Quicherat would analyze the accentuation as follows:[23]

Ad**ieu**, R**ei**ne, victime p**u**re	[2,3,8]
De mes déloy**a**les am**ou**rs	[5,8]
Dans un couv**en**t et sous la b**u**re,	[4,8]
Je m'ensevel**is** pour touj**ou**rs!	[5,8]

A traditional setting with parallel phrases and a standard formulaic accompanimental pattern would have created either awkward rhythms or obvious misaccentuations. Verdi chose conventional regular phrasing supported by a pulsating accompaniment that eschews a clear pattern and occasionally smoothes over the prosodic inadequacies (Ex. 5.3). The first syllable of "Adieu," which falls on the downbeat, is weak and should not receive an accent, while the second syllable, which like the first one covers a set of two quarter notes, requires an accent and should stand in relief. Verdi found the perfect solution by sustaining the A-flat major harmony through the first syllable and moving to an ornamental diminished seventh chord for the second syllable. The return to A-flat major coincides with the next accent on "Reine," but now the harmony persists throughout the entire measure so as not to accent the *e muet*. Beginning with the downbeat of m. 4, Verdi accelerates the harmonic rhythm to a change per pulse. The effect on the prosody is essentially the same as if he

Example 5.4. *Don Carlos*, II,2,6 "O Roi! j'arrive de Flandre" (Rodrigue).

had not changed the harmony at all: through the downbeat of m. 5, every beat receives the same harmonic weight. Only the obligatory accent on "p<u>u</u>re" stands in relief due to the sustained harmony and the climactic pitch. The combination of harmony and melodic rhythm makes it difficult to determine a clear rhythmic middleground, allowing for the following interpretations:

Ad<u>ieu</u>, R<u>ei</u>ne, victime p<u>u</u>re

Verdi continued this approach through the rest of the stanza, albeit not with the same consistency and subtlety. Carlos's "Je l'ai vue, et dans son sourire" (I,2) and Rodrigue's "C'est mon jour, mon jour suprême" (IV,2,1), numbers usually considered conventional, feature similarly ambiguous middleground rhythms, in line with French taste.

In these examples from *Don Carlos*, Verdi either made prosodic changes for dramatic purposes (Ex. 5.1) or he loosened constraints on the melody by avoiding a strong rhythmic accompaniment. In addition, by the time of *Don Carlos*, Verdi's musical language had developed to a degree that allowed him to master highly irregular accents even in a strongly rhythmic context. Here, the composer fulfills Paul Pierson's expectations that the music should reflect not only Lubarsch and Landry's obligatory accents but also their secondary ones.[24]

Verdi had certainly observed every tonic accent as early as *Jérusalem*, but without taking into account the hierarchy of accents and without having been confronted with overly irregular patterns. A greater challenge was presented in the following passage from the highly charged exchange of views between Rodrigue and King Philip, which consists entirely of *vers de sept syllabes* but with accents in a great variety of positions. Verdi's setting (Ex. 5.4) could be used to illustrate the theory of either Quicherat or Lubarsch and Landry, except that the music reflects accents beyond those required by any of these theorists. According to Quicherat, who limits the accents to two per line, one accent must fall on the rhyme, another on either the third or fourth syllable, or sometimes the second or fifth.[25] Rodrigue's narration would be accented as follows:

O R**oi**! J'arrive de Fl**a**ndre,	[2,7]
Ce pa**y**s jadis si be**au**! | |	[3,7]
Ce n'est qu'un dés**e**rt de c**e**ndre,	[5,7]
Un lieu d'horr**eu**r, un tomb**eau**!	[4,7]
Là, l'orphel**in** qui mend**ie**	[4,7]
Et pl**eu**re par les chem**in**s,	[2,7]
Tombe, en fu**ya**nt l'incend**ie**,	[4,7]
Sur des ossem**e**nts hum**ain**s!	[5,7]

Lubarsch and Landry would accentuate somewhat differently:

O R**oi**! J'arrive de Fl**a**ndre,	[2,7]
Ce pa**y**s jadis si be**au**! | |	[3,7]
Ce n'est qu'un dés**e**rt de c**e**ndre,	[5,7]
Un lieu d'horr**eu**r, un tomb**eau**!	[4,7]
L**à**, l'orphelin qui mend**ie**	[1,7]
Et pl**eu**re par les chem**in**s,	[2,7]
T**o**mbe, en fuyant l'incend**ie**,	[1,7]
Sur des ossements hum**ain**s!	[7]

Here Pierson's approach fits like a glove. On the one hand, he requires emphatic reflection of the most important accents (those of Lubarsch and Landry) and on the other, he would also like to see a reflection of virtually all tonic accents. Verdi could not have met the challenge more successfully:

O R**oi**! J'arr**i**ve de Fl**a**ndre,	[2,4,7]
Ce pa**y**s jadis si be**au**! | |	[3,7]
Ce n'est [pl**us**] qu'un dés**e**rt de c**e**ndre,	[3,6,8]
Un l**ieu** d'horr**eu**r, un tomb**eau**!	[2,4,7]
L**à**, l'orphel**in** qui mend**ie**	[1,4,7]
Et pl**eu**re par les chem**in**s,	[2,7]
T**o**mbe, en fu**ya**nt l'incend**ie**,	[1,4,7]
S**ur** des ossem**e**nts hum**ain**s!	[1,5,7]

While Verdi's setting does not employ Pierson's shifting musical meters of Ex. 1.1, it does include considerable rhythmic variety. The accents of the first verse follow at intervals of a half note; the two accents of the second verse follow at the interval of a whole note, etc. When grouping the notes of the first two verses through each subsequent accent (see the demarcation by asterisks), we arrive at the following constellations: a two-note group

("O R<u>oi</u>"), another two-note group ("j'arr<u>i</u>-"), a three-note group ("-ve de Fl<u>an</u>-"), another three-note group ("ce pa<u>y</u>s"), and a four-note group ("jadis si b<u>eau</u>"). After two verses of more uniform groups, two follow with irregular ones: one note ("L<u>à</u>"), three three-note groups ("l'orphel<u>in</u>"; "qui mend<u>i</u>-"; and "-e et pl<u>eu</u>-"), and a five-note group ("-re par le chem<u>in</u>").

These groupings explain the rhythmic irregularity only in part. It also derives from organization at the level of Pierson's segments and Lubarsch and Landry's "conceptually related words" marked by a *Satzton*.[26] These rhythmic groups are textually marked by syntactic incision and musically by a rest or a longer note. Vertical double bars clarify the place of these incisions, which in this stanza occur in a great variety of positions: after the first syllable (as in the fifth verse), after the second (as in the first and seventh verses), after the fourth (as in the fourth verse), or only at the end of a verse.

O Roi! | | J'arrive de Flandre, | |
Ce pays jadis si beau! | |
Ce n'est [plus] qu'un désert de cendre, | |
Un lieu d'horreur, | | un tombeau! | |
Là, | | l'orphelin qui mendie | |
Et pleure par les chemins, | |
Tombe, | | en fuyant l'incendie, | |
Sur des ossements humains!

These incisions create an additional level of irregularity: first a set of two syllables, then sets of five, seven, eight, four, three, and so forth, sometimes delivered within one measure, sometimes within two. A comparison between the setting of the penultimate verse and the setting of its predecessor effectively illustrates the irregularity. By observing the correct accentuation and the syntactic incision of "Tombe, en fuyant l'incendie" (i.e., by having the first syllable of "Tombe" and the penultimate of "incendie" fall on metrically strong beats), Verdi had to account for two additional syllables within the second half of the measure. This adjustment explains the rhythmic variety, even though the phrasing itself remains in regular two-measure groups. This realistic way of grouping the text adds excitement and conviction to the delivery and seems particularly appropriate for Rodrigue's narration, in which he confronts the Spanish king with the dismal state of human rights in the province of Flanders.

This scene solicited contradictory responses from the critics. Although from today's perspective, it abounds in lyrical passages, many reviewers not only considered the political subject unsuitable for opera but "found this oratorical music tiring in the long run" and "would give up its most beautiful discourse for a word of melody."[27] Others, while not denying the focus on recitative and declamation, found the scene highly original:

Mr. Verdi did not conceive this scene according to the traditions of Italian art. He wanted to render it through an effort of lyric declamation and grand development of recitative. The character is very elevated and the contrast of the two people expressed in captivating fashion. The orchestra escorts the thoughts with a variety of tone and originality of detail that must be praised without restriction...[28]

Ernest Reyer found "O Roi, j'arrive de Flandre" "simply one of the best pages of the score."[29]

Two types of stanzas in particular appear more frequently in *Don Carlos* than in *Les Vêpres siciliennes*: those of alexandrines and those of mixed meters. Stanzaic alexandrines would have challenged any composer due to their accentual irregularity and the extended musical periods they seem to imply.[30] The frequency of stanzaic alexandrines in *Don Carlos* did not escape Alexis Azevedo of *L'Opinion nationale*, prompting the following criticism:

With Mr. Verdi, this departure [from his Italian melodic style], so regrettable in our eyes, is deliberate, systematic, [and] a true bias. As evidence, in the libretto of *Don Carlos*, we only [need to] look at the incredible predominance of alexandrines, natural friends of mélopée and declamation and natural enemies of true melody and song. It is too obvious that, if the composer had wanted verses that were shorter and thus more favorable to melody, his librettist would have provided them...[31]

Azevedo had to concede, though, that Verdi was able to overcome the challenge in Élisabeth's act V aria "Toi qui sus le néant."[32] It consists of no fewer than six quatrains of alexandrines, with the last quatrain repeating the first. The following prosodic analysis in the manner of Quicherat illustrates the highly irregular accentual patterns in every stanza but the first:

Toi qui sus le néant des grandeurs de ce monde,	[1,6; 9,12]
Toi qui goûtes enfin la paix douce et profonde,	[1,6; 9,12]
Si l'on repand encor des larmes dans le ciel.	[4,6; 8,12]
Porte en pleurant mes pleurs aux pieds de l'Éternel!	[4,6; 8,12]
Carlos va venir!... Oui, qu'il parte, qu'il oublie...	[5,6; 8,12]
J'ai promis à Posa de veiller sur sa vie.	[3,6; 9,12]
Qu'il suive son chemin glorieux et béni!	[2,6; 9,12]
Pour moi, ma tâche et faite, et mon jour est fini!	[2,6; 9,12]
France, noble pays, si cher à mon jeune âge!	[1,6; 8,12]
Fontainebleau! mon coeur est plein de votre image...	[4,6; 8,12]
C'est là que Dieu reçut notre éternel serment;	[2,6; 10,12]
Et son éternité n'a duré qu'un moment...	[–,6; 9,12]
Beaux jardins Espagnols, à l'heure pâle et sombre,	[3,6; 10,12]
Si Carlos doit encor s'arrêter sous votre ombre,	[3,6; 9,12]
Que vos fleurs, vos gazons, vos fontaines, vos bois,	[3,6; 9,12]
Chantent mon souvenir avec toutes leurs voix!	[1,6; 9,12]
Adieu, rêves dorés... illusions... chimères!...	[2,6; 10,12]
Tout lien est brisé qui m'attache à la terre.	[3,6; 9,12]
Adieu, jeunesse, amour!... succombant sous l'effort,	[4,6; 9,12]
Mon coeur n'a qu'un seul voeu, c'est la paix dans la mort!	[2,6,9,12]

Example 5.5. *Don Carlos*, V,1, "France, noble pays" (Élisabeth).

The first, most regularly accented stanza receives a conventional setting in lyric form, except that verses 1 and 2 lack an orchestral accompaniment. The subsequent stanzas, however, feature irregular accents to a degree that occasionally led Verdi to abandon aria texture in favor of *parlante* or even recitative. The second quatrain, for example, lacks unity of thought on the levels of both the verse and the quatrain. In addition, the first hemistich of the verse has unorthodox accents on subsequent syllables ("ven<u>ir</u>!... **Oui**"). No wonder

Example 5.5 (*Continued*)

Verdi set this quatrain in a variety of styles: recitative for the first distich, lyricism for the third verse, and *parlante armonico* over a regular accompanimental pattern in the final verse.

The third quatrain returns to a focus on a single thought, Élisabeth's memories of her first meeting with Carlos in the forest of Fontainebleau. The irregular sequence of accents, however, seemed to prohibit a conventional lyric design. Verdi assigned the continuous melody to the orchestra, thus allowing the vocal line to unfold freely in *parlante* and in sections of one measure for the vocal transition on "France," two measures for "noble pays, si cher à mon jeune âge," three measures for "Fontainebleau! mon coeur est plain de votre image…," and six measures for the second distich. The setting of this stanza also shows Verdi's increasing reliance on a style that accords with Lubarsch and Landry's prosodic approach. For the most part, he lets the syllables flow in equal note values to the major accent, creating rhythmic groups of varying length: two syllables ("France"), four syllables ("noble pays"), and seven syllables ("si cher à mon jeune âge"). In the context of the *parlante* texture, the result sounds perfectly natural (Ex. 5.5).

Polymetric stanzas presented a particular challenge because accentual irregularity was compounded by verses of varying length. By the time of *Don Carlos*, Verdi must have felt considerably more comfortable setting polymetric stanzas as formal melodies than he had twelve years earlier in *Les Vêpres siciliennes*, as is apparent from the striking increase in the number of polymetric stanzas set.

Such a significant change is bound to leave a mark on the music. Polymeters already appear, although rarely, in the libretto of *Les Vêpres siciliennes*, and some of them are even set as formal melodies. But neither polymetric stanzas mixing verses with their *doppio* form ("O jour de peine" [IV,1]) nor basically monometric ones with a concluding verse of different length ("Au sein de la puissance" [III,3]) required innovative solutions. More complex combinations, however, clearly caused some discomfort: "Fidèle à ses leçons" (I,5), "Ah! l'ai-je bien entendu" (II,3), and "Autour de moi" (IV,1) include awkward text repetition, and the remaining polymeters either include recitative or are not set at all. In *Don Carlos*, Verdi finally seems to have mastered the setting of polymetric stanzas, writing melodies of unsurpassed naturalness, dramatic accuracy, and beauty.

Polymetric stanzas do not necessarily preclude conventional parallel phrases, even though in practice they often led to unorthodox phrase structures, but they most always required adjustments in the accompaniment, in the approach to prosody, or both. The first example, a melody of parallel four-measure phrases from act II of *Don Carlos*, is based on three alexandrines and a *décasyllabe* (accents at the rhyme and obligatory caesura are highlighted).

Par quelle douce v<u>oi</u>x, mon âme est ranim<u>é</u>e?
    Élisab<u>e</u>th... c'est toi, ma bien-aim<u>é</u>e,
Assise à mes côt<u>é</u>s, comme aux jours d'autref<u>oi</u>s?. .
Ah! le printemps verm<u>ei</u>l a reverdi les b<u>oi</u>s!...

To accommodate the changing poetic meters and the resulting irregular sequence of accents, Verdi repeatedly abandoned musical stress in favor of duration (the harp arpeggio on the second beat does not even come close to offsetting the harmonic accent on the first and third beats). He reflected crucial accents at the rhyme and caesura (i.e., "v<u>oi</u>x," "ranim<u>é</u>e," "côt<u>é</u>s," "autref<u>oi</u>s," and "verm<u>ei</u>l") not by placing them on metrically strong beats marked by a change of harmony but by assigning to them relatively longer notes – durational accents on weak beats of the measure. The soft tremolo accompaniment, structured by changes of harmony rather than formulaic rhythmic patterns, allows for maximum effectiveness of the durational accents, which lead to a highly continuous melody, because they extend deep into the measure. This kind of accompaniment not only allows for a natural delivery of the text but also perfectly expresses Carlos's feelings. As in Carlos's declaration of love discussed earlier (see Ex. 5.1), the text can be scanned in iambs and the weak sense of rhythm conveys bliss and delirium (Ex. 5.6).

The stanza beginning with "Carlos n'accusez pas," from the same duet, combines three distinct meters: two alexandrines, a *décasyllabe*, and two *octosyllabes*.

Carlos n'accusez pas mon coeur d'indifférence.
    Comprenez mieux sa fierté... son silence.

Example 5.6. *Don Carlos*, II,2,4, "Par quelle douce voix" (Carlos).

Le devoir, saint flambeau, devant mes yeux a lui,
    Et je marche guidée par lui,
        Mettant au ciel mon espérance!

Verdi took into consideration the rhyme scheme and the resulting stanzaic caesura after the second verse, setting the two portions to distinct melodies. In his attempt to provide them with both symmetry and closure, he resorted to ternary a,a',b structures of $1+1+2$ measures in the first two verses and $2+2+6$ measures in the remaining three. In fact, these ternary structures occurs in *Don Carlos* with great frequency and, as Budden has already pointed out, especially in this duet.³³ They can best be explained by the combination of irregular verse and the need to provide each stanza with some level of musical structure. The following quatrain of *octosyllabes*, for instance, features enjambment from the first to the second verse and again from the second to the third.

Prince, si le Roi veut se rendre
A ma prière... pour la Flandre
Par lui remise en votre main
Vous pourrez partir dès demain!

[Prince, if the King is prepared to grant
What I shall ask him, He will send
You to Flanders to rule in his name.
You will leave for Flanders today!]³⁴

Instead of setting each verse to a phrase or each distich to parallel phrases, the structure of this quatrain once again favors a ternary structure of the melody, with the first one-and-a-half verses set as *a*, the next one-and-a-half verses as *a′*, and the final verse as *b*.

The final polymetric example, from the first tableau of act IV, in which Philippe accuses his wife of unfaithfulness, illustrates particularly well how Verdi accommodated irregular meters by setting them in the manner of Lubarsch and Landry's rhythmic theory. Only the most important syllables receive an accent, by far fewer than would have been required by Quicherat:

Vous me parl<u>ez</u> avec hard<u>ie</u>sse!
Vous ne m'avez conn<u>u</u> qu'en des jours de faibl<u>e</u>sse
Mais la faiblesse un j<u>our</u> peut devenir fur<u>eur</u>.
Al<u>o</u>rs, malh<u>eur</u> sur v<u>ou</u>s... malh<u>eur</u>!

The irregular poetic meter, an *octosyllabe* followed by two alexandrines and another *octosyllabe*, forced Verdi to accelerate the melodic pace in the middle two verses if he wanted to maintain regular phrasing. All the major accents are supported either by harmonic change, by accent of duration, or both. Only the setting of the final verse includes a redundant accent on the first "malh<u>eur</u>" (Ex. 5.7).³⁵

By the time of *Don Carlos*, Verdi had mastered the various approaches to French prosody so fully that even if the rhythmic structure of the verse or stanza was irregular, he was able to write a formal melody and at the same time imbue it with just the right expressive character. In "O ma chère compagne" (Ex. 5.2), Élisabeth, the wife of King Philippe II of Spain, is consoling the Countess d'Aremberg, who had just been banned from court by the King. Despite the King's explicit orders to stay at Élisabeth's side at all times, the Countess had followed the Queen's wish to be left alone for a private conversation with Carlos. Verdi reflected Élisabeth's mood of empathy and sadness at least in part by avoiding strong metric accents, which also allowed him to accommodate the accentual irregularity.

Example 5.7. *Don Carlos*, IV,1,3, "Vous me parlez avec hardiesse" (Philippe).

In "Adieu, reine" (Ex. 5.3), he drew on the same technique to express a similar emotion in a similar dramatic context, Eboli's sad farewell to the Queen brought about by a violation of courtly etiquette.

For other, similarly related dramatic situations, Verdi also drew on related prosodic approaches. For example, in "O Roi! j'arrive de Flandre" (Ex. 5.4), Rodrigue accuses the King of violating human rights in the province of Flanders, and Verdi captured Rodrigue's agitation, already evident in the highly irregular sequence of accents, by reflecting all the accents in the manner of Pierson and emphasizing the irregularities of the melodic rhythm by avoiding word repetition or melismas. In act IV, he applied a related prosodic approach to the opera's only other agitated political narrative, the Grand Inquisitor's "Dans ce beau pays, pur d'hérétique levin [In this beautiful country, free of heretic cells]." Now it is the

Example 5.8. *Don Carlos*, II,2,1, "Au palais de fées" (Eboli).

Inquisitor who criticizes the King, not for violating human rights but for not standing up to Rodrigue's allegedly heretical ideas. Like Rodrigue, the Inquisitor turns to lyricism when conveying his message, and as in Rodrigue's narration, the music accommodates in a relatively fast tempo the highly irregular accents without repeating words or resorting to melismas.[36] While Rodrigue's narrative reflects Pierson's approach, the Inquisitor's narrative primarily reflects that of Lubarsch and Landry, enriched by others. As we have seen in Chapter 1, the approaches of Lubarsch and Landry and of Pierson emphasize declamation and as such are the most appropriate for these agitated narratives. Nevertheless, with regard to declamatory subtlety, "Dans ce beau pays" cannot stand on a par with "O Roi!"; it will be discussed later as an example that effectively mixes prosodic approaches for dramatic effect.[37]

At the opposite end of the expressive spectrum, scanning of verse against some tonic accents tends to appear in lighthearted and picturesque numbers, as in Henri's "La brise souffle" and Hélène's "Boléro," both from act V of *Les Vêpres siciliennes*. Such numbers are rare in *Don Carlos*, but a good example does occur at the beginning of Eboli's "Chanson du voile," where Verdi scans the text in regular trochees, accenting the preposition "des" over the noun "rois" and the first over the second syllable of "devant."[38] As in the numbers at the beginning of act V of *Les Vêpres siciliennes*, this chanson adds local color and functions as a lighthearted relief from the surrounding gloom and desperation (Ex. 5.8). The approaches of Lubarsch and Landry, Quicherat, and especially Pierson would not work well for this chanson, because the resulting irregular rhythm would conflict with the intended mood, just as scanning would contradict the drama of the agitated duets between Philip and Rodrigue and Philip and the Inquisitor.

When scanning does not violate tonic accents and when this scanning occurs in a context that lacks a strong sense of rhythm, Verdi tends to convey not so much lightheartedness or picturesqueness but happiness or bliss; we have seen examples in Carlos's declaration of love in act I (Ex. 5.1) and his delirious confirmation of that love in act II (Ex. 5.6). By contrast, Henri's "De cette voix" (Ex. 4.4), which features similar prosodic and musical characteristics, expresses a longing for reassurance from Hélène rather than happiness or bliss. A partial correspondence between prosody and drama also pertains to Castil-Blaze's weakened sense of rhythm in order to accommodate a text's accentual irregularity. While the farewells of Élisabeth and Eboli express sadness, Carlos's "Je l'ai vue" (I,2) focuses on joyous anticipation and his "C'est vous! ô ma bien-aimée" (III,3,2) on desperate love. In other words, while the approaches of Benloew and Pierson convey specific dramatic situations – the lighthearted, picturesque song and agitated narration – the other approaches lack such a clear association.

When setting a stanzaic passage, Verdi rarely drew on only one prosodic approach, because the musical style of the time sometimes required more, sometimes fewer musical accents than were suggested by the text. He thus combined prosodic approaches, often within a single verse, at the cost of undermining their potential rhetorical force. As in *Les Vêpres siciliennes*, however, the mixing may reinforce a character's emotional development. Unlike Rodrigue, who in "O Roi!" pours out his heart right from the beginning, the Inquisitor in his "Dans ce beau pays" tries to maintain his composure, succumbing to his agitation only gradually. Lubarsch's approach, with its lesser emphasis on secondary accents, was better suited to convey emotional control. When the prelate's agitation takes over after the initial parallel phrases, Verdi's prosodic interpretation becomes accordingly more irregular, often reflecting Pierson's approach. In the following excerpt, bold underlining indicates obligatory accents according to Lubarsch and Landry, simple bold additional obligatory accents according to Quicherat, and simple underlining any additional accents according to Pierson. All the accents required by Quicherat can also be accommodated by Lubarsch and Landry's approach as secondary accents that may or may not be reflected in the music.

Dans ce beau pays, | | pur d'hérétique levain,[39]
Un homme ose saper | | l'édifice divin.
Il est l'ami du Roi, | | son confident intime,
Le démon tentateur | | qui le pousse à l'abîme
Les desseins criminels | | don't vous chargez l'Infant
Ne sont auprès des siens | | que les jeux d'un enfant;
Et moi, l'Inquisiteur, | | moi, pendant que je lève
Sur d'obscurs criminels | | la main qui tient le glaive,
Pour les puissants du monde | | abjurant mon courroux,
Je laisse vivre en paix | | ce grand coupable... et vous!

The first phrase begins in the manner of Lubarsch and Landry with four eighth notes evenly flowing toward the obligatory accent on "pays" and concluding with a measure of greater rhythmic variety and subtle accents beyond the obligatory one on "levain"; the second phrase is in the manner of Quicherat. M. 5 introduces more agitation reflective of Pierson (which, in this case, is synonymous with scanning according to Castil-Blaze and Benloew because the tonic accents alternate with weak ones) while mm. 6–9 reflect Pierson and Lubarsch/Landry (m. 6 can be better explained with Pierson; m. 7 with both Pierson and Lubarsch/Landry, and mm. 8–9 with Lubarsch/Landry). In the remaining measures, Verdi often follows Pierson by accentuating, for instance "auprès" (accent of duration), "pendant" (accent of duration), and "pour" (harmonic accent) (Ex. 5.9).

Example 5.9. *Don Carlos*, IV,1,2, "Dans ce beau pays" (Grand Inquisitor).

Prosody does not characterize a dramatic situation all by itself, because Verdi far too often mixes the various approaches. But when he clearly favors one, it often has a dramatic meaning: when he scans the verse against tonic accents, he emphasizes lightheartedness or local color, and when he treats the verse in the manner of Pierson, he emphasizes a high level of agitation in a confrontational scene. Such a "rhetoric of prosody," which combines prosodic and dramatic considerations, can explain why Verdi would not simply scan any stanza against its tonic accents, even if Benloew's theory would have allowed it; such scanning would have led to monotony and would have suggested a series of exclusively light, picturesque numbers. Neither would Verdi observe all irregular tonic accents of lyrical sections without drawing on melismas or word repetition; this would have suggested an uninterrupted series of confrontational scenes. Verdi's mastery of a wide range of prosodic approaches significantly contributes to his palette of expressive tools and thus to the greater variety and subtlety of his later work. Of course, even if prosody has been able to provide substantial illumination, both stylistic and dramatic, other melodic aspects cannot necessarily be explained by structural characteristics of the text; they reflect a broader French aesthetic.

Aspects of rhythm and phrasing with questionable connection to prosody

The melodic style of *Don Carlos*, which critics so unanimously recognized as new, was in fact not so much new as it was an amplification of the developments already begun in *Les Vêpres siciliennes*. The rhythmic middleground loses definition, the prosodic approach shifts from observing all tonic accents to accentuation in the manner of Lubarsch and Landry's theory, the orchestra increasingly provides the melodic framework, and vocal phrasing becomes more irregular. Sometimes the stylistic changes can be explained with prosody, but other times they simply reflect Verdi's compositional development, probably in reaction to French expectations of melodic originality and variety. *Les Vêpres siciliennes* already features a considerable increase of modified prototypical thematic blocks over Verdi's earlier Italian operas, a trend that continues in *Don Carlos*. Whenever Verdi wrote on a French libretto for a French audience, he substantially broadened his melodic vocabulary. Table 5.1 illustrates this development.

In light of this stylistic development, it is not surprising that critics associated *Don Carlos* with Wagner, even if they were unable to justify their claim beyond citing clichés.[40] Wagner had enjoyed a good press in Paris until Fétis's famous series of articles in the *Revue et gazette musicale* in 1852 began to spoil the composer's reputation. Fétis's call for square phrasing, clearly delineated melody, aesthetic beauty over realism, spontaneity of expression, and music over poetry seems to have provided ammunition both against Wagner and against any composer whose music was controversial for one reason or another.[41] *Don Carlos* was a perfect candidate. It no longer fit the image of the "violent" Verdian opera, and

Table 5.1. Thematic blocks in *Les Vêpres siciliennes* and *Don Carlos*

Type 1. Instant development of a thematic idea in the parallel phrase
   Les Vêpres siciliennes
      "Courage!... du courage" (I,2)
      "Fidèle à ses leçons" (I,4)
      "Vous détournez les yeux" (II,3)
      "La haine égara" (III,3)
      "Adieu, mon pays" (IV,5)
   Don Carlos
      "O Roi, j'arrive de Flandre" (II,2,6)
      "La main de Dieu soit bénie" (II,2,6)
      "J'ai de ce prix sanglant payé la paix du monde" (II,2,6)
      "Je suis dans votre cour indignement traitée" (IV,1,3)
      "Ah! je meurs l'âme joyeuse" (IV,2,1)
Type 2. No phrase parallelism
   Les Vêpres siciliennes
      "A quoi bon" (I,2)
      "Saint amour" (II,1)
      "Près du tombeau" (II,3)
      "O jour de peine" (IV,1)
      "Écoute un instant" (IV,2)
      "La brise souffle" (V,2)
      "La bannière de France" (V,4)
   Don Carlos
      "J'ai pu la voir enfin, ma belle fiancée" (I,2)
      "O bonheur!... sous la nuit claire" (I,3)
      "Voyez! de ces cailloux a jailli l'étincelle" (I,4)
      "De l'inconnu j'ai peur malgré moi-même" (I,4)
      "Ah! je vous aime, et Dieu lui-même" (I.4)
      "Il voulait régner sur le monde" (II,1)
      "Mon fils, les douleurs de la terre" (II,1,2)
      "Les fleurs ici couvrent la terre" (II,2,1)
      "Je viens solliciter de la Reine une grâce" (II,2,4)
      "Quoi! pas un mot, pas une plainte" (II,2,4)
      "Hélas! sa douleur me déchire" (II,2,4,)
      "Viens, Eboli. La fête à peine est commencée" (III,1,1)
      "Pour une nuit me voilà Reine" (III,1,2)
      "Redoutez tout de ma furie!" (III,3,3)
      "Ouvrez-vous, ô portes sacrées" (III,4,2)
      "Vous me parlez avec hardiesse!" (IV,1,3)
      "Maudit soit le soupçon infâme" (IV,1,4)
      "Il faut agir et voici l'heure" (IV,1,4)
      "France, noble pays" (V,1)
      "Beaux jardins espagnols" (V,1)
      "Au revoir dans un monde" (V,2)
Type 3. Including *ad libitum* portions
   Les Vêpres siciliennes
      "Le ciel vient apparaître" (III,3)
   Don Carlos
      none
Type 4. Phrase parallelism only in the orchestra
   Les Vêpres siciliennes
      "Et Dieu disait" (I,2)
      "Quand ma bonté" (III,4)

Table 5.1 (*Continued*)

Don Carlos
    "Voyez! de ces cailloux a jailli l'étincelle" (I,4)
    "Les fleurs ici couvrent la terre" (II,2,1)
    "Hélas! sa douleur me déchire" (II,2,4)
    "Viens, Eboli. La fête à peine est commencée" (III,1,1)
    "France, noble pays" (V,1)
    "Beaux jardins Espagnols" (V,1)

Type 5. Irregular phrasing
  Les Vêpres siciliennes
    "A quoi bon" (I,2)
    "Le ciel vient" (III,3)
    "Ami, le coeur" (IV,2)
    "La bannière" (V,4)
  Don Carlos
    "J'ai pu la voir enfin, ma belle fiancée" (I,2)
    "De l'inconnu j'ai peur malgré moi-même" (I,4)
    "De quels transports poignants et doux" (I,4)
    "Il voulait régner sur le monde" (II,1)
    "Que fait-on à la cour de France" (II,2,3)
    "Je viens solliciter de la Reine une grâce" (II,2,4)
    "Prince, si le Roi veut se rendre" (II,2,4)
    "Quoi! pas un mot, pas une plainte" (II,2,4)
    "O bien perdu... Trésor sans prix!" (II,2,4)
    "O prodige! mon coeur déchiré se console!" (II,2,4)
    "Quel langage nouveau!..." (II,2,6)
    "J'ai de ce prix sanglant payé la paix du monde" (II,2,6)
    "Je dormirai dans mon manteau royal" (IV,1,1)
    "O don fatal et détesté" (IV,1,6)
    "France, noble pays" (V,1)

Type 6. Short initial, basically unaltered parallel phrases of only one design but more than one measure in length
  Les Vêpres siciliennes
    "Viens à nous, Dieu tutélaire" (I,2)
    "Quoi, ma tendresse" (III,4)
    "Autour de moi" (IV,1)
    "Tout un peuple en prière" (IV,5)
    "Trahison! imposture!" (V,4)
  Don Carlos
    "Au palais de fées" (II,2,1)
    "Va! je me sens dans l'âme" (III,1,1)
    "A Dieu vous êtes infidèles" (III,4,4)

Type 7. Long phrases with more than two distinct rhythmic designs
  Les Vêpres siciliennes
    "Et toi, Palerme" (II,1)
    "Adieu, mon pays" (IV,5)
  Don Carlos
    "De l'inconnu j'ai peur malgré moi-même" (I,4)
    "Mon compagnon, mon ami, mon frère" (II,1,3)

critics unfavorably disposed toward Verdi had to look for other objections. The label "Wagnerism" came in handy, for the style of *Don Carlos* seemed to include just the right characteristics: the phrases frequently abandoned the "carrure"; the vocal lines became more declamatory (in accord with the prosodic approaches of Lubarsch and Landry and of Pierson), thus taking on a realistic tone; the increasingly sophisticated melodic style could be interpreted as lacking in spontaneity; and the libretto was complex and powerful. Some of the critics now pretended to miss Verdi's old qualities, which they felt he had sacrificed in favor of imitating Wagner. As Pierre Véron put it: "Verdi, the master of inspiration and melody, began to worship the false gods of musical algebra. Would I believe my ears? He wagnerized!"[42] Critics were puzzled by the ostensible similarity to Wagner's style, not understanding the fundamentally different approaches of the two composers. Théophile Gautier wrote in *Le Moniteur universel*:

The dominating force constituting the foundation of Verdi's genius no longer appears here in the powerful simplicity that made the master from Parma popular and universal; rather, it is sustained by an extraordinary deployment of harmonic means, learned sonorities, and new melodic forms. Did Verdi yield to the direct influence of Richard Wagner or even to the effect of one of these invincible intellectual movements that push man and the arts toward progress and perfection and to which Wagner succumbed as one of the first? This is what is difficult to judge impartially. But one thing is evident: that Verdi completely modified his early procedures in order to adopt principles analogous to those of the German master.

The complete absence in *Don Carlos* of recitative is proof [of this change of style], as is the replacement [of recitative] by declamatory mélopées sustained by a polished accompaniment that completes the librettist's thought. Actual arias imperceptibly dovetail into these mélopées, [and] the opera forms but a single texture, demanding sustained attention on the part of the listener, who in this vast score finds neither recitative to rest his ear nor preparatory ritornellos to alert him of the moment when he should listen more attentively.[43]

As with the modified thematic blocks – which were at least in part responsible for the association of *Don Carlos* with Wagnerism – Verdi took the concept of chaining together independent melodies a step further. The length of passages not interrupted by recitative increases, due in part to Verdi's tendency to set even non-stanzaic verses with formal lyricism.[44] It is thus not surprising that he began to include non-stanzaic links in his melodic chains. For instance, Rodrigue's account of the conditions in Flanders does not come to a harmonic conclusion but is interrupted by a short cantabile ("La main de Dieu soit bénie") in which Rodrigue expresses his gratitude for having the opportunity to freely talk to the King. The latter follows with a new melody, justifying his actions ("J'ai de ce prix sanglant"), but Rodrigue, in the second part of the *septain*, counters Philippe's argument ("Non! en vain votre foudre gronde!"). At this point, non-stanzaic verse would suggest an interruption of the formal melodic flow, but undaunted by the metric irregularity, Verdi continues in the same style: "Le mien" is tagged onto the melody ending with "La marche de l'humanité," and after an orchestral transition of three measures, Rodrigue initiates a slow movement (the adagio of the traditional duet form; "Un souffle ardent"). Philippe's musing over his confidant's outspokenness ("Quel langage nouveau!") concludes a long series of loosely chained melodies, a passage encompassing thirty-one verses overall![45]

    RODRIGUE
    O Roi! j'arrive de Flandre,   [melody 1]
    Ce pays jadis si beau!
    Ce n'est qu'un désert de cendre,
    Un lieu d'horreur, un tombeau!
    Là, l'orphelin qui mendie
    Et pleure par les chemins,
    Tombe, en fuyant l'incendie,
    Sur des ossements humains!
    Le sang rougit l'eau des fleuves,
    Ils roulent, de morts chargés...
    L'air est plein du cri des veuves
    Sur leurs époux égorgés!...
    La main de Dieu soit bénie,   [melody 2]
    Qui fait entendre par moi
    Le glas de cette agonie
    A la justice du Roi!...

    PHILIPPE
J'ai de ce prix sanglant payé la paix du monde;   [melody 3]
Ma foudre a terrassé l'orgueil des novateurs,
Qui vont plongeant la peuple en des rêves menteurs...
La mort, entre mes mains, peut devenir féconde!

    RODRIGUE
    Non! en vain votre foudre gronde!   [melody 4]
    Quel bras a jamais arrêté
    La marche de l'humanité?...

    PHILIPPE
Le mien!...

    RODRIGUE
    Un souffle ardent a passé sur la terre!   [melody 5]
Il a fait tressaillir l'Europe tout entière!
    Dieu vous dicte sa volonté...
Donnez à vos enfants, Sire, la Liberté!...

PHILIPPE
Quel langage nouveau!... Jamais, auprès du trône,　　　[melody 6]
Personne n'éleva la voix si haut... personne!
　　Je n'avais jamais écouté
Cette inconnue ayant pour nom: la Vérité!

A second example, in this case consisting exclusively of stanzaic verse, the act II love duet is developed in a chain of several melodic ideas. Budden analyzes this duet as a sequence of sections in small a, a', b forms.[46] While some melodies fit this concept, others progress more freely, either in a quick succession of rhythmically unrelated ideas or in a chain of independent longer melodies, in either case always reflecting the changing affect of the text. Most of the stanzas in this duet feature the free structures (polymeters, uneven number of verses, etc.) typical of French librettos. Asterisks denote the beginning of a new melody or a rhythmically independent phrase.

CARLOS
*Quoi! pas un mot, pas une plainte
　Une larme pour l'exilé!
*Ah! que du moins la pitié sainte
　Dans votre regard m'ait parlé!
*Hélas! mon âme se déchire...
　Je me sens mourir... *Insensé!
J'ai supplié dans mon délire
　Un marbre insensible et glacé!

ÉLISABETH
*Carlos n'accusez pas mon coeur d'indifférence.
　Comprenez mieux sa fierté... son silence.
*Le devoir, saint flambeau, devant mes yeux a lui,
　　Je marche conduite par lui,
　　Mettant au ciel mon espérance!

CARLOS
*O bien perdu... Trésor sans prix!
　Ma part de bonheur dans la vie!
　Parlez Élisabeth: enivré et ravie,
　Mon âme, à votre voix, rêve du paradis!

As in *Les Vêpres siciliennes*, this manner of chaining melodies did not go unnoticed by the critics. In an otherwise positive review, Auguste Villemot noted: "What perhaps a bit disconcerts the ear this time is that on occasion the melody, instead of ending on a concluding gesture, abruptly turns into another motive or continues in the manner of recitative, according to the method of Wagner."[47]

Example 5.10. *Don Carlos*, IV,2,1 "C'est mon jour" (Rodrigue).

The novelty of the melodic style in *Don Carlos* is often enhanced by a rich harmonic vocabulary, which, however, rarely surpasses the most interesting pages of *La forza del destino*. Verdi's formal melodies remain basically diatonic, but the harmonic rhythm may accelerate to match the pulse of the melody, drawing on harmonies from outside the established key. One of the most beautiful examples appears in Rodrigue's "C'est mon jour," the first of his two arias in act IV. Firmly rooted in E-flat major, the harmonies plunge for just one and a half measures into expressive progressions with a harmonic change every quarter note. Roger Parker eloquently describes this passage:

The music sideslips onto a six-four chord of G *major* (G minor would have been conventionally lachrymose) ... [Rodrigue] restores a melodic B-flat and then, with a second, brief moment of sixteenth-note counterpoint with the accompaniment as he apostrophizes once more his friend ("O mon Carlos"), he brings the music home to the security of the E-flat major tonic. That second, slightly awkward contrapuntal fragment – the unison C, B-flat and E-flat, A-flat and F [see box, Ex. 5.10] – seems to me the affective center of the aria.[48]

Don Carlos marks another significant step in Verdi's melodic development toward *Otello*, possibly the largest step he had ever taken. *Aida*, the opera following *Don Carlos*, has generally been viewed as traditional in form but progressive in harmony, adaptation of exoticism, and perfect integration of the ballet. The opera's melodic significance, on the other hand, has hardly been considered. It is rooted in Verdi's accomplishments in *Don Carlos*.[49]

Aida

Unlike Verdi's collaboration with Méry and Du Locle on *Don Carlos*, his work with Antonio Ghislanzoni on *Aida* is relatively well documented and attests to the composer's concerns about stanzaic form and poetic rhythm. The return to an Italian libretto raised the question whether it should include some of the French forms Verdi so brilliantly mastered in *Don Carlos*. He indeed requested occasional verses modeled on French practice but was also perfectly capable of overturning his original plan and suggesting revisions resembling the most conservative forms of his earlier Italian works.[50] Of the more progressive forms, two types of stanzas deserve special attention: *endecasillabi* and polymeters.

Stanzas of *endecasillabi* are rare in Verdi's operas before *Aida*. With the exception of verses in *doppio* form, the *endecasillabo*, like the French alexandrine, was the longest poetic meter commonly used in librettos at the time. With the lack of a uniform caesura, however, it provided even less structural consistency than its French counterpart. *Aida* includes several stanzas of *endecasillabi*, almost always in interesting musical settings. The unusual number of eleven syllables led to some distinct rhythmic patterns and to stylistic characteristics typical of *Don Carlos*, including vaguely defined middleground rhythms, irregular phrasing, innovative accompaniment, and frequent use of a prosodic approach in accord with Lubarsch and Landry. The tercet from the judgment scene, for instance, might suggest initial parallel phrases on the first two verses and a concluding phrase on the third. Parallel phrases, though, would have created too much repetition for such a short passage. Verdi chose an entirely irregular solution consisting of a two-measure phrase and a five-measure phrase (Ex. 5.11).[51]

Numi, pietà del mio straziato core...	[4,8,10]
Egli è innocente, lo salvate, o Numi!	[4,8,10]
Disperato, tremendo è il mio dolore!	[6,10][52]

The reason for this irregularity most likely lies in the position of the emphatic accents (*accents logiques* in French terminology[53]) on "pietà" early in the first verse and "Numi" at the end of the second. Verdi emphasizes each accent by pitch and duration in a gesture that precludes parallel phrasing. In the first verse, with equal note values flowing toward the three primary accents, Verdi's approach follows Lubarsch and Landry. In the remaining two verses, he reverts to his preferred early practice of emphasizing every tonic accent: "Egli è innocente, lo salvate, o Numi! / Disperato, tremendo è il mio dolore!" The manner in which he emphasizes these syllables, however, recalls French practice because he relies heavily on the cumulative effect of various types of musical accents. In the first verse of the stanza, the initial accent, on "pietà," falls mid-measure and is marked by an accent of duration and the beginning of an accompanimental pattern. The subsequent three quarter notes, including the downbeat on "mio," receive basically equal emphasis and are followed by a durational accent on "straziato," again mid-measure. In verses 2 and 3, the harmonic changes at times support and at times neutralize obligatory accents, causing individual accents to be less prominent. The following syllables receive some kind of accentuation:

è	duration, accompanimental pattern, harmonic
innocente	accompanimental pattern, harmonic
innocente	harmonic, accompanimental pattern
lo	accompanimental pattern
salvate o	harmonic, accompanimental pattern

Example 5.11. *Aida*, IV,1, "Numi, pietà" (Amneris).

N**u**mi	duration, harmonic, accompanimental pattern
Disper**a**to	duration, harmonic
Disperat**o**	harmonic
trem**e**ndo	harmonic
m**i**o	duration, harmonic
d**o**lore	duration, harmonic
dol**o**re	harmonic

The final syllable of "dolore" on the downbeat is drowned out by the sound of the entering chorus. In combination with the two changes of meter, this sequence of strong, medium, and weak accents creates an unpredictable rhythmic flow reminiscent of French opera.[54]

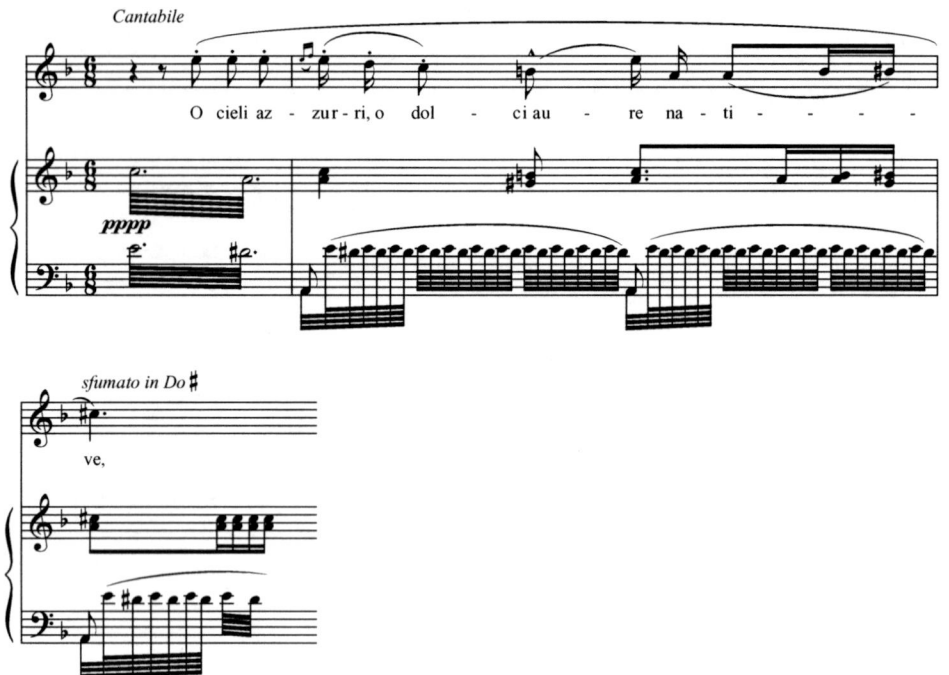

Example 5.12. *Aida*, III, "O cieli azzurri" (Aida).

Two of the melodies on *endecasillabi* rank among Verdi's most popular. The first, "O terra, addio; addio, valle di pianti...," the beautiful slow duet cabaletta concluding the opera, includes little of significance for our purposes. The second, however, Aida's *romanza* at the beginning of act III imitates the French manner of accommodating irregular accents by "not creating too much sense of rhythm." Verdi achieved this effect by means of tremolo accompaniment and a melody that suggests a 2/4 meter despite the notated 6/8 meter, at least in the opening phrase. The accentual structure of the final verse [4,6,10] does not reflect any of the critics' options.[55] It does, however, fit Quicherat's interpretation of the *décasyllabe*, with accents on the fourth and tenth syllables and a movable third accent somewhere in between:

O cieli azz**u**rri... o dolci **au**re nat**i**ve	[4,7,10]
Dove ser**e**no il mio matt**i**n brill**ò**...	[4,8,10]
O verdi c**o**lli... o profum**a**te r**i**ve...	[4,8,10]
O patria m**ia**, mai pi**ù** ti rivedr**ò**.	[4,6,10]

In the context of a vague rhythmic middleground, Verdi could place the accent of "**au**re" on the metrically weak third eighth note and the second, unaccented syllable of the same word on the metrically strong, fourth eighth note. Similarly, the accent of "nat**i**ve" receives a weaker musical emphasis than the word's final syllable (Ex. 5.12).

Why did Verdi not resort to the following, much more conventional solution?

[musical notation in 6/8: O cie-li az-zur-ri o dol-ci au-re na-ti-ve]

Even though this arrangement would make perfect sense in the first verse, it would create an awkward effect in the second. The vague rhythmic middleground accommodates both rhythmic patterns. As with "Numi, pietà del mio straziato core," Verdi combines various types of musical stress (harmonic, accompanimental, dynamic, and durational) to neutralize misaccentuation resulting from the unorthodox metrical position of some syllables: the stress accent on "**au**re" counterbalances the metrical accent on the word's final syllable, and the accent marked by duration and the two-note melisma on "nat**i**ve" counterbalances the softened ("sfumato") metrical and durational accent at the end of the verse. Verdi's musical solution not only minimizes the problems but also perfectly expresses the meaning of the text with its feeling of suspension and airiness.

Polymetric stanzas do not appear in Verdi's Italian operas prior to *Aida*, except for the types mentioned in chapter 1.[56] *Aida* itself, however, includes two prominent examples of polymetric stanzas, one in Aida's act I aria, the other in the final love duet. Because of its explicit connection to French opera, the passage from the duet, "Morir! si pura e bella," is particularly relevant for our purposes. For the first movement, Ghislanzoni originally planned to balance Aida's eight verses of *settenari* ("Vedi?... di morte l'angelo") with a stanza for Radamès. After two suggestions, eventually rejected, Verdi came up with the following idea:

We must avoid monotony by looking for uncommon forms. Yesterday I told you to make eight seven-syllable verses for Radames before the eight of Aida. These two solos, even if I write two dissimilar melodies, would have approximately the same form, the same character; and here we are in the commonplace. The French, even in their stanzas for melodies, sometimes use verses which are longer or shorter. Why could we not do the same? This entire scene can and must be nothing but a scene of pure and simple melody. An unusual verse form for Radames would oblige me to search for a melody diverse from those commonly used for seven- and eight-syllable verse, and would further oblige me to change the tempo and meter for the solo (a kind of *mezz'aria*) for Aida.[57]

Verdi sketched the stanza himself:

Morire! Tu, innocente?	*settenario*
Morire! Tu, sì bella?	"
Tu nell'april degli anni	"
Lasciar la vita?	*quinario*
Quant'io t'amai, no, no'l può dir favella!	*endecasillabo*
Ma fu mortale l'amor mio per te.	"
Morire! tu, innocente?	*settenario*
Morire! Tu, sì bella.[58]	*settenario*

Based on Verdi's model, Ghislanzoni came up with the following solution:

Morir! si pura e bella!	*settenario*
Morir per me d'amore...	"
Degli anni tuoi nel fiore	"
Fuggir la vita!	*quinario*
T'avea il cielo per l'amore creata,[59]	*endecasillabo*
Ed io t'uccido per averti amata!	"
No, non morrai!	*quinario*
Troppo t'amai!...	"
Troppo sei bella!	"

Despite the irregular sequence of three different poetic meters, Verdi maintains regular two-measure phrasing throughout. Closer investigation reveals great rhythmic irregularity within these phrases, however. The first two seem to have been designed for initial phrase parallelism, the second two for a concluding phrase of four measures. With two syllables fewer at his disposal, Verdi could have prolonged existing syllables but decided to repeat words in order to allow for a more natural flow of the text. But repetition of the entire third verse created the problem of having to accommodate more syllables than in the first four measures. Thus, beginning with the repetition of "Degli anni tuoi nel fiore," Verdi resorts to the prosodic approach described by Lubarsch and Landry and lets the weaker syllables flow evenly but in fast note values toward the major accents on "fi**o**re" and "v**i**ta." This solution has consequences for both the rhythmic foreground and the middleground. In the foreground, the immediate repetition of "Degli anni tuoi nel fiore" obliterates the expected rest between the verses, and the rhythmic activity increases dramatically from a dominant quarter-note pulse to a sixteenth-note pulse. The middleground rhythm of the first statement of "Degli anni tuoi nel fiore" continues the half-note pulse originally established by the accompaniment. In the second statement, however, and through the end of the first quatrain, the strongest middleground accents shift first from beat 3 to beat 4 (Ex. 5.13, m. 6, on "fi**o**re") and then from beat 3 to beat 2 (m. 7, on "v**i**ta"). The customarily strong metric positions on beats 1 and 3 are considerably downgraded.

Parallel phrasing on the subsequent two *endecasillabi* was unproblematic after Verdi had synchronized the accentual pattern by first ignoring the elision of "avea il" and then compensating for the additional syllable by truncating the final vowel of "amore":

```
              1    2  3 4  5  6  7 8  9 10 11
libretto:    T'avea il cielo per l'amore creata,    [3,7,10]
              1   2  3 4 5  6    7 8   9 10 11
score        T'avea il cielo per l'amor creata,     [4,8,10]
             Ed io t'uccido per averti amata!       [4,(8),10]
```

Having accented "averti" for reasons of rhythmic parallelism rather than prosodic necessity, Verdi rounds out the stanza by returning to the manner of Lubarsch and Landry for the final three *quinari* and letting each rhythmic group ("No"; "non morrai!"; "troppo t'amai!...";

Example 5.13. *Aida*, IV,2, "Morir! sì pura e bella" (Radamès).

and "Troppo sei bella!") flow evenly to its final accent. As in the conclusion of the quatrain, some of the strongest accents fall on the weak beats 2 and 4 (m. 13), effecting subtle variation of the rhythmic middleground (Ex. 5.13).

The second, less prominent example of a polymetric stanza appears as the second section, "Sventurata! che dissi?...," of Aida's aria in act I.

*L'insana parola,	*senari*
O numi, sperdete!	
Al seno d'un padre	
La figlia rendete;	
Struggete – le squadre	
Dei nostri oppressor!	
Sventurata! che dissi?... *e l'amor mio?...	*endecasillabo*
Dunque scordar poss'io[60]	*settenario*
Questo fervido amor che oppressa e schiava	*endecasillabo*
Come raggio di sol qui mi beava?	*endecasillabo*
Imprecherò la morte	*versi sciolti*
A Radamès... a lui che amo pur tanto!	
Ah! non fu in terra mai	
Da più crudeli angosce un core affranto!	

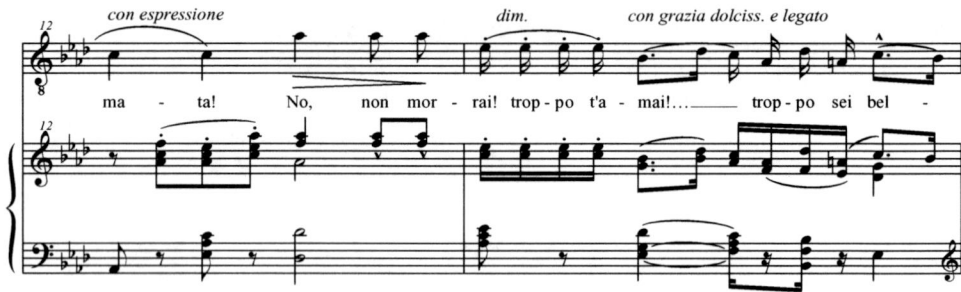

Example 5.13 (*Continued*)

*I sacri nomi di padre... d'amante   *endecasillabi*
    Nè profferir poss'io, nè ricordar...
Per l'un, per l'altro, confusa... tremante...
    Io piangere vorrei... vorrei pregar.
Ma la mia prece in bestemmia si muta:
    Delitto è il pianto a me... colpa il sospir...
In notte cupa la mente è perduta...
    E nell'ansia crudel vorrei morir.

*Numi, pietà – del mio soffrir!   *quinari doppi*
    Speme non v'ha – pel mio dolor...
Amor fatal, – tremendo amor,
    Spezzami il cor, – fammi morir!

Verdi handles the metric irregularity in exactly the same manner as in the third stanza of Élisabeth's act V aria in *Don Carlos*: treatment of "Sventurata! che dissi?" as a vocal transition renders the remainder of the first distich too short for clear phrase parallelism. He thus draws on the orchestra to provide the melodic framework, with the clarinet presenting the parallel four-measure phrases. The voice selectively doubles the clarinet on phrase *a* and then doubles it throughout phrase *a'*. In the second half of phrase *a*, Verdi needed to accommodate only seven syllables ("Dunque scordar poss'io"), the first of which he aligns with the downbeat. At the parallel spot of phrase *a'*, however, he needed to accommodate eleven syllables ("Come raggio di sol qui mi beava?"). Verdi found the perfect solution by anticipating the first five syllables on a long upbeat and once again drawing on the prosodic approach in accord with Lubarsch and Landry. None of the eighth notes of the upbeat is accented over any other, making it perfectly acceptable for the tonic accents of "c_o_me" and "r_a_ggio" to fall on the weakest metric positions of the 4/4 meter (Ex. 5.14).

These examples show that most of Verdi's prosodic accomplishments in *Don Carlos* left a mark on *Aida*; only declamation in the manner of Pierson does not figure prominently. The reasons lie in the absence of appropriate dramatic situations (such as agitated political narratives) and in the overall rhythmic regularity of the *Aida* libretto. Even when this regularity is lacking, Verdi managed, thanks to the acquired prosodic skill, to write largely symmetrical melodies. Scanning against tonic accents, which dates back to *Les Vêpres siciliennes*, does not appear in *Aida* either, because *Aida* does not feature such lighthearted, picturesque numbers as Henri's *mélodie* or Eboli's "Chanson du voile." The absence of numbers on the peripheries of the expressive spectrum – lighthearted character arias and agitated narratives – renders *Aida* prosodically more homogeneous than *Don Carlos*. Verdi compensated for the lack of prosodic variety with variety in other areas, including an enriched harmonic vocabulary and exoticism.

The French concept of conducting a melody continues to play a role in *Aida*. Each of the five sections of Aida's act I aria is set to a new melody, with the exception of the passage in *versi sciolti*, which continues to develop the melody of the previous section (the asterisks inserted in the libretto above indicate the beginning of a new melodic idea). None of the melodies comes to a close; rather, each breaks off and is followed by an entirely new idea. In his Italian operas, Verdi had already adopted this technique in *Un ballo in maschera* and *La forza del destino*, but in this aria, he chains together a greater number of melodies, probably because of his experience with *Don Carlos*.

The case of harmony is less clear-cut. Because chromaticism in the formal melodic portions of *Don Carlos* does not markedly surpass comparable passages in *La forza del destino*, it is difficult to explain the greater harmonic palette of the melodies in *Aida* in terms of Verdi's most recent French opera (in fact, the harmony may be explained more convincingly by Verdi's attempt to evoke an exotic atmosphere).[61] Nevertheless, the harmonic sophistication of *Aida* complied with French taste and, together with the ballet and the sophisticated staging, favored a French production at the Opéra, which eventually took place in 1880.

Example 5.14. *Aida*, I,1, "L'insana parola" (Aida).

Chords are often borrowed from other keys and progress at the pace of the melodic pulse, adding expression without attracting attention to themselves. A good example appears in Radamès's *romanza* "Celeste Aida," especially in the phrase beginning "Del mio pensiero": a melody in B-flat major is harmonized by a diminished seventh chord followed by a string of passing dominant seventh chords (to C, B-flat, G, and F), while the melody itself includes only one short note foreign to the B-flat major scale. The resulting sensuous string of unresolved sevenths perfectly captures Radamès's longing for Aida (Ex. 5.15).

The most telling example of this kind of harmonic virtuosity appears in the act II finale, where Amonasro begs the Egyptian king for clemency, reminding him that the fate of the

Example 5.15. *Aida*, I,1, "Celeste Aida" (Radamès).

Ethiopians today might be the fate of the Egyptians tomorrow. The hymn-like melody is entirely in F major, but the harmonization includes foreign harmonies such as a major triad on the seventh scale degree (at "sign<u>o</u>re"), a major triad on the flat seventh scale degree (at "<u>a</u> costoro"), and a largely coloristic downward slide of six-four chords at the final cadence, to name just the most interesting ones. Verdi's contrapuntal mastery effortlessly ties them all together, creating a feeling of sincerity that betrays Amonasro's desperation (Ex. 5.16).[62]

In the 1992 revision of his *The Operas of Verdi*, Julian Budden predicted that the place of *Don Carlos* in the Verdi canon "will probably fluctuate for many years to come" but that "one can never over-estimate its importance in the evolution of the composer's style."[63] Nevertheless, *Don Carlos* did not exert as great an influence on *Aida* as it could have. A comparison of *La forza del destino* with *Aida* (Table 5.2) in regard to modified thematic blocks confirms this conclusion even though one must keep in mind that the considerably greater length of *Forza* levels off the differences to some degree.

It was not until *Otello* that Verdi's librettist, Arrigo Boito, provided verses of rhythmic and metric variety comparable to those of *Don Carlos* and that, as a consequence, the boundaries between aria texture, *parlante*, and recitative continued to break down.[64] Nevertheless, *Don*

Example 5.16. *Aida*, II,2, "Ma tu, Re, tu signore possente" (Amonasro).

Carlos marked the most significant step in this direction, introducing greater variety of thematic blocks, far fewer passages with formulaic accompaniment, and greater prosodic versatility. In this latter respect, Verdi abandoned the accommodation of every tonic accent, the overwhelming approach in *Jérusalem*, in favor of an approach matching Lubarsch and Landry's theory. In light of such major steps in the composer's development, it is not surprising that the most astute critics of the opera's 1867 production took notice. As Hippolyte Prévost noted, "Verdi himself... created an exclusively French work, which, more surely than his best Italian operas, will carry his name to posterity by gloriously attaching it to the history of an institution already immortalized by illustrious masters of all origins who have passed through it for more than a century."[65]

Otello and *Falstaff*

By the time of *Aida*, French melody had become part of Verdi's dramatic and stylistic vocabulary, and it continued to play an essential role in his last two operas, *Otello* and *Falstaff*. In these works, the melodic, harmonic, and accompanimental characteristics often change quickly, according to the dramatic requirements of the libretto. Verdi's musical language by this time has generally been described as unique, albeit rooted in the language

Table 5.2. Thematic blocks in *La forza del destino* and *Aida*

Type 1. Instant development of a thematic idea in the parallel phrase
   La forza del destino
      "Urna fatale" (III,5)
      "Del mondo i disinganni" (IV,3)
   Aida
      "Ah! pietà... che più mi resta?" (II,1)
      "Su, dunque, sorgete" (III)
      "Flutti di sangue scorrono" (III)
      "Misero appien mi festi" (VI,1)
Type 2. No phrase parallelism
   La forza del destino
      "Ah per sempre" (I,3)
      "Al suon del tamburo" (II,2)
      "Madre, pietosa Vergine" (II,5)
      "Infelice, delusa" (II,9)
      "La Vergine degli Angeli" (II,10)
      "Leonora mia" (III,1)
      "Con voi scendere" (III,2)
      "Non io, fu il destino" (III,11)
      "Morte, ov'io!..." (III,11)
      "Vissi nel mondo" (IV,5)
      "Pace, pace" (IV,6)
   Aida
      "Il tuo bel cielo" (I,1)
      "Son nemici e prodi sono..." (II,2)
      "Padre, a costoro schiava io non sono..." (III)
      "Nel fiero anelito" (III)
      "Sotto il mio ciel, più libero" (III)
      "Morire!... ah!... tu dei vivere!..." (IV,1)
      "Numi, pietà del mio straziato core..." (IV,1)
      "A lui vivo... la tomba!" (IV,1)
      "Sacerdoti! compiste un delitto!" (IV,1)
Type 3. Including *ad libitum* portions
   does not occur
Type 4. Phrase parallelism only in the orchestra
   La forza del destino
      none
   Aida
      Sventurata! che dissi? (I)
Type 5. Irregular phrasing
   La forza del destino
      "Madre, pietosa Vergine" (II,5)
      "Con voi scendere" (III,2)
      "Morte, ov'io!..." (III,11)
      "Pace, pace" (IV,6)

Table 5.2 (*Continued*)

Aida
"Celeste Aida" (I,1)
"Sventurata! che dissi?" (I,1)
"Padre, a costoro schiava io non sono" (III)
"Su, dunque, sorgete" (III)
"Forse... l'arcano amore" (I,1)
"Ebben, qual nuovo fremito" (II,1)
"Numi, pietà del mio straziato core..." (IV,1)
"Sacerdoti! compiste un delitto!" (IV,1)

Type 6. Short initial, basically unaltered parallel phrases of only one design but more than one measure in length
La forza del destino
"Me pellegrina" (I,2)
"Anco una volta" (I,3)
"Guai per chi si lascia illudere" (II,9)
"Se voi scacciate" (II,9)
"Del mondo i disinganni" (IV,3)
"Se i rimorsi" (IV,5)
Aida
"Io son disonorato!" (III)
"Già i sacerdoti adunansi" (IV,1)
"Là tra foreste vergini" (III)
"Morir! si pura e bella!" (IV,2)
"O terra, addio" (IV,2)

Type 7. Long phrases with more than two distinct rhythmic designs
La forza del destino
"Ti lascio, ahimè" (I,2)
"Pace, pace" (IV,6)
Aida
"I sacri nomi di padre..." (I,1)
"Sacerdoti! compiste un delitto!" (IV,1)

of his earlier operas.[66] As far as the melodic style is concerned, *Otello* and *Falstaff* show a concentration of characteristics traditionally associated with French opera, which had been gaining in prominence since *Jérusalem*, as we have seen. By the time of *Otello*, however, it would be problematic to attribute the melodic characteristics to Verdi's own contributions to French opera or for that matter to French opera exclusively. In addition to the work of the latest French composers, especially Massenet, Verdi had learned to appreciate Boito's *Mefistofele* and some operas by Wagner; he was also familiar with Puccini's *Le Villi*.[67] Because all three of these composers – Boito, Wagner, and Puccini – were in turn influenced by French opera, we can no longer claim that by the time of *Otello* and *Falstaff* any of our French melodic characteristics necessarily reflected a direct French influence.

In light of these circumstances, a couple of examples from *Otello* and *Falstaff* must suffice to illustrate the concentration of traditionally French melodic characteristics in Verdi's work. In the love duet at the end of act I of *Otello*, Otello and Desdemona reminisce about the time in their courtship when they told each other of their misfortunes. Desdemona reminds Otello of the story of his captivity, and he reminds her of her tears and sighs, which ennobled his story. The melody on "Ingentilìa di lacrime," a short but distinct link in a long chain of melodies, lacks symmetry and shows the rhythmic variety characteristic of French opera. The beauty of the instrumentation, with its initial combination of high violins, expressive clarinet and bassoon line, and blend of lower strings and winds; the reinforcement of the sighing half step at "di sospir" by horn, bass clarinet, and English horn; and the expansion of the sound at "paradiso" add distinction to this passage while supporting the sense of the text. Even the phrasing, although apparently regular, consists of irregular sub-phrases of 3+1 and 1+2+1 measures respectively (marked by brackets above the staff) (Ex. 5.17).

The harmony is not particularly sophisticated, but the rate of its change varies from eighth-note to half-note, mirroring the ebb and flow of Otello's emotions. The orchestral accompaniment lacks any pattern, allowing for a free unfolding of the melodic rhythm with long upbeats. Even though on the surface the four *endecasillabi* are mostly regular (with obligatory accents on the sixth and tenth syllable) Verdi treats them quite freely, indulging in two instances in purely musical accents (on "di sospir" and "paradiso"). In addition, he ignores the accent on "labbro" in favor of an *accent logique* (derived from the parallelism with "lagrime") on "viso."

Ingentilìa di lagrime l'istoria	[6,10]
Il tuo bel viso e il labbro di sospir;	[6,10]
Scendean sulle mie tenebre la gloria,	[6,10]
Il paradiso e gli astri a benedir.	[6,10]

The "Ave Maria," Desdemona's prayer in act IV, scene 2, also consists (with the exception of a *quinario*), of *endecasillabi*, which include some accentual irregularity, at least at the beginning and the end. The leading nineteenth-century treatises suggest the following prosodic interpretation:

Ave Maria piena di grazia, eletta	[4,8,10]
Fra le spose e le vergini sei tu,	[6,10]
Sia benedetto il frutto, o benedetta,	[6,10]
Di tue materne viscere, Gesù.	[6,10]
Prega per chi adorando a te si prostra,	[6,10]
Prega pel peccator, per l'innocente	[6,10]
E pel debole oppresso e pel possente,	[6,10]
Misero anch'esso, tua pietà dimostra.	[4,8,10]
Prega per chi sotto l'oltraggio piega	[4,8,10]
La fronte e sotto la malvagia sorte;	[4,8,10]
Per noi tu prega	[4]
Sempre e nell'ora della morte nostra.	[4,8,10]

Example 5.17. *Otello*, I,3, "Ingentilìa di lacrime" (Otello).

As in the example from the love duet, traditional prosodic interpretation conveys a misleading picture in several instances because it does not conform with the syntactic structure of Boito's verses. The enjambment at the end of the first verse downgrades the accent on "eletta" and shifts its weight instead to "spose" (the syntactic parallel to "vergini") in the second verse. Verdi treats the entire first quatrain in the manner of Lubarsch and Landry, ignoring numerous tonic accents ("Ave," "eletta," "vergini," "benedetto," and "materne") to convey as natural a flow as possible. Nonetheless, the result is not recitative, because the regularity of the harmonic progressions imbues this passage with a regular pace. As in "Me pellegrina ed orfana" from *La forza del destino*, Verdi begins with a subdued melody and then increases the degree of lyricism, drawing again on a characteristic later found in several verismo arias.

After a more traditional middle section ("Prega per chi adorando") – in m. 15 of which Verdi briefly entrusts the melodic continuity to the orchestra alone – comes the next prosodic idiosyncracy. The most important syntactic accents of the verse "Prega per chi sotto l'oltraggio piega" fall on syllables 1, 8, and 10 (not 4, 8, and 10 as suggested by traditional versification), and the long gap between syllables 1 and 8 forced Verdi to shift the rhythm and once again pace the words in the manner of Lubarsch and Landry: the accent on "ch_i_" falls by the wayside, the one on "p_ie_ga" concedes its prominence to "fr_o_nte," and the one on "s_o_tto" is largely ignored. The final measures before the coda (mm. 29–32) are highlighted by effective, non-functional harmonic progessions (Ex. 5.18).

A single example from *Falstaff* must suffice to attest to the rhythmic freedom with which Verdi has come to treat his formal melodies. As in the examples from *Otello*, they show that the approach of Lubarsch and Landry was gaining in prominence, allowing for an increasingly naturalistic delivery of the words. The phrases in Fenton's sonnet, "Dal labbro il canto estasïato vola," for instance, tend to begin with a series of eighth notes, aiming for the first obligatory accents on either the fourth or sixth syllable, with variety arising from the manner in which the designs end. The passage beginning with "Quivi ripiglia suon" is particularly interesting, not only for its rhythmic variety derived from the irregular textual accents but also for the initial sparseness of the accompaniment (a solo English horn) reminiscent of Raoul's "Plus blanche che la blanche hermine" (Ex. 2.11; accompanied by the solo viola). The absence of a strong metric definition allows for irregular and at the same time natural placement of the textual accents anywhere in the measure: "ripi_g_lia" falls on the fourth beat, "s_uo_n" on the first, "m_a_" (an *accent logique*) on the second eighth-note triplet of the third beat, "c_u_ra" and "un_i_r" on the downbeat, and "dis_u_na," "bac_iai_," and "b_o_cca" on the third beat; "disïata" receives only a very light, diastematic accent while falling naturally within the flow toward the main accent at the end of the verse. This kind of naturalistic declamation is no longer compatible with regular or parallel phrases (Ex. 5.19).

Quivi rip_i_glia s_uo_n, ma la sua c_u_ra   [4,6,10]
Tende sempre ad un_i_r chi lo dis_u_na.   [6,10]
Così bac_iai_ la disïata b_o_cca!   [4,8,10]

Verismo

I have indicated in Leonora's "Me pellegrina ed orfana" and Desdemona's "Ave Maria" connections to a repertoire commonly labeled *verismo*. In light of its strong French roots in literature and music (Georges Bizet and Jules Massenet are most frequently mentioned), it is not surprising that many of the characteristics traditionally associated with French opera continue to play a prominent role in operatic verismo.[68] Parallel phrases and patterned

Example 5.18. *Otello*, IV,2, "Ave Maria" (Desdemona).

accompaniments largely disappear, allowing for ever more varied, free, and thus realistic declamation. Prosodic interpretation in the manner of Lubarsch and Landry and Pierson becomes more prominent, always mixed in the hands of a good composer with more traditional approaches. The gradual dissolution of the stanza goes hand-in-hand with these processes. Although Verdi sounds different from the verists, they build on the same traditions of Italian and French opera. When in Umberto Giordano's *Andrea Chénier* the protagonist poet becomes increasingly agitated as he describes the discrepancy between

Example 5.18 (*Continued*)

the luxury of the nobility and the misery in the streets, traditional French characteristics abound. Luigi Illica's verses constantly change meter and are accordingly set in a melodic style that wavers between distinct rhythmic designs and declamatory strings of short notes rushing to the next significant accent. Although in the first verse of the following excerpt Giordano ignores the secondary accents in the manner of Lubarsch and Landry, he supports them in the subsequent verses by rhythmic or harmonic emphases in the accompaniment. His painstaking reflection of every tonic accent in a passage combining lyricism and declamation recalls the political narrative "Oh Roi, j'arrive de France" from *Don Carlos*, but with the principal distinction that Giordano abandons parallel and regular phrasing (Ex. 5.20).

Example 5.18 (*Continued*)

Example 5.19. *Falstaff*, III,2, "Dal labbro il canto estasïato vola" (Fenton).

Example 5.20. Umberto Giordano, *Andrea Chénier*, I, "Un dì all'azzurro spazio" (Chénier).

ond'io guardato ho a v**oi** sì come a un **a**ngelo.
E d**i**ssi:
ecco la bell**e**zza d**e**lla v**i**ta!
Ma p**oi**,
alle v**o**stre par**o**le,
un nov**e**llo dol**o**r
m'ha c**o**lto in p**ie**no p**e**tto...

    The exact connections between verismo, French opera, and Verdi still await clarification, but it appears that Verdi's music played a more prominent role in the development of verismo than either he or scholars have been willing to admit. Verdi may have railed against foreign influences in opera, especially Wagner's, but he certainly learned his share from the French. While supervising the production of his partly revised *Otello* for the Paris Opéra in 1894, the eighty-one-year-old Verdi found himself in the company of Giulio Ricordi, Illica, Victorien Sardou, and Alberto Franchetti, who at the time was contemplating a setting of *Tosca*. According to Mary Jane Phillips-Matz, Verdi made it clear that he liked *Tosca* and might have composed it himself had he not been so old.[69] He never composed a typical verismo opera, but along with his French colleagues, especially Bizet and Massenet, he helped set the stage for the years to come.

Appendix: Principal theoretical texts cited (arranged in chronological order by date of publication)

Date	Treatise	Relevance to study
1787	Marmontel, Jean François. *Élémens de littérature.*	One of few treatises to include excerpts from librettos. This text is particularly relevant for the definition of a stanza.
1803	Scoppa, Antonio. *Traité de la poésie italienne rapporté à la poésie française, dans lequel on fait voir la parfaite analogie entre ces deux langues ...*	Scoppa claims that French verse can be just as musical as Italian verse if structured by regular accents in line with Italian versification. He is the first in a long line of theorists to prefer regular accentuation of French verse.
1812	Scoppa, Antonio. *Les vrais principes de la versification développés par un examen comparatif entre la langue italienne et la française.* 3 vols.	See Scoppa 1803.
[1831]	Asioli, Bonifazio. *Il maestro di composizione ossia seguito del trattato d'armonia.*	Important for its view of phrasing and versification, especially as practiced by Rossini and Bellini.
1832	Reicha, Antoine. *Traité de mélodie.* 2d ed.	One of the most significant nineteenth-century treatises on melody, mainly due to its systematic approach to the structural analysis of melody.
1833	Reicha, Antoine. *Art du compositeur dramatique ou Cours complet de composition vocale.*	Focuses on all aspects of operatic composition, including versification from the viewpoint of a composer.
1836–39	Choron, Alexandre, and J. Adrien de La Fage. *Nouveau manuel complet de musique vocale et instrumentale, ou, Encyclopédie musicale.*	Combines elements of the two Reicha treatises (1832 and 1833), investigating melody from the perspective of vocal music. In comparison to Castil-Blaze (1858), Choron is more inclined to accept prosodic irregularity.
1841	Ritorni, Carlo. *Ammaestramenti alla composizione d'ogni poema e d'ogni opera appartenente alla musica.*	One of the most important Italian operatic treatises, anticipating structural reforms implemented later in the nineteenth century. Ritorni's rules of versification, less restrictive than those of his contemporaries, reflect practice well.

Date	Treatise	Relevance to study
1843	Boucheron, Raimondo. "Esame dello stato attuale della musica drammatica in Italia."	Accepts for Italian opera some melodic aspects traditionally associated with France (such as unconventional phrasing if required by the sense of the text) but rejects others (such as Reicha's concept of the *chanson*).
1845	Balbi, Melchiorre. *Grammatica ragionata della musica considerata sotto l'aspetto di lingua.*	The most extreme attempt in nineteenth-century Italy of equating the components of language with those of music.
1845	Fétis, François-Joseph. "*Le Prophète* (première représentation le 16 avril): Opéra en 5 actes, paroles de M. Scribe, musique de Meyerbeer" [and related texts].	In a variety of articles and reviews, Fétis deplores the excesses of Italian composers after Rossini (too much declamation, too much emphasis on harmony, noisy accompaniments). He recommends accentual regularity but praises the variety of melodic rhythm in Meyerbeer.
1846	Bourges, Maurice. "Situation mélodique actuelle."	Praises Meyerbeer's operas for all their progressive features and sees in the exploration of irregular rhythmic possibilities a wide-open field.
1850	Quicherat, Louis-Marie. *Traité de versification française.* 2d ed.	One of the most frequently cited nineteenth-century versification manuals. Quicherat interprets the French accents as one of stress and advocates in a given meter a fixed number of accents in partly flexible positions.
1853	Beaulieu, Désiré. *Du rhythme, des effets qu'il produit et de leurs causes.*	Systematizes the effects of rhythmic divisions within a given meter.
1855	Mazzucato, Alberto. "*Il profeta*" [and related texts].	An admirer of Meyerbeer, Mazzucato provides a particularly useful description of French and Italian melodic styles.
1856	Basevi, Abramo. "Se Meyerbeer scrivesse oggi un'opera italiana" [and related texts].	Basevi advocates a *stile italo-germanico*, (i.e., a style that combines Italian melody with German harmony). A good melody should take the character of the poetry into consideration and be ready to abandon square phrasing. Basevi holds up Meyerbeer as the model for Italian composers to follow.
1858	Blaze, François Henri Joseph [Castil-Blaze]. *L'art des vers lyriques.*	The most famous French treatise advocating accentual regularity for the purpose of facilitating good melodic writing. Castil-Blaze calls verse without such regularity "prose rimée [rhymed prose]"
1862	Benloew, Louis. *Précis d'une théorie des rhythmes.* Vol. 1, *Rhythmes français et rhythmes latins.*	Offers guidelines for the rhythmic interpretation of verse depending on its purpose (recitation or musical setting). The more a melody wishes to "flatter the ear," the more appropriate scanning becomes. A French philologist specializing on accentuation in indo-european languages, Benloew has particular authority.

Date	Treatise	Relevance to study
1865	Pacini, Giovanni. *Le mie memorie artistiche.*	Exemplifies the struggle of Italian composers for rhythmically innovative melodic designs, especially in cabalettas.
1871	Weigand, Gustave. *Traité de versification française.* 2d ed.	Includes an interesting section on stanzaic theory.
1872	Bertrand, Gustave. *Les nationalités musicales étudiés dans le drame lyrique.*	Paints Verdi as a hopeless Italian, who (although he came close in *Don Carlos*) could never compose a truly French work.
1879	Lubarsch, E. Otto. *Abriss der französischen Verslehre.*	Goes beyond mechanical rules of determining syllables and accents, pointing to the rhythm of actual spoken French.
1883	Tobler, Adolf. *Vom französischen Versbau alter und neuer Zeit: Zusammenstellung der Anfangsgründe.* 2d ed.	Helpful regarding such issues as enjambment and caesura. Issues of rhythm beyond the accents at the rhyme and caesura are largely ignored.
1884	Pierson, Paul. *Métrique naturelle du langage.*	Suggests that composers embrace the accentual irregularity of French verse by adjusting the melodic rhythm.
1891	Banville, Théodore de. *Petit traité de poésie française.*	Allows for more freedom regarding caesura and enjambment than most other manuals of versification.
1894	Combarieu, Jules. *Les rapports de la musique et de la poésie considérés au point de vue de l'expression.*	Recognizes the ambiguity of the French accent and claims that the *accent oratoire* or *logique* is the only accent a composer must rigorously observe.
1904	Saran, Franz. *Der Rhythmus des französischen Verses.*	Distinguishes three approaches to French verse: "altnational," describing verse in terms of rhyme, number of syllables, and caesuras (as in Tobler and Banville); "alternierend," in terms of metric feet (as in Benloew's scanning); and "accentuierend," in terms of tonic (stress) accents (as in Quicherat).
1911	Landry, Eugène. *La théorie du rythme et le rythme du français déclamé.*	Focuses less on the tonic accent (which has only theoretical value) than on rhythmic groups determined by sense.
1912	Martinon, Philippe. *Les strophes: Étude historique et critique sur les formes de la poésie lyrique en France...*	The most thorough discussion of stanzaic structure, organized by length of stanza and metric composition.

Notes

Introduction

1. Alain Arnaud, "Ton ennemi Meyerbeer...," in *Verdi: Les Vêpres siciliennes*, ed. Michel Orcel, *L'Avant-scène opéra opérette*, no. 75 (Paris: Avant-scène, 1985), 90.
2. Letter of October 28, 1854, to Nestor Roqueplan, quoted in Gaetano Cesari and Alessandro Luzio, eds., *I copialettere di Giuseppe Verdi* (Milan: n.p., 1913), 154.
3. Letter of April 21, 1868, quoted in translation in Budden, *The Operas of Verdi*, rev. ed., 3 vols. (Oxford: Clarendon Press, 1992), 3:26.
4. Verdi almost always conceived his melodies with a specific text already in hand. See Philip Gossett, *Divas and Scholars: Performing Italian Opera* (University of Chicago Press, 2006), 371–4.
5. Many mid-nineteenth-century Italian melodies based, for example, on *ottonari* (verses of eight syllables with fixed accents on the third and seventh syllables) belong to a small number of rhythmic types. For a taxonomy of rhythmic types based on individual poetic meters, see Friedrich Lippmann, "Der italienische Vers und der musikalische Rhythmus: Zum Verhältnis von Vers und Musik in der italienischen Oper des 19. Jahrhunderts, mit einem Rückblick auf die 2. Hälfte des 18. Jahrhunderts," *Analecta musicologica* 12 (1973): 253–369; 14 (1974): 324–410; 15 (1975): 298–333.
6. *Il Figaro*, February 11, 1864, quoted in Arrigo Boito, *Tutti gli scritti*, ed. P. Nardi (Milan: Mondadori, 1942), 1119 and translated in Budden, *The Operas of Verdi*, 2:16–17. Among the Italian critics, Abramo Basevi most clearly pointed to the advantages of French verse. For example, see "*Gli ugonotti (Anglicani)* del celebre M.º Giacomo Meyerbeer al teatro Ferdinando," *L'armonia* 5 (1857): 69–70. The composer Giovanni Pacini (*Le mie memorie artistiche* [Florence: G. G. Guidi, 1865, reprint, Lucca: Maria Pacini Fazzi, 1981], 70–1) commented on the same problem.
7. Julian Budden ("L' influenza della tradizione del grand opéra francese sulla struttura ritmica di *Don Carlo*," in *Atti del II° congresso internazionale di studi verdiani, Verona, Parma, Busseto, 30 luglio–5 agosto 1969*, ed. Marcello Pavarani [Parma: Istituto di studi verdiani, 1971], 311–18), for example, points out the greater rhythmic variety of *Les Vêpres siciliennes* and *Don Carlos* but does not attempt to show whether and how such changes derive from the properties of French verse. Jeffrey Langford's essays ("Text Setting in Verdi's *Jérusalem* and *Don Carlos*," *Verdi Newsletter*, no. 12 [1984]: 19–31; and "Poetic Prosody and Melodic Rhythm in *Les Vêpres siciliennes*," *Verdi Newsletter*, no. 23 [1996]: 8–18), on the other hand, do not take into account the broad theoretical foundation of French versification. Finally, Damien Colas is in the process of evaluating Verdi's setting of French verse but so far has not focused on the rich theoretical discourse about French prosody. His study is in progress, with a lengthy portion on the alexandrine already published. See Damien Colas, "'Quels accents! quel langage!': Examen du traitement de l'alexandrin dans *Les Vêpres siciliennes*," in *L'opéra en France et en Italie (1791–1925): Une

scène privilégiée d'échanges littéraires et musicaux, ed. Hervé Lacombe, Publications de la Société française de musicologie, III/8 (Paris: Société française de musicologie, 2000), 187–214.
8. Abramo Basevi, *Studio sulle opere di Giuseppe Verdi*, rev. and enl. ed. (Florence: Tofani, 1859), 245–7.
9. Pietro Torrigiani, "*I vespri siciliani* a Parma," *L'armonia* 1, no. 2 (1856): 6.
10. Hector Berlioz, "Opinion de Berlioz sur *Les Vêpres siciliennes* de Verdi," *La France musicale* 19 (1855): 314.
11. The most important bibliographic tool in this respect is the *Retrospective Index to Music Periodicals* (formerly *Répertoire International de la Presse Musicale*; Ann Arbor: UMI, 1988–), an ongoing effort to catalogue the contents of old music journals. Equally important are collections of reviews such as Hervé Gartioux, ed., *Giuseppe Verdi*, Les Vêpres siciliennes: *Dossier de presse parisienne (1855)*, Critiques de l'opéra français du XIXème siècle, vol. 6 (n.p.: Lucie Galland, 1995); and Hervé Gartioux, ed., *Giuseppe Verdi*, Don Carlos: *Dossier de presse parisienne (1867)*, Critiques de l'opéra français du XIXème siècle, vol. 9 (Heilbronn: Lucie Galland, 1997).
12. "Ieri sera sono stato all' Opéra: mi sono annojato molto ma sono anche restato sbalordito della *mise en scene*: era la *Juive* d' Halévy." Quoted in Claudio Sartori, "La Streppoli e Verdi a Parigi nella morsa quarantottesca," *Nuova rivista musicale italiana* 2 (1974): 249.
13. Letter to Clarina Maffei of March 2, 1854, quoted in translation in Mary Jane Phillips-Matz, *Verdi: A Biography* (Oxford University Press, 1993), 339–40.
14. Verdi used these words in a letter of March 4, 1869, to the Florentine critic Filippo Filippi, quoted in Luigi Magnani, "'L'ignoranza musicale' di Verdi e la biblioteca di Sant'Agata," in *Il teatro e la musica di Giuseppe Verdi: Atti del III° congresso internazionale di studi verdiani (Milano, Piccola Scala, 12–17 giugno 1972)*, ed. Mario Medici and Marcello Pavarani (Parma: Istituto di studi verdiani, 1974), 250.
15. Ibid., 253.
16. Letter of March 27, 1847, quoted in translation in Phillips-Matz, *Verdi*, 207–8.

Chapter 1 Rhythm and stanza in French and Italian librettos

1. Only toward the end of the century did librettos emerge in what Louis Gallet called *poésie mélique* (short lines without rhyme or fixed length, connected by dashes). See Graham Sadler et al., "Versification," in *The New Grove Dictionary of Opera*, ed. Stanley Sadie, 4 vols. (London: Macmillan, 1992), 4:967. Charles Gounod's early attempt at setting a prose libretto (*Georges Dandin*, 1874) did not materialize. It took some fifteen years more until Alfred Bruneau and Claude Debussy set the first prose librettos. See Steven Huebner, *The Operas of Charles Gounod* (Oxford: Clarendon Press, 1990), 88.
2. Only a small number of theorists discuss a wide variety of technical aspects of French librettos: Castil-Blaze, *L'Art des vers lyriques* (Paris: A. Delahays, 1858); Jean François Marmontel, *Élémens de littérature*, 6 vols. (n.p., 1787), vols. 5–6; and Antonio Scoppa, *Les vrais principes de la versification développés par un examen comparatif entre la langue italienne et la française*, 3 vols. (Paris: Courcier, 1811–1814).
3. Examples refer to works by Verdi unless otherwise noted. The quotations from *Jérusalem* are taken from Gustave Vaëz and Alphonse Royer, Jérusalem: *Opéra en quatre actes, musique de G. Verdi, représenté, pour la première fois, à Paris, sur le théâtre de l'Académie Royale de Musique,*

le 26 novembre 1847 (Brussels: Lelong, 1847). In creating this work, the librettists adapted most of the text to fit the music composed to the original Italian libretto (*I lombardi*), which therefore followed the principles of Italian and not French versification. To avoid any misleading conclusions, the citations are drawn from the newly composed portions of this opera, unless otherwise noted. The numbering of the acts and scenes follows the one given in the libretto from which the citation is taken.

4. Théodore de Banville, *Petit traité de poésie française* (Paris: A. Lemerre, 1891); and Léon Emile Kastner, *A History of French Versification* (Oxford: Clarendon Press, 1903), 14. The quotations from *Les Vêpres siciliennes* are taken from Eugène Scribe and Charles Duveyrier, *Les Vêpres siciliennes, musique de M. Verdi; représenté pour la première fois, sur le théâtre de l'Académie impériale de Musique, le 13 juin 1855* (Paris: Michel Lévy frères, 1855).

5. Louis-Marie Quicherat, *Traité de versification française où sont exposées les variations successives des règles de notre poésie et les fonctions de l'accent tonique dans les vers français*, 2d ed. (Paris: Hachette, 1850), 3; Banville, *Petit traité de poésie française*, 33; and Adolphe Tobler, *Le vers français ancien et moderne*, 2d ed., trans. Karl Breul and Léopold Sudre (Paris: F. Vieweg, 1885), 78–9. A complete alphabetical list of sets of vowels and their interpretations as synerisis or dieresis appears, along with some general guidelines, in Andreas Giger, "The Role of Giuseppe Verdi's French Operas in the Transformation of His Melodic Style" (Ph.D. diss., Indiana University, 1999), 299–301.

6. See Quicherat, *Traité*, 518. Although such attempts date back to the fifteenth century, Antoine de Baïf (1532–1589) was unquestionably the most prominent promoter of measured verse. One of Baïf's followers, Nicolas Rapin (1539–1608), wrote verses in which stress accent and quantitative accent tended to coincide. He thus forms a link between Baïf's *vers mesuré* and a system based on regular stress accents first proposed by Louis de Gardin in 1630 as a reaction to earlier writers of quantitative verse. See Kastner, *History*, 295–308.

7. Alexandre Choron and J. Adrien de La Fage, *Nouveau manuel complet de musique vocale et instrumentale, ou, Encyclopédie musicale*, part II, vol. 3, *Instrumentation, union de la musique avec la parole, genres* (Paris: Roret, 1836–1839), 132 and 138–53 passim.

8. Castil-Blaze, *L'Art des vers lyriques*, 13–27.

9. "Mais le principe était trouvé, et ce principe est incontestable: 'Dans les vers d'une langue quelconque, il est impossible d'admettre aucune harmonie sans rhythme, *ni aucun rhythme sans accent.*' ... Le système moderne diffère essentiellement du système ancien, en ce que l'accent a été substitué à la quantité: au lieu de syllabes *longues*, on a pris des syllabes *accentuées*, et des syllabes *muettes*, au lieu de syllabes *brèves*." To strengthen his point, Quicherat (*Traité*, 516) draws here on a quotation from Antonio Scoppa. See also Tobler, *Le vers français*, 1–2; and Kastner, *History*, 1, 295–308.

10. Scoppa, *Les vrais principes*, 1:78–9, 2:500. Antoine Reicha (*Art du compositeur dramatique ou Cours complet de composition vocale*, 2 vols. [Paris: Farrenc, 1833], 1:4, 10) agrees with Scoppa but typically uses the same term (*accent grammatical ou tonique*) for both quantitative and stress accents. He makes his point using the words *patte* and *pâte*, which he says are undoubtedly pronounced differently, but in a musical setting the stress accent on the first syllable requires both first syllables be long (scanned – ˘). His scansion tables make it clear, however, that the signs – and ˘ refer to the placement of the syllables on weak and strong beats of the measure, rather than to their length. See Reicha, *Art du compositeur dramatique*, 2:1–2. In 1812, the Institut de France

commissioned François-Joseph Gossec, André-Ernest-Modeste Grétry, Étienne-Nicolas Méhul, and Alexandre Choron to review the first volume of Scoppa's *Les vrais principes*. The convoluted report they provided states that French versification relies "on the number of syllables and the distribution of the accents." Other occurrences in the report of the term "accent" imply stress accent, but the members of the commission consistently avoid the question as to whether this accent is one of stress or duration. Their criticism of Scoppa's theory suggests that stress accents should also be long and maintain that French verse resists the regular accent patterns found in Italian. See Alexandre Choron et al., *Rapport présenté au nom de la section de musique, et adopté par la classe des beaux-arts de l'institut impérial de France, dans ses séances du 18 avril et des 2 et 9 mai 1812, sur un ouvrage intitulé*: Les vrais principes de la versification, développés par un examen comparatif entre les langues française et italienne, etc., par M. A. Scoppa (Paris: Firmin Didot, 1812), 9–10.

11. See Antonio Scoppa, *Traité de la poésie italienne rapporté à la poésie française, dans lequel on fait voir la parfaite analogie entre ces deux langues ...* (Paris: Renouard, 1803).

12. Henri Morier, *Dictionnaire de poétique et de rhétorique* (Paris: Presses universitaires de France, 1961), 1; see also Eugène Landry, *La théorie du rythme et le rythme du français déclamé avec une étude expérimentale de la déclamation de plusieurs poètes et comédiens célèbres, du rhythme des vers italiens, et des nuances de la durée dans la musique* (Paris: Honoré Champion, 1911), 159n, 396. Both Morier and Landry, who measure the length of the spoken syllables in hundredths of a second, do not deny that the lengthened syllables may also have a stress accent.

13. Castil Blaze suggests the following interpretations: "châtelain," "pâlissant," "violon," and "sûreté," etc. *L'Art des vers lyriques*, 14. These views confirm the weakness of the tonic accent of an isolated word.

14. Jules Combarieu, *Rapports de la musique et de la poésie considérées au point de vue de l'expression* (Paris: Alcan, 1894), 275.

15. E. Otto Lubarsch, *Abriss der französischen Verslehre* (Berlin: Weidmann, 1879), 10.

16. For example, Banville, *Petit traité*; and Tobler, *Le vers français*. The following portion outlining the four basic approaches to French prosody also appears in my article "The Triumph of Diversity: Theories of French Accentuation and Their Influence on Verdi's French Operas," *Music & Letters* 84 (February 2003): 59–72.

17. "Il ne faut pas confondre avec la syllabe forte un autre élément qui contribue plus encore que celle-ci au mouvement harmonieux du vers, je veux parler du *temps fort*. Lui aussi se fait sentir, comme l'accent moderne, par un appui, un coup de la voix; et lorsque, comme cela arrive très-souvent, il vient se poser sur la syllabe accentuée, il échappe complétement [*sic*] à l'observateur superficiel. Ce n'est que lorsqu'il vient frapper une syllabe faible qu'il devient sensible même à l'oreille la moins exercée ...

> On lira:
>   il est un Dieu devant lui je m'incline
>   pauvre et content sans lui demander rien.
> Mais on chantera:
>   il est un Dieu devant lui je m'incline
>   pauvre et content sans lui demander rien ...

Il existe donc une disconvenance très-marquée entre les syllabes fortes et les temps forts ... Mais il est évident que cette disconvenance ne saurait être absolue. A la césure et à la rime, temps fort et syllabe forte coïncident toujours; il n'est pas nécessaire que cette coïncidence se rencontre ailleurs ...

Lorsqu'en récitant des vers on veut frapper surtout l'intelligence, on appuiera sur les syllabes fortes, en négligeant un peu les temps forts. Lorsqu'au contraire on veut flatter l'oreille, et surtout lorsqu'on veut chanter, on scandera inévitablement. La syllabe forte est inhérente au mot, au sens; elle est toujours la même. Le temps fort est inhérent au rhythme, et se poste indifféremment sur des syllabes fortes ou des syllabes faibles, sur des mots à sens plein ou à sens vide. La syllabe forte a une valeur logique, le temps fort n'a qu'une valeur poétique et musicale." Louis Benloew, *Précis d'une théorie des rhythmes*, vol. 1, *Rhythmes français et rhythmes latins* (Paris: Franck, 1862), 20–2, 24. The mark for the *temps fort* on "lui" of the version to be sung is accidentally left out in the source, but it is clear from the subsequent text that it should be there.

18. Paul Pierson, *Métrique naturelle du langage* (Paris: Vieweg, 1884), 227; and Ferdinand de Gramont, *Les vers français et leur prosodie* (Paris: Hetzel, 1876), 4.
19. Writings influenced by Scoppa include, among others, Jean-Ambroise Ducondut, *Essai de rythmique française: Introduction théorique, manuel lyrique et préludes* (Paris: M. Lévy frères, 1856); Jean Marie Lurin, *Éléments du rythme dans la versification et la prose française* (Lyons: Bauchu, 1850); A. Fleury, "Du rythme dans la poésie chantée," *Études religieuses, philosophiques* ... 60 (November 1893), 326–63; Castil-Blaze, *L'Art des vers lyriques*; and Choron, *Nouveau manuel*.
20. Quoted in Castil-Blaze, *L'Art des vers lyriques*, 64.
21. Quoted in translation in Steven Huebner, "Italianate Duets in Meyerbeer's Grand Operas," *Journal of Musicological Research* 8 (1989): 204–5.
22. See Huebner, *The Operas of Charles Gounod*, 223. Italian influences have already been suggested by Franz Saran, *Der Rhythmus des französischen Verses* (Halle: Niemeyer, 1904), 189, 195; and more recently by Frits Noske, *French Song from Berlioz to Duparc*, rev. Rita Benton and Frits Noske, trans. Rita Benton (New York: Dover, 1970; reprint, New York: Dover, 1988), 52.
23. "Il arrivera quelquefois qu'on ne sera pas d'accord sur la place des accents; on le sera toujours sur leur nombre." Quicherat, *Traité*, 134n.
24. Jeffrey Langford, "Text Setting in Verdi's *Jérusalem* and *Don Carlos*," 28–9.
25. All quotations from the *Don Carlos* libretto are taken from the original publication unless otherwise indicated: Joseph Méry and Camille Du Locle, *Don Carlos, opéra en cinq actes, musique de G. Verdi, représenté, pour la première fois, à Paris, sur le théâtre impérial de l'Opéra le 11 mars 1867* (Paris: Michel Lévy, 1867). If the short citations list three numbers (e.g., *Don Carlos*, III,1,2), the act is divided by *tableau* and scene.
26. The *vers de neuf syllabes* is very rare in Verdi.
27. "Le sens, c'est-à-dire ici l'importance et la liaison des mots, doit s'accorder avec le rythme, c'est-à-dire avec un besoin d'art, pour déterminer la place de l'accent emphatique, sa force et son retour. Sens et rythme jouent un rôle également positif et négatif, c'est-à-dire d'élection et d'exclusion. Ici c'est le sens qui dicte le premier ses lois, tant à l'auteur qu'au diseur, mais elles sont bien moins sévères que celles du rythme. En thèse générale, ils sont en conflit. Le sens demanderait des accents variés, des groupes longs et inégaux. Le rythme tend à égaliser et à multiplier les accents, et à en rendre le retour régulier. Au reste ... il règne beaucoup d'incertitude et de latitude en cette matière." Landry, *La théorie du rythme*, 225–6.
28. Ibid., 223, 230, 267.
29. Ibid., 223.

30. "Der Wortton oder die Betonung des Einzelwortes erleidet im Französischen eine bedeutende Herabsetzung durch den Satzton ... Der französische Satzton vereinigt eine Reihe begrifflich zusammengehöriger Worte auch für das Ohr, indem er dem letzten Glied der Wortreihe eine höhere Betonung als den übrigen Gliedern verleiht. Z. B. der Satz

> Cette maison est agré**able**,

welcher nur eine Begriffsreihe bildet, wird so ausgesprochen, dass die Betonung seines Schlusswortes *agréable* viel stärker hervortritt als die Betonungen aller übrigen in ihm vorkommenden Wörter. Er wird zu einer gleichmässig hinfliessenden Silbenreihe, welche mit dem Hauptton ihres Endwortes schliesst, während sie durch ihre inneren Betonungen nur schwach gegliedert wird. Aus gleichem Grunde hat in dem Satze

> C'est une agréable nou**velle**

das Wort *agréable* eine ungleich schwächere Betonung als in dem zuerst angeführten Satze, denn der Satzton trifft hier auf *nouvelle*." Lubarsch, *Abriss der französischen Verslehre*, 5–6.

31. "Le simple accent du mot, qui est un faible accent d'énergie et de durée sur la dernière voyelle ou la pénultième, joue dans la déclamation, comme dans les autres dictions du français, un rôle tout intellectuel, qui consiste à séparer les vocables, à distinguer un mot composé de ses composants ..." Landry, *La théorie du rythme*, 191–2. See also Kastner, *History*, 1; and Choron, *Nouveau manuel*, 140.

32. "Cette accentuation de deux en deux serait insupportable à la lecture, surtout lorsqu'elle ferait tomber un ictus sur une syllabe naturellement faible; aussi, dans la déclamation des vers, se contente-t-on aujourd'hui de faire sentir le dernier ictus de chaque hémistiche qui doit toujours concorder avec un ictus naturel de la voix, et, le plus souvent, on fait entendre dans l'intérieur de chaque hémistiche un autre ictus placé facultativement sur la syllabe le plus naturellement désignée par le sens ...

Il faut bien avoir le courage de l'avouer, le vers français prononcé, non pas de la façon monotone en usage dans les écoles, mais avec toute l'expression que réclame le sens de la phrase, n'a plus aucun rythme déterminé et ne se distingue plus en rien, sinon peut-être par l'allure du style, de la simple déclamation prosaïque; du reste, on doit plutôt s'en féliciter que s'en plaindre, tout le monde conviendra qu'il n'est pas de rythme plus pauvre que celui des vers scandés; plus on mettra d'expression dans la déclamation du vers, plus l'indigence du vieux rythme disparaîtra sous la riche improvisation du sentiment; en un mot, plus les vers déclamés ressembleront à une belle prose, plus il plairont." Pierson, *Métrique naturelle du langage*, 225–7. Pierson did not seem to realize that Benloew, too, favored irregular accentuation when declaiming (as opposed to singing).

33. "Chaque segment part de l'étape marquée par la césure précédente pour s'acheminer vers une nouvelle étape qui sera marquée par la césure qui le termine ... C'est donc suivre une marche tout-à-fait naturelle ... Le mot considéré en lui-même, abstraction faite de toute phrase de laquelle il fasse partie, peut être une entité idéale, mais sitôt qu'on veut le faire passer du domaine abstrait dans un organisme concret, il perd son individualité idéale et n'est plus qu'un assemblage de syllabes concourant avec les syllabes d'un ou de plusieurs autres mots à former une entité rythmique désigné par nous sous le nom de *segment* ... On sait déjà que tout segment a pour noyau un accent général de la période, celui-ci devient l'accent culminant du segment ...; en dessous de cet accent culminant et unique, règnent un ou plusieurs accents faibles par rapport à

lui, mais doués individuellement d'une force suffisante pour commander à un système d'accents plus faibles." Pierson, *Métrique naturelle du langage*, 157–8.

34. "[L'accent oratoire] consiste dans une certaine inflexion de la voix, et dans l'expression imitative du sentiment qui s'exhale par cet organe: il est tout ce que la passion, la vivacité, le goût, le génie peuvent ajouter à la parole pour la rendre frappante, pour lui donner plus d'âme et de vivacité, comme les couleurs animent et relèvent la beauté d'un dessin pour ébranler les sens et agir sur l'imagination. Il n'est pas une propriété de la langue qui parle, mais du coeur qui sent; il n'est pas inhérent aux mots, il est inhérent aux passions." Scoppa, *Les vrais principes*, 2:494.

35. "Ces mots ne sont pas bien difficiles à reconnaître et à sentir, en lisant avec attention ce que l'on doit mettre en musique. Les mots soulignés dans les phrases suivantes, par exemple, exigent un accent logique:

   1°. "................ Dans un age si *tendre*
   "Quel éclaircissement en pouvez vous attendre.
   2°. "Je vois que la sagesse elle *même* t'inspire.

   Pour que le Déclamateur récitant ou le Chanteur puissent appuyer suffisamment sur ces mots, il faut que le Compositeur leur donne une valeur de note un peu longue, et les mette sur des notes un peu élevées." Reicha, *Art du compositeur dramatique*, 1:10–11.

36. Quicherat, *Traité*, 13–15. A caesura can, however, separate the auxiliary verb from the participle or infinitive, if any other word lies between the two parts: "Vous devez de Montfort | | admirer la clémence!" (*Les Vêpres siciliennes*, I,4). Some sources provide very general definitions of the caesura: "The caesura is a repose of the voice, marked within a verse by a tonic syllable more strongly accentuated than the other tonic syllables of the verse." Charles Le Goffic and Édouard Thieulin, *Nouveau traité de versification française à l'usage des classes de l'enseignement classique et de l'enseignement moderne des lycées et collèges des écoles normales, du brevet supérieur et des classes de l'enseignement secondaire des jeunes filles*, 3d ed. (Paris: Masson, 1897), 86.

37. "Observer toutes les règles de l'art dans l'emploi de la césure est un des points les plus difficiles de la technique poétique, surtout dans des poèmes qui, du commencement à la fin, emploient le même vers ... Le principe ... est celui-ci: la césure peut séparer l'une de l'autre même les parties de la phrase qui ont entre elles un étroit rapport, à condition qu'il ne survienne pas après elle une pause plus forte, parce qu'alors ... il serait à craindre que la nature du vers ne fût méconnue." Tobler, *Le vers français*, 131.

38. Victor Hugo, "Préface [to *Cromwell*]," in *Théâtre complet de Victor Hugo*, ed. J.-J. Thierry and Josette Mélèze (Monaco: Gallimard, 1967), 441.

39. The first example from *Don Carlos* does not appear in the original libretto; it replaces three verses of irregular length.

40. Reicha, *Art du compositeur dramatique*, 6. Quicherat (*Traité*) contradicts himself as far as the requirement of a caesura for the *vers de neuf syllabes* is concerned. Compare his statement on p. 11 (caesura not required) with the one on p. 185 (caesura required). For the *décasyllabe*, Kastner (*History*, 103) gives examples with the caesura after the fourth, fifth, and even sixth syllables, which has to do with the fact that he codifies all divisions known to him.

41. Banville (*Petit traité*, 113–14) refers here to Wilhelm Ténint's *Prosodie de l'école moderne* (Paris: Didot, 1844). See also the variety of divisions in the verses assembled by Gustave Weigand in his *Traité de versification française*, 2d ed. (Bromberg: E. S. Mittler, 1871), 105–38.

42. Quicherat, *Traité*, 66; and Banville, *Petit traité*, 93. Kastner (*History*, 112) defines the term more loosely, including cases in which the overflow takes up the entire subsequent verse.
43. Tobler, *Le vers français*, 23. In his attempt to define enjambment in Italian librettos, Robert Moreen ("Integration of Text Forms and Musical Forms in Verdi's Early Operas," [Ph.D. diss., Princeton University, 1975], 39–47) encountered the problem of determining on what level the sense had to finish with the verse. If the verse finishes a sentence, it obviously avoids overflow; if it finishes with the article for the noun that opens the next verse, the two lines present a clear-cut example of overflow. Between these two extremes, however, one finds a wide spectrum of solutions.
44. Quicherat, *Traité*, 66. Boileau, a member of the *Académie française*, codified the rules of good verse in his *L'Art poétique* (1674), which controlled versification up to the time of the Romantics.
45. Scoppa (*Les vrais principes*, 1:325) commented on the discrepancy between theory and practice as follows: "It is very strange that the French, while constantly inveighing against enjambment of the verses, always employ it with success."
46. At the end of a century that had dispensed with many rules of versification, Banville called for complete freedom in the use of the technique, claiming that a strong rhyme was the only device needed to create rhythm and harmony. Banville, *Petit traité*, 91–115.
47. For an example of stanzas within a drama, see Pierre Corneille, *Le Cid*, I,6 and V,2. The French use the term *lyrique* in two ways: to refer either to operatic compositions (e.g., as in *tragédie lyrique*) or to lyric poetry, as contrasted with dramatic or epic poetry.
48. The poem is quoted from *Selected Poems of Victor Hugo: A Bilingual Edition*, trans. E. H. and A. M. Blackmore (University of Chicago Press, 2001), 550.
49. See M. Elizabeth C. Bartlet, ed., *Gioachino Rossini*: Guillaume Tell, *Edizione critica delle opere di Gioachino Rossini*, I/39, *Commento critico – testi* (Pesaro: Fondazione Rossini, 1992), 14–16. All quotations from French librettos are indented in this way. Some contemporary librettos distinguish *each* meter by indention, i.e., the *vers de cinq syllabes* would be indented slightly more than the *vers de six syllabes*. See, for example, Eugène Scribe, L'Africaine, *opéra en cinq actes, musique de Giacomo Meyerbeer* (Paris: Brandus et Dufour, [1865]). We follow this practice only if a stanza includes such adjacent meters.
50. Unfortunately, modern editions of Italian librettos (including Luigi Baldacci's *Tutti i libretti di Verdi*, 4th ed. [Milan: Garzanti, 1992]) fail to reproduce the stanzaic arrangements. The following example appears, together with an extensive discussion of the intricacies of translating librettos, in Philip Gossett, "Translations and Adaptations of Operatic Texts," in *Palimpsest: Editorial Theory in the Humanities*, ed. George Bornstein and Ralph G. Williams (Ann Arbor: The University of Michigan Press, 1993), 295; and idem, *Divas and Scholars*, Chapter 11.
51. Temistocle Solera, I lombardi alla prima crociata, *dramma lirico posto in musica dal Sig. Maestro Giuseppe Verdi, da rappresentarsi nell'I. R. Teatro alla Scala il carnevale 1843* (Milan: Gaspare Truffi, 1843).
52. A condensed version of this section on stanzaic analysis has been published in my "Defining Stanzaic Structure in Verdi's French Librettos and the Implications for the Musical Setting," *Acta musicologia* 73 (2001): 141–63.
53. See, for example, Quicherat, *Traité*, 217; and Le Goffic and Thieulin, *Nouveau traité*, 115–16.
54. "La *Stance* est une période poétique symétriquement composée. Il est bien vrai qu'assez souvent elle contient plusieurs sens finis, et qu'aussi quelquefois le sens n'est que suspendu; mais je la

prends, pour la définir dans sa forme la plus régulière; et au gré de l'oreille comme au gré de l'esprit, la *Stance* la mieux arrondie est celle dont le cercle embrasse une pensée unique, et qui se termine comme elle et avec elle par un plein repos." Marmontel, *Élémens de littérature*, 6:158–9.
55. Weigand, *Traité*, 146.
56. Ellipses in librettos do not indicate an omission of text, but rather a suspended thought.
57. Weigand, *Traité*, 146. Philippe Martinon (*Les strophes: Étude historique et critique sur les formes de la poésie lyrique en France depuis la renaissance avec une bibliographie chronologique et un répertoire général* [Paris: H. Champion, 1912], vi–viii) classifies stanzas in the following order of priority: according to number of verses, rhyme scheme, longest verse within the stanza, and type of final rhyme (masculine or feminine).
58. Quicherat, *Traité*, 219. According to Martinon (*Les strophes*, 433), rhyming couplets do not create enough rhythmic suspense. Marmontel (*Élémens de littérature*, 6:159), too, objects to the sequence of rhyming couplets; he claims that "[d]istichs strung together cannot produce a harmonious stanza." This aspect plays a lesser role in poetry intended for musical setting, which might explain why librettists did not mind using rhyming couplets in their stanzas.
59. Martinon, *Les strophes*, 441.
60. Quicherat (*Traité*, 219–21), for example, does not even mention the distich, whereas he quotes some tercets from librettos. Martinon (*Les strophes*) omits the distich but includes the tercet. Most other sources consulted, however, discuss both distichs and tercets. For variety, Romantic poets (and Victor Hugo always figures prominently among them) revived asymmetrical stanzas, especially the *quintil* but also the *septain*. See Martinon, *Les strophes*, 68, 70.
61. Martinon (*Les strophes*, 69) calls it a "form used by Romantics to obtain variety." See also Weigand, *Traité*, 146. The pattern *abc abc* or even *abcd abcd* sometimes occurs in poetry of the Middle Ages; by the nineteenth century, however, it is out of date. See Le Goffic and Thieulin, *Nouveau traité*, 85.
62. Eugène Scribe, "*Dom Sébastien, Roi de Portugal*: Opéra en cinq actes, musique de M. G. Donizetti (Académie royale de Musique – 13 novembre 1843)," in Eugène Scribe, *Théâtre de Eugène Scribe de l'académie française: opéras* – Le Dieu et la bavadère, Le Serment, Guido et Ginevra, La Xacarilla, Les Martyrs, Dom Sébastien, Le Juif errant (n.p.: Éditions d'aujourdhui, 1984), 220. This is a reprint from the 1857 Paris edition in twenty volumes of the same title, published by Michel Lévy.
63. Martinon, *Les strophes*, 442; and Quicherat, *Traité*, 219.
64. Martinon, *Les strophes*, 442.
65. Alphonse Royer and Gustave Vaëz, La Favorite, *opéra en quatre actes, musique de M. G. Donizetti, divertissements de M. Albert, représenté pour la première fois, à Paris, sur le théâtre de l'Académie royale de musique le 2 décembre 1840* (Paris: Dondey-Dupré, 1840), 9.
66. "On fera mieux de les regarder comme des vers sans césure, parce qu'il est contraire à la nature de la poésie strophique de joindre des vers de structure différente autrement que d'après un type déterminé." Tobler, *Le vers français*, 113–14.
67. See John N. Black, *The Italian Romantic Libretto: A Study of Salvadore Cammarano* (Edinburgh: The University Press, 1984), 250.
68. Verses are quoted as they appear in the original publication: [Temistocle Solera and Antonio Piazza], Oberto, Conte di S. Bonifacio: *Dramma in due atti da rappresentarsi nell'I. R. Teatro alla Scala l'autunno 1839* (Milan: Gaspare Truffi, 1839).

69. I am aware of only one example with interior *tronco* endings: Germont's "Di Provenza."

> Di Provenza il mare, il suol – Chi dal cor ti cancellò?
>   Al natio fulgente sol – Qual destino ti furò? ...
>   Oh rammenta pur nel duol – Ch'ivi gioia a te brillò,
>   E che pace colà sol – Su te splendere ancor può.
>   Dio mi guidò!

Francesco Maria Piave, La traviata, *musica di Giuseppe Verdi, espressamente composta pel Gran Teatro La Fenice, da rappresentarsi nella stagione di Carnovale e Quadragesima 1852–1853* (Venice: Gattei, n.d.), 20.

70. Francesco Maria Piave, I due Foscari: *Tragedia lirica posta in musica dal maestro Giuseppe Verdi pel teatro di Torre Argentina l'autunno del 1844* (Rome: Tipografia Ajani, [1844]).
71. Silvana Ghiazza, *Elementi di metrica italiana e cenni di retorica* (Bari: Edizione Levante, 1985), 43–4; and W. Theodor Elwert, *Italienische Metrik*, 2d ed. (Wiesbaden: Steiner, 1984), 48.
72. Choron does not define "caesura" according to the manuals of versification.
73. "Lorsque la voix qui déclame s'appuie dans les vers sur la dernière syllabe d'un mot, c'est ce qu'on appelle une *césure*; lorsque la syllabe sur laquelle on s'arrête n'est pas la dernière, mais seulement une longue suivie de brèves ou de muettes, et sur laquelle porte l'accent, c'est ce que j'appelle un *simple repos*; comme dans ces vers italiens:

>   1 2 3
>   Così bollono, etc.
>   1 2   3
>   Le lor gelide, etc.

les syllabes *bol* de *bollono*, et *ge* de *gelide*, sont longues et portent l'accent; c'est sur elles que la voix s'arrête: les suivantes sont brèves, et font partie du second hémistiche; la voix ne pourrait s'y reposer non plus que sur l'*e* muet français. Il en est de même des syllabes qui s'élident par la rencontre de deux voyelles, comme *or che niega i doni*; la syllabe *ga* se confond avec la suivante *i*, comme s'il y avait *or che nieg' i doni*, etc." Choron, *Nouveau manuel*, 143.
74. "Ma siccome per le incursioni de' Vandali, e de' Goti rimase corrotto l'idioma latino, e si perdette la notizia, e l'uso vero delle *Quantità*, e degli *Accenti*; così la nostra favella Italiana, che dalla Latina riconosce le leggi, o il nascimento, non conosce più ora sensibilmente quella distinzione di *Accento*, e di *Quantità* di sillaba; anzi confondendo queste due cose, fa, che l'accento acuto, e la sillaba lunga presso di noi fia tutt'uno; e tutt'uno ancora fia l'accento grave, e la sillaba breve. Per esempio; in questa parola *Favore* la sola sillaba *vo* è acutamente accentata, ed è insieme lunga; le altre due sillabe *fa*, e *re* restano con l'accento grave, e passano per brevi." Gianbattista Bisso, *Introduzione alla volgar poesia in due parti divisa*, 4th ed. (Venice: Giuseppe Orlandeli, 1791), 2. See also W. Theodor Elwert, *Versificazione italiana dalle origini ai giorni nostri* (Florence: Felice le Monnier, 1973), 45.
75. Landry, *La théorie du rythme*, 386–96; and Francesco Zambaldini, *Il ritmo dei versi italiani* (Turin: Loescher, 1874), 19–20.
76. See, for example, Carlo Ritorni, who states at the beginning of his discussion of versification: "In speech, a word consists of long and short syllables, that is, of accented or unaccented ones ...

In an Italian word, we single out a long syllable, called accent; and all the others, if there are any, are short." In his examples (pp. 106–8), however, Ritorni deals with equal durations and stress accents (called arsis and thesis). Carlo Ritorni, *Ammaestramenti alla composizione d'ogni poema e d'ogni opera appartenente alla musica* (Milan: Pirola, 1841), 103, 106–8.

77. "[L'alexandrine], en effet, a plus d'ampleur et de variété que l'*endecasillabo*, mais moins de force, et cette différence répond à celle de l'accent, qui chez nous, dans l'emphase, est plus marqué pour la durée, et chez les autres peuples romans l'est d'avantage pour l'énergie ... La force des accents a pour effet de rendre plus nettes et plus indépendantes les divisions rythmiques ... Cette force ... multiplie les pauses." Landry, *La théorie du rythme*, 274–5, 388. The types of verses chosen here could be replaced by any other.

78. This table appears in an expanded version in Scott L. Balthazar, "The Rhythm of Text and Music in 'Ottocento' Melody: An Empirical Reassessment in Light of Contemporary Treatises," *Current Musicology*, no. 49 (1992): 7.

79. Ibid., 7–8.

80. See Verdi's letter of October 18, 1870, to Antonio Ghislanzoni, quoted in *I copialettere di Giuseppe Verdi*, 658. The letter is dated by Philip Gossett in "Verdi, Ghislanzoni and *Aida*: The Uses of Convention," *Critical Inquiry* 1 (December 1974): 298.

81. For examples of *metri lirici* and *metri drammatici*, see Rocco Murari, *Ritmica e metrica razionale italiana*, 3d ed. (1909; reprint, Milan: Istituto Editoriale Cisalpino-Goliardica, 1977), 95–180.

82. Elwert, *Italienische Metrik*, 98; Pietro G. Beltrami, *La metrica italiana* (Bologna: Il Mulino, 1991), 357; and Ghiazza, *Elementi di metrica italiana*, 99.

83. Moreen, "The Integration of Text Forms and Musical Forms in Verdi's Early Operas," 22.

84. *Versi in selva* literally means "verses in the woods"(i.e., organized as irregularly as trees). They consist of an irregular mixture of *endecasillabi* and *settenari* without strophic arrangements and only occasional rhymes or none at all. Elwert, *Italienische Metrik*, 144; and Beltrami, *La metrica italiana*, 322–7. Paolo Fabbri ("Metrik und Form," in *Geschichte der italienischen Oper*, ed. Lorenzo Bianconi and Giorgio Pestelli, vol. 6, *Theorien und Techniken, Bilder und Mythen*, trans. Claudia Just and Paola Riesz [Laaber: Laaber Verlag, 1992], 181) claims that passages that alternate verses of seven and eleven syllables – especially in canzonas and madrigals – had been interpreted throughout as virtual *endecasillabi*, sometimes complete (*intero*) and sometimes shortened to a *settenario* (*rotto*). Such an interpretation would indeed justify the application of the term "versi sciolti" but nevertheless it implies a greater degree of organization than is usually found in the opening (and sometimes transitional) sections of a scene.

85. For example, Elwert, *Italienische Metrik*, 102; Alberto Del Monte, *Retorica, stilistica, versificazione: Introduzione allo studio della letteratura* (Turin: Loescher, 1955; reprint, Turin: Tipografia Gravinese, 1989), 134; and Ghiazza, *Elementi di metrica italiana*, 115.

86. Francesco Paolo Memmo, *Dizionario di metrica italiana* (Rome: Edizioni dell'Ateneo, 1983), 154.

87. Elwert, *Italienische Metrik*, 137.

88. Elwert, *Versificazione italiana*, 159; and idem, "Lo svolgimento della forma metrica della poesia lirica italiana dell'*ottocento*," *Estudis Romànics* 2 (1949–1950): 117.

89. Salvadore Cammarano, *Alzira: Tragedia lirica, divisa in prologo e due atti; da rappresentarsi nel Real Teatro S. Carlo* (Naples: Dalla tipografia Flautina, 1845).

90. Elwert, *Versificazione italiana*, 158; Black, *The Italian Romantic Libretto*, 257; and Fabbri, "Metrik und Form," 190.
91. Temistocle Solera, *Attila: Dramma lirico in un prologo e tre atti, musica di Giuseppe Verdi; da rappresentarsi nel Gran Teatro La Fenice nella stagione di carnovale e quadragesima del 1845–46* (Venice: Dalla tipografia di Giuseppe Molinari, [1845]).
92. See, for example, the manuscript libretto in Piave's hand of "*Il duca di vendome* [*Rigoletto*], libretto di F. M. Piave da musicarsi nella stagione di Carnovale e Quadragesima del 1850–1185 pel gran teatro la Fenice dal maestro Giuseppe Verdi," available in a photocopy at the American Institute for Verdi Studies at New York University (+ML40 V48 R4a).
93. See, for example, the manuscript libretto of *Macbeth*, available in a microfilm copy (Film ML49 V48 v.5) at the American Institute for Verdi Studies at New York University.
94. Moreen, "Integration of Text Forms and Musical Forms in Verdi's Early Operas," 20. The example from *Alzira*, I,3 quoted above exemplifies this case.
95. Memmo, *Dizionario di metrica italiana*, 154.
96. See Black, *The Italian Romantic Libretto*, 263.
97. For a list of polymetric stanzas, see Moreen, "Integration of Text Forms and Musical Forms in Verdi's Early Operas," 149.
98. The passage has repeatedly attracted attention. See, for example, Gossett, "Verdi, Ghislanzoni, and *Aida*," 328–30; Moreen, "Integration of Text Forms and Musical Forms in Verdi's Early Operas," 147–56; and Wolfgang Osthoff, "Musica e versificazione: Funzioni del verso poetico nell'opera italiana," in *La drammaturgia musicale*, ed. Lorenzo Bianconi (Bologna: Il Mulino, 1986), 136–9.
99. Arrigo Boito, *Otello: Dramma lirico in quattro atti, musica di Giuseppe Verdi; Teatro alla Scala, carnevale–quaresima 1886–87* (Milan: Ricordi, [1886]). The original libretto correctly renders Boito's autograph. However, the verse "Spento è quel sol, quel sorriso, quel raggio" could possibly be interpreted as the beginning of a separate distich. The autograph libretto is available in a microfilm copy at the American Institute for Verdi Studies at New York University.

Chapter 2 French and Italian melodic aesthetics and practice ca. 1830–1870

1. "La musica che vuolsi adattare al libretto domanda quindi tutta l'attenzione e lo studio del critico rispetto alla melodia, alle frasi, al ritmo, al taglio, alle armonie, ed agl'accompagnamenti che adopransi." Abramo Basevi, "Le riforme," *L'armonia* 1 (1856): 2.
2. "Di qual opera francese parla qui il periodico di Berlino? La vera fisonomia della melodia francese noi non la sapremmo ravvisare che nelle opere comiche. Nell'opera seria, il cui maggior tempio è il grand'*Opéra*, com'altri osservò, la musica francese è cosmopolita; ed infatti ben rado nelle grandi opere che si rappresentano a quel teatro ci viene fatto di scorgere i vizi inerenti alla melodia ed alla musica francese in generale." "Aristocrazie musicali," *Gazzetta musicale di Milano* 18 (1860): 57.
3. A. de Lauzières, "La musica in Francia," *Gazzetta musicale di Milano* 24 (1869): 436. Much later, Carl Dahlhaus ("Französische Musik und Musik in Paris," 6) claimed that specifically French music did not exist.
4. "Nous venons de parler de musique, d'école, de style français; à ce sujet, nous entendons dire que la musique française proprement dite est un mythe, qu'il n'existe pas ... puisque les plus

belles oeuvres que nous qualifions comme nôtres, sont dues, la plupart, à des compositions étrangers. On cite Grétry, pour l'opéra comique et Gluck pour l'opéra.

A ce point de vue, il est vrai, notre bagage ne se composerait que d'emprunts plus ou moins habiles faits, d'un côté, à l'Italie, cette divine source mélodieuse, de l'autre, à l'Allemagne, cette patrie de l'harmonie. Mais il en est autrement; tout en s'assimilant les qualités des écoles italienne et allemande, la musique française a toujours su dégager son originalité: la grâce, l'élégance, le goût, l'esprit surtout s'y retrouvent toujours. Gluck était Allemand, mais ce n'est que dans la langue française qu'il a rencontré une prosodie à la fois plus ferme, plus accentuée que l'italienne, plus douce et plus harmonieuse que l'allemande; la seule prosodie à laquelle il ait pu rigoureusement appliquer sa théorie dramatique." A. Thurner, "L'opéra comique et ses transformations," *La France musicale* 27 (1863): 78.

5. "But neither is Meyerbeer French, nor still less can his music, his melody be said to share in the nature of French music." "Aristocrazie musicali," 58.

6. Fabrizio Della Seta, "L'immagine di Meyerbeer nella critica italiana dell'ottocento e l'idea di 'dramma musicale,'" in *L'opera tra Venezia e Parigi*, ed. Maria Teresa Muraro, Studi di musica veneta, vol. 14 (Florence: Olschki, 1988), 148.

7. "Avevamo opinato che la musica, adoperata come la vediamo dal sublime ingegno di Meyerbeer, poteva sola servire di modello agli Italiani per uscire da questo stato di transizione che minaccia scadimento, ed entrare in un periodo di rigenerazione dell'arte musicale." Abramo Basevi, "Se Meyerbeer scrivesse oggi un'opera italiana." Abramo Basevi, "Se Meyerbeer scrivesse oggi un'opera italiana," *L'armonia* 1 (1856): 22. Similar opinions appear in the anonymous "La novità nella musica," *L'armonia* 1 (1856): 109–10; and "Perchè non si ripetono *Gli ugonotti* nel teatro della Pergola?" *L'armonia* 4 (1857): 25.

8. François-Joseph Fétis, "*Le Prophète* (première représentation le 16 avril): Opéra en 5 actes, paroles de M. Scribe, musique de Meyerbeer," *Revue et gazette musicale de Paris* 16 (1849): 170.

9. See James H. Johnson, *Listening in Paris: A Cultural History*, Studies on the History of Society and Culture, vol. 21 (Berkeley: University of California Press, 1995), 213–15, 219, 226. Jean Mongrédien (*French Music from the Enlightenment to Romanticism, 1789–1830*, trans. Sylvain Frémaux [Portland, OR: Amadeus Press, 1996], 79–82, 84) offers Julia's "Ô des infortunés déesse tutélaire" from Spontini's *La Vestale* as a good example of the "suave melodies" foreshadowing Bellini. On Cherubini's *Médée*, see ibid., 101.

10. Johnson, *Listening in Paris*, 219, 226; and Mongrédien, *French Music from the Enlightenment to Romanticism*, 89, 106, 138. See also Fabrizio Della Seta, *Italia e Francia nell'ottocento*, Storia della Musica, vol. 9 (Turin: E.D.T., 1993), 80 (virtuosity) and 82 (harmony). Sabine Henze-Döhring (*Oper und Musikdrama im 19. Jahrhundert*, vol. 13 of *Handbuch der musikalischen Gattungen* [Laaber: Laaber, 1997], 16) calls Rossini's feat of combining vocal virtuosity and expressive intensity "quadrature of the circle."

11. Halévy and Auber studied with Cherubini, Meyerbeer with Clementi (later imitating Rossini's style). Many of the French writers did not perceive Berlioz as an exemplary French melodist. The Italians, however, believed that he shared the problems they associated with the French style.

12. "La melodia nostra e piana, fluida, a proporzioni che direbbersi architettoniche; è simmetrica, rispondentesi nelle sue diverse frasi, rotonda, periodata, concludente. Ha principio, mezzo, fine omogenei. Scorre naturale insomma nell'esplicazione di ambo i suoi elementi, tonalità, cioè, e ritmo.

La melodia oltramontana rifugge con istudio, quasi sembrerebbe con affettazione, persino con ripugnanza, da questa naturalezza, da questa spontaneità ... Quanto al ritmo, e precisamente al suo naturale esplicamento, il periodo, la bisogna procede ben diversamente. Nelle cantilene del *Profeta*, salvo qualche eccezione, non l'ordinaria regolarità, non rigore di proporzioni, non simmetria, non rispondenza ritmica di frasi, non rotondità di periodo, non naturali conclusioni. La melodia il più sovente si arresta, si frange, vien troncata; e se non sempre da principio, certamente nel mezzo, od immancabilmente verso la fine." Alberto Mazzucato, "*Il profeta*," *Gazzetta musicale di Milano* 13 (1855): 187. See also Geremia Vitali, *La musica ne' suoi principj nuovamente spiegata* (Milan: Ricordi, [1847]), 6–7.

13. See, for example, Adrien de La Fage, "Lettres sur l'état actuel de la musique en Italie (septième lettre)," *Revue et gazette musicale de Paris* 16 (1849): 411. Instead of "exaggerated declamation," La Fage advocated "a music as natural and simple as possible."

14. Fétis, "*Le Prophète*," 154.

15. De La Fage, "Lettres sur l'état actuel de la musique en Italie," 411; Fétis, "Dangers de la situation actuelle de la musique dramatique: Causes du mal – moyens de régénération," *Revue et gazette musicale de Paris* 12 (1845): 3; Luigi Ferdinando Casamorata, "Cicalate: II. Il canto," *Gazzetta musicale di Milano* 23 (1868): 394.

16. The *Gazzetta musicale di Milano* was published by Ricordi, *L'Italia musicale* by Francesco Lucca, *L'art musical* by Léon Escudier (Verdi's French publisher) and the *Revue et gazette musicale* by Brandus (Meyerbeer's publisher).

17. "Quanto alla *melodia* preferirei quasi di non parlarne; di questo elemento essenziale della musica vi sono tanti concetti diversi, che giudicando un'opera non si può mai asserire, nè negare, se la *melodia* esista o manchi. Per certuni la *melodia* è il motivo triviale, che gratta, come suole dirsi, le orecchie, ed a cui è serbato l'onore finale degli organini; per altri la *melodia* è quella qualunque frase musicale che ricerca loro le fibre del cuore, che li fa piangere ed intenerire, e sono quelli che ne hanno un migliore concetto; per Wagner, la melodia è l'infinito, è il mormorio della foresta, la melopea senza ritmo, senza proporzioni, senza ritorni, che vaga e divaga, e che può produrre un eccitamento metafisico, lasciando incontentato l'orecchio ed arido il cuore." Filippo Filippi, "Studio analitico sul *Don Carlos* di Giuseppe Verdi," *Gazzetta musicale di Milano* 24 (1869): 35.

18. Mazzucato ("A Filippo Filippi [lettera quarta ed ultima]," *Gazzetta musicale di Milano* 22 [1867]: 251) had at an earlier point encouraged Italian composers to look "beyond the Alps," but in 1867 he believed that it was time to stop. Antonio Ghislanzoni ("Conversazioni musicali," *Gazzetta musicale di Milano* 21 [1866]: 74–5) spoke out against imitating Gounod and Meyerbeer and believed that the Italians should become original while remaining true to themselves. Basevi and Raimondo Boucheron, on the other hand, repeatedly encouraged their composers to look for fresh ideas in the north.

19. See Chapter 1, 16–17.

20. Reicha, *Art du compositeur dramatique*, 10; and Vitali, *La musica ne' suoi principj nuovamente spiegata*, 11. Vitali, who calls this accent *drammatico* or *patetico*, does not elaborate on its application at all. On the other hand, Lubarsch (*Abriss der französischen Verslehre*, 6) defined *accent logique* (which he calls *Satzton*) along the lines of Landry's primary accent, namely as the accent on the last word of a syntactic unit. In this case, the *accent logique* no longer constitutes

an "additional" prosodic accent but the only essential one. At the end of the century, Jules Combarieu (*Les rapports de la musique et de la poésie*, 276) claimed that the *accent oratoire* or *logique* was the only accent a composer had to observe rigorously.

21. For example, in Giuseppe Baini, *Saggio sopra l'identità de' ritmi musicale e poetico* (Florence: Piatti, 1820), 5; Ritorni, *Ammaestramenti*, 104; Choron, *Nouveau manuel*, 135; J.-B. Rongé, "De la poésie lyrique," *Revue et gazette musicale de Paris* 30 (1863): 188–9; and Castil-Blaze, *L'art des vers lyriques*, 20.
22. See Chapter 1, 36–7.
23. It is true that Ritorni speaks out against rounded musical periods ("rotondi periodi musicali"), emphasizing that the meter does not have to follow the forms of the text but rather the requirements of dramatic expression (*Ammaestramenti*, 131, 135). He makes these comments, however, in the context of a futuristic concept involving a type of opera based solely on lyric verse ("metro cantabile"), pointing to the *Baccanali* of Girolamo Baruffaldi as a model. Even a cursory investigation of these *Baccanali*, with constantly changing lengths of verse and stanza, reveals that melodic writing could not follow the rhythm of such forms in any detail. See Girolamo Baruffaldi, *Volume primo de' Baccanali*, 2d ed. (Bologna: Lelio dalla Volpe, 1758).
24. Ritorni, *Ammaestramenti*, 106. Ritorni uses "arsis" for "unaccented beat of the measure," "thesis" for "accented beat of the measure."
25. In fact, Asioli suggests using such verses only in recitative. See Bernardoni, "La teoria della melodia vocale nella trattatistica italiana (1790–1870)," *Acta musicologica* 62 (1990): 43.
26. Similar cases also occur in the works of other composers. See, for example, Lucia's "Regnava nel silenzio" (Donizetti, *Lucia di Lammermoor*, I,4) with "regnava" accented on the first syllable, or Climene's cabaletta "Il cor non basta a reggere" (Pacini, *Saffo*, II) with "labbro" accented on the second syllable. See also Salvatore D'Anna's citation of "Di quella pira," in which, at the beginning of the first two verses, the weak syllables fall on the downbeat while the secondary accents fall on weak beats. Salvatore D'Anna, *Grammatica riguardante i principii elementari di musica in corrispondenza a quei del linguaggio in correlazione all'antico* (Palermo: Michele Amenta, 1866), 55.
27. "L'uso poi di questi accenti produce nella musica una condizione *qualificativa* di molta rilevanza, giacchè la regolare uniformità dei primi tre rende equabile e *tranquilla* l'espressione, e l'accento apparente rompe in certa guisa quella monotona equabilità, e rende l'espressione più *fluttuante* ed *agitata*." Balbi, *Grammatica ragionata della musica considerata sotto l'aspetto di lingua* (Milan: G. Ricordi, 1845), 149.
28. See Chapter 1, 10–11 (Benloew); 11 (Scoppa); 12–13 (Quicherat); 12–14 (Lubarsch and Landry).
29. See, for example, François-Joseph Fétis, "Dangers de la situation actuelle de la musique dramatique," 1; Paul Lacome, "De la poésie française au point de vue du chant," *L'art musical* 6 (1866): 250; and A. Thurner, "L'opéra comique et ses transformations," *La France musicale* 27 (1863): 78.
30. See Luca Zoppelli, "'Stage Music' in Early Nineteenth-Century Italian Opera," *Cambridge Opera Journal* 2 (1990): 31–2; despite the title of the article, Zoppelli's examples here refer to French opera. See also Sebastian Werr, *Musikalisches Drama und Boulevard: Französische Einflüsse auf die italienische Oper im 19. Jahrhundert* (Stuttgart: Metzler, 2002), 189.

31. This is the text actually set by Halévy. The version of the libretto printed in the complete edition of Scribe's works adds irregular verse length to the irregular accent pattern:

> Quelle est donc cette voix secrète,
> Qui du fond de mon coeur s'élève et la défend?
> Ah! je pleure sur elle, et mon ame [sic] inquiète
> Frémit du destin qui l'attend.

Théâtre complet de M. Eugène Scribe, membre de l'Académie française, 2d ed., 24 vols. (Paris: Aimé André, 1835), 14:444.

32. Castil-Blaze, *L'art des vers lyriques*, 60; and Choron, *Nouveau manuel complet*, 149.

33. See, for example, Choron, *Nouveau manuel*, 142–5; Fétis, "Du rhythme de la poésie lyrique," *Revue et gazette musicale de Paris* 30 (1863): 81; Andrew Porter, "Don't Blame Scribe!" *Opera News* 39, no. 20 (1975): 27; and Steven Huebner, "Italianate Duets in Meyerbeer's Grand Operas," 204–5. Castil-Blaze (*L'art des vers lyriques*) was the most notorious advocate of rhythmic and metric regularity and as such undoubtedly invoked Italian standards.

34. "Il y a ... une accommodation entre le rythme des vers et celui des sons qui doit être réalisée sous peine de compromettre l'harmonie de leur association. Rapports mystérieux et complexes dont les lois échappent presque entièrement à l'analyse, qu'il faut sentir et non rechercher péniblement." René Brancour, "Mélodie," in *La grande encyclopédie: Inventaire raisonné des sciences, des lettres et des arts*, 31 vols., ed. Camille Dreyfus (vols. 1–18) and André Berthelot (vols. 19–31) (Paris: H. Lamirault [vols. 1–22] and Société anonyme de la grande encyclopédie [vols. 23–31], 1886–1902); vol. 23 (1896–1898): 613.

35. "Dans une langue comme celle qui se parle en France, y a-t-il si grand inconvénient à faire une faute de prosodie pour obtenir une phrase de chant d'un tour heureux ou neuf, et les musiciens de nos jours ont-ils eu si grand tort de secouer les chaînes dont il plaisait à MM. les poëtes de les charger? Je ne le pense pas." Adrien de La Fage, "Revue critique: *Méloprosodie française, ou guide du chanteur*," *Revue et gazette musicale de Paris* 14 (1847): 318. See also Combarieu, *Les rapports de la musique et de la poésie*, 274.

36. Mathis Lussy (*Musical Expression, Accents, Nuances, and Tempo, in Vocal and Instrumental Music*, trans. from the 4th ed. by M. E. von Glehn [London: Novello, n.d.], 102), demanded that long syllables fall on strong beats; in case such a coincidence did not take place, he suggested that the note on an unaccented beat "should ... be prolonged by several notes."

37. "Il faut qu[e le musicien] choisisse entre ces trois partis: ou qu'il change de rythme à chaque vers, ce qui serait insupportable; ou qu'il viole la prosodie en coupant les notes et en plaçant les bonnes notes sur les mauvaises syllabes, ce qui n'est guère moins vicieux; ou enfin qu'il fasse un chant *vague, sans caractère déterminé*, qui ne fasse pas trop sentir le rythme, et qui ne choque pas trop la prosodie. Ce dernier procédé est le *moins mauvais*, mais *il n'est pas bon*." Quoted in Fleury, "Du rythme dans la poésie chantée," 345.

38. Maurice Bourges ("*L'Africaine*: Opéra de G. Meyerbeer. La partition," *Revue et gazette musicale de Paris* 32 [1865]: 199) characterized the combination of beats divided in (eighth-note) triplets and sixteenth-notes as "rhythme indécis" and particularly appropriate to the "ivresse" of Sélika's "Scène du mancenillier" in the final act of Meyerbeer's *Africaine*.

39. Huebner, *The Operas of Gounod*, 224.

40. "La marche de notre musique doit être lente et ennuyeuse. Pour peu qu'on voulût en précipiter le movement, la vîtesse ressembleroit à celle d'un corps dur et anguleux qui roule sur le pavé." Quoted in "Lettre de M. de Chabanon, sur les propriétés musicales de la langue françoise," *Le mercure de France*, 3 vols. (January 1773): 1:179.

41. "La servilité intellectuelle d'*il signor poeta* de l'Italie doit cesser, car la monotonie du vers et du rhythme de complaisance produit nécessairement la monotonie mélodique; et il n'y a que les compositeurs médiocres qui doivent désirer la continuation des vers lyriques comme on les a faits jusqu'à ce jour, ces vers

    D'une moitié de rime habillés au hasard,
    Seuls et jetés par ligne exactement pareille,
    De leur chute uniforme importunant l'oreille,
    Ou bouffis de grands mots qui se choquent entr'eux,
    L'un sur l'autre appuyés, se traînant deux à deux.

    Les vieux maîtres de notre école musicale, et surtout Gluck, se sont montrés scrupuleux observateurs de la prosodie et des règles de la déclamation dans leurs mélodie, qui souvent même n'a pas de carrure; et en cela ils sont plus vrais que nos compositeurs modernes, pour qui l'harmonie apprise est presque tout." Henri Blanchard, "Mélodie et poésie," *Revue et gazette musicale de Paris* 20 (1853): 301. The rhyming translation of the verse was generously provided by Thomas J. Mathiesen. Defending the Italian standpoint, Antonio Ghislanzoni warned Italian composers not to draw on librettos structured in the French manner with their "insubordination of meters and verses that to an Italian ear can never be pleasant." Antonio Ghislanzoni, "Conversazioni musicali II," *Gazzetta musicale di Milano* 21 (1866): 75.

42. "[Quest'opera del Verdi] ha delle eleganze d'armonie squisitissime e delle eleganze di ritmo non frequentissime nelle altre opere del grande compositore; il verso francese, meno misurato del nostro, ad accenti più blandi ed indeterminati, giovò alla musica togliendole l'uggia della cantilena, della simmetria, dote grandissima e grandissima pecca della prosodia italiana, che genera quasi inevitabilmente nella frase musicale povertà e grettezza di ritmo. Ma di questa magagna si seppero quasi tutti i nostri grandi forbire, quando musicarono su testo francese." Arrigo Boito, "Cronache dei teatri," in *Tutti gli scritti*, 1119.

43. "Meyerbeer per ottenere l'efficace unione della poesia e della musica, ha rotto quelle catene sotto il peso delle quali i nostri maestri pare che non di mala voglia scrivano. Questo agire independente fruttò a Meyerbeer l'accusa di strano, e capriccioso da quelli che per camminare guardano sempre indietro e mai dinanzi. D'altra parte, coloro che, privi di buon gusto, vogliono nelle belle arti, e per ciò ancora nella musica, la servile imitazione e nulla più, pretendendo che il canto si accosti talmente alla declamazione da scambiarsi quasi tra loro. Ma la musica drammatica non avrebbe ragione di esistere, ove tale fosse la sua mira, e la commedia e la tragedia dovrebbero cacciar del tutto dalla scena l'intruso melodramma, come avvisano alcuni." Abramo Basevi, "*Gli ugonotti* (*Anglicani*) del celebre Mº. Giacomo Meyerbeer al teatro Ferdinando," *L'armonia* 5 (1857): 70.

44. "La subdivision du temps fort peut se faire par deux, par trois, par quatre, par six, etc., comme celle du temps faible; elle a pour résultat de changer complètement le caractère du rhythme; car elle invertit l'ordre naturel, né de ce besoin de régularité dans le mouvement inné chez l'homme;

elle ôte sa force au temps fort, la fait passer au temps faible, et même, dans la mesure à trois temps, au plus faible des trois, au second temps. Aussi, selon les différens degrés de mouvement, et suivant le caractère de la mélodie, elle est propre à exprimer tout ce qui est opposé à l'ordre, depuis la simple négligence jusqu'au désordre le plus absolu ... [L'exemple suivant est empreint] de ce laisser-aller, de cette grâcieuse négligence, dont l'expression a tant de charme." Désiré Beaulieu, *Du rhythme, des effets qu'il produit et de leurs causes* (Paris: Dentu, 1853), 65–6, 68. See also Ex. 2.8.

45. Héctor Berlioz, "Strauss et l'avenir du rythme," in *Cauchemars et passions*, ed. Gérard Condé (Paris: J. C. Lattès, 1981), 127.

46. "Peu de compositeurs ont, au même degré que Meyerbeer, le sentiment du rhythme à la fois original et régulier. J'en trouve un exemple digne de remarque dans cette romance à deux voix, dont j'indique l'harmonie de mémoire [musical example]

D'après les traditions rhythmiques ordinaires, on aurait divisé le premiers [*sic*] vers ainsi:

Un | jour dans les | flots de la | Meuse, etc.

Mais l'auteur du *Prophète*, au lieu de commencer au temps levé de la mesure, a trouvé une forme beaucoup plus originale en commençant au second temps; ce qui donne un caractère inusité, piquant, à toute cette première partie de la phrase musicale. Mais par cette disposition, le second vers: *J'allais périr ... Jean me sauva*, n'aurait produit qu'une phrase de deux mesures, mal cadencé avec la phrase de quatre du premier. Meyerbeer, par la répétition de deux rhythmes nouveaux, a donné à toute la phrase sa carrure complète, tout en conservant une allure libre à ces rhythmes originaux. Dans l'effet général d'une grande oeuvre musicale, le public ne remarque pas ces résultats d'un art très-soigneux des détails, mais le connaisseur en tient compte à l'artiste." Fétis, "*Le Prophète*," 154.

47. Even some French writers commented on this characteristic with bewilderment. For example, in the context of an overall positive evaluation, Gustave Bertrand (*Les nationalités musicales étudiées dans le drame lyrique* [Paris: Didier, 1872], 219) referred to the "tourment" and "inconsistance" of Meyerbeer's rhythms.

48. "Il bello nella melodia drammatica sarà egli solo riposto nella facilità di imprimersi nella memoria sì che si possa ripetere questo o quel tratto subito dopo la prima recita? Non sappiamo crederlo, e stimiamo anzi che al dramma meglio si convenga una certa libertà, una certa artifiziosa trascuranza, purchè diretta ad accrescere evidenza all'espressione, e dignità al carattere, e novità al concetto." Raimondo Boucheron, "Esame dello stato attuale della musica drammatica in Italia," *Gazzetta musicale di Milano* 2 (1843): 210. For criticism of artful melody, see the anonymous "Il maestro Halévy," 101, and Mazzucato, "*Il profeta*," 187–8.

49. Luigi Ferdinando Casamorata, "*Macbeth*, melodramma di F. Piave musicato da Giuseppe Verdi," *Gazzetta musicale di Milano* 6 (1847): 140; and Philoxène Boyer, "Compositeurs du dix-neuvième siècle: Verdi," *La France musicale* 21 (1857): 243. Casamorata claims that predominantly syllabic setting was introduced in France by Gluck, unaware of the fact that it had characterized French opera ever since Lully.

50. "Le mie *cabalette* non scaturivano come acque limpide da purissima fonte, ma erano bensì frutto di qualche meditazione, conciossiacosachè studiava il modo di dare un accento diverso ai metri della poesia, onde non cadere in melodie che ricordassero qualche altro pensiero; cosa troppo facile a verificarsi, specialmente nella *prima battuta*. Adduco l'esempio del modo come

fu trattato il *quinario* dal sommo Rossini e da me: [examples follow.] Lo stesso sistema posi in pratica quasi sempre per tutti gli altri metri, procurando in pari tempo di ottenere più uniformità di pensiero fra la prima parte del tèma e la seconda." Pacini, *Le mie memorie artistiche*, 70. The Rossini examples are from *La donna del lago* (I,7) and *Tancredi* (I,5); the first Pacini example is from *L'ultimo giorno di Pompei* (I,2); the second example, which in Pacini's *Memorie* includes a typo (the eighth notes on the second syllable of "rapidi" should surely be sixteenth notes), is unidentified. I am grateful to Denise Gallo, Francesco Izzo, and Hilary Poriss for their help in trying to identify the Pacini examples.

51. "Solo dirò che quelli che più ammirai, furono Mehul [sic], Boieldieu, poichè più melodici e quadrati degli altri nelle loro composizioni, per quanto la lingua natale il permettesse loro. Ed a proposito di ciò, mi farei lecito osservare che niun'altra nazione potrà mai toglierci il primato in fatto d'ispirazione; imperocchè il nostro dolce idioma, e per conseguenza la nostra poesia regolata dal ritmo e dall'uniformità del verso, sono cause precipue del nostro melodica fraseggiare." Pacini, *Le mie memorie artistiche*, 31–2.

52. See also his *Filosofia della musica o estetica applicata a quest'arte* (Milan: Ricordi, 1842), 120.

53. "Quel restringere i periodi in otto, dodici, o sedici battute come si fa per lo più, quell'appajare i ritmi e le frasi sè, che ciascuna sia seguita da una seconda corrispondente, se può essere indispensabile in una musica da ballo, o in altri generi di piccole proporzioni, può molte volte nuocere alle composizioni grandiose e sconvenire alla ragione drammatica, la quale vuole che tutti i mezzi siano subordinati allo scopo di dipingere i fatti che si rappresentano colla maggior illusione possibile. Da questa servilità proviene in gran parte l'uniformità che guasta molte delle moderne melodie, e la difficoltà di crearne di nuove. Da questa l'esclusione di alcuni metri nella poesia drammatica, i quali potrebbero essere opportuni a coadiuvare l'espressione, e le leggi quasi sempre arbitrarie con cui i maestri martoriano spesso i poeti." Boucheron, "Esame dello stato attuale," 210. See also Basevi, "Se Meyerbeer oggi scrivesse un opera italiana," 22.

54. See Blanchard, "Mélodie et poésie," 301; Choron, *Nouveau manuel*, 136; Bourges, "Situation mélodique actuelle," *Revue et gazette musicale* 13 (1846): 236; Berlioz, "Strauss et l'avenir du rythme," 125–6; and Huebner, *The Operas of Gounod*, 223–50 passim.

55. For a good example by Berlioz with hardly any parallelism, see his *La Damnation de Faust*, particularly Faust's aria "Merci, doux crépuscule!" (IV,9).

56. "L'influenza dell'opera francese si sente nelle opere di Verdi più che in quelle di qualunque altro maestro italiano. Questo nuovo elemento si rivela non solamente nell'armonia, ma penetrò altresì nella melodia turbandone il tranquillo corso con ritmi corti, e duri accenti." Quoted in Italian in "Aristocrazie musicali," 57.

57. "Diremo per ultimo della struttura della melodia, la quale sembra si vada sempre più accostando alle forme della canzonetta, anzichè assumere un fare largo qual si conviene alla drammatica; specialmente se trattasi di argomento serio." Boucheron, "Esame dello stato attuale," 210." See also the reference to "frasi concise" in A. Berti, "Sulla musica di *Roberto il diavolo*," *Gazzetta musicale di Milano* 1 (1842): 202–3.

58. See Mazzucato's review of *Le Prophète* cited above; "Di alcune recenti opinioni intorno al *Simon Boccanegra*," *Gazzetta musicale di Milano* 17 (1859): 46; and Ghislanzoni, "Conversazioni musicali II," 75. The phrase "conducting a melody" is derived from Italian treatises by Francesco Galeazzi (Bathia Churgin, "Francesco Galeazzi's Description [1796] of Sonata Form," *Journal of the American Musicological Society* 21 [1968], 190; "motivo ben condotto" or "ben condotta

Melodia"); or Carlo Gervasoni (*La scuola della musica in tre parti divisa*, 2 vols. [Piacenza: N. Orcesi, 1800], 1:435–6; "la melodia condotta").
59. See Abramo Basevi, *Introduzione ad un nuovo sistema d'armonia* (Florence: Tofani, 1862), 13.
60. Mazzucato, "Il profeta," 187.
61. *Théâtre complet de M. Eugène Scribe*, 14:419.
62. For further examples of this French type of melodic development, see Fidès's arioso "Ah! mon fils" (II,6) from *Le Prophète*; Alice's *romance* "Va, dit-elle" (I,4) and Isabelle's *cavatine* "Robert, toi que j'aime" (IV,2), both from *Robert le diable*; and Halévy's "Ah! sur ton front de rose" (I,8) from *Le Juif errant*. A related way of developing a melody appears also in Italian arias but usually only in connection with a declamatory beginning. For a detailed discussion, see Chapter 3.
63. See, for example, the overwhelming concentration on expression in the reviews of Meyerbeer's operas as collected and annotated by Marie-Hélène Coudroy, *La critique parisienne des "grands opéras" de Meyerbeer*: Robert le diable – Les Huguenots – Le Prophète – L'Africaine (Saarbrücken: Musik-Edition Lucie Galland, 1988).
64. For the former concept, see Fétis, "Le Prophète," 173; for the latter, Aldino Aldini, "Premières représentations. Théâtre impérial italien: *Un ballo in maschera*, opéra en quatre actes, par G. Verdi," *La France musicale* 25 (1861): 18.
65. "Il n'est pas facile d'analyser la partition de M. Verdi, et, ce qui rend surtout notre tâche laborieuse, c'est le défaut capital que nous nous permettons de lui reprocher d'abord. M. Verdi ... est un VÉRITABLE ITALIEN pour qui l'expression dramatique n'a été jusqu'ici qu'un accessoire très secondaire, et à qui il manque surtout de savoir développer une idée ... Je veux parler de cet art (de développement) dont LES HUGUENOTS et ROBERT LE DIABLE nous offrent de si admirables modèles." Excerpt from the *Journal des débats*, quoted in "Jérusalem, opera in quattro atti, parole di Royer e Vaëz, musica di Verdi," *Gazzetta musicale di Milano* 6 (1847): 385.
66. See Vitali, *La musica ne' suoi principj nuovamente spiegata*, 11–12.
67. Alberto Mazzucato, "Problemi musicali: A proposito di una traduzione nuova [by Predari] di un libro vecchio [by Fétis]. Al redattore della gazzetta musicale (lettera settima)," *Gazzetta musicale di Milano* 17 (1859): 2. For criticism of artificiality, see, for example, "Il maestro Halévy," 97–8, 101–2; and "*L'ebrea* di Halévy al T. Carlo Felice di Genova," *L'armonia* 5 (1858): 115–16.
68. See Friedrich Lippmann, *Vincenzo Bellini und die italienische Opera Seria seiner Zeit: Studien über Libretto, Arienform und Melodik*, Analecta musicologica, vol. 6 (Cologne: Böhlau, 1969), 138–9. Lippmann points out that in Bellini, verses 5 and 6 almost always constitute an undivided *b* section.
69. "La novità nella musica," 109–10.
70. "La vera difficoltà per un italiano che scriva sopra un libretto francese, consiste nel dovere musicare dei pezzi che richiedono nuove forme; perchè la poesia destinata al cantabile ora è troppo breve, ora troppo lunga, e quando si ripete molte volte, e quando s'interrompe con dei recitativi. Queste e tante altre cose impediscono di adoprare le forme musicali omai accetate oggigiorno in Italia. Il cambiamento della forma portando seco inevitabilmente un mutamento nella condotta dei pezzi, ne nasce, che, ove si voglia rimanere nello stile italiano, si è obbligati a passare lestamente sopra i versi quando eccedono l'ampiezza richiesta nella forma italiana, o a trattenervisi di troppo ove sieno pochi. Italianizzare adunque un libretto francese equivale in ogni modo ad ampliare la musica italiana, a sopraccaricarla di pleonasmi musicali." Abramo

Basevi, "*Giovanna di Guzman* (*Vespri siciliani*) al teatro Pegliano di Firenze," *L'armonia* 1 (1856): 65.

71. "Ecco che cos'è il canto italiano, l'elemento melodico della nostra musica: egli è indipendente da tutto ciò che non è canto, cioè dire dall'armonia; e non pertanto è bello, sempre bello nella sua sostanza, sia che lo sentiate modulato dalla rozza voce del bifolco, sia dal più abile artista." Pietro Siciliani, *Sulla differente ragione estetica nell'indole della musica tedesca e della musica italiana: Dialogo fra un critico ed un filosofo* (1868), quoted in Mazzucato's review of the book in the *Gazzetta musicale di Milano* 23 (1868): 209–10.

72. See, for example, Marie Escudier, "Mélodies nouvelles par V. Massé," *La France musicale* 25 (1861): 397; and "*Les Troyens à Carthage*: Opéra en cinq actes, paroles et musique de M. Hector Berlioz," *La France musicale* 27 (1863): 350.

73. Fétis seems to have been unaware that harmonic innovation came to France with Italian composers. See pp. 44–5.

74. "A peine eut-il touché le sol de la France, que ses tendances de transformations prirent une détermination plus décidée: *Guillaume Tell* est la plus haute manifestation de ces tendances. Rossini y entre complétement [*sic*] dans le domaine de l'harmonie attractive, et ses mélodies y prennent le caractère harmonique." François-Joseph Fétis, "Troisième lettre aux compositeurs dramatiques." *Revue et gazette musicale de Paris* 20 (1853): 445.

75. "'Maître, lui dit-il, je viens vous soumettre mon grand ouvrage à double choeur et à double orchestre, intitulé *le Jugement dernier*, et vous demander, comme un service, de me dire franchement si je suis né pour la composition et si je dois persister à suivre cette carrière. Je vous prie, surtout, de porter votre attention sur le point capital de mon oeuvre. Au moment où les morts se lèvent de leur sépulcre, on entend un morceau qui sera terrible, par la raison qu'il est tout entier distribué aux instruments de cuivre, jouant à huit parties réelles, avec huit paires de timbales, huit petites flûtes et trois cents enfants de choeur qui, jusque là, n'avaient pas articulé un son.'

Rossini jeta sur l'auteur du *Jugement dernier* un coup d'oeil méfiant, examina la partition et lui dit: —C'est très-bien; maintenant, faites-moi un petit air accompagné sur le piano, par deux accords seulement, l'accord de tonique et l'accord de dominante, et je verrai si vous êtes né pour la composition et si je dois, en conscience, vous engager à poursuivre cette carrière.'" Oscar Comettant, "De l'expression en musique," *L'art musical* 1 (1861): 178. This anecdote was very likely intended as a satire on Hector Berlioz.

76. See François-Joseph Fétis, "Dangers de la situation actuelle de la musique dramatique, 4.

77. Fétis specifically applies the term to Théodora's *strophe* from act III of Halévy's *Le Juif errant*. The first two parallel phrases consist of four clearly separated motives in a short 2/4 meter, two elements that cannot be responsible for the style's breadth. The harmonies include only I and V^7, the latter from measures 3 to 7. The resistence to resolution in both harmony and melody must have led to Fétis's characterization. See François-Joseph Fétis, "*Le Juif errant*: Grand opéra en cinq actes. La musique," *Revue et gazette musicale de Paris* 19 (1852): 153. Melodies with considerable harmonic interest, often for purely coloristic reasons, also appear in Meyerbeer's operas, for example Isabelle's cavatine "En vain j'espère" (*Robert le diable*, II,1); Valentine's melody "Mais comment, par quelle adresse" from the duet Valentine-Marcel "Dans la nuit où seul je veille" (*Les Huguenots*, III,3); and Fidès's "Comme un éclair" (*Le Prophète*, V,3). For a good example by Auber, see Alphonse's "O toi jeune victime" from *La Muette de Portici*, I,1.

78. "Si le maestro à la mode manque d'originalité et d'invention dans la mélodie, son imagination n'est pas plus riche dans l'instrumentation et dans le rhythme des accompagnements. Il n'a qu'une manière, qu'une formule pour chaque chose, et depuis sa première partition jusqu'à la dernière, il se montre partout le même, avec une obstination désespérante. Pour les airs et les duos, il s'est emparé d'une forme d'accompagnement des thèmes mis en usage par Bellini et Donizetti. Cette forme est toujours celle-ci: [example follows.]" Fétis, "Verdi," *Revue et gazette musicale de Paris* 17 (1850): 323.
79. "Dès ses premiers ouvrages, dès *Ernani* et *Les Lombards*, on remarqua cette inspiration chaude et fougueuse qui oublie d'être distinguée, ces violences de rhythme et de sonorité qui se dispensent souvent d'invention mélodique ... Quand ses romances parlent d'amour et de soupirs, il n'en faut pas croire un mot: au fond cela crie: Aux armes!" Bertrand, *Les nationalités musicales étudiées dans le drame lyrique*, 341–2.
80. R., "*Nabuco* et les Verdistes," *Revue et gazette musicale de Paris* 12 (1845): 357. The rhyming translation was generously provided by Philip Gossett.
81. For a detailed study of French orchestration, see William Edward Runyan, "Orchestration in Five French Grand Operas" (Ph.D. diss., University of Rochester, 1983).
82. Raoul's "Plus blanche que la blanche hermine" (*Les Huguenots*, I,2) offers a particularly good example (see Ex. 2.11).
83. "Meyerbeer ne se borne pas, comme les Italiens, à loger tout l'intérêt dans la mélodie vocale, dont il soigne pourtant au plus haut degré les formes, les allures, les rhythmes appropriés franchement au sujet. Il fait plus: il confie à l'accompagnement un rôle qui a toujours de l'importance. Pour lui, l'accompagnement est le jeu de physionomie, le geste, la pantomime éloquente qui révèle tout ce que la voix ne dit pas et n'a pu dire. De l'accompagnement il fait un interprète habile, une paraphrase, une glose [*sic*] intelligente qui détaille toutes les sensations et met en relief les accessoires, sans pousser cependant jusqu'à l'abus du pittoresque, ce fléau de l'art contemporain. Aussi, point de formules banales, friperies qui traînent sous les plus folies pensées italiennes, françaises, et même dans les *lieder* allemands des dernières années." Maurice Bourges, "Quarante mélodies à une et à plusieurs voix, par G. Meyerbeer (deuxième article)," *Revue et gazette musicale de Paris* 17 (1850): 158.
84. "Ma poi, a poco a poco, sera per sera, tendendo l'orecchio, il pubblico s'avvisò che l'aurora di Münster aveva qualche cosa di bello e di vero che non era nell'apparato elettrico, nelle bandiere sventolanti, nei ghiacci argentati, ma in una cert'aria, in una certa atmosfera, in un certo ...

    incognito indistinto ...,

che volitava in orchestra, nei cori, nei ritmi, nelle note potenti, e sentì in cuore il misterioso contatto d'un genio novissimo." Boito, "Cronaca dei teatri [Dal *Figaro*, 18 Feb. 1864]," in *Tutti gli scritti*, 1121.

Episode: Design, middleground rhythm, and phrase

1. See, for example, Francesco Galeazzi, *Elementi teorico-pratici di musica con un saggio sopra l'arte di suonare il violino analizzata, ed a dimostrabili principi ridotta, opera utilissima a chiunque vuol applicar con profitto alla musica e specialmente a' principianti dilettanti, e professori*

di violino, 2 vols. (Rome: Pilucchi Cracas, 1791; Rome: Michele Puccinelli, 1796); Gervasoni, *La scuola della musica*; Bonifazio Asioli, *Il maestro di composizione ossia seguito del trattato d'armonia*, 4 vols. (Milan: Ricordi, [1832?]); Geremia Vitali, *La musica ne' suoi principj nuovamente spiegata*; and Antoine Reicha, *Traité de mélodie: Abstraction faite de ses rapports avec l'harmonie, suivi d'un supplément sur l'art d'accompagner la mélodie par l'harmonie, lorsque la première est prédominante, le tout appuyé sur les meilleurs modèles mélodiques*, 2d ed. (Paris: S. Richault, 1832).

2. Joseph Kerman, "Lyric Form and Flexibility in *Simon Boccanegra*, *Studi verdiani* 1 (1982): 55–7. Nor does Budden define his concept of phrase, relying instead on intuition. In his analysis of the act II duet between Don Carlos and Élisabeth, the *b* phrases of an *aab* complex could often be divided into separate phrases (*The Operas of Verdi*, 3:76, ex. 36e), or some shorter phrases could be taken together to form longer parallel phrases (3:74, ex. 36c). Budden's approach suggests that he would have labeled the beginning of "L'atra magion vedete" differently from Kerman, substituting for the *a* and *a'* phrases a complete *aab* set.

3. See Grosvenor W. Cooper and Leonard B. Meyer, *The Rhythmic Structure of Music* (University of Chicago Press, 1960); Maury Yeston, *The Stratification of Musical Rhythm* (New Haven: Yale University Press, 1976); and Joel Lester, *The Rhythms of Tonal Music* (Carbondale: Southern Illinois University Press, 1986).

4. For a survey of this aspect of Italian music theory during the first half of the nineteenth century, see Friedrich Wedell, *Annäherung an Verdi: Zur Melodik des jungen Verdi und ihren musiktheoretischen und ästhetischen Voraussetzungen* (Kassel: Bärenreiter, 1995), 19–145.

5. Italian discussions of phrasing in terms of harmony lose prominence in the course of the first half of the century. While Galeazzi (*Elementi teorico-pratici di musica*, 2:260–3) and Gervasoni (*La scuola della musica*, 409–14, 430–3) still treat various types of cadences and their relation to phrasing, later theorists, such as Asioli, Ritorni, or Vitali, prefer to focus on aspects of text–music relationship. In our analyses, we apply with some small modifications the commonly used modern terminology as described in the original *MGG*. See Wilhelm Pfannkuch, "Kadenz und Klausel," in *Die Musik in Geschichte und Gegenwart*, ed. Friedrich Blume (Kassel: Bärenreiter, 1958), 7:412–13.

6. The term "quarter cadence" is borrowed from Reicha, who uses it, however, to describe a type of melodic cadence. He fails to define it clearly.

7. We follow the standard way of counting, according to which upbeats are ignored and measures with only a cadential downbeat count as a full measure.

8. In its italianized form as *disegno*, the term *dessin* also made its way into Italian treatises as in, for example, Vitali's *La musica ne' suoi principj nuovamente spiegata*. Reicha's term *rhythme* primarily refers to the phrase length and the regular sequence of melodic cadences at the end of each phrase; the term *membre*, however, aims at the thematic composition of a phrase.

9. "Quand un dessin mélodique est aussi court, et qu'il a une cadence aussi faible, il faut au moins qu'il soit répète [*sic*], avec d'autres notes, et qu'il ait la seconde fois une cadence plus marquée; alors la Mélodie aura un sens plus déterminé, parce que cette répétition la fixe davantage ... Une pareille répétition nous l'appellerons un *rhythme* ...

Un dessin, pour qu'on puisse le distinguer d'un dessin suivant, doit avoir au moins un quart de cadence, c'est-à-dire un petit point de repos, qui existe, 1°. dans une pause, ou, 2°. dans une note plus longue. Bref, il faut qu'il se trouve nécessairement quelque chose à la fin d'un dessin, aussi petite que cette différence puisse être, pour le distinguer du commencement du suivant." Reicha, *Traité de mélodie*, 9, 14.

10. Reicha developed a theory of melody that entirely disregards harmonic cadences. In a *supplément*, he admits, however, that harmony and melody must correspond because discrepancies would destroy the overall effect: "The harmonic cadences must correspond with the melodic ones, i.e., when the melody makes a half cadence, the harmony must do the same. Because if under a perfect melodic cadence the harmony makes a different one (a deceptive cadence, for example), the melodic period, which should come to a close, is interrupted and does not end at all. In short, badly placed harmonic cadences destroy the melodic cadences and consequently the rhythm of the melody. This means that a melody, however well phrased, produces, when considered without its harmony, the effect of a badly phrased melody... It is one of the most important points in this marriage that [the composer] have a profound knowledge and carefully observe the correspondence between harmonic and melodic cadences, without which the melodic points of rest and rhythms are infallibly destroyed – and thereby the melodic interest." Reicha, *Traité de mélodie*, 89–90. Our method of grouping notes is related to that of Cooper and Meyer and is based on musical parameters ranging from various kinds of proximity (pitch, instrumentation, harmony) to patterns, articulation, and the tendency toward end-accentuation. See Cooper and Meyer, *The Rhythmic Structure of Music*, Chapter 2. The requirement of some sort of cadence, however, usually leads to designs that may be considerably longer than Cooper and Meyer's first-level rhythmic groups.
11. See also Peter M. Landey's introduction to Anton Reicha's *Treatise on Melody*, trans. Peter M. Landey, Harmonologia, vol. 10 (Hillsdale, NY: Pendragon Press, 2000), xv.
12. The term *middleground rhythm* is borrowed from Yeston, *The Stratification of Musical Rhythm*, but the concept also appears in other studies, including Cooper and Meyer, *The Rhythmic Structure of Music*.

Chapter 3 *Jérusalem* and its influence on the subsequent Italian operas

1. Verdi in a letter of June 27, 1847, to Giuseppina Appiani. *Copialettere*, 458.
2. Verdi in a letter of August 22, 1847, to Giuseppina Appiani. *Copialettere*, 462.
3. David R. B. Kimbell, "Verdi's First *Rifacimento*: *I lombardi* and *Jérusalem*," *Music & Letters* 60 (1979): 1–2. For another extensive discussion of the revisions, see Giuseppe Pugliese, *Gerusalemme*, Quaderni dell'istituto di studi verdiani, ed. Mario Medici, vol. 2 (Parma: Istituto di studi verdiani, [1963]).
4. Kimbell, "Verdi's First *Rifacimento*," 23; see also Budden, *The Operas of Verdi*, 1:348; and Pugliese, *Gerusalemme*, 58–9.
5. Kimbell, "Verdi's First *Rifacimento*," 23.
6. In the coda, too, Verdi avoided strong accentuation on an *e muet*: he removed the syncopation on "così da te lontan<u>o</u>" (which would have led to "en vain en vain espèr<u>e</u>") and replaced it with a smoother rhythmic figure.
7. For Benloew's approach, see Chapter 1, 10–11.
8. This rare case of borrowing was first discussed in David Rosen and David Lawton's "Verdi's Non-Definitive Revisions: The Early Operas," in *Atti del III° congresso internazionale di studi*

verdiani, 199; and Roger Parker, "'Infin che un brando vindice' e le cavatine del primo atto di *Ernani*," in *Verdi: Bollettino dell' Istituto di studi verdiani*, no. 10 (1987): 144–5, 160.

9. See Moreen, "Integration of Text Forms and Musical Forms in Verdi's Early Operas," 128–30.
10. In this particular case, Verdi may have believed that the contrast of a long note on "t'a" and a series of subsequent shorter notes on "livré sa" would better reflect the violent emotion of the text.
11. Where sketches allow tracing the compositional process from continuity draft to the final version of the same opera, we occasionally notice that Verdi removed syncopations during a later stage of a work's gestation. See, for instance, the final portion of example 7 in Kathleen Kuzmick Hansell's "Compositional Techniques in *Stiffelio*: Reading the Autograph Sources," in *Verdi's Middle Period, 1849–1859: Source Studies, Analysis, and Performance Practice*, ed. Martin Chusid (University of Chicago Press, 1997), 76.
12. Kimbell repeatedly refers to smoother rhythms. See his "Verdi's First *Rifacimento*," 28, 31.
13. See Chapter 1, 36.
14. The prosodic interpretation above follows Quicherat; see Chapter 1, 12–13.
15. For an extensive treatment of this problem, see Gossett, "Translations and Adaptations of Operatic Texts."
16. "[C]ette scène est celle de la dégradation, qui ne se trouve pas dans *I Lombardi*, et que le compositeur a écrite entièrement en collaboration avec MM. Royer et Vaëz. Le succès a couronné cette alliance. La grande supériorité du cinquième tableau sur tous les autres est d'heureux augure pour l'avenir lyrique de M. Verdi, et nous révèle ce que nous pourrions attendre de son talent, s'il travaillait jamais, non plus sur un canevas italien, mais sur un libretto et avec les conseils de M. Scribe. Ici du moins, tout est profondément dramatique: la marche funèbre du cortége [*sic*] qui vient se ranger autour de l'échafaud, la prière si pathétique adressée par Gaston à ses frères d'armes, sa fureur, son désespoir, et quand tout lui manque sur la terre, cet appel à Dieu, son dernier, son unique refuge! M. Verdi a compris et rendu en maître chacun des détails de cette belle situation; il a trouvé des accens simples et pénétrans pour la prière, des élans d'indignation pour l'honneur révolté, et surtout il a cette fois obéi à la règle dont nous parlions plus haut, il a été l'interprète fidèle de la passion de son personnage, il l'a suivie dans tous ses développemens, repoussant toute tradition d'école, toute routine de système; en un mot, il a été vrai, et il doit sentir maintenant ce qui peut sortir d'émotions et de puissance de cette source sacrée à laquelle il vient peut-être de puiser pour la première fois." E. Ds., "Feuilleton du *Journal des débats* du 28 Novembre 1847. Académie Royale de Musique, Première représentation de *Jérusalem* ...," *Journal des débats politiques et littéraires*, November 28, 1847.
17. "Une pièce de vers destinée à la musique doit donc, autant que possible, n'être que le développement d'un même sentiment ou de sentiments similaires et présenter peu d'images ou des images sans grand relief, et du même caractère général que celui du morceau." Charles Beauquier, *La musique et le drame: Étude d'esthétique*, 2d ed. (Paris: Fischbacher, 1884), 62.
18. For other typical examples, see "Tremin gl'insani" (*Nabucco*, I,7) and "T'arretri e palpiti" (*Giovanna d'arco*, I,4). Like Verdi, Rossini frequently begins his arias with a melody lacking a sustained accompaniment. But unlike Verdi, he greatly embellishes the melodic line, occasionally following it with not one but (as in Amenaide's cavatina "Come dolce all'alma mia" from *Tancredi*)

two lyrical melodies. It is possible that Rossini's works introduced such multi-melody arias to France early in the century before they returned to Italy as a French influence.
19. See Chapter 2, 72.
20. For the approach of Lubarsch and Landry, see Chapter 1, 12–14.
21. See Kimbell, "Verdi's First *Rifacimento*," 21.
22. The operas considered in this context are *Il corsaro* (1848), *La battaglia di Legnano* (1849), *Luisa Miller* (1849), and *Stiffelio* (1850). *Il corsaro* has long been viewed as having one foot in the pre- and one in the post-*Jérusalem* period. Phillips-Matz (*Verdi*, 226) and Budden (*The Operas of Verdi*, 1:364), for example, state that one of the most interesting numbers, the prison duet of Act III, had been at least sketched out as early as August 1846. In her critical edition of *Il corsaro*, however, Elizabeth Hudson questions this assumption, advancing the lack of evidence (a continuity draft of this number, for example). See Elizabeth Hudson, introduction to *Il corsaro*, The Works of Giuseppe Verdi, I/13 (University of Chicago Press, 1998), xix.
23. In the version with parallel eight-measure phrases, the prototype may include four designs per phrase.
24. For a musical example, see "La mia letizia infondere" (Ex. 3.1). The term "thematic block" is borrowed from Lippmann ("Der italienische Vers und der musikalische Rhythmus," 15:309–10). See also Giorgio Pagannone, "Mobilità strutturale della *lyric form*: Sintassi verbale e sintassi musicale nel melodramma italiano del primo ottocento," *Analisi* 7 (1996): 4–5.
25. For example in Foresto's "Che non avrebbe il misero" (*Attila*, III,2). Other instances of this thematic block in the four operas following *Jérusalem* include: "Tutto parea sorridere" in *Il corsaro* (I,2); "La pia materna mano" (I,1), "Quante volte come un dono" (I,4), and "Vendetta d'un momento" (III,10) in *La battaglia di Legnano*; "O meco incolume" in *Luisa Miller* (II,4); and "Vidi dovunque gemere" (I,4) and "Me disperato abbruciano" (II,7) in *Stiffelio*.
26. "Noble guerrier" (Ex. 3.8) conforms with the basic phrase structure $a,a',a''/b$ but not with the durational proportion of the phrases of 1:1:2.
27. Another example of a French ternary form is the Marchesa's "Si mostri a chi l'adora" (*Un giorno di regno*, II,6). In this aria, however, the contrast between the two melodies is deliberately exaggerated in order to indicate to the audience that the second quatrain is an aside.
28. Budden, *The Operas of Verdi*, 1:398.

Chapter 4 *Les Vêpres siciliennes* and its influence on the subsequent Italian operas

1. Phillips-Matz (*Verdi*, 338) claims that the two men met in the summer of 1854 but does not provide any supporting evidence.
2. See Andrew Porter, "*Les Vêpres siciliennes*: New Letters from Verdi to Scribe," *19th Century Music* 2 (1978): 95; idem, "Don't Blame Scribe!," 26; and Andreas Giger, "Neue Briefe von Scribe an Verdi und das 'Problem' des fünften Aktes von *Les Vêpres siciliennes*," in *Eugène Scribe und das europäische Musiktheater des 19. Jahrhunderts*, ed. Sebastian Werr and Daniel Brandenburg, Forum Musiktheater, vol. 6 (Berlin: LIT, 2007), 189–214.
3. "Je vous envoye les vers que vous me demandez, vous les trouverez sur la page à coté et s'ils ne vous vont pas bien, je vous en ferai d'autres [I am sending you the verses you request from me; you'll find them on the facing page, and if you don't like them, I'll make you others]." Letter of June 9, 1854, from Scribe to Verdi, located at Sant'Agata and available on microfilm at the

American Institute for Verdi Studies at New York University. This letter and four others from Scribe to Verdi appear in my "Neue Briefe von Scribe an Verdi," 191.

4. "Je viens solliciter votre complaisance pour un petit changement dans le second acte – J'aurais besoin que le choeur: *O bonheur! O delice* au lieu d'avoir des vers de *sept* en eut *de huit* comme par example

O martyr de la patrie
Pour briser la tyrannie

vous pouvez conserver /si ca vous convient/ les mêmes idées, les mêmes rimes, seulement soyez assez bon pour en changer le rhythme en vers de *huit*." Quoted in Porter, "New Letters from Verdi to Scribe," 101. Porter preserves Verdi's spelling. Verdi is counting the syllables according to the Italian system.

5. "Huit vers pour les siciliens, huit pour les Francais /ou si vous voulez seulement huits vers ensemble Siciliens et Francais/ plus huits vers pour les femmes qui presentent les fleurs à Hélène. J'aimerais que le rhitme fut comme ces vers

Fortune cruelle
Tu viens m'accabler:
Mais un seul mot d'elle
Peut me consoler!

Ils se pretent fort bien pour un 3/8." Quoted in ibid., 103.

6. See Table 1.3 in Chapter 1, 36.

7. "Pour le moment j'aurais besoin d'avoir un beau *Cantabile* à la place de '*Tout respire un air de fête*'. Sur trois vers c'est impossible pour moi de faire une frase melodique. Il m'en faudrait quatre, c'est a dire 8. Tachez de leur donner une tournure plus pathétique, et que le rhythme soit comme

'Ami! le coeur d'Hélène,
Pardonne au repentir -'"

Quoted in Porter, "New Letters from Verdi to Scribe," 106.

8. See Chapter 1, 36.

9. For the approaches according to Benloew and Quicherat, see Chapter 1, 10–11 and 12–13, respectively.

10. See Chapter 2, 49–51; and Damien Colas, "'Quels accents! quel langage!': Examen du traitement de l'alexandrin dans *Les Vêpres siciliennes*," in *L'Opéra en France et en Italie (1791–1925): Une scène privilégiée d'échanges littéraires et musicaux*, ed. Hervé Lacombe, Publications de la Société française de musicologie, III/8 (Paris: Société française de musicologie, 2000), 213–14, where he points out that Verdi usually avoids isometric interpretation in noble situations.

11. The number is inexplicably labeled "Sicilienne" in the score. Only the libretto includes the heading "Bolero."

12. Honorat du Bueil, Seigneur de Racan, 1589–1670. French poet. He was one of the earliest members of the Académie Française (1635) and author of bucolic and religious poems.

13. Jean Regnault de Segrais, 1624–1701. French poet. His works include *Bérénice* (novel, 1648–1651), *Athys* (verse, 1653), *Poésies diverses* (1658), and verse translations of Virgil's *Aeneid* and *Georgics*.
14. "La romance de Henri continue le genre harmonieux et doux adopté par le musicien pendant tout ce début de l'acte. Ici les vers sans être rivaux de ceux de Lamartine, avaient une certaine grâce de style qui pouvait jusqu'à un certain point l'inspirer:

    La brise souffle ...

    C'est du Racan ou du Ségrais [sic] tout pur. Verdi ne pouvait que suivre cette pente et faire du genre pittoresque et imitatif: il y a parfaitement réussi et son orchestration est très-agréablement colorée." Quoted in Gartioux, *Giuseppe Verdi*, Les Vêpres siciliennes, 75.
15. See Chapter 2, 61–2.
16. See Scribe's letter to Charles Duveyrier, quoted (without date) in Paul Bonnefon, Les métamorphoses d'un opéra: Lettres inédites d'Eugène Scribe," *Revue des deux mondes* 41 (1971): 892; and Porter, "New Letters from Verdi to Scribe," 105.
17. Anselm Gerhard, *Die Verstädterung der Oper: Paris und das Musiktheater des 19. Jahrhunderts* (Stuttgart: Metzler, 1992), 338–42.
18. I am trying to balance Gerhard's view in my "Neue Briefe von Scribe an Verdi."
19. See Chapter 2, 58.
20. The accent on "un" is a typical *accent logique*. See Chapter 1, 16–17.
21. See Chapter 1, 12–14.
22. The approach of Lubarsch and Landry, of course, is often applied to *versi sciolti* and non-stanzic verse, neither of which is the focus of this study.
23. For stanzaic requirements, see Chapter 1, 19–33.
24. It may be for this reason that the *décasyllabes* of "Et toi, Palerme" was translated into *quinari doppi*, not into *endecasillabi*. See Gossett, "Translations and Adaptations of Operatic Texts," 290–1.
25. For examples, see Lippmann, *Der italienische Vers und der musikalische Rhythmus*, 12:321–69.
26. Colas, "'Quels accents! Quel langage!,'" 212.
27. For the concept of middleground rhythm, see the Episode, 83–5.
28. See Chapter 1, 8–9.
29. For a discussion of mid-century lyric form, see Chapter 2, 70–2.
30. See Aimé Victor Becq de Fouquières, *Traité général de versification française* (Paris: G. Charpentier, 1879), 188–93, 308–13.
31. Porter, "New Letters from Verdi to Scribe," 106.
32. Alberto Mazzucato, "*Giovanna de Guzman*," *Gazzetta musicale di Milano* 14 (1856): 82, 105.
33. "Parliamo della magniloquenza ritmica. E difatti è mestieri convenire che sebbene le melodie della *Giovanna de Guzman* sieno ben lungi da quell'eccesso di dimensione, di che abbiam più volte fatto rimprovero alla scuola di Mercadante, presentano tuttavia una *larghezza* di concetti sensibilmente più marcata che in tutti i precedenti spartiti di Verdi. Dal che un aumento di severità, di solennità, ed in conseguenza una qualche diminuzione di popolarità, di impeto, di concisione." Ibid., 106. The reference to Saverio Mercadante is no coincidence. Between 1835

and 1840, Mercadante reformed his style according to French aesthetics, including a more heavy focus on declamation. See David Kimbell, *Italian Opera* (Cambridge University Press, 1991), 477–8.

34. Most notably by Berlioz in "Opinion de Berlioz sur *Les Vêpres siciliennes*," 314.
35. Other prominent examples with corresponding melodic pulse and middleground rhythm in the opening designs: "Fidèle à ses leçons" (Henri; I,5), "Je suis libre" (Henri; I,5), "Au sein de la puissance" (Montfort; III,3), "Malheureux et non coupable" (Henri; IV,2), and "Pour moi rayonne" (Henri; IV,2).
36. This discussion of thematic blocks has previously been published in Andreas Giger, "Reconsidering *Les Vêpres siciliennes* in the Context of French Aesthetic Thought," in *Verdi 2001: Atti del Convegno internazionale / Proceedings of the International Conference (Parma – New York – New Haven, 24 January–1 February 2001)*, ed. Fabrizio Della Seta, Roberta Montemorra Marvin, and Marco Marica, 2 vols. consecutively paginated (Florence: Leo S. Olschki, 2003), 534–6.
37. In the printed libretto, this quatrain appears as a perfectly rhyming stanza; in the score, verses 1 and 3 no longer rhyme.
38. Phrases must be more than one measure long. Phrases of an odd number of measures are considered irregular unless a measure of orchestral transition turns the phrase into a phrase of an even number of measures.
39. The irregularity is created by the repetition of the motto "Morrò" at the very beginning of the cabaletta. Had Verdi left out the emphatic first "Morrò," the thematic block would have been perfectly regular.
40. "In tempo *largo*, si manifesta il motivo *Deh tu calma*, nella forma tante volte adoprata da Verdi, che consiste nel ripetere la *mossa* d'un *motivo* senza risolverla, creando in tal modo la prima frase del motivo medesimo. Questa forma, oltre ad essere il più delle volte contraria all'espressione drammatica, rivela per se stessa gran povertà d'immaginazione." Basevi, "*Giovanna di Guzman*," 66.
41. Budden (*The Operas of Verdi*, 1:323) identifies Carlo's "O mio castel paterno" (*I masnadieri*, I,1) as Verdi's first example of this kind of non-developmental thematic block. On another occasion ("Verdi and Meyerbeer in Relation to *Les Vêpres siciliennes*," *Studi verdiani* 1 [1982]: 11–13), he criticizes this style in Meyerbeer's operas.
42. Basevi, "*Giovanna di Guzman*," 67.
43. Compare this principle with Halévy's "Si la rigueur" (*La juive*, I,4), discussed in Chapter 2, 73–5. I do not mean to suggest that all of Verdi's thematic blocks prior to *Les Vêpres siciliennes* follow the simple harmonic progressions of "Dite alla giovine." "Tutto parea sorridere" (*Il corsaro*, I,2), for example, which also begins with a long arch, touches on the third scale degree (C major) of its key (A-flat major).
44. Some critics saw in *Les Vêpres siciliennes* a purely Italian work – Mazzucato in a positive sense, Basevi in a negative one.
45. "Fra i difetti notati in questo spartito è capitale quello che si riferisce alla mancanza di nesso e di relazione fra i pensieri melodici; di guisa che più presto che fusi appariscono cuciti fra loro, con danno del linguaggio musicale il quale, comunque composto di frazioni regolarissime in sè, sembra così procedere senza intendimento alcuno." Pietro Torrigiani, "*I vespri siciliani* a Parma," 6.

46. Transitional sections in Verdi's early and middle-period operas often help clarify the customary large-scale form, but sometimes they also link unusual sequences of stanzas. See, for example, the long duet between Violetta and Giorgio Germont in *La traviata* (II,5). It features the following structure:

versi sciolti (*scena*)
"Pura siccome un angelo" (stanza of *settenari*)
versi sciolti
"Non sapete quale affetto" (two stanzas of *ottonari*)
"È grave il sagrifizio" (*settenari* often divided, not inviting full-fledged lyrical setting)
"Un dì, quando le veneri" (stanza of *settenari*)
"Così alla misera, – ch'è un dì caduta" (stanzas of *quinari doppi*)
versi sciolti
"Morrò!... la mia memoria" (stanzas of *settenari*)

47. "Noi non abbiamo sott'occhio il testo francese: ma sembra per altro che lo Scribe nel pezzo di sortita del soprano intendesse a che il compositore vi ordisse una di quelle arie a strofe, o a couplets, assai comuni nel teatro francese, e non forse abbastanza usate invece nell'opera italiana: sembra, diciamo; dacchè per verità nella traduzione italiana la fattura poetica dei tre couplets non appare, quanto al metro, simmetrica come sarebbe di dovere, mentre la prima coppia di strofe ha metro differente da quello delle altre due coppie: ed inoltre, guardando separatamente queste due ultime, il sentimento de' primi quattro versi dell'una è troppo opposto a quello de' primi quattro versi dell'altra perchè possano sopportare un'identica od almeno analoga melodia; stantechè è il primo un sentimento di coraggio, l'altro di sconforto. Nondimeno è manifesto che il pezzo avrebbe dovuto presentare la forma lirica, simmetrica, dell'ode, della ballata, della canzone, dell'inno." Alberto Mazzucato, "*Giovanna de Guzman*," 260.

48. Eugène Scribe, *Giovanna de Guzman (musica de' Vespri siciliani): Opera-ballo in 5 atti posta in musica dal M. Cavaliere Giuseppe Verdi da rappresentarsi al Teatro Regio nel Carneval-Quaresima 1855-1856* (Turin: Giuseppe Fodratti, [1855]), 11.

49. Such chains of basically short melodies explain why critics often did not point to specific arias but to individual sections. For example: "Nothing more pure than the phrase 'Ami, le coeur d'Hélène pardonne au repentir,' nothing more tenderly passionate than the one 'Je t'aime heureuse et fière / De mourir en t'aimant'" (A. Basset, "Théâtre impérial de l'Opéra: Première représentation des *Vêpres siciliennes*, opéra en 5 actes, de MM. Scribe et Duveyrier, musique de M. Verdi," *La patrie*, July 10, 1855, quoted in Gartioux, *Giuseppe Verdi*, Les Vêpres siciliennes, 104); "One certainly noticed this phrase filled with charm and sentiment: 'Pour moi, quelle ivresse inconnue, / De contempler ses traits chéris!'" (P.-A. Fiorentino, "Théâtre de l'Opéra. *Les Vêpres siciliennes*, opéra en cinq actes, paroles de MM. E. Scribe et Charles Duveyrier, musique de M. Verdi," *Le constitutionnel*, June 15, 1855, quoted in Gartioux, *Giuseppe Verdi*, Les Vêpres siciliennes, 43); and "The duo following this aria is one of the most developed and best pieces of the work. In the *largo*, one loudly applauded, and rightly so, a wonderful phrase: 'Tu vois mon trouble et mes alarmes / Et ton coeur n'est pas étonné!'" (A. De Rovray, "Théâtre impérial de l'Opéra. *Les Vêpres siciliennes*, Opéra en cinq actes; paroles de MM. Eugène Scribe et Charles Duveyrier, musique de M. Verdi," *Le moniteur universel*, June 17, 1855, quoted in Gartioux, *Giuseppe Verdi*, Les Vêpres siciliennes, 50).

50. Torrigiani, "*I vespri siciliani* a Parma," 6; Basevi, "*Giovanna di Guzman*," 66.
51. Ibid.
52. See Harold Powers, "Aria sfasciata, duetto senza l'insieme: Le scene di confronto tenore-soprano nello *Stiffelio/Aroldo* di Giuseppe Verdi," in *Tornando a Stiffelio: Popolarità, rifacimenti, messinscena, effettismo e altre 'cure' nella drammaturgia del Verdi romantico*, ed. Giovanni Morelli (Florence: Olschki, 1987), 187.
53. *Copialettere*, 709.
54. For a detailed article on the *Trouvère* revisions, see David Lawton, "*Le trouvère*: Verdi's Revision of *Il trovatore* for Paris," *Studi verdiani* 3 (1985): 79–119. I am grateful to Professor Lawton for an advance copy of his introduction to the critical edition of *Le trouvère*. In this introduction, he no longer questions Verdi's authorship, unambiguously referring to the "important revisions by the composer." See also Budden, *The Operas of Verdi*, 2:107–12.
55. The musical examples of the French version are taken from Lawton's "*Le trouvère*: Verdi's Revision of *Il trovatore* for Paris," 114.
56. The list of sources discussing Verdi's revisions for the Paris *Macbeth* is much longer than that for *Jérusalem* or *Le trouvère*. The most important study, which also includes most of the deleted sections of the 1847 *Macbeth* in vocal score, remains David Rosen and Andrew Porter's *Verdi's Macbeth: A Sourcebook* (New York: Norton, 1984). See also Giuseppe Verdi, *Macbeth*, 2 vols., ed. David Lawton, The Works of Giuseppe Verdi, I/10 (University of Chicago Press, 2005).
57. In the duet cabaletta "Vieni altrove! ogni sospetto" (I,15) for example, the revisions in the setting of Macbeth's quatrain ("Deh potessi il mio delitto") can be explained more convincingly by Verdi's attempt to avoid loss of momentum than by French aesthetics. Furthermore, the subsequent text ("Deh, sapessi, o Re trafitto / L'alto sonno a te spezzar!") does not justify the new broad melody of the first version, since the distich mirrors the preceding one in both structure and emotional content.
58. Scanning against accents had long been common in Italian operas, especially in *quinari*, regardless of the dramatic situation. See, for example, "L<u>a</u> tomba è un l<u>e</u>tto – sp<u>a</u>rso di f<u>io</u>ri" (*Luisa Miller*, III,2), "D<u>i</u> quella p<u>i</u>ra – l'<u>o</u>rrendo f<u>o</u>co" (*Il trovatore*, III,6), and "L<u>a</u> donna è m<u>o</u>bile" (*Rigoletto*, III,2).
59. See Budden, *The Operas of Verdi*, 2:329.
60. A vague sense of rhythm also appears in settings of poetic meters other than the *ottonario*. A comparison of "Consentimi, o Signore" (*Un ballo in maschera*, I,9) with "E pur l'aere," Carlo's culminating melody from the duet with Giovanna (*Giovanna d'Arco*, I,4), demonstrates the new melodic breadth after *Les Vêpres siciliennes*, achieved mainly through even note values and a rhythmically amorphous tremolo accompaniment.
61. Pierluigi Petrobelli, "De l'alexandrin à l'anapeste chez Verdi: Structure poétique et composition musicale dans *Un ballo in maschera*," in *L'opéra en France et en Italie (1791–1925)*, 215–22.
62. See Chapter 2, 62.
63. Pierluigi Petrobelli, "The Fusion of Styles," in *A Masked Ball/Un ballo in maschera*, ed. Nicholas John, English National Opera Guide, vol. 40 (London: Riverrun Press, 1989), 12.
64. See Exx. 2.13 and 2.14 and Episode, 85–6.
65. Budden, *The Operas of Verdi*, 2:450–1.
66. Examples from types 1 and 2 are often closely related. The shift of examples from type 1 to type 2 between *Vêpres* and *Forza* is the result of an increasing number of melodies in which

development in the second phrase goes just far enough to disqualify the thematic block from belonging to type 1.
67. Even though the short ensuing coda clearly draws on rhythmic elements from the second melody, it begins with a two-measure phrase that could possibly count as an additional melody.
68. Other examples include Riccardo's *canzone* "Di' tu se fedele" (*Un ballo in maschera*, I,10), with new melodies at "Con lacere vele" and "Sollecita esplora"; Leonora's "Me pellegrina ed orfana (*La forza del destino*, I,2), with two new melodies at "Ti lascio, ahimè con lagrime"; and Leonora's "Pace, pace" (*La forza del destino*, IV,6), with new melodies at "Cruda sventura," "L'amai, gli è ver," and "Oh Dio! Dio fa ch'io muoia." "David Kimbell points to the unusual string of melodies of Riccardo's *canzone* from *Un ballo in maschera* in his *Italian Opera*, 555; Budden (*The Operas of Verdi*, 3:107) calls this style the "*Aida* manner."
69. See, for example, Gustave Chadeuil's review in *Le siecle* (June 21, 1855), quoted in Gartioux, *Giuseppe Verdi*, Les Vêpres siciliennes, 84.

Chapter 5 *Don Carlos* and after

1. "C'est du Meyerbeer! disait la foule en sortant, après avoir applaudi." Timothée Trimm on *Don Carlos*, quoted in Gartioux, *Giuseppe Verdi*, Don Carlos, 42.
2. "Somme toute, l'oeuvre est ce qu'elle devait être, un opéra français, non pas un opéra italien." M. de Thémines on *Don Carlos*, quoted in Gartioux, *Giuseppe Verdi*, Don Carlos, 94.
3. See the famous letter of June 19, 1865, to Léon Escudier, quoted in translation in Phillips-Matz, *Verdi*, 500.
4. The history of *Don Carlos* is documented in Ursula Günther, "La genèse de *Don Carlos*, opéra en cinq actes de Giuseppe Verdi, représenté pour la première fois à Paris le 11 mars 1867," *Revue de musicologie* 58 (1972): 16–64 and 60 (1974): 87–158; and in Budden, *The Operas of Verdi*, 3:5–39. Verdi wrote to Arrivabene: "The libretto is completely ready, and it seems in good shape." Annibale Alberti, *Verdi intimo: Carteggio di Giuseppe Verdi con il Conte Opprandino Arrivabene (1861–1886)* (Verona: Mondadori, 1931), 71, quoted in Günther, "Genèse," 38.
5. Ursula Günther, "Le livret français de *Don Carlos*: Le premier acte et sa révision par Verdi," in *Atti del II° congresso internazionale di studi verdiani, 30 luglio–5 agosto 1969*, ed. Marcello Pavarani (Parma: Istituto di Studi Verdiani, 1971), 90. The gestation of the libretto for the revised *Don Carlos* is documented in great detail. See Ursula Günther, "Der Briefwechsel Verdi-Nuitter-Du Locle zur Revision des *Don Carlos*," *Analecta musicologica* 14 (1974): 414–44; and 15 (1975): 334–401.
6. Some of the markings are in Du Locle's hand, but the majority are in Verdi's. Günther, "Genèse," 37.
7. Even though Verdi requested accentuation on syllables 4 and 8, his model clearly indicates that he meant syllables 3 and 8. Verdi's model reads (as cited in Alessandro Luzio, ed., *Carteggi verdiani*, 4 vols. [Rome: Reale accademia d'Italia, 1935–47], 4:163):

    .... rèmords .... tristesse amère.

Du Locle's solution reads:

    O remords! amère tristesse!

8. See Luzio, *Carteggi verdiani*, 4:164; and Günther, "Genèse," 95. This passage was cut during the rehearsal period (Günther, "Genèse," 95) but appears in the critical edition of the vocal score. *Giuseppe Verdi*, Don Carlos: *Edizione integrale delle varie versioni in cinque e in quattro atti (comprendente gli inediti verdiani a cura di Ursula Günther)*, ed. Ursula Günther and Luciano Petazzoni (Milan: Ricordi, 1974; reprint, 1990), 484–5.
9. See Chapter 1, 36.
10. See Günther, "Le livret français de *Don Carlos*," 119.
11. For the approach of Lubarsch and Landry, see Chapter 1, 12–14.
12. "Mais ces fautes ne sont pas fréquentes, et elles n'existent même pas pour le public ni pour la majorité des compositeurs." J. Weber in *Le temps*, March 19, 1867, quoted in Gartioux, *Giuseppe Verdi*, Don Carlos, 139. I am aware of only two other reviews that mention prosodic problems in *Don Carlos*: Etienne Arago in *L'avenir national*, March 19, 1867; and F. de Langevais (L. Buloz) in *La Revue des deux mondes*, April 1, 1867, quoted in Gartioux, *Giuseppe Verdi*, Don Carlos, 130 and 198, respectively.
13. See Günther, "Genèse," 43.
14. Auguste Villemot's account in *Le Soleil*, March 20, 1867, is particularly revealing in this respect. Having attended the second performance, the author reported that members of the audience, negatively predisposed by reports on the premiere, realized when experiencing the opera for themselves at the second performance that it was "beautiful" and "superb." See Gartioux, *Giuseppe Verdi*, Don Carlos, 169.
15. "Nous ne rendrons pas compte du premier acte de *Don Carlos*, par cette raison toute simple que nous ne l'avons pas vu. L'affiche indiquait le début du spectacle pour sept heures et demie, ce qui, suivant les habitudes connues, semblait donner au public une demi-heure de latitude pour arriver. Cette fois seulement l'administration n'a pas pu accorder de grâce à ses invités. La toile s'est levée et le spectacle a commencé à l'heure fixe, malgré le bruit des portes de loges, malgré le langage muet des stalles inoccupées dont les bras de velours semblaient mimer une protestation." Nestor Roqueplan in *Le constitutionnel*, March 18, 1867, quoted in Gartioux, *Giuseppe Verdi*, Don Carlos, 95.
16. As evidence, Günther ("La Genèse," 157) quotes a review published on September 14, 1867, in *The Musical World*: "On Thursday last we had the last performance of *Don Carlos* at the Opera, previous to the *congé* of Mr. Faure. This gentleman, as *Posa*, and Obin as *Philipp II*, were both first rate in the personification of their caracter [sic] as well as in the execution of the music allotted to them. Morère, *Don Carlos* is really an inferior artist as regard [sic] figure, acting and singing, and I cannot understand why Verdi did not confide this important part to a better one, having two other tenors at his disposition. Madame Gueymard is very far from giving to this brillan [sic] part the due vocal and dramatic importance like Mme Fricci did at Covent garden [sic] last season. However she is a good artist and makes something of it. Shocking was the way how Mme Sass akted [sic] and sang the part of *Elisabeth*. Walking up and down the stage indifferently. Laughing and joking openly with her companions in the most dramatical moments, throwing down the part altogether. Singing the music without any expression at all, as if she was rehearsing it at the piano. Without any artistical dignity, and without any respect for the public, for the art, for the composer, for herself!"
17. "Il faut tout d'abord écarter le nom de l'auteur, chasser les souvenirs du *Trovatore*, de *Rigoletto*, de la *Traviata*, ne pas chercher dans *Don Carlos* le Verdi violent, brutal, passionné, mais toujours

saisissant par le jet et l'inspiration de l'idée mélodique. Ce Verdi-là n'existe plus: le compositeur que nous avons sous les yeux a rompu avec les formules de l'école italienne. Meyerbeer lui-même lui semble attardé: il incline avec Wagner vers la mélopée et la déclaration [sic] lyrique." Gérome in *L'Univers*; quoted in Gartioux, *Giuseppe Verdi*: Don Carlos, 181.

18. Hippolyte Prévost's review for *La France* as reprinted in Léon Escudier's *L'Art musical* of March 28, 1867, quoted in ibid., 213; and the critic of *La France* as quoted in ibid., 12.
19. See Chapter 1, 10–11 (Benloew) and Chapter 2, 58 (avoiding a strong sense of meter and 54–6, mixing of prosodic approaches).
20. See Chapter 1, 12–13.
21. See Chapter 2, 74–5.
22. By "isolated" quatrains, I mean quatrains that are not part of a series of stanzaic structures in continuous formal lyricism.
23. Even though the highlighting undoubtedly reflects Quicherat's theory, he certainly would have censored the two consecutive accents of "Ad**ieu**" and "R**ei**ne."
24. See Chapter 1, 12–14 (Lubarsch and Landry), and 15–16 (Pierson).
25. Quicherat, *Traîté de versification française*, 193. See Giger, "The Triumph of Diversity," 76–9.
26. See Chapter 1, 12–16.
27. "Cette musique oratoire fatigue à la longue: on donnerait pour un mot de mélodie ses plus beaux discours." Paul de Saint-Victor in *La Presse*, March 18, 1867, quoted in Gartioux, *Giuseppe Verdi*: Don Carlos, 110.
28. "M. Verdi n'a pas conçu cette scène suivant les traditions de l'art italien, il a voulu la rendre par un effort de déclamation lyrique et un grand développement de récitatif; le caractère en est très-élevé et le contraste des deux personnages exprimé d'une façon saisissante. L'orchestre escorte la pensée avec une variété de ton et une originalité de détails qu'il faut louer sans réserve ..." G. de Saint-Valry in *Le Pays*, March 20, 1867, quoted in Gartioux, *Giuseppe Verdi*: Don Carlos, 165.
29. *Le Journal des débats*, March 20, 1867, quoted in ibid., 162.
30. Reicha, *Art du compositeur dramatique*, 1:15.
31. "[C]ette déviation, si regrettable à nos yeux, est, chez M. Verdi, voulue, systématique, un véritable parti pris. Nous n'en cherchons pour preuve que l'incroyable prédominance dans le livret de *Don Carlos*, des vers alexandrins, naturellement amis de la mélopée et de la déclamation, et naturellement ennemis de la véritable mélodie et du chant. Il est trop visible que si le compositeur eût voulu des vers plus courts, et, partant, plus propices à la mélodie, son librettiste les lui eût facilement accordés ..." Alexis Azevedo in *L'Opinion nationale*, March 19, 1867, quoted in Gartioux, *Giuseppe Verdi*, Don Carlos, 145.
32. Ibid., 149.
33. Budden, *The Operas of Verdi*, 3:72.
34. Translation by Andrew Porter. For the musical setting, see the vocal score, 184.
35. Verdi slightly changed the order of the words from "Alors, malheur sur vous ... malheur!" to "Alors, malheur, malheur sur vous!"
36. Two two-note melismas are the only exception.
37. Although not a narrative but a politico-religious reproach like "Dans ce beau pays," Philippe's "A Dieu vous êtes infidèles [To God you are unfaithful]" (III,4,4; p. 402 of the vocal score) directed toward the six deputies from Flanders also features a stanza with highly irregular accents that, in the context of an animated tempo, are interpreted according to Lubarsch and Landry.

38. Another example is Thibault's "Les fleurs ici couvrent la terre" (II,2,1). Regular scanning of regular verse, the approach recommended by Castil-Blaze, is also rare in *Don Carlos*. Text that could easily be scanned is not scanned (e.g., "Malheur sur toi, fils adultère, / Mon cri vengeur va retentir ... / Malheur sur toi, demain la terre / S'entr'ouvrira pour t'engloutir" [III,3,3]) or is treated over a neutral accompaniment that conceals the scanning (see Exx. 5.1 and 5.6).
39. This first verse has the obligatory caesura after the fifth instead of the sixth syllable. The hiatus created by accented adjacent syllables would have been censured by nineteenth-century theorists.
40. Vincent d'Indy remarked, referring to a year as late as 1875, that anything out of the ordinary was immediately qualified as "wagnerian." See Danièle Pistone, "Wagner et Paris (1839–1900)," *Revue internationale de musique française* 1 (1980): 64.
41. See Katharine Ellis, *Music Criticism in Nineteenth-Century France: La Revue et Gazette musicale de Paris, 1834–1880* (Cambridge University Press, 1995), 206–7.
42. "Verdi, le maître de l'inspiration et de la mélodie, il s'est mis à sacrifier aux faux dieux de l'algèbre musicale. En croirai-je mes oreilles? Il a wagnérisé!" Pierre Véron in *Le Journal amusant*, March 16, 1867, quoted in Gartioux, *Giuseppe Verdi*, Don Carlos, 57. Scholarship generally agrees that Verdi's innovations in *Don Carlos* are fundamentally different from the style Wagner promoted in *Opera and Drama*. Pinpointing these differences, however, continues to be a challenge. See, for example, Dietmar Holland, "Der späte Verdi," in *Verdi-Theater*, ed. Udo Bermbach (Stuttgart: Metzler, 1997), 74–8.
43. "La force dominatrice qui fait le fond du génie de Verdi apparaît ici, non plus dans la puissante simplicité qui a rendu populaire et universel le maître parmesan, mais soutenue par un déploiement extraordinaire de moyens harmoniques, de sonorités recherchées et de formes mélodiques nouvelles. Verdi a-t-il obéi à l'influence directe de Richard Wagner, ou bien à l'effet d'un de ces mouvements invincibles des esprits qui poussent les hommes et les arts au progrès et au perfectionnement, et auquel Wagner a su céder un des premiers? C'est ce qu'il est difficile de juger impartialement: mais une chose est évidente, à savoir que Verdi a modifié complètement ses procédés premiers pour adopter des principes analogues à ceux du maître allemand.

    L'absence complète de récitatif dans le *Don Carlos* en est la preuve, ainsi que son remplacement par des mélopées déclamatoires, soutenues par un accompagnement travaillé qui complète la pensée du poète. Les airs proprement dits s'enchâssent par des soudures imperceptibles à ces mélopées, l'opéra ne forme qu'une seule trame, et exige une attention soutenue de la part de l'auditeur, qui ne trouve dans cette vaste partition ni récitatif pour reposer son oreille, ni ritournelle préparatoire pour l'avertir du moment où il faut écouter plus particulièrement." Théophile Gautier in *Le Moniteur universel*, March 18, 1867, quoted in Gartioux, *Giuseppe Verdi*, Don Carlos, 104. See also Gérome in *L'Univers illustré*, March 20, 1867; Eugène Tarbé in *Le Figaro*, March 13, 1867; Pierre Véron in *Le Journal amusant*, March 16, 1867; Paul de Saint-Victor in *La Presse*, March 18, 1867; and B. Jouvin in *Paris-Magazine*, March 17, 1867, all quoted in Gartioux, *Giuseppe Verdi*, Don Carlos.
44. Verdi's approach to irregularly accented and polymetric stanzas has shown how comfortable he had become setting them to formal lyricism. I further investigate this issue in "Translation of Librettos and Lyrical Perception in Verdi's *Gerusalemme, Giovanna de Guzman*, and *Don Carlo*," in *La traduction des livrets: Aspects théoriques, historiques et pragmatiques*, ed. Gottfried Marschall (Paris: Presses de l'université Paris-Sorbonne, 2004), 107–30.
45. See vocal score, 236–45.

46. Budden, *The Operas of Verdi*, 3:72.
47. "Ce qui, cette fois, déroute peut-être un peu l'oreille, c'est que, parfois, la mélodie, au lieu d'aboutir au trait final, tourne brusquement à un autre motif, ou se continue en manière de récitatif, selon la méthode de Wagner." Auguste Villemot in *Le Soleil*, March 20, 1867, quoted in Gartioux, *Giuseppe Verdi, Don Carlos*, 169.
48. Roger Parker, *Leonora's Last Act: Essays in Verdian Discourse* (Princeton University Press, 1997), 17.
49. See, for example, Budden, *The Operas of Verdi*, 3:197–8; and Uwe Schweikert, "*Aida*," in *Verdi Handbuch*, ed. Anselm Gerhard and Uwe Schweikert in collaboration with Christine Fischer (Stuttgart: Metzler, 2001), 472.
50. Gossett, "Verdi, Ghislanzoni, and *Aida*," 310–34, *passim*.
51. The excerpts from *Aida* are cited according to the 1871 Cairo libretto: Aida, *opera in 4 atti e 7 quadri, parole di A. Ghislanzoni, musica del Commandatore G. Verdi, scritta per commissione di Sua Altezza il Kedive per il Teatro dell'Opera del Cairo e rappresentata per la prima volta su queste scene nel mese di Decembre 1871* (Cairo: Tipografia francese Delbos-Demouret, 1871).
52. Italian theorists do not require an accent on the third syllable. See Chapter 1, 36.
53. See Chapter 1, 16–17.
54. Egbert Kahlke analyzes this passage in "Vers und Musik in der *Aida*," *Studi verdiani* 11 (1996): 101–2, pointing to the great diversity with which Verdi sets *endecasillabi*. Kahlke, however, does not seem to distinguish between passages in *versi sciolti* and those in *versi lirici*.
55. See Chapter 1, 36.
56. See p. 41.
57. Letter of November 13, 1870, quoted in translation in Gossett, "Verdi, Ghislanzoni, and *Aida*," 329. See also Kahlke, "Vers und Musik in der *Aida*," 110–1.
58. Quoted in Gossett, "Verdi, Ghislanzoni, and *Aida*," 329.
59. This and the previous line appear in the hand of Giuseppina Strepponi in the margin of the manuscript. J. Richard Kitson, "Verdi and the Evolution of the *Aida* Libretto" (Ph.D. diss., University of British Columbia, 1985), 929. The Cairo libretto includes the emended version discussed below.
60. The Cairo libretto does not indent this verse, implying a passage in *versi sciolti*. The complete rhyme scheme, however, suggests stanzaic verse.
61. See, for example, Ralph P. Locke, "Beyond the Exotic: How 'Eastern' Is *Aida*?" *Cambridge Opera Journal* 17 (2005): 119–23.
62. According to Budden (*The Operas of Verdi*, 3:231), this melody is "typical of the Aida style – regular and periodic, with swift and unpredictable changes of harmony (note the E-flat at the start of the second phrase – an almost sixteenth-century touch) and chromatic inflexions that caress without cloying." For a more detailed analysis of this passage and an approach that interprets the harmonic surprises here and elsewhere in *Aida* as resulting from a counterpoint between conflicting linear implications, see David Lawton, "The Harmonic Language of *Aida*" (paper presented at the annual meeting of the American Musicological Society, New York, 3 November 1979). I am grateful to Professor Lawton for generously providing a copy of his paper.
63. Budden, *The Operas of Verdi*, 3:157.

64. See Andreas Giger, "The French Influences," in *The Cambridge Companion to Verdi*, ed. Scott L. Balthazar (Cambridge University Press, 2004), 136–8.
65. "Verdi a donc fait à son tour l'oeuvre exclusivement française qui, plus sûrement que ses meilleurs opéras italiens, portera son nom à la postérité, en le rattachant glorieusement à l'histoire même d'une institution immortalisée par des maîtres illustres de toutes les origines qui s'y sont succédé depuis plus d'un siècle." Hippolyte Prévost's review for *La France* as reprinted in Léon Escudier's *L'Art musical* of March 28, 1867, quoted in Gartioux, *Giuseppe Verdi*, Don Carlos, 213.
66. Kimbell, *Italian Opera*, 604.
67. Phillips-Matz, *Verdi*, 638; *The Verdi-Boito Correspondence*, ed. Marcello Conati and Mario Medici, trans. William Weaver (University of Chicago Press, 1994), lii–liii; Julian Budden, *Verdi*, The Master Musicians, rev. ed. (New York: Schirmer, 1996), 153; and Mary Jane Phillips-Matz, *Puccini: A Biography* (Boston: Northeastern University Press, 2002), 53–4.
68. On the history of the term verismo, see Andreas Giger, *Verismo*, Handwörterbuch der musikalischen Terminologie (Wiesbaden: Steiner, 2004); and idem, "Origin, Corruption, and Redemption of an Operatic Term," *Journal of the American Musicological Society* 60 (2007): 271–315. For references to Bizet and Massenet, see M. Carner, *Puccini: A Critical Biography* (New York: Knopf, 1959), 242; and Julian Budden, "Puccini, Massenet and 'Verismo,'" *Opera* 34 (May 1983): 477–81.
69. Phillips-Matz, *Puccini*, 109.

Bibliography

A. Primary Sources

a. Books

Asioli, Bonifazio. *Il maestro di composizione ossia Seguito del trattato d'armonia*. Milan: Ricordi, 1831?

Balbi, Melchiorre. *Grammatica ragionata della musica considerata sotto l'aspetto di lingua*. Milan: Ricordi, 1845.

Banville, Théodore de. *Petit traité de poésie française*. Paris: Alphonse Lemerre, 1891.

Baruffaldi, Girolamo. *Volume primo de' Baccanali*. 2d ed. Bologna: Lelio dalla Volpe, 1758.

Basevi, Antonio. *Studio sulle opere di Giuseppe Verdi*. Rev. and enl. ed. Florence: Tofani, 1859.

———. *Introduzione ad un nuovo sistema d'armonia*. Florence: Tofani, 1862.

Beauchemin, Charles. *Méloprosodie française ou Guide du chanteur*. Paris, 1847.

Beaulieu, Désiré. *Du rhythme, des effets qu'il produit et de leurs causes*. Paris: Dentu, 1853.

Beauquier, Charles. *La musique et le drame*. Paris: Fischbacher, 1884.

Becq de Fouquières, L. Aimé Victor. *Traité général de versification française*. Paris: G. Charpentier, 1879.

Benloew, Louis. *Précis d'une théorie des rhythmes*. Vol. 1, *Rhythmes français et rhythmes latins*. Paris: Franck, 1862.

Berlioz, Hector. *Cauchemars et passions*. Edited by Gérard Condé. Paris: J. C. Lattes, 1981.

Bertrand, Gustave. *Les nationalités musicales étudiées dans le drame lyrique*. Paris: Didier, 1872.

Bisso, Gianbattista. *Introduzione alla volgar poesia in due parti divisa*. 4th ed. Venice: Giuseppe Orlandeli, 1791.

Blaze, François Henri Joseph. *L'art des vers lyriques*. Paris: A. Delahays, 1858.

Boito, Arrigo. *Tutti gli scritti*. Edited by P. Nardi. Milan: Mondadori, 1942.

Boucheron, Raimondo. *Filosofia della musica o estetica applicata a quest'arte*. Milan: Ricordi, 1842.

Chabanon, Michel-Paul. *De la musique considérée en elle-même et dans ses rapports avec la parole, les langues, la poésie, et le théâtre*. Paris: Pissot, 1785.

Choron, Alexandre, and J. Adrien de La Fage. *Nouveau manuel complet de musique vocale et instrumentale, ou, Encyclopédie musicale*. Paris: Roret, 1836–1839.

Choron, Aléxandre, et al. *Rapport présenté au nom de la section de musique, adopté par la classe des beaux-arts de l'Institut impérial de France, dans ses séances du 18 avril et des 2 et 9 mai 1812, sur un ouvrage ... de Scoppa*. Paris: Firmin Didot, 1812.

Combarieu, Jules. *Les rapports de la musique et de la poésie considérées au point de vue de l'expression*. Paris: F. Alcan, 1894.

D'Anna, Salvatore. *Grammatica riguardante i principii elementari di musica in corrispondenza a quei del linguaggio in correlazione all'antico*. Palermo: Michele Amenta, 1866.

Ducondut, Jean-Ambroise. *Essai de rhythmique française: Introduction théorique, manuel lyrique et préludes*. Paris: M. Lévy frères, 1856.

Galeazzi, Francesco. *Elementi teorico-pratici di musica con un saggio sopra l'arte di suonare il violino analizzata, ed a dimostrabili principi ridotta, opera utilissima a chiunque vuol applicar con profitto alla musica e specialmente a' principianti dilettanti, e professori di violino*. 2 vols. Rome: Pilucchi Cracas, 1791; Rome: Michele Puccinelli, 1796.

Gervasoni, Carlo. *La scuola della musica in tre parti divisa*. 2 vols. Piacenza: N. Orcesi, 1800.

Gramont, Ferdinand de. *Les vers français et leur prosodie*. Paris: Hetzel, 1876.

Hugo, Victor. "Préface [to *Cromwell*]." In *Théâtre complet de Victor Hugo*, ed. J.-J. Thierry and Josette Mélèze, 409–54. Monaco: Gallimard, 1967.

———. *Selected Poems of Victor Hugo: A Bilingual Edition*. Translated by E. H. and A. M. Blackmore. University of Chicago Press, 2001.

Le Goffic, Charles, and Édouard Thieulin. *Nouveau traité de versification française à l'usage des classes de l'enseignement classique et de l'enseignement moderne des lycées et collèges des écoles normales, du brevet supérieur et des classes de l'enseignement secondaire des jeunes filles*. 3d ed. Paris: Masson, 1897.

Lubarsch, E. Otto. *Abriss der französischen Verslehre*. Berlin: Weidmann, 1879.

Lurin, Jean Marie. *Éléments du rythme dans la versification et la prose française*. Lyons: Bauchu, 1850.

Lussy, Mathis. *Musical Expression, Accents, Nuances, and Tempo in Vocal and Instrumental Music*. Translated from the 4th ed. by M. E. von Glehn. London: Novello, n.d.

Marmontel, Jean François. *Élémens de littérature*. 6 vols. N.p., 1787.

Marselli, Nicola. *Saggi critici sulla ragione della musica moderna*. Naples: Detken, 1859.

Pacini, Giovanni. *Le mie memorie artistiche*. Florence: G. G. Guidi, 1865; reprint, Lucca: Maria Pacini Fazzi, 1981.

Pierson, Paul. *Métrique naturelle du langage*. Paris: Vieweg, 1884.

Arthur Pougin, ed. *Biographie universelle des musiciens et bibliographie générale de la musique par François-Joseph Fétis, supplément et complément*. 2 vols. Paris: Firmin Didot, 1878–1880.

Quicherat, Louis-Marie. *Traité de versification française*. 2d ed. Paris: L. Hachette, 1850.

Reicha, Antoine. *Traité de mélodie: Abstraction faite de ses rapports avec l'harmonie, suivi d'un supplement sur l'art d'accompagner la mélodie par l'harmonie, lorsque la première est prédominante: Le tout appuyé sur les meilleurs modèles mélodiques*. 2d ed. Paris: S. Richault, 1832.

———. *Art du compositeur dramatique ou Cours complet de composition vocale*. 2 vols. Paris: A. Farrenc, 1833.

———. *Treatise on Melody*. Translated by Peter M. Landey. Harmonologia, vol. 10. Hillsdale, NY: Pendragon Press, 2000.

Ritorni, Carlo. *Ammaestramenti alla composizione d'ogni poema e d'ogni opera appartenente alla musica*. Milan: Pirola, 1841.

Scoppa, Antonio. *Traité de la poésie italienne rapporté à la poésie française, dans lequel on fait voir la parfaite analogie entre ces deux langues ...* Paris: Renouard, 1803.

———. *Les vrais principes de la versification développés par un examen comparatif entre la langue italienne et la française*. 3 vols. Paris: Courcier, 1812.

Siciliani, Pietro. *Della differente ragione estetica nell'indole della musica tedesca e della musica italiana: Dialogo fra un critico ed un filosofo*. Bologna: Monti, 1868.

Tobler, Adolf. *Vom französischen Versbau alter und neuer Zeit: Zusammenstellung der Anfangsründe.* 2d ed. Leipzig: Hirzel, 1883.

Tobler, Adolphe. *Le vers français ancien et moderne.* 2d ed. Translated by Karl Breul and Léopold Sudre. Paris: Vieweg, 1885.

Vitali, Geremia. *La musica ne' suoi principj nuovamente spiegata.* Milan: Ricordi, 1847.

Weigand, Gustave. *Traité de versification française.* 2d ed. Bromberg: E. S. Mittler, 1871.

Zambaldini, Francesco. *Il ritmo dei versi italiani.* Turin: Loescher, 1874.

b. Articles and Reviews

Aldini, Aldino. "Premières représentations. Théâtre impérial italien: *Un ballo in maschera*, opéra en quatre actes, par. G. Verdi." *La France musicale* 25 (1861): 17–18, 25–6, 33–4.

"Aristocrazie musicali." *Gazzetta musicale di Milano* 18 (1860): 57.

Balbi, Melchiorre. "*Gli Anglicani* di Meyerbeer al Teatro nuovo di Padova (17 giugno 1844)." *Gazzetta musicale di Milano* 3 (1844): 102.

———. "Della nazionalità musicale." *Gazzetta musicale di Milano* 4 (1845): 174–5.

Basevi, Abramo. "Rapporto della declamazione col canto." *L'Italia musicale* 6 (1854): 134.

———. "Storia fantastica della melodia." *L'Italia musicale* 7 (1855): 326, 334–5.

———. "Le riforme." *L'armonia* 1 (1856): 1–2.

———. "Se Meyerbeer scrivesse oggi un'opera italiana." *L'armonia* 1 (1856): 22–3.

———. "Il poeta il maestro ed il cantante [Per la riforma musicale in Italia]." *L'armonia* 1 (1856): 41–2.

———. "Il linguaggio musicale [come espressione degli "affetti": analisi]." *L'armonia* 1 (1856): 45–6.

———. "La melodia antica e moderna in Italia [Dissertazione storica e tecnica (continua)]." *L'armonia* 1 (1856): 61–2, 69–70, 73–4, 85–6, 89, 93–4.

———. "*Giovanna di Guzman* (*Vespri siciliani*) al teatro Pegliano di Firenze." *L'armonia* 1 (1856): 65–7.

———. "La proprietà letteraria ed i libretti." *L'armonia* 1 (1856): 103.

———. "*Gli Ugonotti* (*Anglicani*) del celebre M.º Giacomo Meyerbeer al Teatro Ferdinando [Firenze]." *L'armonia* 5 (1857): 69–70.

Berlioz, Hector. "Opinion de Berlioz sur *Les Vêpres siciliennes* de Verdi." *La France musicale* 19 (1855): 314.

———. "Strauss et l'avenir du rythme." In *Cauchemars et passions*, ed. Gérard Condé, 122–8. Paris: J. C. Lattes, 1981.

Berti, A. "Sulla musica di *Roberto il diavolo*." *Gazzetta musicale di Milano* 1 (1844): 202–3.

Blanchard, Henri. "Mélodie et poésie." *Revue et gazette musicale de Paris* 20 (1853): 293–4, 301–2.

Boucheron, Raimondo. "Esame dello stato attuale della musica drammatica in Italia." *Gazzetta musicale di Milano* 2 (1843): 205–6, 209–10.

Bourges, Maurice. "Situation mélodique actuelle." *Revue et gazette musicale de Paris* 13 (1846): 235–6.

———. "Quarante mélodies à une et à plusieurs voix, par G. Meyerbeer (deuxième article)." *Revue et gazette musicale de Paris* 17 (1850): 158–9.

———. "*L'Africaine*: Opéra de G. Meyerbeer. La partition." *Revue et gazette musicale de Paris* 32 (1865): 161–4, 169–71, 177–80, 189–91, 197–9.

Boyer, Philoxène. "Compositeurs du dix-neuvième siècle: Verdi." *La France musicale* 21 (1857): 241–3.

Brancour, René. "Mélodie." In *La grande encyclopédie: Inventaire raisonné des sciences, des lettres et des arts*, ed. André Berthelot et al., 23:612–16. Paris, 1896–1898.

C. "Della poesia da musica [La riforma del libretto alla base dell'auspicata riforma musicale in Italia]." *L'armonia* 1 (1856): 37.

———. "*I vespri siciliani (Giovanna di Guzman)* a Roma." *L'armonia* 1 (1856): 63.

Casamorata, Luigi Ferdinando. "*Macbeth*, melodramma di F. Piave musicato da Giuseppe Verdi." *Gazzetta musicale di Milano* 6 (1847): 113–15, 129–33, 139–41, 153–5, 163–5, 172–4.

———. "Cicalate: II. Il canto." *Gazzetta musicale di Milano* 23 (1868): 369–73, 393–5.

"Cenni su Meyerbeer." *L'armonia* 5 (1857): 70.

Chabanon, Michel-Paul. "Lettre sur les propriétés musicales de la langue françoise." *Mercure de France* (January 1773): 171–91.

Comettant, Oscar. "De l'expression en musique." *L'art musical* 1 (1861): 177–8.

"Della declamazione." *L'Italia musicale* 7 (1855): 294–5.

"Dell'ultima opera del M.º Verdi giudicata dal sig. Rovani nella *Gazzetta ufficiale di Milano* [A proposito de *I vespri siciliani*: Confronto tra l'opera italiana e l'opera francese; lo stile delle precedenti opera verdiane]." *L'armonia* 1 (1856): 35.

"Di alcune recenti opinioni intorno al *Simon Boccanegra*." *Gazzetta musicale di Milano* 17 (1859): 43–7.

Ds., E. "Feuilleton du *Journal des débats* du 28 Novembre 1847. Académie Royale de Musique, première représentation de *Jérusalem*." *Journal des débats politiques et littéraires*, 28 November 1847.

Escudier, Marie. "Mélodies nouvelles par V. Massé." *La France musicale* 25 (1861): 397.

———. "*Les Troyens à Carthage*: Opéra en cinq actes, paroles et musique de M. Hector Berlioz." *La France musicale* 27 (1863): 349–51.

Fétis, François-Joseph. "Dangers de la situation actuelle de la musique dramatique: Causes du mal – moyens de régénération." *Revue et gazette musicale de Paris* 12 (1845): 1–5, 17–20, 33–7, 57–61, 97–102.

———. "*Le Prophète* (première représentation le 16 avril): Opéra en 5 actes, paroles de M. Scribe, musique de Meyerbeer." *Revue et gazette musicale de Paris* 16 (1849): 121–6, 137–40, 153–7, 169–74.

———. "Verdi." *Revue et gazette musicale de Paris* 17 (1850): 308–11, 322–5.

———. "*Le Juif errant*: Grand opéra en cinq actes. La musique." *Revue et gazette musicale de Paris* 19 (1852): 137–40, 145–7, 153–5.

———. "Troisième lettre aux compositeurs dramatiques." *Revue et gazette musicale de Paris* 20 (1853): 443–6.

———. "Seconda lettera ai compositori drammatici del signor Fétis [musica e parola nel melodramma]." *L'Italia musicale* 6 (1854): 98, 102, 122–3, 146, 166.

———. "Quarta ed ultima lettera di Fétis ai compositori drammatici [irregolarità e invenzione melodica]." *L'Italia musicale* 6 (1854): 294, 314–15.

_____. "Du rhythme de la poésie lyrique et des études rhythmiques de M. A. van Hasselt." *Revue et gazette musicale de Paris* 30 (1863): 81–3.

Filippi, Filippo. "Studio analitico sul *Don Carlos* di Giuseppe Verdi." *Gazzetta musicale di Milano* 24 (1869): 17–18, 33–5, 49–52, 57–8, 83–5, 225–8, 241–4, 259–62, 279–82, 287–90, 296–8, 311–14, 327–30; 25 (1870): 79–80, 95–7, 143–5.

Fleury, A. "Du rythme dans la poésie chantée." *Études religieuses, philosophiques ...* 60 (November 1893): 326–63.

Gambini, Carlo Andrea. "La *Giovanna di Guzman* di G. Verdi al Teatro Carlo Felice di Genova la sera del 21 corrente." *L'armonia* 1 (1856): 86.

_____. "Polemica [con il giornale "Staffile" in merito alla rappresentazione a Genova della *Giovanna de Guzman* di Verdi]." *L'armonia* 1 (1856): 103.

Gartioux, Hervé, ed. *Giuseppe Verdi, Les Vêpres siciliennes: Dossier de presse parisienne (1855)*. Critiques de l'opéra français du XIXème siècle, vol. 6. N.p.: Lucie Galland, 1995.

_____, ed. *Giuseppe Verdi, Don Carlos: Dossier de presse parisienne (1867)*, Critiques de l'opéra français du XIXème siècle, vol. 9. Heilbronn: Lucie Galland, 1997.

Ghislanzoni, Antonio. "Conversazioni musicali II." *Gazzetta musicale di Milano* 21 (1866): 17–18, 25–8, 49–51, 57–8, 73–6, 161–2, 185–8, 201–3.

_____. "Reminiscenze artistiche: La musica di Verdi a Parigi nell'anno 1851." *Gazzetta musicale di Milano* 21 (1866): 105–9.

_____. "*L'africana* al R. Teatro alla Scala." *Gazzetta musicale di Milano* 21 (1866): 217–21.

"Il canto Italiano." *L'Italia musicale* 4 (1852): 297–8, 306, 310.

"I libretti d'opera in prosa." *Gazzetta musicale di Milano* 30 (1875): 363–4.

"Il maestro Halévy." *L'Italia musicale* 4 (1852): 97–8, 101–2.

Lacome, Paul. "De la poésie française au point de vue du chant." *L'art musical* 6 (1866): 249–50, 257–9.

La Fage, Adrien de. "Revue critique: *Méloprosodie française, ou Guide du chanteur* par Charles Beauchemin." *Revue et gazette musicale de Paris* 14 (1847): 318–19.

_____. "Lettres sur l'état actuel de la musique en Italie (septième lettre)." *Revue et gazette musicale de Paris* 16 (1849): 410–12.

Lauzières, A. de. "La musica in Francia." *Gazzetta musicale di Milano* 24 (1869): 436–7.

"*L'ebrea* di Halevy al T. Carlo Felice di Genova." *L'armonia* 5 (1858): 115–16.

Mazzucato, Alberto. "*Il profeta*." *Gazzetta musicale di Milano* 13 (1855): 169–71, 177–8, 187–9, 220–1, 281–3, 337–8, 404–5.

_____. "*Giovanna de Guzman*." *Gazzetta musicale di Milano* 14 (1856): 57–9, 65–7, 81–2, 105–6, 258–60.

_____. "Problemi musicali: A proposito di una traduzione nuova [by Predari] di un libro vecchio [by Fétis]. Al redattore della gazzetta musicale (lettera settima)." *Gazzetta musicale di Milano* 17 (1859): 1–3.

_____. "A Filippo Filippi (lettera quarta ed ultima)." *Gazzetta musicale di Milano* 22 (1867): 249–52.

_____. "Della differente ragione estetica nell'indole della musica tedesca e della musica italiana: Dialogo fra un critico ed un filosofo per Pietro Siciliani." *Gazzetta musicle di Milano* 23 (1868): 209–10.

_____. "Wagner e la melodia." *Gazzetta musicale di Milano* 26 (1871): 21–2.

"La novità nella musica." *L'armonia* 1 (1856): 109–10.

"Perché non si ripetono *Gli ugonotti* nel Teatro della Pergola? Un buon consiglio ai sigg. impresarj maestri Ronzi." *L'armonia* 4 (1857): 25.

R. "*Nabuco* [sic] et les Verdistes." *Revue et gazette musicale de Paris* 12 (1845): 357–9.

Raffaelli, Pietro. "Lamenti e consigli di alcuni illustri italiani intorno al melodramma [Per la riforma del libretto d'opera]." *L'armonia* 1 (1856): 37–8.

———. "Sulla riforma del melodramma." *L'armonia* 1 (1856): 74–5, 78, 98–9, 101–2.

Redazione. "*Jérusalem*, opera in quattro atti, parole di Royer e Vaëz, musica di Verdi." *Gazzetta musicale di Milano* 6 (1847): 385–7.

Rongé, J.-B. "De la poésie lyrique." *Revue et gazette musicale de Paris* 30 (1863): 188–9, 195–6.

Thurner, A. "L'opéra comique et ses transformations." *La France musicale* 27 (1863): 53–4, 61–3, 69–70, 77–9, 85–6, 93–4, 109–10, 125–6, 133–4, 141–2, 149–50, 157–8, 165–6, 189–90, 197–8, 205–7, 221–2, 229–30, 245–6, 253–5, 261–2, 269–71, 277–8, 285–6, 293–5, 301–3, 310–11, 326–8, 334–6, 352–3, 357–8, 365–6, 373–4, 382–3, 390–1.

Torrigiani, Pietro. "*I vespri siciliani* a Parma." *L'armonia* 1, no. 2 (1856): 6.

"*Un ballo in maschera*. Musica del Maestro Verdi. Eseguita la prima volta al Teatro Apollo di Roma la sera del 17 Febbraio 1859." *L'armonia* 6 (1859): 206–7.

"Un quesito [sulla crisi dell'opera contemporanea: I compositori, i cantanti, il pubblico]." *L'armonia* 6 (1859): 211.

"Varietà: Ridicolezze musicali [Sul rapporto tra musica e testo poetico]." *L'armonia* 1 (1856): 31–2.

Westphal, Rudolf. "Der Rhythmus des gesungenen Verses." *Allgemeine Musik Zeitung*, 15 June 1888.

c. Letters

Alberti, Annibale, ed. *Verdi intimo. Carteggio di Giuseppe Verdi con il conte Oprandino Arrivabene (1861–1886)*. Milan: Mondadori, 1931.

Baker, Evan. "Lettere di Giuseppe Verdi a Francesco Maria Piave 1843–1865: Documenti della Frederick R. Koch Foundation Collection e della Mary Flagler Cary Collection presso la Pierpont Morgan Library di New York." *Studi verdiani* 4 (1986–1987): 136–66.

Bonnefon, Paul. "Les métamorphoses d'un opéra: Lettres inédites d'Eugène Scribe." *Revue des deux mondes* [Paris] 41 (September-October 1917), 877–99.

Cesari, Gaetano, and Alessandro Luzio, eds. *I copialettere di Giuseppe Verdi*. Milan, 1913; reprint, Bologna: Forni, 1968.

Garibaldi, Luigi Agostino. *Giuseppe Verdi nelle lettere di Emanuele Muzio ad Antonio Barezzi*. Milan: Fratelli Treves, 1931.

Luzio, Alessandro, ed. *Carteggi verdiani*. 4 vols. Rome: Reale accademia d'Italia, 1935–1947.

Medici, Mario, and Marcello Conati, eds. *Carteggio Verdi-Boito*. 2 vols. Parma: Istituto di studi verdiani, 1978.

Morazzoni, Giuseppe, and Giulio Maria Ciampelli, eds. *Verdi. Lettere inedite. ... Le opere verdiane al Teatro alla Scala (1839–1929)*. Milan: Libreria Editrice Milanese, 1929.

Mossa, Carlo Matteo. "Le lettere di Emanuele Muzio alla Casa Ricordi." *Studi verdiani* 4 (1986–1987): 167–201.

Pascolato, Alessandro. *"Rè Lear" e "Ballo in maschera": Lettere di Giuseppe Verdi ad Antonio Somma*. Città del Castello: Lapi, 1902.

Porter, Andrew. "*Les Vêpres siciliennes*: New Lettres from Verdi to Scribe." *19th Century Music* 2 (1978): 95–109.

Prod'homme, Jacques Gabriel. "Unpublished Letters from Verdi to Camille Du Locle." *The Musical Quarterly* 7 (1921): 73–103.

———. "Verdi's Letters to Léon Escudier." *Music and Letters* 4 (1923): 62–70, 184–96, 375–7.

———. "Lettres inédites de G. Verdi à Léon Escudier." *Rivista musicale italiana* 35 (1928): 1–28, 171–97, 519–52.

Schneider, Herbert, ed. *Correspondance d'Eugène Scribe et de Daniel-François-Esprit Auber*. Sprimont: Mardaga, 1998.

d. Scores and Librettos

Baldacci, Luigi, ed. *Tutti i libretti di Verdi*. 4th ed. Milan: Garzanti: 1992.

Boito, Arrigo. Otello: *Dramma lirico in quattro atti, musica di Giuseppe Verdi; Teatro alla Scala, carnevale–quaresima 1886–1887*. Milan: Ricordi, 1886.

Cammarano, Salvadore. Alzira: *Tragedia lirica, divisa in prologo e due atti; da rappresentarsi nel Real Teatro S. Carlo*. Naples: Dalla tipografia Flautina, 1845.

Donizetti, Gaetano. Anna Bolena, *opera completa per canto e pianoforte. Edizione comprendente la scena e duetto "Si, son io che a te ritorno."* Edited by Philip Gossett. Milan: Ricordi, 1986.

Ghislanzoni, Antonio. Aida, *opera in 4 atti e 7 quadri, musica del Commandatore G. Verdi, scritta per commissione di Sua Altezza il Kedive per il Teatro dell'Opera del Cairo e rappresentata per la prima volta su queste scene nel mese di Decembre 1871*. Cairo: Tipografia francese Delbos-Demouret, 1871.

Méry Joseph, and Camille Du Locle. Don Carlos, *opéra en cinq actes, musique de G. Verdi, représenté, pour la première fois, à Paris, sur le théâtre impérial de l'Opéra le 11 mars 1867*. Paris: Michel Lévy, 1867.

Metastasio, Pietro. La Semiramide riconosciuta: *Dramma per musica; da rappresentarsi nel nuovo privilegiato imperiale teatro, in occasione del gloriosissimo giorno natalizio della sac. ces. real maestà di Maria Teresa*. Vienna: Giovanni Pietro van Ghelen, 1748; reprint, New York: Garland, 1983.

Piave, Francesco Maria. I due Foscari: *Tragedia lirica posta in musica dal maestro Giuseppe Verdi pel teatro di Torre Argentina l'autunno del 1844*. Rome: Tipografia Ajani, 1844.

———. Il corsaro, *musica di Verdi. Da rappresentarsi nel Teatro grande di Trieste l'autunno del 1848*. Milan: Francesco Lucca, [1848].

———. La traviata, *musica di Giuseppe Verdi, espressamente composta pel Gran Teatro La Fenice, da rappresentarsi nella stagione di Carnovale e Quadragesima 1852–53*. Venice: Gattei, n.d.

Scribe, Eugène. *Théâtre complet de M. Eugène Scribe, membre de l'Académie française*. 2d ed. 24 vols. Paris: Aimé André, 1834–1842.

———. Le prophète, *opéra en cinq actes, musique de G. Meyerbeer, représenté pour la première fois, à Paris, sur le théâtre de l'Opéra, le 16 avril 1849*. Paris: M. Lévy frères, 1855.

———. Les Vêpres siciliennes, *musique de M. Verdi; représenté pour la première fois, sur le théâtre de l'Académie impériale de Musique, le 13 juin 1855*. Paris: Michel Lévy frères, 1855.

———. Giovanna de Guzman *(musica de' Vespri siciliani): Opera-ballo in 5 atti posta in musica dal M. Cavaliere Giuseppe Verdi da rappresentarsi al Teatro Regio nel Carneval-Quaresima 1855–1856*. Turin: Giuseppe Fodratti, [1855].

———. L'africaine, *opéra en cinq actes, musique de Giacomo Meyerbeer*. Paris: Brandus et Dufour, [1865].

———. *Oeuvres complètes*. 76 vols. Paris: E. Dentu, 1874–1885.

———. *Théâtre de Eugène Scribe: Opéras*. Paris: Editions d'aujourd'hui, 1984.

Scribe, Eugène, and Charles Duveyrier. Giovanna de Guzman, *opera in cinque atti, musica del maestro Giuseppe Verdi, ufficiale della Legion d'Onore, da rappresentarsi al teatro regio di Parma il Carnevale-Quaresima 1855–56*. Translated by E. Caimi. Milan: Ricordi, [1855].

Solera, Temistocle. I lombardi alla prima crociata, *dramma lirico posto in musica dal Sig. Maestro Giuseppe Verdi, da rappresentarsi nell'I. R. Teatro alla Scala il carnevale 1843*. Milan: Gaspare Truffi, 1843.

———. Attila: *Dramma lirico in un prologo e tre atti, musica di Giuseppe Verdi; da rappresentarsi nel Gran Teatro La Fenice nella stagione di carnovale e quadragesima del 1845–1846*. Venice: Dalla tipografia di Giuseppe Molinari, 1845.

[Solera, Temistocle, and Antonio Piazza]. Oberto, conte di S. Bonifacio: *Dramma in due atti da rappresentarsi nell'I. R. Teatro alla Scala l'autunno 1839*. Milan: Gaspare Truffi, 1839.

Vaëz, Gustave, and Alphonse Royer. La Favorite, *opéra en quatre actes, musique de M. G. Donizetti, divertissements de M. Albert, représenté pour la première fois, à Paris, sur le théâtre de l'Académie Royale de Musique le 2 décembre 1840*. Paris: Dondey-Dupré, 1840.

———. Jérusalem: *Opéra en quatre actes, musique de G. Verdi, représenté, pour la première fois, à Paris, sur le théâtre de l'Académie Royale de Musique, le 26 novembre 1847*. Brussels: Lelong, 1847.

Verdi, Giuseppe. Jérusalem: *Grand opéra en quatre actes*. [Vocal Score]. [Paris]: Bureau Central de Musique, [1849].

———. Les Vêpres siciliennes, *partition piano et chant, accompagnement de piano par H. Potier*. Paris: Léon Escudier, [1855].

———. Les Vêpres siciliennes. [Complete French edition with Additional Aria. Vocal Score]. Paris: Léon Escudier, [1856].

———. Simon Boccanegra [1857]. [Vocal Score]. Paris: Léon Escudier, [1858].

———. La forza del destino: *Opera in quattro atti del maestro cavaliere Giuseppe Verdi ..., poesia di F. M. Piave. Rappresentata per la prima volta al Teatro Imperiale Italiano di Pietroburgo il 10 novembre 1862. Canto e pianoforte*. Milan: Ricordi, 1862.

———. Don Carlos: *Edizione integrale delle varie versioni in cinque e in quattro atti (comprendente gli inediti verdiani a cura di Ursula Günther)*. Edited by Ursula Günther and Luciano Petazzoni. Milan: Ricordi, 1974; reprint, 1990.

———. Oberto, Conte di San Bonifacio. *Dramma in due atti [per] canto e pianoforte*. Milan: Ricordi, n.d.; reprint, 1975.

———. Macbeth. *Opera completa per canto e pianoforte*. Milan: Ricordi, n.d.; reprint, 1978.

———. Il finto Stanislao (Un giorno di regno). *Opera completa per canto e pianoforte*. Milan: Ricordi, n.d.; reprint, 1980.

———. I due Foscari. *Opera completa per canto e pianoforte*. Milan: Ricordi, n.d.; reprint, 1981.

———. La battaglia di Legnano. *Opera completa per canto e pianoforte*. Milan: Ricordi, n.d.; reprint, 1983.

———. Rigoletto. *Melodramma in Three Acts by Francesco Maria Piave*. Reduction for Voice and Piano Based on the Critical Edition of the Orchestral Score Edited by Martin Chusid. University of Chicago Press, 1985.

———. Un ballo in maschera. *Opera completa per canto e pianoforte, riduzione di L. e A. Truzzi*. Milan: Ricordi, n.d.; reprint, 1992.

———. Attila. *Opera completa per canto e pianoforte, riduzione di Luigi Truzzi*. Milan: Ricordi, n.d.; reprint, 1993.

———. Giovanna D'Arco. *Opera completa per canto e pianoforte*. Milan: Ricordi, n.d.; reprint, 1993.

———. I masnadieri, *riduzione per canto e pianoforte*. Milan: Ricordi, n.d.; reprint, 1993.

———. I lombardi alla prima crociata. *Opera completa per canto e pianoforte*. Milan: Ricordi, n.d.; reprint, 1994.

———. Ernani. *Dramma lirico in Four Acts by Francesco Maria Piave*. Reduction for Voice and Piano Based on the Critical Edition of the Orchestral Score Edited by Claudio Gallico. University of Chicago Press, 1995.

———. Nabucodonosor. *Dramma lirico in Four Parts by Temistocle Solera*. Reduction for Voice and Piano Based on the Critical Edition of the Orchestral Score Edited by Roger Parker. University of Chicago Press, 1996.

———. I masnadieri. *A Tragic Opera [in Four Acts], Libretto by Andrea Maffei*. Edited by Roberta Montemorra Marvin. The Works of Giuseppe Verdi, I/11. University of Chicago Press, 2000.

———. La traviata. *Melodramma in Three Acts by Francesco Maria Piave*. Reduction for Voice and Piano Based on the Critical Edition of the Orchestral Score Edited by Fabrizio Della Seta. 2 vols. University of Chicago Press, 2001.

———. Il trovatore. *Dramma in Four Parts by Salvadore Cammarano*. Reduction for Voice and Piano Based on the Critical Edition of the Orchestral Score Edited by David Lawton. University of Chicago Press, 2002.

———. Macbeth. *Melodramma in Four Acts, Libretto by Francesco Maria Piave and Andrei [sic] Maffei*. 2 vols. Edited by David Lawton. The Works of Giuseppe Verdi, I/10. University of Chicago Press, 2005.

B. Secondary Sources

Abbiati, Franco. *Giuseppe Verdi*. 4 vols. Milan: Ricordi, 1959.

Abert, Anna Amalie. "Verdi und Wagner." *Analecta musicologica* 11 (1972): 1–13.

Arnaud, Alain. "Ton ennemi Meyerbeer …" In *Verdi: Les Vêpres siciliennes*, ed. Michel Orcel, 90–1. L'Avant-scène opéra opérette, no. 75. Paris: Avant-scène, 1985.

Baldacci, Luigi "I libretti di Verdi." In *Il melodramma italiano dell'Ottocento: Studi e ricerche per Massimo Mila*, ed. Giorgio Pestelli, 113–23. Turin: Einaudi, 1977.

Balthazar, Scott L. "Evolving Convention in Italian Serious Opera: Scene Structure in the Works of Rossini, Bellini, Donizetti, and Verdi, 1810–1850." Ph.D. diss., University of Pennsylvania, 1985.

———. "Ritorni's *Ammaestramenti* and the Conventions of Rossinian Melodramma." *Journal of Musicological Research* 8 (1989): 281–311.

———. "Analytic Contexts and Mediated Influences: The Rossinian *Convenienze* and Verdi's Middle and Late Duets." *Journal of Musicological Research* 10 (1990): 19–45.

———. "The Rhythm of Text and Music in 'Ottocento' Melody: An Empirical Reassessment in Light of Contemporary Treatises." *Current Musicology*, no. 49 (1992): 5–28.

Baroni, Mario. "Le formule d'accompagnamento nel teatro del primo Verdi." *Studi verdiani* 4 (1986–1987): 18–64.

Bartlet, M. Elizabeth C. ed. *Gioachino Rossini:* Guillaume Tell. Edizione critica delle opere di Gioachino Rossini, I/39. Vols. 5–6, *Commento critico – testi.* Pesaro: Fondazione Rossini, 1992.

Becker, Heinz. "Giacomo Meyerbeers Mitarbeit an den Libretti seiner Opern." In *Bericht über den Internationalen musikwissenschaftlichen Kongress: Bonn 1970,* ed. Carl Dahlhaus et al., 155–62. Kassel: Bärenreiter, 1971.

Beltrami, Pietro G. *La metrica italiana.* Bologna: Il Mulino, 1991.

Bernardoni, Virgilio. "La teoria della melodia vocale nella trattatistica italiana (1790–1870)." *Acta musicologica* 62 (1990): 26–61.

Beyer, Barbara. "Selbstverständigung and Verselbständigung: Eine Analyse von Giuseppe Verdis *Don Carlos.*" Ph.D. diss., Technische Universität Berlin, 1988.

Bianconi, Lorenzo, ed. *La drammaturgia musicale.* Bologna: Mulino, 1986.

Black, John N. *The Italian Romantic Libretto: A Study of Salvadore Cammarano.* Edinburgh: The University Press, 1984.

Bloom, Peter. "A Note on Verdi in Paris." *Verdi Newsletter,* no. 16 (1988): 18–22.

Bogianckino, Massimo. "*Simon Boccanegra*: Il testo in prosa, i libretti, le prime esecuzioni delle due versioni al teatro alla Scala e la critica milanese del tempo." *Annali della Facoltà di lettere e filosofia dell'Università degli studi di Perugia* 14 (1976–1977): 231–59.

Bourgeois, Jacques. "Verdi et Paris." In *Verdi:* Les Vêpres siciliennes, ed. Michel Orcel, 98–101. L'Avant-scène opéra opérette, no. 75. Paris: L'Avant-scène, 1985.

Breque, Jean-Michel. "Travail de Scribe ou scibouillard." In *Verdi:* Les Vêpres siciliennes, ed. Michel Orcel, 17–22. L'Avant-scène opéra opérette, no. 75. Paris: L'Avant-scène, 1985.

Budden, Julian. "L'influenza della tradizione del grand opéra francese sulla struttura ritmica di *Don Carlo.*" In *Atti del II° congresso internazionale di studi verdiani, Verona, Parma, Busseto, 30 luglio–5 agosto 1969,* ed. Marcello Pavarani, 311–18. Parma: Istituto di studi verdiani, 1971.

———. "Varianti nei *Vespri siciliani.*" *Nuova rivista musicale italiana* 6 (April–June 1972): 155–81.

———. "Verdi and Meyerbeer in Relation to *Les Vêpres siciliennes.*" *Studi verdiani* 1 (1982): 11–20.

———. *The Operas of Verdi.* Rev. ed. 3 vols. Oxford: Clarendon Press, 1992.

Celletti, Rodolfo. "Lo stile vocale di Verdi e di Wagner." *Analecta musicologica* 11 (1972): 328–42.

Chusid, Martin. "The Inquisitor's Scene in Verdi's *Don Carlos*: Thoughts on the Drama, Libretto and Music." In *Studies in Musical Sources and Style: Essays in Honor of Jan LaRue,* ed. Eugene K. Wolf and Edward H. Roesner, 505–34. Madison: A-R Editions, 1990.

Clémeur, Marc. "Eine neu entdeckte Quelle für das Libretto von Verdis *Don Carlos.*" *Melos/Neue Zeitschrift für Musik* 6 (1977): 496–9.

Cohen, H. Robert. "Verdi in Paris: Reflections in *L'illustration.*" *Periodica musica* 7 (1989): 5–12.

Colas, Damien. "'Quels accents! Quel langage!' Examen du traitement de l'aléxandrin dans *Les Vêpres siciliennes.*" In *L'Opéra en France et en Italie (1791–1925): Une scène privilégiée d'échanges littéraires et musicaux. Actes du colloque franco-italien tenu à l'Académie musicale de Villecroze (16–18 octobre 1997),* ed. Hervé Lacombe, 187–214. Paris: Société française de musicologie, 2000.

Colombo, Paola. "Fétis – Verdi: Cronaca di una polemica." *Nuova rivista musicale italiana,* nos. 3–4 (1991): 391–425.

Conati, Marcello. "Verdi, il grand opéra e il *Don Carlos.*" In *Atti del II° congresso internazionale di studi verdiani, Verona, Parma, Busseto, 30 luglio–5 agosto 1969,* ed. Marcello Pavarani, 242–79. Parma: Istituto di studi verdiani, 1971.

---. "'E quasi si direbbe prosa strumentata.' (L'aria 'a due' nello *Stiffelio*)." In *Tornando a Stiffelio: Popolarità, rifacimenti, messinscena, effettismo e altre 'cure' nella drammaturgia del Verdi romantico*, ed. Giovanni Morelli, 243–63. Florence: Leo S. Olschki, 1987.

---. "Verdi et la culture parisienne des années 1830." In *La vie musicale en France au XIXe siècle*, vol. 4, *La musique à Paris dans les années mil huit cent trente*, ed. Peter Bloom, 209–25. Stuyvesant: Pendragon Press, 1987.

---. "Le mura di Gerico. (La crisi dell'opera italiana negli anni 1860 e l'affermazione del 'grand opera')." In *Teatro Regio, città di Parma, stagione lirica 1987–1988*, 59–67. Parma: Grafiche STEP, 1988.

---. *Simon Boccanegra di Giuseppe Verdi*. Milan: Ricordi, 1993.

Cooper, Grosvenor W., and Leonard B. Meyer. *The Rhythmic Structure of Music*. University of Chicago Press, 1960.

Coudroy, Marie-Hélène. *La critique parisienne des "grands opéras" de Meyerbeer: Robert le diable – Les Huguenots – Le Prophète – L'Africaine*. Saarbrücken: Musik-Edition Lucie Galland, 1988.

Dahlhaus, Carl. "Französische Musik und Musik in Paris." *Lendemains* 31–2 (1983): 5–10.

Dalmonte, Rossana. "La canzone nel melodramma italiano del primo ottocento: Ricerche di metodo strutturale." *Rivista italiana di musicologia* 11 (1976): 230–313.

Della Seta, Fabrizio. "L'immagine di Meyerbeer nella critica italiana dell'ottocento e l'idea di 'dramma musicale.'" In *L'opera tra Venezia e Parigi*, ed. Maria Teresa Muraro, 147–76. Studi di musica veneta, vol. 14. Florence: Leo S. Olschki, 1988.

---. *Italia e Francia nell'ottocento*. Storia della Musica, vol. 9. Turin: E.D.T., 1993.

Del Monte, Alberto. *Retorica, stilistica, versificazione. Introduzione allo studio della letteratura*. Turin: Loescher, 1955; reprint, Turin: Tipografia Gravinese, 1989.

Detels, Claire. "Giuseppe Verdi's *Simon Boccanegra*: A Comparison of the 1857 and 1881 Versions." Ph.D. diss., University of Washington, 1982.

---. "*Simon Boccanegra*: Notes on the 1857 Version." *Opera Journal* 18 (1985): 12–20.

De Van, Gilles. "Théâtre et musique dans les opéras de Giuseppe Verdi." Ph.D. diss., Université de la Sorbonne Nouvelle Paris III, 1989.

---. "Musique et narration dans les opéras de Verdi." *Studi verdiani* 6 (1990): 18–54.

---. "La musique de la langue: Le français de *Don Carlos*." In *D'un opéra à l'autre: Hommage à Jean Mongrédien*, ed. Jean Gribenski, Marie-Claire Mussat, and Herbert Schneider, 124–32. Paris: Presses de l'Université de Paris-Sorbonne, 1996.

Ellis, Katharine. *Music Criticism in Nineteenth-Century France: La Revue et Gazette musicale de Paris, 1834–1880*. Cambridge University Press, 1995.

Elwert, W. Theodor. "Lo svolgimento della forma metrica della poesia lirica italiana dell'*ottocento*." *Estudis Romànics* 2 (1949–1950): 113–33.

---. *Versificazione italiana dalle origini ai giorni nostri*. Florence: Felice Le Monnier, 1973.

---. *Italienische Metrik*. 2d ed. Wiesbaden: Steiner, 1984.

Fabbri, Paolo. "Metrik und Form." In *Geschichte der italienischen Oper*, ed. Lorenzo Bianconi and Giorgio Pestelli, trans. Claudia Just und Paola Riesz, vol. 6, *Theorien und Techniken, Bilder und Mythen*, 179–242. Laaber: Laaber Verlag, 1992.

Finscher, Ludwig. "Wort und Ton in den Opern Verdis." *Analecta musicologica* 11 (1972): 255–71.

Freeman, John W. "Berlioz and Verdi." In *Il teatro e la musica di Giuseppe Verdi. Atti del III° congresso internazionale di studi verdiani: Milano, Piccola Scala, 12–17 giugno 1972*, ed. Mario Medici and Marcello Pavarani, 148–65. Parma: Istituto di studi verdiani, 1974.

Gartioux, Hervé, ed. *Giuseppe Verdi,* Les Vêpres siciliennes: *Dossier de presse parisienne (1855)*. N.p: Musik-Edition Lucie Galland, 1995.

Gerhard, Anselm. "Verdi face au grand opéra français." In *Verdi*: Les Vêpres siciliennes, ed. Michel Orcel, 92–6. L'Avant-scène opéra opérette, no. 75. Paris: L'Avant-scène, 1985.

———. "'Ce cinquième acte sans intérêt': Preoccupazioni di Scribe e di Verdi per la drammaturgia de *Les Vêpres siciliennes*." *Studi verdiani* 4 (1986–1987): 65–86.

———. *Die Verstädterung der Oper: Paris und das Musiktheater des 19. Jahrhunderts*. Stuttgart: Metzler, 1992.

Gerhard, Anselm, and Uwe Schweikert, eds. *Verdi Handbuch*. Stuttgart: Metzler, 2001.

Ghiazza, Silvana. *Elementi di metrica italiana e cenni di retorica*. Bari: Edizione Levante, [1985].

Ghislanzoni, Antonio. "Conversazioni musicali." *Gazzetta musicale di Milano* 21 (1866): 74–5.

Giger, Andreas. "The Role of Giuseppe Verdi's French Operas in the Transformation of His Melodic Style." Ph.D. diss., Indiana University, 1999.

———. "Defining Stanzaic Structure in Verdi's French Librettos and the Implications for the Musical Setting." *Acta musicologia* 73 (2001): 141–63.

———. "Reconsidering *Les Vêpres siciliennes* in the Context of French Aesthetic Thought." In *Verdi 2001: Atti del Convegno internazionale / Proceedings of the International Conference (Parma – New York – New Haven, 24 January–1 February 2001*, ed. Fabrizio Della Seta, Roberta Montemorra Marvin, and Marco Marica, 519–43. 2 vols. consecutively paginated. Florence: Leo S. Olschki, 2003.

———. "The Triumph of Diversity: Theories of French Accentuation and Their Influence on Verdi's French Operas." *Music and Letters* 84 (2003): 55–83.

———. "The French Influences." In *The Cambridge Companion to Verdi*, ed. Scott L. Balthazar, 111–39. Cambridge University Press, 2004.

———. *Verismo*. Handwörterbuch der musikalischen Terminologie, ed. Hans Heinrich Eggebrecht and Albrecht Riethmüller. Wiesbaden: Steiner, 2004.

Gossett, Philip. "Verdi, Ghislanzoni and *Aida*: The Uses of Convention." *Critical Inquiry* 1 (December 1974): 291–334.

———. "Music at the Théâtre Italien." In *La musique à Paris dans les années mil huit cent trente*, ed. Peter Bloom, 327–64. Stuyvesant: Pendragon Press, 1987.

———. "Translations and Adaptations of Operatic Texts." In *Palimpsest: Editorial Theory in the Humanities*, ed. George Bornstein and Ralph G. Williams, 285–304. Ann Arbor: The University of Michigan Press, 1993.

———. *Divas and Scholars: Performing Italian Opera*. University of Chicago Press, 2006.

Goury, Jean. "Verdi et la France." In *Atti del II° congresso internazionale di studi verdiani, Verona, Parma, Busseto, 30 luglio–5 agosto 1969*, ed. Marcello Pavarani, 565–72. Parma: Istituto di studi verdiani, 1971.

Groth, Renate. *Die französische Kompositionslehre des 19. Jahrhunderts*. Beihefte zum Archiv für Musikwissenschaft, vol. 22. Wiesbaden: Franz Steiner, 1983.

Günther, Ursula. "Le livret français de *Don Carlos*: Le premier acte et sa révision par Verdi." In *Atti del II° congresso internazionale di studi verdiani, Verona, Parma, Busseto, 30 luglio–5 agosto 1969*, ed. Marcello Pavarani, 90–140. Parma: Istituto di studi verdiani, 1971.

———. "Die Pariser Skizzen zu Verdis *Don Carlos*." In *Bericht über den Internationalen Musikwissenschaftlichen Kongress: Bonn 1970*, ed. Carl Dahlhaus et al., 412–14. Kassel: Bärenreiter, 1971.

———. "La genèse de *Don Carlos*, opéra en cinq actes de Giuseppe Verdi, représenté pour la première fois à Paris le 11 mars 1867." *Revue de musicologie* 58 (1972): 16–64; 60 (1974): 87–158.

———. "Documents inconnus concernant les relations de Verdi avec l'Opéra de Paris." In *Il teatro e la musica di Giuseppe Verdi. Atti del III° congresso internazionale di studi verdiani: Milano, Piccola Scala, 12–17 giugno 1972*, ed. Mario Medici and Marcello Pavarani, 564–83. Parma: Istituto di studi verdiani, 1974.

———. "Der Briefwechsel Verdi – Nuittier – du Locle zur Revision des *Don Carlos*." *Analecta musicologica* 14 (1974): 414–4; 15 (1975): 334–401.

———. "Wagnerismen in Verdis *Don Carlos* von 1867?" In *Wagnerliteratur – Wagnerforschung*, ed. Carl Dahlhaus and Egon Voss, 101–8. Mainz: Schott, 1985.

Hansell, Kathleen Kuzmick. "Compositional Techniques in *Stiffelio*: Reading the Autograph Sources." In *Verdi's Middle Period, 1849–1859: Source Studies, Analysis, and Performance Practice*, ed. Martin Chusid, 45–97. University of Chicago Press, 1997.

Harwood, Gregory. "Verdi's Reform of the Italian Opera Orchestra." *19th Century Music* 10 (1986): 108–34.

Henson, Karen. "Exotisme et nationalités: *Aida à l'Opéra* de Paris." In *L'Opéra en France et en Italie (1791–1925): Une scène privilégiée d'échanges littéraires et musicaux. Actes du colloque franco-italien tenu à l'Académie musicale de Villecroze (16–18 octobre 1997)*, ed. Hervé Lacombe, 263–97. Paris: Société française de musicologie, 2000.

Hepokoski, James A. "Genre and Content in Mid-Century Verdi: 'Addio, del passato' (*La traviata*, Act III)." *Cambridge Opera Journal* 1 (1989): 249–76.

———. "*Ottocento* Opera as Cultural Drama: Generic Mixtures in *Il trovatore*." In *Verdi's Middle Period, 1849–59*, ed. Martin Chusid, 147–96. University of Chicago Press, 1997.

Holland, Dietmar. "Der späte Verdi." In *Verdi-Theater*, ed. Udo Bermbach, 71–88. Stuttgart: Metzler, 1997.

Huebner, Steven. "Italianate Duets in Meyerbeer's Grand Operas." *Journal of Musicological Research* 8 (1989): 203–58.

———. "Paris Opera Audiences, 1830–1870." *Music and Letters* 70 (1989): 203–56.

———. *The Operas of Charles Gounod*. Oxford: Clarendon Press, 1990.

———. "Lyric Form in Ottocento Opera." *Journal of the Royal Musical Association* 117 (1992): 123–47.

Johnson, James. H. *Listening in Paris: A Cultural History*. Studies on the History of Society and Culture, vol. 21. Berkeley: University of California Press, 1995.

Kahlke, Egbert. "Vers und Musik in der *Aida*." *Studi verdiani* 11 (1996): 75–118.

Kastner, Léon Emile. *A History of French Versification*. Oxford: Clarendon Press, 1903.

Kerman, Joseph. "Lyric Form and Flexibility in *Simon Boccanegra*." *Studi verdiani* 1 (1982): 47–62.

Kimbell, David. "Verdi's First *Rifacimento*: *I lombardi* and *Jérusalem*." *Music and Letters* 60 (1979): 1–36.

———. *Verdi in the Age of Italian Romanticism*. Cambridge University Press, 1981.

———. *Italian Opera*. Cambridge University Press, 1991.

Kitson, J. Richard. "Verdi and the Evolution of the *Aida* Libretto." Ph.D. diss., University of British Columbia, 1985.

Landry, Eugène. *La théorie du rythme et le rythme du français déclamé*. Paris: Champion, 1911.

Langford, Jeffrey. "Text Setting in Verdi's *Jérusalem* and *Don Carlos*." *Verdi Newsletter*, no. 12 (1984): 19–31.

———. "Poetic Prosody and Melodic Rhythm in *Les Vêpres siciliennes*." *Verdi Newsletter*, no. 23 (1996): 8–18.

Lawton, David. "The Harmonic Language of *Aida*." Paper presented at the annual meeting of the American Musicological Society, New York, 3 November 1979.

———. "*Le trouvère*: Verdi's Revision of *Il travatore* for Paris." *Studi verdiani* 3 (1985): 79–119.

Lester, Joel. *The Rhythms of Tonal Music*. Carbondale: Southern Illinois University Press, 1986.

Lippmann, Friedrich. *Vincenzo Bellini und die italienische Opera Seria seiner Zeit*. Analecta musicologica, vol. 6. Cologne: Böhlau, 1969.

———. "Der italienische Vers und der musikalische Rhythmus: Zum Verhältnis von Vers und Musik in der italienischen Oper des 19. Jahrhunderts, mit einem Rückblick auf die 2. Hälfte des 18. Jahrhunderts." *Analecta musicologica* 12 (1973): 253–369; 14 (1974): 324–410; 15 (1975): 298–333.

Longarini, Enzo. "*Vêpres siciliennes/I vespri siciliani* – studio sui libretti." Tesi di laurea, Università degli studi di Parma, 1977–1978.

Magnani, Luigi. "L' 'ignoranza musicale' di Verdi e la Biblioteca di S. Agata." In *Il teatro e la musica di Giuseppe Verdi. Atti del III° congresso internazionale di studi verdiani: Milano, Piccola Scala, 12–17 giugno 1972*, ed. Mario Medici and Marcello Pavarani, 250–7. Parma: Istituto di studi verdiani, 1974.

Marchesi, Gustavo. "L'ambiente culturale e artistico parigino al tempo dei *Vespri*: Appunti per una definizione." In *Universalità della musica, prestigio dell'Italia, attualità di Verdi: Studi in onore di Mario Medici*, ed. Giuseppe Vecchi, 21–68. 2 vols. Bologna: Amis, 1986.

Martinon, Philippe. *Les Strophes: Étude historique et critique sur les formes de la poésie lyrique en France depuis la renaissance avec une bibliographie chronologique et un répertoire général*. Paris: H. Champion, 1912.

Meloncelli, Raoul. "Giuseppe Verdi e la critica francese." *Studi verdiani* 9 (1993): 97–122.

Memmo, Francesco Paolo. *Dizionario di metrica italiana*. Rome: Edizioni dell'Ateneo, 1983.

Mila, Massimo, ed. *Giuseppe Verdi: Les Vêpres siciliennes; opéra en cinq actes, paroles de Eugène Scribe et Charles Duveyrier*. Opera: Collana di guide musicali, I/1. Turin: Unione Tipografico-Editrice Torinese, 1973.

———, "Fétis e Verdi, ovvero gli infortuni della critica." In *Il teatro e la musica di Giuseppe Verdi. Atti del III° congresso internazionale di studi verdiani: Milano, Piccola Scala, 12–17 giugno 1972*, ed. Mario Medici and Marcello Pavarani, 312–21. Parma: Istituto di studi verdiani, 1974.

Mirabelli, Ubaldo. "La rivoluzione negata e *I vespri siciliani*." *La rivista illustrata del museo teatrale alla Scala* 2, no. 5 (1989–1990): 2–25.

Mongrédien, Jean. *French Music from the Enlightenment to Romanticism, 1789–1830*. Translated by Sylvain Frémaux. Portland, OR: Amadeus Press, 1996.

Moreen, Robert Anthony. "Integration of Text Forms and Musical Forms in Verdi's Early Operas." Ph.D. diss. Princeton University, 1975.

Morier, Henri. *Dictionnaire de poétique et de rhétorique*. Paris: Presses universitaires de France, 1961.

Murari, Rocco. *Ritmica e metrica razionale italiana*. 3d ed. Milan: Ulrico Hoepli, 1909; reprint, Milan: Istituto Editoriale Cisalpino-Goliardica, 1977.

Neuls-Bates, Carol. "Verdi's *Les Vêpres siciliennes* (1855) *and Simon Boccanegra* (1857)." Ph.D. diss., Yale University, 1970.

Nicastro, Aldo. "Il teatro francese nell'evoluzione del melodramma verdiano." In *Il teatro e la musica di Giuseppe Verdi. Atti del III° congresso internazionale di studi verdiani: Milano, Piccola Scala, 12–17 giugno 1972*, ed. Mario Medici and Marcello Pavarani, 338–48. Parma: Istituto di studi verdiani, 1974.

Noske, Frits. "Melodia e struttura in *Les Vêpres siciliennes* di Verdi." *Ricerche musicali* 4 (1980): 3–8.

———. *French Song from Berlioz to Duparc: The Origin and Development of the Mélodie*. Revised by Rita Benton and Frits Noske. Translated by Rita Benton. New York: Dover, 1988.

Osthoff, Wolfgang. "Musica e versificazione: Funzioni del verso poetico nell'opera italiana." In *La drammaturgia musicale*, ed. Lorenzo Bianconi, 125–41. Bologna: Società editrice il Mulino, 1986.

Pagannone, Giorgio. "Mobilità strutturale della *Lyric Form*: Sintassi verbale e sintassi musicale nel melodramma italiano del primo ottocento." *Analisi* 7 (1996): 2–17.

Parker, Roger. "'Infin che un brando vindice' e le cavatine del primo atto di *Ernani*." *Verdi: Bollettino dell'Istituto di studi verdiani*, no. 10 (1987): 142–60.

———. *Leonora's Last Act: Essays in Verdian Discourse*. Princeton University Press, 1997.

Pendle, Karin. *Eugène Scribe and French Opera of the Nineteenth Century*. Studies in Musicology, vol. 6. Ann Arbor: UMI Research Press, 1979.

Petit, Pierre. "Verdi et la France." In *Giuseppe Verdi: Raccolti in occasione delle celebrazioni verdiane dell'VIII settimana musicale 16–22 settembre 1951*, ed. Guido Chigi Saracini, 37–47. Siena: Casa editrice Ticci, 1951.

Petrobelli, Pierluigi. "The Fusion of Styles." In *A Masked Ball/Un ballo in maschera*, ed. Nicholas John, 9–14. English National Opera Guide, vol. 40. London: Riverrun Press, 1989.

———. "De l'alexandrin à l'anapeste chez Verdi: Structure poétique et composition musicale dans *Un ballo in maschera*." In *L'Opéra en France et en Italie (1791–1925): Une scène privilégiée d'échanges littéraires et musicaux. Actes du colloque franco-italien tenu à l'Académie musicale de Villecroze (16–18 octobre 1997)*, ed. Hervé Lacombe, 215–22. Paris: Société française de musicologie, 2000.

Phillips-Matz, Mary Jane. *Verdi: A Biography*. Oxford University Press, 1993.

———. *Puccini: A Biography*. Boston: Northeastern University Press, 2002.

Pistone, Danièle. "Wagner et Paris (1839–1900)." *Revue internationale de musique française* 1 (1980): 7–84.

Poindefert, Bruno. "*Les Vêpres siciliennes*: Commentaire littéraire et musical." In *Verdi:* Les Vêpres siciliennes, ed. Michel Orcel, 27–89. L'Avant-scène opéra opérette, no. 75. Paris: L'Avant-scène, 1985.

Porter, Andrew. "The Making of *Don Carlos*." *Proceedings of the Royal Musical Association* 98 (1971–1972): 73–88.

———. "Verdi's Ballet Music, and 'La Pérégrina.'" In *Atti del II° congresso internazionale di studi verdiani, Verona, Parma, Busseto, 30 luglio–5 agosto 1969*, ed. Marcello Pavarani, 355–67. Parma: Istituto di studi verdiani, 1971.

———. "Don't Blame Scribe." *Opera News* 39, no. 20 (1975): 26–7.

———. "*Don Carlos* in the Original Language." *Opera* (London) 34 (1983): 365–8.

Powers, Harold. "Aria sfasciata, duetto senza l'insieme: Le scene di confronto tenore-soprano nello *Stiffelio/Aroldo* di Giuseppe Verdi." In *Tornando a* Stiffelio: *Popolarità, rifacimenti, messinscena, effettismo e altre 'cure' nella drammaturgia del Verdi romantico*, ed. Giovanni Morelli, 141–88. Florence: Leo S. Olschki, 1987.

———. "'La solita forma' and 'the Uses of Convention.'" *Acta musicologica* 59 (1987): 65–90.

Pugliese, Giuseppe. *Gerusalemme*. Quaderni dell'istituto di studi verdiani, vol. 2. Parma: Istituto di studi verdiani, [1963].

Rosen, David. "Le quattro stesure del duetto Filippo-Posa." In *Atti del II° congresso internazionale di studi verdiani, Verona, Parma, Busseto, 30 luglio–5 agosto 1969*, ed. Marcello Pavarani, 338–88. Parma: Istituto di studi verdiani, 1971.

Rosen, David, and David Lawton. "Verdi's Non-Definitive Revisions: The Early Operas." In *Il teatro e la musica di Giuseppe Verdi. Atti del III° congresso internazionale di studi verdiani: Milano, Piccola Scala, 12–17 giugno 1972*, ed. Mario Medici and Marcello Pavarani, 189–237. Parma: Istituto di studi verdiani, 1974.

Rosen, David, and Andrew Porter, eds. *Verdi's* Macbeth: *A Sourcebook*. New York: W. W. Norton, 1981.

Ross, Peter. "Studien zum Verhältnis von Libretto und Komposition in den Opern Verdis." Ph.D. diss., Universität Bern, 1980.

———. "Amelias Auftrittsarie im *Maskenball*: Verdis Vertonung im dramaturgisch-textlichen Zusammenhang." *Archiv für Musikwissenschaft* 40 (1983): 126–45.

Sala, Emilio. "Verdi and the Parisian Boulevard Theatre, 1847–1849." *Cambridge Opera Journal* 7 (1995): 185–205.

Saran, Franz. *Der Rhythmus des französischen Verses*. Halle: Max Niemeyer, 1904.

Sartori, Claudio. "La Strepponi e Verdi a Parigi nella morsa quarantottesca." *Nuova rivista musicale italiana* 2 (1974): 239–53.

Smith, Martin Dennis. "Antoine Joseph Reicha's Theories on the Composition of Dramatic Music." Ph.D. diss., Rutgers University, 1979.

Strohm, Reinhard. "Zum Verhältnis von Textstruktur und musikalischer Struktur in Verdis Arien." In *Atti del I° congresso internazionale di studi verdiani, Venezia, Isola di San Giorgio Maggiore, Fondazione Giorgio Cini, 31 luglio–2 agosto 1966*, ed. Marcello Pavarani and Pierluigi Petrobelli, 247–51. Parma: Istituto di studi verdiani, 1969.

Wedell, Friedrich. *Annäherung an Verdi: Zur Melodik des jungen Verdi und ihre musiktheoretischen und ästhetischen Voraussetzungen*. Kassel: Bärenreiter, 1995.

Weiss, Piero. "Verdi and the Fusion of Genres." *Journal of the American Musicological Society* 35 (Spring 1982): 138–56.

Werr, Sebastian. *Musikalisches Drama und Boulevard: Französische Einflüsse auf die italienische Oper im 19. Jahrhundert*. Stuttgart: Metzler, 2002.

Witzenmann, Wolfgang. "Grundzüge der Instrumentation in den Opern Verdis und Wagners." In *Colloquium "Verdi-Wagner," Rom 1969*, ed. Friedrich Lippmann, 304–27. Analecta musicologica, vol. 11. Cologne: Böhlau Verlag, 1972.

Yeston, Maury. *The Stratification of Musical Rhythm*. New Haven: Yale University Press, 1976.

Zoppelli, Luca. "'Stage Music' in Early Nineteenth-Century Italian Opera." *Cambridge Opera Journal* 2 (1990): 29–39.

Index

Note: Italicized page numbers indicate the presence of an illustration.

Accent: acute, 36, 242; culminating, 15–16; diastematic, 58–9, 100, 134, 223; durational, 9, 16, 36, 53, 57–8, 63, 100, 134–7, 194, 196, 199, 208, 211, 236, 238, 243; final, 33, 213; fixed, 47, 52, 103, 113, 166, 230, 233; French, 11, 36, 56, 230–31; grave, 36, 242; harmonic, 93, 103, 194, 196, 199, 211; harsh, 65; hierarchy of, 188; idiosyncratic, 133; interior, 53, 99, 103, 133, 170; irregular, 11, 15, 29, 52, 58–61, 103–5, 122, 126, 129–31, 133, 135–7, 166, 186, 188, 191, 193–4, 196–8, 201, 210, 221, 223, 231, 238, 248, 266–7; Italian, 35–36; melodic, 159; metric, 12, 42, 47–8, 52–4, 64, 126, 133, 135, 137, 185, 190, 196, 211, 223; migrating, 47; musical, 45–7, 56, 125, 186, 199, 208, 221; obligatory, 10, 12, *13*, 16, 34, 55, 126, 129, 183, 186, 188, 199, 208, 221, 223; pattern, 8, 29, 36, 37, 47, 56, 70, *70*, 103, 122, 126, 166, 212, 213; prosodic, 11, 51, 84, 130, 134, 136, 247; punctuating, 53, 129; quantitative, 9; regular, 52, 121–2, 137, 169, 192, 229–30, 236; rhythmic, 2, 10, 12, 48, 60, 76, 84–5, 93, 96, 129, 186–8, 209, 235; secondary, 14, 15, 17, 130, 133, 168–9, 188, 199, 225, 247; stress, 8–9, 11, 16, 56–7, 134, 137, 194, 211, 230–1, 235–6, 243; and structure, 17, 48, 58, 60, 63, 69, 91, 98–9, 107, 112, 116, 124, 141, 143, 181, 194, 210, 263; textual, 13, 45, 47, 53, 56, 58, 104, 168, 181, 223; tonic, 2–3, 9, 12, 16–18, 47, 49–50, 52–3, 56, 58, 91, 94, 99, 116, 122–6, 131, 166, 181, 183–4, 188–9, 198–9, 201, 208, 215, 218, 222, 225, 231, 236; and versification, 8–16, 47, 54, 58–61, 133, 187–8, 208. *See also Accent; Accento;* Syllable – accented

Accent logique, 10, 16–17, 46, 133, 208, 221, 223, 231, 237, 239, 246–7, 260

Accent oratoire, 10, 16–17, 231, 239, 247, 266

Accent tonique ou temporel, 9, 235. *See also* Accent – tonic

Accento apparente, 47–8, 247

Accento casuale, 36–7

Accento drammatico, 246

Accento eccezionabile, 48

Accento e ritmo, 182. *See also* Accent – rhythmic

Accento maggiore, 48

Accento massimo o metrico, 48. *See also* Accent – metric

Accento minore, 48

Accento obbligato, 36, 37. *See also* Accent – obligatory

Accento patetico, 246

Accentuation: *See* Accent

Adam, Adolphe: *Le Brasseur de Preston*, 51, *51*

Aesthetics, 1, 3, 61, 100, 105, 201, 263; French, 3, 47, 72, 76–8, 93–4, 99, 103, 113, 137, 141, 161, 170, 181, 201, 261; Italian, 3, 47, 72, 77, 141; melodic, 3, 47, 72, 77, 87, 161

Affect, 91, 107, 112, 138, 141, 168, 179, 206–7

Alberti, Annibale, 264

Aldini, Aldino, 252

Appiani, Giuseppina, 256

Arago, Etienne, 265

Aria, 8, 19, 43, 58, 73–4, 85, 91, 107, 112–13, 118, 120, 122, 125, 129, 141, 143, 146, 156, 159, 161, 172–3, 175, 178, 207, 213, 215, 223, 251, 252, 258, 262; strophic, 2, 143, 171; substitute, 96; ternary, 25. *See also* Texture – aria

L'armonia, 3, 44, 141, 234, 244–5, 249, 252–3

Arnaud, Alain, 233

Arrivabene, Conte Opprandino, 264

L'Art musical, 73, 246–7, 253, 266, 269

Asioli, Bonifazio, 36–7, 47, 229, 247, 255

Auber, Daniel-François-Esprit, 43, 45–6, 63, 65, 245; *Le Domino noir*, 49, 50, *50*, 57, *57*, 66, *66*; *La Muette de Portici*, 253

Azevedo, Alexis, 191, 266

Baïf, Antoine de, 235

Baini, Giuseppe, 36, 37, 47, 247

Balbi, Melchiorre, 47–8, 230, 247

Baldacci, Luigi, 240

Ballad, 144

Ballata, 170

Balthazar, Scott L., 243, 269

Banville, Théodore de, 18, 231, 235–6, 239–40

Bartlet, M. Elizabeth C., 240

Baruffaldi, Girolamo: *Baccanali*, 247

Basevi, Abramo, 3, 43–4, 61, 66, 116, 138, 141, 156, 166, 230, 233–4, 244–6, 249, 251–3, 261, 263

Basset, A., 262

Bassi, Calisto, 20, 105–6

Beauchemin, Charles, 57

Beaulieu, Désiré, 62, 125, 230, 250

Beaumont, Alexandre, 157

Beauquier, Charles, 113, 257

Becq de Fouquières, Amié Victor, 136, 260
Bellini, Vincenzo, 45, 74, 229, 245, 252, 254; *La sonnambula*, 73–4, 74
Beltrami, Pietro, 243
Benloew, Louis: *See* Versification – according to Benloew
Benton, Rita, 237
Berlioz, Hector, 3, 45–6, 62, 65, 76, 234, 237, 245, 250–1, 253, 261; *La Damnation de Faust*, 251; *Les Troyens à Carthage*, 253
Bermbach, Udo, 267
Bernardoni, Virgilio, 247
Berti, A., 251
Berthelot, André, 248
Bertrand, Gustave, 75, 187, 231, 250, 254
Bianconi, Lorenzo, 243–4
Bisso, Gianbattista, 35, 242
Bizet, Georges, 223, 228, 269
Black, John N., 241, 244
Blanchard, Henri, 60, 249, 251
Blaze, François Henri Joseph: *See* Castil-Blaze
Blume, Friedrich, 255
Boieldieu, François Adrien, 64, 251
Boileau, Nicolas, 18, 240
Boito, Arrigo, 2, 41–2, 61, 126, 217, 222, 233, 244, 249, 254, 269; *Mefistofele*, 220
Bolero, 122–3, 259
Boléro, 198
Bonnefon, Paul, 260
Bornstein, George, 240
Boucheron, Raimondo, 63–5, 230, 246, 250–1
Bourges, Maurice, 75–6, 230, 248, 251, 254
Boyer, Philoxène, 250
Brancour, René, 56, 248
Brandenburg, Daniel, 258
Breul, Karl, 235
Bruneau, Alfred, 234
Budden, Julian, 173, 195, 206, 217, 233, 255–6, 258, 261, 263–4, 266–9
Bueil, Honorat du: *See* Racan, Seigneur de
Buloz, L.: *See* Langevais, F. de

Cabaletta, 38, 63–4, 75, 96, 98, 116, 120, 129, 145, 210, 231, 247, 250, 261, 263

Cadence, 60, 63, 74, 81, 86, 107, 113, 166, 172–3, 217; definition of, 78–9; melodic, 79–81, 107, 179, 255–6; typology of, 80. *See also* Design – and cadence; Phrase – and Cadence
Caesura, 9–13, 15, 17–18, 23, 29–30, 33–5, 106, 123, 194, 208, 231, 236, 239, 242, 267; stanzaic, 22–3, 25, 29, 32–3, 131, 195
Cammarano, Salvadore, 38, 241, 243
Cantabile, 72, 122, 133, 137, 204, 247, 252, 259
Cantilena, 2, 61, 246, 249
Canzona, 37, 243, 262
Canzone, 144, 170–1, 264. *See also* Couplet
Canzonetta, 37–8, 65
Carner, Mosco, 269
Casamorata, Luigi Ferdinando, 246, 250
Castil-Blaze: *See* Versification – according to Castil-Blaze
Cavatina, 38, 257
Cavatine, 73, 252–3
Cesari, Gaetano, 233
Chadeuil, Gustave, 264
Chaining melodies, 143, 150–2, 155–6, 179, 204–6, 215, 221, 262, 264. *See also* Conducting a melody
Chenier, André, 19. *See also* Giordano, Umberto – *Andrea Chénier*
Cherubini, Luigi, 44, 245; *Médée*, 245
Chiabrera, Gabriello, 37
Choron, Alexandre, 8, 29, 35, 56, 229, 235–8, 242, 247–8, 251
Churgin, Bathia, 251
Cleopatra, 182
Chusid, Martin, 257
Clementi, Muzio, 245
Combarieu, Jules, 9, 231, 236, 247–8
Comettant, Oscar, 253
Colas, Damien, 134, 233, 259–60
Conati, Marcello, 269
Condé, Gérard, 250
Conduct of the melody: *See* Conducting a melody
Conducting a melody, 66, 70, 72, 107, 117, 120, 156, 161, 166, 178, 181, 215, 251–2
Conducting the melody: *See* Conducting a melody

Cooper, Grovesnor, 78, 255–6
Corneille, Pierre: *Le Cid*, 240
Coudroy, Marie-Hélène, 252
Couplet, 143, 145, 170–1, 241, 262
Critics: *See* Musical Press

D'Anna, Salvatore, 247
Dahlhaus, Carl, 244
Debussy, Claude, 234
Declamation, 12, 14–15, 45, 49, 60–1, 69, 137, 173, 190–1, 198, 230–1, 236, 238, 246, 249, 261, 266–7; lyric, 113, 143, 185, 190, 225, 266; naturalistic, 2, 212, 223; realistic, 224. *See also* Text Setting – declamatory
Del Monte, Alberto, 243
Della Seta, Fabrizio, 245, 261
De Rovray, A., 262
Design: and cadence, 86, 118, 120, 256; melodic, 79, 81, 107, 113, 133, 138, 141, 143, 223, 225, 231, 255; and phrase, 79, 83, 85, 107, 113, 118, 140, 170, 178, 203, 220, 255, 258; of Anton Reicha, 78, 81, 83, 85, 255–6
Dieresis, 7–8, 235
D'Indy, Vincent, 267
Donizetti, Gaetano, 74, 254; *Anna Bolena*, 49, 70, *71*, 72; *Dom Sébastien*, 27, 241; *La Favorite*, 29–30, 241; *Lucia di Lammermoor*, 247
Drama, 3, 19, 56, 63–4, 70, 113, 138, 141, 170–1, 183, 188, 194, 198, 201, 218, 247; effect of, 185, 198; French, 1, 8. *See also* Melody – dramatic; *Accento drammatico*; *Metri drammatici*
Dramaturgy, 1, 99, 120, 125, 263; agitated narratives, 197, 199, 201, 215; dramatic situations, 61, 91, 94, 106–7, 125–6, 131, 170–1, 197, 199, 201, 215, 263; lighthearted numbers, 2, 49, 51, 116, 122, 123, 125–6, 129, 166, 171, 183–4, 198–9, 201, 215; picturesque numbers, 2, 198–9, 201, 215
Dreyfus, Camille, 248
Ducondut, Jean-Ambroise, 29, 237
Du Locle, Camille, 182–3, *183*, 207, 237, 264
Duparc, Henri, 237

Duponchel, Charles, 91
Duveyrier, Charles, 235, 260, 262

Elision, 8, 17, 34–5, 133, 168, 212
Ellis, Katharine, 267
Elwert, W. Theodor, 38, 242–4
E muet, 7–9, 17, 35, 59, 96, 100, 183, 187, 235, 242, 256
Enjambment: See Verse – enjambment in
Escudier, Léon, 91, 182, 246, 264, 266, 269
Escudier, Marie, 91, 253

Fabbri, Paolo, 243–4
Fétis, François-Joseph, 44–5, 56, 62–3, 73–5, 187, 201, 230, 245–8, 250, 252–4
Filippi, Filippo, 46, 234, 246
Fiorentino, P.-A., 262
Fischer, Christine, 268
Fleury, A., 58, 237, 248
Foreground rhythm: See Rhythm – foreground
La France musicale, 43, 157, 234, 245, 250, 252–3, 266, 269
Franchetti, Alberto, 228
Frémaux, Sylvain, 245
Frugoni, Carlo Innocenzo, 37–8

Galeazzi, Francesco, 251, 254–5
Gallo, Denise, 251
Gardin, Louis de, 235
Gartioux, Hervé, 234, 260, 262, 264–9
Gautier, Théophile, 204, 267
Gazzetta musicale di Milano, 43, 45, 143, 244, 246, 249–3, 260
Gerhard, Anselm, 125, 260, 268
Gérome, 266–7
Gervasoni, Carlo, 252, 255
Ghiazza, Silvana, 242–3
Ghislanzoni, Antonio, 207, 212, 243–4, 246, 249, 251, 268
Giger, Andreas, 235–6, 240, 258–61, 266, 269
Giordano, Umberto: *Andrea Chénier*, 22–5, 227, 228
Giusti, Giuseppe, 3
Gluck, Christoph Willibald, 43–4, 60, 65, 245, 249–50
Gossec, François-Joseph, 236
Gossett, Philip, 233, 240, 243–4, 254, 257, 260, 268

Gounod, Charles, 45–6, 65, 234, 237, 246, 248, 251; *Faust*, 65, 65
Grétry, André-Ernest-Modeste, 43, 46, 49, 236, 245; *Richard Coeur-de-lion*, 49, 50
Gramont, Ferdinand de, 237
Gueymard, Pauline, 185
Günther, Ursula, 185, 264–5

Halévy, Jacques Fromental, 45–6, 59, 63, 65, 73, 76, 245, 248, 250; *L'ebrea*, 252; *La Juive*, 3, 52–3, 54, 55, 56, 66, 66–9, 69–70, 70, 73, 75, 261; *Le Juif errant*, 58, 59, 76, 241, 252–3
Hansell, Kathleen Kuzmick, 257
Harmony: See Accent – harmonic; Cadence; Melody – and harmony; *Mélodie harmonique*; Meter – and harmony; Rhythm – and harmony
Henze-Döhring, Sabine, 245
Hérold, Ferdinand: *Le Pré aux clercs*, 62
Hiatus, 8
Holland, Dietmar, 267
Hudson, Elizabeth, 258
Huebner, Steven, 234, 237, 248, 251
Hugo, Victor, 17, 239–41; "L'Oiseau" from *Toute la lyre*, 19

Ictus: See *Temps fort*
Illica, Luigi, 225, 228
Indentation: See Indention
Indention, 2, 20, 37, 40–2, 145–6, 240, 250, 268
Izzo, Francesco, 251

Johnson, James H., 245
Journal des débats, 70, 106, 252, 257, 266
Jouvin, B., 267
Just, Claudia, 243

Kastner, Léon Emile, 235, 238–40
Kerman, Joseph, 78, 79, 255
Khalke, Egbert, 268
Kimbell, David, 94, 256–8, 261, 264, 269
Kitson, J. Richard, 268

Lacombe, Hervé, 234, 259
Lacome, Paul, 247

La Fage, Adrien de, 57, 229, 235, 246, 248
Lamartine, 125, 260
Landey, Peter M., 256
Landry, Eugène. See Versification – according to Landry
Langevais, F. de, 265
Langford, Jeffrey, 12, 233, 237
Lauzières, Achille de, 43, 244
Lawton, David, 96, 157, 256, 263, 268
Le Goffic, Charles, 239–41
Lester, Joel, 78, 255
Libretto: French, 1, 2, 7, 11, 18–21, 33, 33, 38, 42, 46, 72, 91, 135, 143, 145, 145, 146, 157, 182, 184, 191, 201, 206, 240, 252, 264, 265; Italian, 2, 20, 33, 35, 37, 42, 46, 105, 124, 126, 143, 145, 145, 165, 207, 240, 252; manuscript, 39, 244; printed, 37–9, 39, 40–1, 52, 130, 133, 237, 248, 261; properties of, 106, 182, 204, 218, 234, 264; structural aspects of, 3, 19–20, 24, 27, 32, 37, 39, 42, 70, 91, 103, 121–2, 143–4, 156, 191, 194, 208, 215, 235, 239, 249, 266, 268
Lippmann, Friedrich, 233, 252, 258, 260
Locke, Ralph P., 268
Lubarsch, E. Otto: See Versification – according to Lubarsch
Lully, Jean-Baptiste, 250
Lurin, Jean Marie, 237
Lussy, Mathis, 248
Luzio, Alessandro, 233, 264–5
Lyric form, 96, 107, 116–17, 120, 131, 146, 150, 155, 190, 192–3, 198, 201, 223, 255, 258, 262; mid-century, 70, 72, 135, 178, 187, 260. See also Declamation – Lyric
Lyric poetry, 7, 19, 27–8, 231, 240–1, 243
Lyric verse: See Verse – lyric
Lyricism, formal, 2, 20, 187, 204, 266–7

Maffei, Clarina, 3, 234
Magnani, Luigi, 234
Malherbe, François, 18
Marica, Marco, 261
Marini, Ignazio, 96

Marmontel, François, 22, 229, 234, 241
Marschall, Gottfried, 267
Martinon, Philippe, 231, 241
Marvin, Roberta Montemorra, 261
Massenet, Jules Emile Frédéric, 220, 223, 228, 269
Mathiesen, Thomas J., 249
Mazzucato, Alberto, 45, 69, 76, 137, 143–5, *145*, 230, 246, 250–3, 260–2
Medici, Mario, 234, 269
Méhul, Étienne Nicholas, 64, 236, 251
Mélèze, Josette, 239
Melisma, 2, 133–4, 137, 183, 197–8, 201, 211, 266
Melodia, 174, 246, 250
Mélodie, 215
Mélodie harmonique, 73
Melody: borrowed, 103; characteristics of, 65, 76, 94, 107, 125, 129, 131, 137, 141, 143, 194, 201, 204, 210, 220–1, 230, 245, 250; and contrast, 70, 112–13, 143, 258; distinct, 141, 156, 162, 164–6, *167*, 179, 181, 195; dramatic, 63, 65, 137, 250; French, 1–4, 12, 42–5, 47, 62–3, 65–6, 73, 76, 105, 107, 112, 157, 159, 162, 218, 220, 230, 244–5, 252; formal, 2–3, 19, 31, 130, 133, 166, 193–4, 196, 204, 207, 223; and harmony, 43, 45, 58, 60, 72–3, 81, 100, 113, 118, 120, 128, 138, 141, 155, 162, 166, 168, 170–4, 187, 204, 207, 215–18, 221–3, 253, 255–6, 268; independent, 72, 155, 166, 178, 204, 206; innovative, 134, 166, 185; inventive, 62–3, 74–5, 254; Italian, 12, 42, 45, 66, 72–3, 76, 96, 98, 107, 162, 230, 233; parallel, 79, 131, 175; philosophy of, 46; and rhythm, 2–3, 43, 45–7, 58, 62, 65, 69–70, 74, 76, 81, 84, 106, *106*, 112–13, 120, 127, 137–8, 170–1, 178–9, 184, 188, 206, 223, 225, 231, 243, 247, 254, 256, 264; simple, 73, 211; structure of, 3, 46, 65, 72, 76, 99, 112–13, 117–18, 120, 128, 168, 172–3, 196, 229, 251; symmetrical, 76, 130, 215, 221; and text setting, 46, 51–2, 56, 59, 60, 64, 69, 93, 99, 107, 122, 126, 128–9, 144, 164, 168, 179, 190–1, 193, 196, 201, 215, 218, 230, 233, 243; trivial, 3; truncated, 66, 69; vague, 58–9, 126. *See also* Accent – melodic; Aesthetics – melodic; Cadence; Chaining melodies; Conducting a melody; Design – melodic; *Melodia*; *Mélodie*; *Mélodie harmonique*; Meter – and melodic pulse; Phrase – melodic; Rhythm – melodic; Stanza – and melody; Style – melodic; Texture – *parlante melodico*
Mélopée, 185, 191, 204, 246, 266–7
Melopoeia, 46. *See also Mélopée*
Memmo, Francesco Paolo, 243–4
Mercadante, Giuseppe Saverio, 137, 260–1
Méry, Joseph, 182, 207, 237
Meter: alternation of, 22; ambiguous, 63, 168, 170–1, 186–7; classical, 8, 36; compound, 136; duple, 136, 168; duple, 136, 168; French and Italian, 103, 105, 126, 185, 242–3, 249; and harmony, 28, 59; irregular, 96, 131, 196, 204, 215; long, 7, 65–6; and melodic pulse, 53, 83, 137–8, 168, 207, 216, 261; musical, 116, 133, 168–9, 189, 210–11, 239, 247; poetic, 1, 7, 19, 20–1, 23, 25, 27, 29, 33, 35, 64–5, 91, 104–5, 113, 121, 123, 136, 141, 143, 145, 162, 166, 168–70, 184, 194, 196, 208, 212, 233, 249, 263; regular, 15, 103, 121, 130, 146; and rhyme, 29; and rhythm, 7, 10, 28, 42, 44, 47, 58, 61–3, 76, 113, 126, 129–30, 184, 209, 215, 225, 230; short, 19, 65–6, 73, 170; triple, 126, 168; uniform, 7; vague, 127, 137, 186. *See also* Accent – metric; *Accento massimo o metrico*; *Metri drammatici*; Metric feet; Polymeter; Rhythm – and meter; Stanza – and meter; Stanza – mixed meter; Verse
Metric feet: anapest, 11, 55; dactyl, 55, 104, 131, 133; iamb, 11, 55, 96, 99, 122, 125, 127–9, 133, 183, 194; trochee, 11, 55–6, 125, 198
Metri drammatici, 37, 243
Metri lirici: *See* Lyric poetry
Meyer, Leonard B., 78, 255–6
Meyerbeer, Giacomo, 1, 11, 44–6, 59, 61–2, 64–5, 72–3, 76, 138, 141, 182, 185, 230, 233, 237, 245–6, 248–52, 254, 261, 264, 266; *L'Africaine*, 28, 185, 240, 248, 252; *L'Étoile du Nord*, 3; *Les Huguenots*, 51–2, *52*, 59, *60*, 70, 156, 252–4; *Le Prophète*, 44, 45, 62, *62*, 63, 245–6, 250–3; *Robert le diable*, 70, 251–3
Mid-century lyric form: *See* Lyric form – mid-century
Middleground rhythm: *See* Rhythm – middleground
Mongrédien, Jean, 245
Le Moniteur universel, 204, 262, 267
Moreen, Robert, 240, 243–4, 257
Morelli, Giovanni, 263
Morère, Jean, 185
Morier, Henri, 9, 236
Murari, Rocco, 243
Muraro, Maria Teresa, 245
Music critics: *See* Musical press
Musical press: 1, 3, 8–9, 18, 43–6, 49, 61, 64–5, 70, 72–3, 75–6, 106, 116, 125, 137–8, 141, 143–4, 146, 156–7, 166, 182, 184–5, 190–1, 201, 204, 206, 210, 218, 233–4, 244–6, 248–54, 260, 265, 266–7
Musical style: *See* Style – French musical; Style – musical

Noske, Frits, 237
Nuitter, Charles, 157

Oltremontani, 44–5, 64, 120, 246
Opera: comic, 43, 49, 65, 244–5; foreign influences in, 44, 228; French, 1–3, 11, 43, 45–6, 48, 63, 65–6, 74, 76, 87, 98, 103, 113, 116–17, 120, 125, 129, 141, 143, 169–70, 181–2, 184–5, 187, 204, 208–9, 211, 215, 218, 220–1, 223–4, 228, 231, 233–5, 247, 250–1, 264;

French grand, 1, 11, 43, 51, 233, 237, 244, 248, 252–4; Italian, 2, 11, 41, 45–6, 48, 72, 74, 76, 94, 103–4, 116, 120, 129, 134, 138, 143, 166, 168–9, 178, 182, 185, 201, 208, 211, 215, 218, 224, 229–30, 233, 245, 247, 251–2, 261–4, 269
Opéra, Paris, 1, 43, 44, 76–7, 91, 157, 182, 185, 215, 218, 228
Opéra comique (Paris), 44
Opéra comique: *See* Opera – Comic
L'Opinion nationale, 191, 266
Orcel, Michel, 233
Osthoff, Wolfgang, 244

Pacini, Émilien, 157, 251
Pacini, Giovanni, 63–4, 231, 233; *Saffo*, 247
Pagannone, Giorgio, 258
Parker, Roger, 96, 207, 257, 268
Parlante: *See* Texture – *parlante*
La Patrie, 182, 262
Pavarani, Marcello, 233–4, 264
Perrin, Émile, 182
Pestelli, Giorgio, 243
Petazzoni, Luciano, 265
Le petit journal, 182
Petrobelli, Pierluigi, 263
Pfannkuch, William, 255
Phillips-Matz, Mary Jane, 228, 234, 258, 264, 269
Phrase: balanced, 69–70, 104–5; and cadence, 78–9, 86, 105, 107, 113, 118, 136, 250, 255; concept of, 15–17, 45, 61, 66, 74, 78, *79*, 87, 117, 143, 171, 204, 206, 208; irregular, 49, 65, 140, 177, 187, 201, 203, 208, 219, 221, 261; long, 65, 140, 178, 255; melodic, 3, 46, 57, 64, 78, 85, 87, 118, 122, 194, 256; parallel, 65, 69, 78, 85–6, 107, 113, 116–18, *118*, 120, 131, 135–6, 138–40, 166, 170, 176–9, 187, 194, 196, 199, 202–3, 208, 212, 215, 219–20, 223, 225, 253, 255, 258; regular, 64, 130, 138, 175, 187, 196, 212, 221, 225; short, 65, 86, 168, 170–1, 178, 255; square, 201, 230; structure, 56, 63, 66, 69, 70, *70*, 73, 76, 113, 125, 129, 136, 138, 187, 190, 194, 199, 210, 212, 229–30, 255; symmetric, 64, 125–6; truncated, 66. *See also* Design – and phrase
Phrasing: *See* Phrase
Piave, Francesco Maria, 38, 242, 244, 250
Piazza, Antonio, 241
Pierson, Paul: *See* Versification – according to Pierson
Pistone, Danièle, 267
Polymeter, 103, 194, 196, 206, 208. *See also* Stanza – polymetric
Porter, Andrew, 248, 258–60, 263, 266
Poriss, Hilary, 251
Powers, Harold, 263
Practice: *See* Style
Prévost, Hippolyte, 218, 266, 269
Prosody: approaches to, 2–3, 12, 17, 48–9, 51–2, 54, 56–8, 60–1, 93–4, 96, 100, 105, 107, 116, 121, 125, 129–31, 133, 137, 141, 168, 183, 185, 188, 193–4, 196–9, 201, 204, 208, 212, 215, 218, 223, 233, 249, 266; characteristics of, 3, 91, 99, 135, 184, 185, 187, 201, 229, 265; French, 1, 3, 12–13, 23–35, 43–4, 76, 87, 94, 105, 117, 137, 184, 196, 233, 236–7; and interpretation, 16, *16*, 48, 59, 78, 94, 129, 136, 199, 221–2, 224; Italian, 2, 34–5, 37, 61, 185, 249; theory of, 2–3, 96, 191. *See also* Accent – prosodic; Rhetoric of prosody; Scanning – prosodic; Versification
Prototype, 38, 70, 117–18, *118*, 120, 138, 201, 258
Puccini, Giacomo, 269; *Le Villi*, 220; *Tosca*, 228
Pugliese, Giuseppe, 256

Quicherat, Louis-Marie: *See* Versification – according to Quicherat

Racan, Seigneur de (Honorat du Bueil), 125, 259–60
Racconto, 78, 175
Rapin, Nicolas, 235
Recitative, 2, 7, 19, 20, 22, 31, 46, 72, 103, 190, 206, 247, 252, 266. *See also* Texture – recitative
Reicha, Antoine, 16–18, 46, 78, 83, 229–30, 235, 255–6; *Art du compositeur dramatique*, 229, 235, 239, 246, 266; *Traité de mélodie*, 79, 81, 83, 229, 255–6. *See also* Design – of Anton Reicha
Repose, 35
Revue et gazette musicale, 60, 75, 201, 245–9, 251, 253–4, 267
Reyer, Ernest, 191
Rhetoric of prosody, 2, 12, 125, 183, 199, 201
Rhyme: *See* Meter – and rhyme; Stanza – and rhyme pattern; Verse – and rhyme scheme
Rhythm: ambiguity of, 61, 63, 188; binary, 125; diversity of, 49, 61, 63, 123; and effect, 35; even, 102; expressive, 36, 48; foreground, 83, 113, 212; French poetic, 1, 3, 22, 106, 207; and harmony, 44, 59, 61, 74, 76, 84, 85, 96, 107, 118, 129, 187–8, 194, 207, 225, 235, 240; irregular, 3, 10, 56, 60, 129, 136, 166, 183, 190, 197–8, 212, 230; melodic, 45, 47, 98, 107, 112, 166, 168, 171, 178, 188, 197, 221, 230–1, 233; and meter, 47, 63, 74, 99, 113, 126, 129–30, 166, 169, 184, 212, 217, 233, 243, 248; middleground, 83–5, 107, 134, 137–8, 187–8, 201, 208, 210–13, 256, 260–1; monotonous, 18–19, 47, 60, 249; musical, 47, 59, 61–2, 123, 141, 183, 199, 233, 255, 260; and originality, 63–4, 103, 250; parallelism in, 66, 212; patterns of, 45, 53, 56, 58–9, 66, 70, 74–6, 83–4, 99, 100, 102, 104, 107, 156, 181, 194, 208, 211; punctuated, 15; regular, 7, 11, 35, 45, 62, 104, 122, 125, 127, 135, 215, 250; repetitive, 65, 73; and sense, 12–13, 15, 17, 58, 231, 237; short, 65; simple, 62; and structure, 3, 22, 56, 60, 69, 78, 81, 98, 100, 120, 141, 175, 196, 255; surface, 83–4; theory of, 78, 196, 237; trochaic, 52; uneven, 102, 248; variety of, 62, 156, 221, 223, 233; and

Rhythm (*cont.*)
   text/verse, 17, 19, 34, 35, 37–8, 47, 52, 56, 58–1, 64, 69, 104–6, 121–2, 126, 129, 131, 133–4, 136–7, 165, 178, 182, 186–7, 189–90, 193, 196, 206, 220, 223, 230–1, 236–7, 242, 248; weak sense of, 126, 128, 166, 181, 185, 187, 194, 198, 210, 263. *See also* Accent – rhythmic; Melody – and rhythm; Meter – and rhythm
Ricordi, Giulio, 157, 228, 246
Ricordi, Tito, 1
Riesz, Paola, 243
Rifacimento, 94
Ritorni, Carlo, 36, 47, 229, 242–3, 247, 255
Romance, 49, 59, 62, 66, 75, 79, 125, 186, 252
Romanza, 107, 112–13, 120, 166, 210, 216
Romani, Felice, 38
Rongé, J.-B., 247
Roqueplan, Nestor, 91, 233, 265
Rosen, David, 96, 256, 263
Rossini, Gioachino, 1, 44, 64, 73, 229–30, 245, 251, 253, 257–8; *La donna del lago*, 251; *Guillaume Tell*, 20, 73, 240, 253; *Tancredi*, 251, 257
Rousseau, Jean-Jacques, 59–60
Royer, Alphonse, 91, 93–4, 96, 102, 105–6, 234, 241, 252, 257
Runyan, William Edward, 254

Sadie, Stanley, 234
Sadler, Graham, 234
St.-Étienne, Sylvain, 125
Saint-Saëns, Camille, 12
Saint-Valry, G. de, 266
Saint-Victor, Paul de, 266–7
Sant'Agata, 182, 258; library at, 4, 182, 234
Saran, Franz, 231, 237
Sardou, Victorien, 228
Sartori, Claudio, 234
Sasse, Marie-Constance, 185
Satzton 14, 190, 238, 246
Scanning: mechanical, 2, 47, 49, 51, 231; prosodic, 122–3, 134; regular, 2; and text/verse, 10–11, 15, 48–50, 52–3, 55–7, 96, 98, 104, 116, 122–3, 125–6, 129, 131, 133–4, 166, 170, 175, 181, 183–4, 194, 198–9, 201, 215, 230–1, 263, 267. *See also* Versification
Schweikert, Uwe, 268
Scoppa, Antonio: *See* Versification – according to Scoppa
Scribe, Eugène, 1, 11, 28, 69–70, 91, 106, 121–2, 130, 137, 143, 145, 184, 230, 235, 240–1, 245, 248, 252, 257–60, 262
Segrais, Jean Regnault de, 125, 260
Siciliani, Pietro, 72, 253
Solera, Temistocle, 38, 240–1, 244
Spontini, Gaspare, 44; *La Vestale*, 245
Stanza: distich, 23, 27, 31, 37, 38, 49, 126, 146, 179, 196, 215, 241, 244, 263; *dixain*, 23; *douzain*, 23; French, 2, 3, 33, *33*, 103, 116; *huitain*, 27; Italian theory of, 37, 42; and melody, 19, 143, 146, 155–6, 162, 179, 211; and meter, 46, 133, 185–6, 209–1, 225, 230–1, 240, 249, 253, 266; of mixed meter, 22, 191; poetic, 2, 30–1, 143, 145; polymetric, 41, 193–4, 196, 206, 211, 213, 244, 267; quatrain, 11, 14, 22, 27, 29, 32, 41–2, 51, 53, 103–4, 116, 126, 129–31, 133, 135, 143, 162, 178, 183, 185, 187, 191–3, 196, 212, 222, 258, 261, 263, 266; *quintil*, 241; regularly accented, 11, 104; and rhyme pattern, 22–5, 27–8, 32–3, 37–40, 50, 56, 130, 194–5, 241, 261; tercet, 22, 27, 32–3, 103, 130, 208, 241; and unity of thought, 21, 22, 30, 33, 37, 42, 103. *See also* Indention; Stanzaic; Tercet; Text setting; Verse
Stanzaic: form, 2–3, 7, 19–20, 28–9, 130, 133, 169–70, 178, 182–3, 187, 191, 204, 206–8, 224, 229, 240–1, 260; passages, 53, 199; structure, 2–3, 7, 19–22, 24, 37–8, 40–2, 96, 131, 159, 161, 185, 188, 191, 193, 196, 212, 215, 231, 240, 247, 262, 266; theory, 3, 231. *See also* Caesura – stanzaic; Stanza
Strepponi, Giuseppina, 1, 234, 268

Style: French musical, 1, 43–6, 51, 60, 63, 65, 76, 96, 99, 103, 106–7, 112–13, 120, 141, 143, 156, 161, 164, 170, 172, 174–5, 181, 187–8, 207–8, 210, 215, 230, 244–5, 249; melodic, 1, 3, 43–6, 48, 76, 116, 120, 137–8, 181, 184–5, 190–1, 201, 204, 207, 220, 230, 235; musical, 1, 7, 54, 72, 113, 116, 179, 204, 229
Sudre, Léopold, 235
Syllable: accented, 9–10, 13, 17, 22, 35–6, *36*, 53, 57, 93, 99, 125, 129, 183, 185–7, 189–90, 193, 196, 208–10, 212, 233, 235–6, 239, 242, 247, 267, 268; counting, 2, 7–8, 10, 13, 18, 20, 27–8, 33–4, 36, 47, 59, 98, 103–6, 123, 131, 133–4, 183, 190, 193, 198, 208, 211–2, 215, 221, 223, 233, 236, 239, 242–3, 259, 264, 267–8; empty, 11, 58; French, 8–9, 33, 121–2; long, 10–12, 35–6, 126, 235–6, 242–3, 248; short, 10–12, 35–6, 126, 235, 242–3; stressed, 9, 35–6, 57, 96, 186, 236; strong, 9–10, 134, 136, 235–7, 248; unaccented, 22, 34, 56, 242; weak, 9–10, 15, 47–8, 96, 130, 187, 235, 237–8, 247. *See also* E muet
Symmetry, 2, 22, 41–2, 45, 47, 49, 56, 58, 61, 65–6, 72–3, 83, 103, 113, 117, 120, 126, 143–4, 195, 221, 241, 245–6, 249, 262. *See also* Melody – symmetrical; Phrase – symmetric
Syneresis, 7, 8, 235
Syntactic group, 12–14, 17–19, 21, 35, 49, 53, 246
Syntactic pause, 34–5
Syntax, 2, 10, 17, 37, 54, 56, 190, 222–3

Tarbé, Eugène, 267
Taste: *See* Style
Temps fort (ictus), 10–11, 15, 17, 56, 125, 236–7, 249–50, 237–8, 249–50
Ténint, Wilhelm, 18, 239
Text setting: declamatory, 15, 35, 113, 129–31, 133, 143, 204,

225, 238, 242, 252; French, 3, 61, 63, 72, 92–4, 96, 98–9, 107, 136, 143; and structure, 19–21, 24–5, 35, 41, 46, 47, 51–2, 58–9, 61, 65, 69–70, 81, 83, 85, 93–4, 125–7, 130–1, 133, 135–6, 141, 143, 150, 159, 165, 168, 170, 174–5, 178–9, 186, 189–90, 192–6, 199, 201, 211, 221–2, 229, 233, 235, 237, 241, 247, 250, 255. *See also* Melody – and text setting; Rhythm – and text/verse; Scanning – and text/verse

Texture: aria, 192, 204, 217; *parlante*, 192–3, 217; *parlante armonico*, 193; *parlante melodico*, 66; recitative, 192–4, 204, 217, 222

Thematic block, 117, *118*, 120, *139–40*, 141, 156, 166, *167*, 168, 175, *176–8*, 181, 201, *202–3*, 204, 217–8, *219–20*, 258, 261, 264

Thémines, M. de, 264

Thierry, J.-J., 239

Thieulin, Édouard, 239–1

Thomas, Ambroise: *Mignon*, 53, *55*

Thurner, A., 245, 247

Tobler, Adolphe, 17–18, 30, 231, 235–6, 239–41

Torrigiani, Pietro, 3, 141, 155, 234, 261, 263

Tonic accent: *See* Accent – tonic

Tremolo, 102, 137, 166, 168, 172–3, 194, 210, 263

Trimm, Timothée, 264

L'ultimo giorno di Pompei, 251

Unity of thought: *See* Verse – and unity of thought; Stanza – and unity of thought

Vaëz, Gustave, 91, 93–4, 96, 102, 105–6, 234, 241, 252, 257

Verdi, Giuseppe, 18, 45, 70, 74, 75, 77–8, 85, 87, 91, 93–4, 96, 99, 103–4, 107, 112–13, 116–17, 120–1, 137–8, 141, 185, 201, 231, 234, 240, 243, 246, 249, 251–2, 254–62, 268; *Aida*, 3, 41–2, 207–9, *209*, 210, *210*, 211–14, *213–14*, 215–16, *216*, 217, *217*, 218, *219–20*, 243–4, 264, 268; *Alzira*, 38, 243–4;

Aroldo, 94, 157, 263; *Attila*, 39, 113, *114*, 244, 258; *Un ballo in maschera*, 136, *136*, 166, 169–70, *170*, 171, *171*, 173–4, *175*, *176–8*, 215, 252, 263–4; *La battaglia di Legnano*, 118, *119*, 120, 175, 258; *Il corsaro*, 258, 261; *Don Carlos*, 1–3, 13, 18–19, 23, 24, 28, 30, 46, 94, 181–3, *183*, 184, *184*, 185–6, *186*, 187, *187*, 188, *188*, 189, 190–2, *192–3*, 193–5, *195*, 196–7, *197*, 198, *198*, 199, *200*, 201, *202–3*, 204–7, *207*, 208, 215, 217–8, 225, 231, 233–4, 237, 239, 246, 264–9; *I due Foscari*, 34–5, 39, 242; *Ernani*, 75, *84*, 96, 98, *99*, 100, 106, 254, 257; *Falstaff*, 218, 220, 223, *226*; *La forza del destino*, 166, 171–2, *172–3*, 174, *174*, 175, *176–8*, 178–9, *179–81*, 207, 215, 217, *219–20*, 222, 263; *Un giorno di regno*, 258; *Giovanna d'Arco*, 257, 263; *Giovanna de Guzman*, 137, 156, 253, 260–3, 267; *Jérusalem*, 1, 3, 8, 10, 13, 19, 21, 23–4, 29, 91–3, *92–3*, 94, *95*, 96, *96–7*, 99–100, *100*, *101*, 102, *102*, 100–4, *104*, 105, *105*, 106, *106*, 107, 108–9, 112–13, 116–17, *117*, 118, 120, 126, 138, 143, 175, 181–2, 188, 218, 220, 233–4, 237, 252, 256–8, 263, 267; *I lombardi*, 1, 21, 33, 40–1, 75, 91–4, *92–3*, *95*, 96, *96–7*, 99, *101*, 102, *102*, 106, 116, 175, 235, 254, 256–7; *Luisa Miller*, 120, 258, 263; *Macbeth*, 81, *81*, *82*, 94, *106*, 157, 159, 161–2, *161–5*, 164–6, 182, 244, 250, 263; *I masnadieri*, 91, 113, *115*, 261; *Nabucco/Nabucodonosor*, 47, 48, *48*, 75, 112, *112*, 254, 257; *Oberto*, 34, 96, 98, 107, *110–11*, 241; *Otello*, 41–2, 207, 217–18, 220–2, *222*, 222–4, *224–6*, 228, 244; *Rigoletto*, 43, 65, 138, *139–40*, 185, 244, 263, 265; *Simon Boccanegra*, 78, *79*, 94, 166, *167*, 168, *168*, 169, *169*, 251, 255; *Stiffelio*, 94, 157, 257–8, 263; *La traviata*, *82*, *83*, 120, 125, 127, *127*, *139–40*,

141, *142*, 185, 242, 262, 265; *Le trouvère*, 157, 159, *160*, 263; *Il trovatore*, 3, *139–40*, 157, *160*, 175, 185, 263, 265; *Les Vêpres siciliennes*, 1–3, 8, 13, 17–8, 21, 22, 25–2, 34–5, 61, 79, *80*, 84, 85, 86, *86*, 87, *87*, 98, 120–3, *123*, 124, *124*, 125–8, *128*, 129–1, *132*, 133–4, *134*, 135, *135*, 136, *136*, 137–8, *138*, *139–40*, 141, *142*, 143–4, *144*, 145–6, *146–9*, 150–2, *150–5*, 155–7, *157–9*, 159, 161, 166, 168, 174–5, *176–8*, 178, 179, 181, 183–5, 187, 191, 194, 199, 201, *202–3*, 206, 215, 233–5, 239, 253, 258, 260–4

Verismo, 173, 223–4, 228, 269

La Vérité, 125

Véron, Pierre, 204, 267

Vers de cinq syllabes, 121, 185, 240

Vers de neuf syllabes, 18, 237, 239

Vers de six syllabes, 33, 122, 185, 240

Vers de sept syllabes, 121, 185

Verse: alexandrine, 12–3, 17–19, 21–2, 29, 36, 46, 103, 123, 131, 133, 191, 194, 196, 208, 233, 243, 259, 263, 266; *decasillabo*, 36, 113, 145, 169; *décasyllabe*, 18, 29, 131, 194, 210, 239, 260; *doppio*, 34, 194, 208; *endecasillabo*, 36–7, 41, 47, 131, 175, 208, 210–14, 221, 243, 260, 268; enjambment in, 18–19, 23, 196, 222, 231, 240; French, 2–4, 7–12, 15, 20, 33–7, 42, 61, 91, 96, 121, 126, 130, 134, 136–7, 165–6, 181, 229, 231, 233, 235–40; irregular, 30, 56–8, 61, 69, 130, 196, 239, 243, 248; Italian, 2–3, 9, 11–12, 21, 33–5, 37, 60, 64, 126, 134, 166, 178, 229, 233, 236, 242, 244; lyric, 60, 70, 116, 235–7, 247–8, 268; *novenario*, 36, 105, 126, 168; *octosyllabe*, 14, 21–2, 53, 103, 105, *106*, 113, 126, 129, 135, 187, 194, 196; *ottonario*, 34, 36, *106*, 113, 121, 145, 168, 185, 233, 262–3; *piano*, 33–4, 41, 81, 83, 106, 133; *quinario*, 36, 47, 64, 145, 170, 211–12, 221, 251, 263; *quinario doppio*,

Verse (*cont.*)
21, 34, 105–6, *106*, 113, 126, 131, 162, 214, 260, 262; and rhyme scheme, 12–3, 17, 19, 20–1, 24–5, 27–8, 32, 34, 37–8, 40–1, 53, 56, 60, 103, 121, 133, 175, 230–1, 243, 261, 268; *sdrucciolo*, 33–4, 37, 40, 81, 83, 133; *senario*, 36, 121–2, 178, 185, 213; *settenario*, 33, 36–7, 41, 47, 103, 127, 133, 145, 162, 175, 183, 185, 211–13, 243, 262; *settenario doppio*, 123, 133; *tronco*, 33–4, 38–9, 41–2, 106, 242; and unity of thought, 22, 42. *See also* Rhythm – and text/verse; Scanning – and text/verse; Text setting – and structure; *Vers*; *Versi*

Versi in selva, 37, 243

Versi lirici: *See* Verse – lyric

Versi sciolti, 20, 37, 143, 213, 215, 243, 260, 262, 268

Versi tronchi, 33–4, 37–42, 106

Versification: according to Benloew, 10–11, 13, 15, 47, 48–9, 51, 54, 55–6, 96, 100, 123, 125, 133, 185, 199, 201, 230–1, 237–8, 247, 256, 259, 266; according to Castil-Blaze, 11, 29, 56, 58, 122, 126, 128, 166, 185, 187, 198–9, 229–30, 234–7, 247–8, 267; according to Landry, 12–16, 36, 49, 53–6, 116, 129–31, 133, 166, 181, 183, 188–90, 193, 196, 198–9, 201, 204, 208, 212, 215, 218, 222–5, 231, 236–8, 242–3, 246–7, 258, 260, 265–6; according to Lubarsch, 14–16, 49, 53–6, 116, 129, 130–1, 133, 166, 181, 183, 188–90, 193, 196, 198–9, 201, 204, 208, 212, 215, 218, 222–5, 231, 236, 238, 246–7, 258, 260, 265–6; according to Pierson, 15–16, *16*, 188–90, 197–9, 201, 204, 215, 224, 231, 237–9, 266; according to Quicherat, 9, 12–13, *13*, 14–16, 48, 50–3, 55, 69, 126, 129, 131, 133, 134, 136, 186–9, 191, 196, 198–9, 210, 230–1, 235, 237, 239, 240–1, 247, 257, 259, 266; according to Scoppa, 11, 48, 122, 229, 234–7, 240, 247; French, 1–2, 7, 9, 11, 14, 33, 35–7, 42, 46, 48, 134, 136, 185, 231, 233–7, 239–40, 242, 260; Italian, 11, 33–6, *36*, 42, 46, 48, 185, 229, 235, 242–4

Villemot, Auguste, 206, 265, 268
Vitali, Geremia, 46, 70, 246, 252, 255
Von Glehn, 248

Wagner, Richard, 46, 185, 201, 204, 206, 220, 228, 246, 266–8
Wagnerism, 204
Weaver, William, 269
Weber, J., 265
Wedell, Friedrich, 255
Weigand, Gustave, 22, 231, 239, 241
Werr, Sebastian, 247, 258
Williams, Ralph G., 240

Yeston, Maury, 78, 255–6

Zambaldini, Francesco, 242
Zoppelli, Luca, 247